SANCTUARIES OF SPANISH NEW MEXICO

SANCTUARIES OF

MARC TREIB

SPANISH NEW MEXICO

Drawings by Dorothée Imbert

Foreword by J. B. Jackson

University of California Press
Berkeley
Los Angeles
Oxford

University of California Press
Berkeley and Los Angeles, California

University of California Press, Ltd.
Oxford, England

Grateful acknowledgment is made
to The Program for Cultural
Cooperation Between Spain's
Ministry of Culture and United
States Universities for a grant in
support of this publication.

Designed by Marc Treib

Treib, Marc.
Sanctuaries of Spanish New
Mexico / Marc Treib;
drawings by Dorotheé Imbert;
foreword by J.B. Jackson.
p.   cm.
Includes bibliographical
references and index.
ISBN 0-520-06420-8 (acid-free paper)
1. Church architecture—New
Mexico. 2. Architecture,
Spanish colonial—New Mexico.
I. Imbert, Dorotheé. II. Title.
NA5230.N6T74   1993
726′.5′09789—dc20   93-7058

1 2 3 4 5 6 7 8 9

Printed in the United States of
America

The paper used in this publication
meets the minimum requirements
of American National Standard for
Information Sciences—Permanence of Paper for Printed Library
Materials, ANSI Z39.48-1984. ⊗

In memory of my mother,
Rita Treib

Color Plates follow page 75.

Unless otherwise noted in the caption, photographs are by the author. The date in brackets indicates the year the photograph was made.

FOREWORD

J. B. Jackson

In a few years' time we will be marking the four hundredth anniversary of the first Spanish settlement in New Mexico, which Don Juan de Oñate founded in July 1598. He had set out from Mexico a year earlier as leader of an expedition to explore and take possession of the northern frontier region, which was largely unknown to Europeans, and to convert its Indian inhabitants to Christianity. Together with a small party of officers he went on ahead of the main party and traveled north up the valley of the Rio Grande until he reached a landscape suited to colonization. Here the group discovered an abandoned Indian village. Oñate decided that this was the place to stop, that in a sense this was the goal of the expedition.

A brief ceremony ensued. Mass was said, and Oñate solemnly declared the village to be the future capital of the Province of New Mexico, of which he was to be governor. He gave the village the name of San Juan de los Caballeros and brought the ceremony to a close by planting a standard especially designed in Mexico for the occasion: a white silk banner adorned with gold and crimson tassles and bearing the images of the Virgin and Saint John the Baptist.

Ironically enough, the capital of the province was soon moved to another place, and Oñate, ostensibly captain general and governor for life, fell into disgrace and was removed from office. Yet the short, largely improvised ritual, witnessed by no more than a scattering of silent Indians, survived (and still survives) as a Hispanic New Mexican tradition.

The custom of celebrating as formally, splendidly, and publicly as possible a significant historical event was already popular in sixteenth- and seventeenth-century Europe. Such celebration was a visible expression of a widely held belief that history was a preordained sequence of trials and triumphs, that time was a stately procession of events leading to a transcendent climax. Although entirely alien to the thinking of the Native American population, these formal rituals took root among the colonists as proof of their Old World civic and religious heritage and as an effective way of heralding their accomplishments.

Other, more elaborate celebrations of the Conquest soon followed, each of them carefully displaying a hierarchical social order and each marking, so it was supposed, a further advance toward the creation of a baroque commonwealth in New Mexico. There was a celebration—procession, mass, sermon—when the main body of the expedition finally arrived, a celebration on the completion of the first irrigation ditch, a celebration of the building of the first church, and a three-day celebration on the occasion of the public submission of several local Pueblo leaders to the authority of Spain. This event included a mock battle between the Moors (on horseback) and the Christians (on foot, although equipped with firearms). A sermon concluded the event.

The euphoria of the Conquest soon evaporated, for the Province of New Mexico fell on evil days. Some pueblos rebelled, soldiers mutinied, and many settlers fled back to the safety of Mexico. Disorder and discouragement were the result, and the modern landscape of New Mexico contains few visible reminders of the first two centuries of colonization.

Those few are likely to be the remote rural churches built by the Franciscan missionaries. Church architecture thus provides us with the most reliable evidence of continuity in much of New Mexico's history. Marc Treib's impressive study of a number of those churches, their origin, their construction, and their subsequent modification up to the present will have a strong appeal not only to those interested in architectural history but also to readers wanting to know more about New Mexico's turbulent past. But this book's chief value is Treib's ability—rare among architectural critics—to marry aspects of the everyday world to the world of ideas. The churches he describes in detail are shown to us as both religious symbols and products of a frontier economy and Indian labor; they are interpreted as provincial variations on Mexican baroque but also as influences on Indian converts. Treib's breadth of historical and architectural learning is paradoxically best revealed in his discussion of prosaic details: the limited choice of materials, the limited choice of tools, the restraints imposed by soil and climate. The merging of two very different perspectives gives the reader a stereoscopic view: the church as artifact separated from the Pueblo villages by its European complexity and the church as an integral part of the economy and society of a workaday Spanish colonial landscape.

Most of us are aware that the prehistoric pueblos—at least those in the basin of the Rio Grande—were built out of adobe; and anyone acquainted with the Southwest knows that the Spanish conquerors introduced the use of adobe brick. But very few writers on southwestern architecture have anything to say about the contrast between Pueblo and Spanish construction techniques. It is generally assumed that the transition from one to the other was smooth when in fact it took several generations. Treib provides us with a concise and objective description of the two ways of using adobe, and by simply enumerating the characteristics of each, he alerts the reader to an important fact: building with standardized adobe bricks represented a totally new approach to architecture in the eyes of the Pueblo Indians.

The prehistoric Pueblo adobe building technique was an example of what is known as puddling, which involves taking handfuls of mud (without any binding ingredient such as grass or straw), squeezing them into lumps or balls, and then placing them in rows or courses, one after another up to a convenient height. This produces a very thin wall without any reinforcing frame; moreover, there is little or no preparation of the site—to say nothing of a foundation for the house. As Marc Treib notes, the puddling technique closely resembled the way Pueblo Indian women made pots by using rolled coils of clay; both activities were in fact the exclusive occupation of women.

A puddled wall was rarely sturdy enough to support a second story, and yet second stories on top of puddled houses seem to have been common. How many such structures collapsed is anyone's guess, but there is ample evidence that they *did* often collapse. It is surprising that no method of reinforcing puddled walls was ever devised, for Pueblo builders frequently showed great skill and ingenuity. All that we can assume is that two-story puddled houses were not thought to be worth much investment in labor and were never considered to be long-lasting. They were easy to build and easy to abandon.

The Spanish invaders brought with them from Mexico (and ultimately from Spain) the knowledge of how to make strong, uniform, adobe bricks and how to use them in construction. This was much more than rudimentary building material. Ordinances drawn up in Mexico City in 1599 called for the licensing of adobe masons, who were required to know how to build a foundation, how to calculate the weight of a roof in relation to the thickness of walls, how to erect scaffolding, and even how to read plans. Whether these regulations were ever enforced in New Mexico is very doubtful, but their memory persisted among the priests, soldiers, and settlers, and the prototypal building they sought to reproduce amid the New Mexican landscape was one with strong foundations, sturdy walls supporting heavy roof beams, and precautions against settling, collapsing, and eroding.

To the Indians who did the heavy work, much of the building activity must have been bewildering: the use of plumb lines and measuring rods and the frequent consulting of a plan or drawing. But one thing must have been obvious to them all: that the design of the church and all the work done on it were intended to achieve a single purpose—the creation and protection of a number of interior spaces. This meant building a structure so strong, so massive, and so firmly attached to its site that it could resist the ravages of time and weather and could last for many generations.

The use of adobe bricks and the use of puddling are so totally unlike in every respect that there seems no point in trying to compare the two. Yet the average Pueblo Indian of the colonial period probably had no trouble seeing the essential difference: the house of adobe bricks was meant to be the most important space, or collection of spaces, in the daily existence of its occupants, a substitute for life outdoors; whereas the house of puddled mud was simply a useful adjunct designed to hold things or serve as a part-time shelter. The church was a particularly fearsome example of adobe brick architecture not only because it was monstrous in size and permanent but also because people were compelled to enter its labyrinthine rooms at regular intervals and for a prescribed length of time.

Once entrapped in the church, the outsider became a helpless participant in an elaborate, highly organized pageant progressing down the center of the nave to the altar. The otherworldly atmosphere of the interior was enriched by darkness, music, incense, and the sombre costumes of the officiating priest. To the European members of the congregation—priests, soldiers, and settlers—this was not only a familiar scene but also a reminder of another well-established public event, the baroque outdoor celebration of earlier and happier times. Although far smaller, far less splendid, and far less varied in composition, the New World church pageant nevertheless retained the basic elements of its origin: symbols, hierarchy, and a slow procession building to a dramatic climax at the altar. Both kinds of ceremony illustrated the Western concept of the interaction of time and space; progress, movement in either dimension, inevitably led to a wished-for goal.

How did the Indian participant respond? The bells, the measured tread of the processioners, the rhythmic order of the service itself, and the reminders of the church calendar culminating in the observance of Easter all produced an ever-increasing expectation of a final moment. But this was not the time by which Indians lived: theirs was the cyclical, neverending recurrence of cosmic events; the movement of heavenly bodies; the sequence of seasons; the dance of night and day; the ordering of the outdoor world, not of the world of dark interiors. To escape from the enclosed spaces of the church was to escape from the tyranny of an incomprehensible architecture and to return to traditional ways of thinking.

In an essay on Hopi architecture, Benjamin Lee Whorf suggested that the Hopi (and presumably other Pueblo societies) had an ambivalent attitude toward all interior, three-dimensional spaces. He wrote that although the Hopi had terms for many architectural structures, they had no term for the room. "Hollow spaces like room, chamber, hall are not really *named* as objects but rather as locations; i.e., positions of other things are specified so as to show their location in such hollow spaces." This tendency to perceive the room or any other interior space (such as the nave of the church) simply as a container with no inherent quality or function of its own was consistent with the use of the flimsy, essentially short-lived puddled dwelling. Its few contents and its intermittent functions indicated all the Pueblo required of architecture: shelter and necessary containment.

An unusual element in this study of missionary churches is Treib's account of the decay that occurred among many of them when their missionary role was reduced or eliminated. It was then that they acquired an archaeological appeal, and Treib's discussion of preservation and restoration policies clarifies the dangers residing in a too-strict attempt to restore the churches to something like their original condition. For much of the "incorrect" or inaccurate restoration in the nineteenth century was the work of the Pueblo Indians themselves and indicated how their attitudes toward architectural spaces had changed. More than a century ago Victor Mindeleff, in his study of Pueblo architecture, noted how the Zuñi Indians had attempted to patch up their decaying churches by using adobe but with little understanding of the nature of adobe bricks. "When molded adobe bricks have been used by the Zuni, in house dwelling," he wrote, "they have been made from the raw material just as it was taken from the fields. As a result these bricks have none of the durability of the Spanish work." He added that "walls in Zuni were only as thick as necessary . . . evidently modelled directly after the walls of stone masonry which had already been pushed to the limit of thinness." It was as if the nineteenth-century Pueblo builders were reverting to the short-lived construction of pre-Conquest times.

If this neglect of the church buildings had any deeper significance, it was that the Pueblo people were turning away from a built environment in which they had never felt at home. It was then that the ceremonies they most cherished—the traditional dances, endlessly repetitive and without climax either in time or on the surface of the plaza— were once again freely honored and held outdoors.

Those who still believe in the persistence of a baroque heritage among the Hispanic population of New Mexico can take heart in the survival of many church traditions. The cultural, as distinguished from the doctrinal, influence of the Catholic church is particularly strong in northern, predominantly rural counties. Despite a dwindling population, increasing poverty, and an omnipresent Anglo culture, there are still villages that look upon the church and its priest as defenders of a formal Spanish way of life. It is in the church that they expect to hear correct Spanish and to observe correct behavior and dress. It is in the church that they celebrate marriages and baptisms and gather to mourn a death. There are few other occasions for a display of formality and family ties. But it is on the day (or the eve) of the local patron saints that something like the ceremonial procession reappears. The church bell rings, bonfires are set at intervals around the outside of the church, and the image of the saint heads the procession as the congregation walks slowly three times around the church, singing as it goes. The flames light up the rough adobe walls and earnest faces. All the elements of celebration are present, all the symbols of order, reverence, and an undying love for this particular time, this particular place.

PREFACE

On my first visit to New Mexico some ten years ago I was taken by the power of the landscape and the beauty of the buildings. The appropriateness of both their forms and materials, the quality of light, and the subtle variations of the colors of the adobe in the various locales all make an indelible impression on the first-time visitor to New Mexico, and I was certainly no exception. The vividness of the reds near Jemez and Pecos, for example, are indelibly etched in my memory.

With many questions about the architecture I had seen, I began to search for answers first in books and then in articles. I was surprised to find that George Kubler's pioneering work, *The Religious Architecture of New Mexico*, first issued in 1940, remained the classic study and that little had been published since that examined the churches of New Mexico not only as architecture but also as the products of a unique environmental and social history. Although many insightful writings explained land settlement patterns, title disputes, and the ethnology of New Mexico, the need still remained for an architectural history that synthesized material from these studies and bolstered them with fieldwork and formal analysis. Naively assuming that I must already be sufficiently familiar with the subject to produce a book of my own, I made the fateful mistake of beginning this project outside my usual area of expertise. The gravity of my error soon became apparent, and I realized that I would have to undertake two to three times as much research and study to reach, at least, a minimally informed point of view.

I began this book in 1982 as a guide to the *missions* of New Mexico that would include an introductory essay examining the environmental, social, and political history of New Mexico and an analysis and description of the churches built in response to these constraints. To complement period images, I would make new photographs of the churches and prepare architectural plans at a consistent scale. Although this seemed a considerable task, the goals of the project also seemed simply enough formulated.

But problems in limiting the scope of the book arose almost immediately. If geographical circumscription were used as the primary selection criterion, the existing churches of today's El Paso and

Juarez would need to be included since they were part of the same supply-route system. Alternatively, if the mission building type were the main criterion, how could one include the Santuario at Chimayo, which is neither a mission nor a church but a votive chapel? And what of the parish church of San José at Las Trampas, in certain respects the most complete example of late-eighteenth-century New Mexican religious architecture? Surely, the book must include them. Should the demolished Castrense chapel—which once figured prominently on the plaza of Santa Fe and for which the most elaborate altarpiece in New Mexico was created—also be presented? Should churches such as Tome and Belen—originally missions but now parish churches—be included, although their message appeared in other, better preserved structures and they had been treated in other studies?

Since there are certain to be readers who will take issue with my selection of some churches over others, perhaps a word or two on my reasoning is in order. I wanted to study existing buildings, rather than historical documents, so I chose not to discuss those churches I was unable to visit because I would have been forced to rely solely on previously published texts and historic photos, which distort even as they document. Thus, Santa Ana is left out, not because it is any less valuable than other churches described here, but because the pueblo is virtually closed to visitors year round. Moreover, because the total length of the text was also a consideration, certain sacrifices had to be made. Accordingly, both the text and the title of the book were adjusted to reflect the churches necessary to the telling of the story. I settled on a more generic, although perhaps somewhat more ambiguous, term and architectural corpus, choosing *sanctuary* instead of church or mission. In this case, sanctuary is used broadly to describe religious structures such as the mission, the church, the chapel, the *oratorio*, and the *morada*. The core of the book centers on the mission church, while the Hispanic parish church or chapel constitutes the remainder of the text. For the most part the construction of all the structures described herein extended from the 1620s to the 1820s, although the current form of the buildings may be of more recent construction. For example, in spite of

its long history, the existing church of San Ildefonso was rebuilt to new plans in the late 1960s. In addition, the small village churches that commonly date from the post-1820s are barely touched on in this book. Their number, pattern, and role in their respective villages make it clear that they warrant an independent study, as the surveys conducted during the 1980s by the Santa Fe architectural firm Johnson/Nestor/Molier/Rodríguez clearly demonstrate.

For those structures that have been omitted—Belen, Tome, Cordova, Nambe, Socorro, and Santa Ana, for example—references can be found in other sources: principally Kubler's works, the classic Adams and Chavez translation and annotation of Domínguez's *The Missions of New Mexico in 1776*, Kessell's *The Missions of New Mexico Since 1776*, and Prince's *Spanish Mission Churches of New Mexico*, for an earlier (1915) point of view.

Although this book has outgrown its original formulation as a guide, the organization still reflects its beginnings. In Part I of the text I have tried to concisely outline the environmental conditions of New Mexico, the patterns of exploration and settlement by the Spanish, and their influence on the development of New Mexico's colonial architecture. Politics always plays a key role in the generation and understanding of architecture, whether implicitly through funding or explicitly through legislation. In New Mexico the relations and interrelations among the Pueblo Indians, the Franciscans, the military, and the colonists were often convoluted and antagonistic. Whether constructed for worship, defense, or administration, the architecture of the province reflected this volatile condition. Those articles that guided, however weakly, the settlement of the northern provinces and that were formalized at the end of the sixteenth century as the Royal Ordinances of Colonization (commonly referred to as the Laws of the Indies) are discussed because they are necessary for understanding the form taken by Spanish settlement and the architecture that filled the subsequent town plan.

Following the discussion of the environmental and social underpinnings of Spanish cities and architecture in New Mexico, the focus shifts to the buildings themselves: the forms of domestic and religious structures, their siting and construction, their furnishing and decoration. In the middle of the nineteenth century New Mexico became part of the United States, and the impact of this political shift was registered on the form of many important church buildings. The aftermath and the successive attempts to modify and later "restore" the mud or stone fabric of the sanctuaries conclude Part I. Nevertheless, issues remain that warrant further research: for example, the exact nature and practice of the mass and other liturgy during the sixteenth and seventeenth centuries, the relationship between daily and annual religious practice, and the specific form of the church and the Franciscan domestic quarters.

Part II comprises individual chapters on the churches and their histories. Because I intended the book to be useful as a guide, these entries are more or less self-contained, and some overlap exists between these chapters and Part I. For the most part, cultural material, architectural precedents, and construction techniques appear in Part I, while specific architectural descriptions of the sanctuaries appear in the individual chapters in Part II. In each case I have tried to chronicle the history of the structure and comment on it, focusing where appropriate on a particular issue or characteristic and discussing it within the context of a single church. For example, the power of light and the complex problems of restoration are both presented in the chapter on Isleta, while the issue of church siting in relation to the pueblo is discussed in the chapters on Pecos and Taos. For detailed descriptions of adobe construction techniques, see Taos pueblo; for stone, Abo. The use of mud plaster versus cement stucco is central to the history of the Ranchos de Taos church and its restoration, while the Cochiti chapter chronicles the major stylistic changes that came with the wave of Anglo immigration and trade at the turn of the twentieth century. The scope and role of mission decorative programs are illustrated by the Laguna pueblo church of San José.

A church of mud or even stone is mutable, and the forms of the New Mexican churches have changed drastically even in the last century. Both historical and contemporary photographs accompany the text of most chapters, although several of the Pueblo communities, including Cochiti, San Felipe, Santo Domingo, and Zia, permit neither photography nor note taking and are represented only by period photographs. The communities' right to privacy took precedence over my desire for complete documentation of the churches.

Where available sources or permission allowed, architectural plans of the churches were prepared, and these are included with the individual entries. Reproducing all the plans at the same scale may limit the amount of perceivable detail, but it allows a ready reference to the relative sizes and configurations of the various structures. Windows drawn without shadows lie more than eight feet above floor level.

A word of warning: these plans must be taken in almost all instances as "conjectural." In some cases, such as San Francisco at Ranchos de Taos and Laguna, the plans derive from Historical American Buildings Survey (HABS) drawings and can be considered relatively accurate, although the basic data upon which they are based may date as far back as fifty years. Where possible, data from field observations have been used to bring these drawings up to date. But for other churches, such as San Felipe and Santo Domingo, where no photography or note taking is allowed, a hypothetical plan was pieced together from aerial and historical photos, verbal descriptions, and memory. The plans are meant to illustrate only relative size and rough configuration and should not be taken as truly accurate and current (1989) records of the churches.

The orthography of cities, towns, and pueblos is based on *New Mexico Place Names: A Geographical Dictionary*, edited by T. M. Pearce. Church names, however, retain those accents in common use.

If one begins a book in naïveté, one ends in humility. It is unavoidable, given all the points that were unconsciously overlooked and questions that remain unanswered. I hope the reader will find in these pages a comprehensive introduction to New Mexican church architecture and some answers to the questions that their very existence raises.

Marc Treib
Berkeley, December 1989

ACKNOWLEDGMENTS

It has been said that any writing stands at the tip of a pyramid supported by the work of other scholars. This book is no exception. Certain of these authors are credited in the introduction; the bibliography lists others. To begin, I must mention John Brinckerhoff Jackson, a close friend and inspiration, whose exact profession eludes classification. He is a scholar, an author, a geographer, and a historian of the American cultural landscape. Today he likes to say that he has retired to his home in La Cienaga, although this is far from the truth. As the founder, publisher, and editor (for seventeen years) of *Landscape* magazine, he has had an enormous impact on thought in the field and has given many a knowledgeable personal view of the Southwest. While claiming no expert knowledge of the subject of New Mexican religious architecture, he has been highly influential to my view of the subject in conversation and criticism; as the contributor of the Foreword to this book, he has provided additional insight. For both I am extremely grateful.

I was also fortunate to have had the opportunity to meet Bainbridge Bunting, whose books and articles constitute the most succinct explanation of the state's architecture, including the colonial period church. When I first met him at a gathering of the Society of Architectural Historians some years ago, I suggested timidly that I was thinking of writing a book on his subject, and he warmly encouraged me in the undertaking. His untimely death deprived New Mexico of its strongest architectural advocate.

Several of my colleagues at the University of California, Berkeley, especially Professors Spiro Kostof and Dell Upton, graciously reviewed the text in manuscript form and offered valuable suggestions for improving it. Architectural historian Christopher Wilson also contributed critical insight, comments, and help with source materials. Robert Nestor, who is primarily responsible for my interest in the architecture of New Mexico, provided not only material on the churches on which his firm has worked but also valuable information on their history and construction.

Several other scholars, including George Kubler, Marc Simmons, John Kessell, E. Boyd, and D. W. Meinig, have contributed unknowingly to this text. Their many works on social and political history, geography, popular arts, and architecture are cited in the bibliography and are recommended as further reading.

Even during the century that photography has documented the effects of environment and society on the earthen churches, the changes have been great, and the photographic records are critical to our understanding of their environment and architectural form. I must thank Arthur Olivas and Richard Rudisill, photo archivists at the Museum of New Mexico, for their help and advice. It was a pleasure to work with two people so knowledgeable about their institution's collections. Sanda Alexandride, the former archivist at the Heye Foundation, Museum of the American Indian, was helpful in locating and having printed certain images of ceremony on Pueblo lands. I also thank James Ivey, historian with the National Park Service, who provided base plans of the Salinas missions and shared his recent archaeological findings and interpretations. McHugh-Lloyd and Associates, Architects, also loaned drawings from which several of the plans were prepared. In addition to the Museum of New Mexico, the National Park Service, the Smithsonian Institution, and the Tourism and Travel Division of the State of New Mexico have generously permitted reproduction of their photographs.

The Bancroft Library at the University of California, Berkeley, has proved an invaluable resource. I also wish to acknowledge the aid of Laura J. Holt, librarian at the Laboratory of Anthropology in Santa Fe, and Jan Barnhart, librarian of Special Collections including the John Gaw Meem Archives at the Zimmerman Library, University of New Mexico, for their help in tracking both obvious and obscure information. Sarah Nestor, formerly editor at the Museum of New Mexico Press, deserves my gratitude for helping initiate and encourage this project.

To Jean Sugiyama, Jan Kristiansson, and especially Barbara Ras, go my gratitude for making the task of editing both challenging and bearable. The text is all the better due to their efforts. Steve Renick generously lent his design expertise and criticism.

For research assistance, thanks go to Diane Favro, currently teaching at the University of California, Los Angeles. Her ability to track and find the difficult fact is an innate gift. Credit is also due to two people who helped produce the manuscript: Sylvia Russell and D'vora Treisman. Kevin Gilson printed most of the photographs from my negatives, getting the best from what they offered. Heather Trossman helped develop the original graphic vocabulary for the plans, although Dorothée Imbert executed all the plans and other drawings and aided me in the final library searches and the last-minute rushes to the Bancroft Library to track the elusive footnote. Her help and encouragement have been crucial to the completion of the book; her sense of humor helped me maintain my own during some trying situations.

Portions of this work were aided by grants from the Committee on Research, University of California at Berkeley. I would also like to acknowledge the gracious support for color reproductions provided by The Program for Cultural Cooperation Between Spain's Ministry of Culture and the United States Universities.

SAN JERÓNIMO
Taos pueblo
Entry portal.
[1986]

PART I

AN ARCHITECTURAL FOOTPRINT ON THE NORTHERN FRONTIER

AN ARCHITECTURAL FOOTPRINT
ON THE NORTHERN FRONTIER

To understand the churches of New Mexico, one must consider more than the architectural ideas that shaped the form of these structures or the building methods used to construct them. The limits imposed by the physical environment, the patterns of exploration and settlement by the Spanish, and the politics practiced by them as they settled among the Pueblo Indians all contributed to the development of New Mexico's colonial architecture.

Although the churches of New Mexico are rooted in European religious tradition, they are neither completely alien to native soil nor merely provincial variations of European or Mexican church structures because they differ so substantially from their architectural precedents. Rather, the New Mexican church represents the mutual influence or conflation of indigenous American building practices with those of the Iberian Peninsula. The single-naved church with its thick adobe walls, crude structural beams, and transverse clerestory benefited as much from the building traditions of the Pueblo Indians as from the ideas of the Spanish missionaries, military engineers, and civilian builders. Churches in the far northern frontiers differed from high-style churches in Spain and Mexico in part because Franciscan visions and aspirations were constrained by a severe physical environment and limited building technology. In the tension between aspiration and reality resided (and still resides) the source of both the power and beauty of these buildings.

THE SETTING

Only with the advance of climatic management has architecture been provided the means to distance itself from its immediate environment. For centuries prior to our own, building reflected the impact of the elements on its form, engaging in an exchange between the forces of nature and those of artifice. The needs of individuals and societies also tempered the contour of architecture as habitation acquired concrete form. In time, an architecture balancing these imperatives resulted; in New Mexico the process was no different.

The landscape of New Mexico can stagger with its endlessness [Plate 1]. The land cannot be described as lush in any but a few isolated valleys, and at times desolate is a more appropriate adjective. But even amid the aridity and sparse vegetation there is always the promise of beauty to come: for example, when the cottonwoods are in autumn color or the desert flowers in spring bloom. But the land and the vegetation are only the raw ingredients of New Mexico's landscape. To them must be added

1–1

1–1
NEW MEXICAN LANDSCAPE
Stuart Davis
1923
[Amon Carter Museum, Fort Worth,
Texas]

the desert light. "The high desert plain is a land where distance is lost, and the eye is a liar, a land of ineffable lights and sudden shadows; of polytheism and superstition, where the rattlesnake is a demigod," as Charles Lummis waxed poetically.[1] The chroma of grays, browns, reds, and even blacks of the earth and stone constantly change as the hot, unrelenting light of noon passes into the oblique shadows of approaching sunset. From spring to fall, the sky can be a piercingly clear blue unhampered by reflective dust or refractive moisture. The thunderstorms of summer create fluid skies that layer cloud on cloud, gray on gray continually dissolving like ink on water. Only in winter, when storm clouds obscure the sun, is the bowl of the sky lowered onto the land.

In *Sky Determines*, Ross Calvin proposed that the aridity of the land endowed the state with its particular character. From the sun, from the desert, came the vegetation and, later, the architecture. Although Calvin's thesis may be too rigidly deterministic, its basic premise is plausible. Nevertheless, the availability of water was only one of the major factors that affected settlement; other environmental conditions also influenced the form that human presence took on the land.

New Mexico occupies a plateau high in elevation, with Santa Fe, the capital, located in the state's northeastern quadrant [Plate 2]. Its ecology is classified as High Sonoran Desert: low in humidity despite the altitude. Elevations above six thousand feet enjoy an annual precipitation of about fourteen inches, a radical contrast to the three inches or less that water the deserts below. The plateau falls sharply just north of the small town of La Bajada (about twenty-five miles south of Santa Fe), and at the foot of this drop lies the pueblo of Cochiti, set against the clearly visible strata of black volcanic rock. Further south, the plain descends an additional several hundred feet as it slopes gradually to Albuquerque and beyond to Las Cruces on the Mexican border.

Cutting across New Mexico from roughly north to south are great ranges of mountains bracketing the fertile river valleys that have sustained both indigenous and colonial settlements. A somewhat milder extension of the Rocky Mountains, the Sangre de Cristo (Blood of Christ) Mountains lie to the east of Santa Fe, isolating the eastern plains from the Rio Grande drainage and peaking at roughly thirteen thousand feet above sea level. The two major gaps in these mountains—the Raton and Glorieta passes—have been strategically important throughout history.

To the northwest of Santa Fe lie the Jemez Mountains, geologic survivors of a massive prehistoric volcanic explosion. The meadows and farms within its caldera contrast sharply with the colors of the desert that surrounds it four thousand feet below. Steep and pine-forested, the source of streams and rivers that eventually drain into the Rio Grande, these mountains form the backdrop to the pueblos of Jemez, Zia, and Santa Ana. The mountains are home to the piñon pine (source of pine nuts) and the scrubby juniper, which rarely grows higher than fifteen feet or so and whose twisted configuration yields little usable wood for major construction. The mountains also provide the tall and straight ponderosa pine used for roof beams, and thus to the mountains the builders went, no matter the distance or the difficulty in transporting the huge logs once they were cut.

Albuquerque is dominated by the hulking backdrop of the Sandia Crest, whose round contour terminates the view of the city when it is approached from the west. Further south the Manzano Mountains turn slightly to the southeast, demarcating the Salinas district, whose dried lakes provided the precious commodity of salt for domestic use and trade. The Salinas district was the site of the missions of Abo, Quarai, and Gran Quivira, known in combination with several smaller settlements—more poetically than accurately—as the "Cities That Died of Fear."[2] The Jicarilla Range beyond marks the southernmost boundary of colonial church building from the beginning of the Spanish settlement to the end of the seventeenth century.

The longest and the largest river in New Mexico, the Rio Grande del Norte is the aorta of the New Mexican landscape [Plate 3]. When the Spanish came upon this river as they moved east from Zuñi, they were aware neither of its source in the mountains of southern Colorado nor of its extent. Broad, yet shallow in its southern parts, the river's majesty increases in the north, culminating in the great Rio Grande gorge south of Taos. Here the deep cut and swiftness of the current suggest the sleeping giant capable of eroding banks and destroying villages. (The river swept away the Santo Domingo church in 1886.) Although always a river of intermittent flow—full and swift during the spring thaw, slow and gentle in late summer—its dimensions today are no longer what they were in the past. Modern water-management systems have significantly modified the Rio Grande: the dam above Cochiti, for example, has reduced the river to a stream during certain times of the year, affecting life along its length. A number of major tributaries feed the river, and

1–2

1–2
LANDFORMS
[Adapted from Beck and Haase, *Histori-cal Atlas of New Mexico*]

these, too, have fostered settlement. To the north the Chama River provides water to the villages around Abiquiu. Rivers flowing from the Truchas Peak and other nearby mountains sustain the fertile valleys that support the villages of Las Trampas, Chimayo, Cordova, and Santa Cruz. Further south the Jemez drainage serves the pueblos of Jemez, Zia, and Santa Ana before its rivers and streams empty into the Rio Grande.

Roughly paralleling the Rio Grande is the Pecos River drainage, the second major valley system to the east. Here the mountains join the plains, and the sedentary Pueblo Indians were forced to confront the nomadic Plains Indians tribes that included, in time, the Comanche and the Apache. To the west of Albuquerque stretch hundreds of miles of deserts and mesas, a dry landscape of flat-topped landforms that provide the background for the pueblos of Laguna, the Sky City of Acoma, and the Zuñi pueblos near the Arizona state line.

Topography and climate were not the sole determinants of architectural form in New Mexico. They were but two, albeit important ones, of a constellation of factors that included defense, available building materials and technology, and social practices.

THE NATIVE CULTURE

New Mexico's Pueblo story begins in prehistory and centers in two major areas: Mesa Verde in the Four Corners area of what is today Colorado and Chaco Canyon in western New Mexico. These two areas served as home to the Anasazi, the ancestors of the Pueblo peoples. The climate about a thousand years ago is believed to have been more hospitable than it is today; moisture was in greater abundance, and winters were considerably milder. Although a detailed investigation of early Indian settlement and culture is beyond the scope of this book, three points bear directly on the development of the colonial New Mexican church: what the native people built, where they built, and how they built. All had a significant impact on the refinement of Pueblo construction methods during the sixteenth and seventeenth centuries, and these in turn eventually influenced the construction of the Spanish colonial churches.

The first substantial archaeological evidence of construction at Mesa Verde records structures termed pit dwellings that date from about the sixth century. Their basic living space consisted of a shallow pit excavated two to three feet below ground level, above which a wooden superstructure was fashioned, covered first with twigs, and then fin-

ished in mud. Even though archaeological findings situate some of these dwellings at the base of cliffs, most of them seem to have been built on mesa tops near cultivated plots. The ease of obtaining building ground, defense, and proximity to fields, rather than any geometric organizing principle, governed the arrangement of Anasazi villages.

During the subsequent Developmental Pueblo period (750–1100), several major changes in construction methods were adopted. Pit construction was abandoned as a house form and was retained only in the underground ceremonial structures called *kivas*. For domestic use numerous cells constructed of fieldstone were joined in a loose, linear manner to form terraces and defensive structures and to express village identity. It was during this period that clustered building units were first constructed and a sense of collective architectural form emerged.[3]

Sometime during the eleventh century, unascertained forces occasioned a transfer of dwelling sites from the mesa tops to the caves formed by water seepage and wind erosion in the sides of the cliffs. Defense is usually given as the most plausible reason for this shift. Whatever the impetus, it must have been considerable to instigate such a drastic change in living conditions. The cave dwellings were carefully constructed of stone, and because working practices did not allow for refined dressing of the stone, the material was used as it was found. In spite of these limitations, the quality of the craft is impressive even by today's standards. All the walls were laid up dry, or set in adobe mortar, with smaller stone fragments inserted between the larger pieces to ensure stability. The entirety was finished with a layer of mud plaster on both the interior and exterior surfaces. To support the roof, wooden beams spanned the walls to create a structure subsequently covered by wooden crosspieces and a thick layer of mud. The village developed incrementally, with each new room fitted to the existing construction and the superstructure of the cave. The beauty of Mesa Verde architecture derives from the perfect harmony of materials throughout and the soft contrast among the natural contours of the cave, the rectangular forms of the apartments, and the roofs of the round kivas.

In response to a different environmental setting, the Chaco Canyon culture in western New Mexico developed an architecture of a more apparent formal order. Unlike Mesa Verde, there were no large caves for habitation or defense in the Chaco River valley, although the villagers probably had to restrict access to exist. In place of the physical super-

1–4

1–3
CLIFF PALACE
Mesa Verde, Colorado
11–13th centuries
The conglomeration of cellular units is fitted to the superstructure of the cave.
[1986]

1–4
PUEBLO BONITO
Chaco Canyon
12–13th centuries
Over a century's time the individual residential and storage units completed the form of a loose "*D*."
[1983]

8

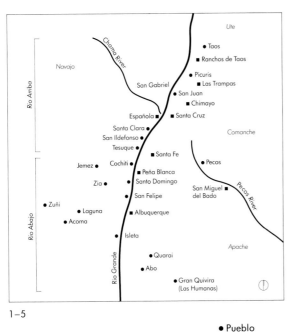

1–5

● Pueblo
■ Spanish town

1–5
PUEBLO AND SPANISH SETTLEMENTS
[Source: Meinig, *Southwest*]

structure provided by the cave to which all construction was secondary, a coherent form emerged from several building phases that required a century to refine. In the case of the multistory Pueblo Bonito, a sweeping D-shaped plan positioned the dwellings and storerooms in a great semicircle that opened toward the river. Like construction at Mesa Verde, the walls of the dwellings were finished with a covering of plaster so that little or none of the exquisite artisanry remained visible. Regardless of whether or not plastering was intended primarily to achieve a sense of architectonic unity, the additional insulation protected the dwellings from wind infiltration and immediate deterioration. In their strength and simplicity the Chaco Canyon structures are impressive. When the refinement of this architectural achievement is set against the barrenness of the surrounding desert and the scarce resources, the stature of the accomplishment increases substantially.

In both these Anasazi culture areas one finds that cellular construction was realized in stone and wood. By piling and agglomeration, whether in response to the cave's aperture or to the surface of the canyon at the lower elevations, the construction method was logical and straightforward. Only trees of limited size were available for construction. A log was cut to estimated length, and if found too long, it was allowed to extend beyond the wall surface even if exposed to rot. Variations of these basic techniques are found in almost all the native groups throughout the Southwest, building practices that not only formed the basis of construction for the succeeding Rio Grande pueblos but also neatly paralleled the methods brought by the Spanish to construct their houses and churches as well.

From 1276 to 1299 Mesa Verde and Chaco Canyon suffered a severe drought, which may have prompted the desertion of the mesa about that time. During the ensuing decades a segment of the population emigrated, presumably toward the Rio Grande. Moving eastward, they are believed to have settled with groups of the Chaco peoples in the region around the Pajarito plateau near today's Santa Clara, San Ildefonso, and Frijoles Canyon, now Bandelier National Monument. Although arable land was limited and the proportions of the canyon severely restricted the amount of sunlight that reached the fields, the indigenous settlers were able to utilize the natural caves and the soft volcanic tufa of the hillsides for their homesteads. To increase the volume of their living spaces, they excavated the caves and constructed stone dwellings against the bases of the cliff. Despite the threat of floods and attack by the Plains Indians, villages were established along the banks of the Rio Grande and other rivers where water flowed year-round, redepositing alluvial soils rich in minerals and fertilizers. When the Spanish arrived in the sixteenth century, they found the pueblos concentrated along the river and its tributaries, although other communities were found to the southeast in the Salinas area and further west at Acoma, Zuñi, and Hopi (located in what is today Arizona).

EXPLORATION

For Spain, the centuries preceding New Mexican settlement in 1598 were charged with the spirit of conquest. After enduring centuries of foreign occupation in Andalusia, the Castillians were able to drive the Moors back to North Africa during the thirteenth century and reestablish Catholicism as the predominant religion throughout the Iberian Peninsula. Quests for the riches of the Orient— spices, silk, and precious minerals—enjoyed some success, as evidenced by Christopher Columbus's 1492 voyage and Europe's "discovery" of the New World. The search for instant wealth, whose perceived reality was heightened by rumor, continued throughout the century and into the next. The risks were great, the stakes were high, the losses were many, and the monetary returns, at times, were incredible.

The uniting of the independent realms of Spain and Portugal in 1581 bolstered the economic resources of the kingdom and made further exploration possible. Throughout the following century, however, fiscal pressures on Spain's treasury continued to mount.[4] A ready source of economic relief could be found in the conquest of the New World. According to popular myth, the vast riches of Indian monarchs lay in Mexico and Peru waiting only to be located, plundered, and finally returned to Spain— to the king, of course—but not without great personal, social, and economic reward for the conqueror. At this time "home, foreign and economic problems were completely intermingled."[5]

Earlier in the fifteenth century, the Catholic nations of Spain and Portugal had announced their intentions to settle and evangelize in the newly explored lands. To reduce potential territorial conflicts, Alexander VI issued a papal bull in 1493 dividing the world more or less into halves, with Spain receiving the majority of the Western Hemisphere. Of equal importance, however, was the pope's grant to the monarch of the right to select the clergy in these lands. As a result, the Spanish

aristocracy became thoroughly enmeshed in the ecclesiastical governance of the new colonies. Power was endowed in a series of appointed delegates who ultimately answered to the king. This system did little to eliminate or ameliorate inevitable conflicts of interest between church and civil authorities, problems that continued to plague the government throughout its centuries of administration.

Within three decades after Columbus's landing, Hernán Cortés had conquered most of Mexico and Central America, claiming for Spain the great native populations there as subject peoples. The Spanish turned to the tasks at hand. They extracted the wealth of the land to fill royal coffers denuded by war and recession, established colonies to stabilize control of the lands and ensure a continued flow of revenue to the Iberian state, and attempted to Christianize the native peoples and bring them within the influence of the Catholic church.

The Spanish friars were also compelled by other pressures. The religious fervor of the missionaries was at a peak. The Muslim Reconquest was still fresh in the spirit of the time; one foe of the church had been vanquished and Spain was united again. The second enemy, the Protestant Reformation, would require a struggle extending, at least in architecture and the arts, for almost a century. In painting and sculpture, and not least of all in architecture, the resurgence of religious fervor would propel the rise of an aesthetic that manifested the power of the church.

Shortly after Cortés's conquest, a group of Friars Minor of the Observance, later known as The Twelve, arrived in Mexico to bolster the limited missionary activity.[6] The philosophy that guided the evangelical programs of the mendicant orders operating in Mexico (the Augustinians, the Dominicans, and particularly the Franciscans) was often characterized by an idealism little less than utopian. Bishop Vasco de Quiroga of Michoacán became auditor of New Spain in 1530. Influenced by the humanism of Sir Thomas More's *Utopia*, Quiroga tried to implement a philosophy that regarded the indigenous people of Mexico as the potential "equals" of the Europeans.[7] In his view, although these natives existed in a lesser stage of development, they were capable of "improvement" and, in time through tutelage, Christianization. With continued exposure to European civilization, they, too, would be capable of leading what he deemed to be full and worthy lives as good Catholics and royal subjects. These questionable intentions were not always fully reflected in the actions of the Spanish clergy and administrators, however.

For the upwardly aspiring Spaniards of the six-teenth and seventeenth centuries, the New World was a place to increase their position or lead a new life. For commoners, it was a road from servitude or debt, although a considerable portion of their re-maining years might be required to accomplish any material advancement. Many of the settlers were lured not only by the uncertain promise of wealth but also by the certain attainment of social status; they were to be granted the title of *hijosdalgo*, "illus-trious men of known ancestry."[8] To impoverished nobles, residence in the colonies might help resur-rect a family name with glory primed by coin. Set-tlement was viewed as an investment: extract a re-ward from the land quickly and leave. This social group constituted a continual nuisance to religious and civil authorities alike because its members usu-ally considered manual labor beneath their station. For all these groups, settlement in Mexico and later in New Mexico was regarded not only as a social experiment but also as a purposeful transplanting of an old culture for both economic and religious gain.[9]

MOVING NORTH

By the opening of the sixteenth century, pressures for expansion and the desire for new wealth had lured explorers and missionaries out of central Mex-ico northward to the barren lands of New Mexico. Myths fueled their quest. The blind pursuit of El Dorado (the tribal chieftain of the Americas who was first covered with vegetal pitch and then dipped in gold dust to create a golden man) and the source of his gold had taken the Spanish throughout South America. He was never found. Further north, it was said, lay the legendary Seven Cities of Cíbola and the land of Quivira—kingdoms of gold, precious stones, and wealth unimaginable.[10]

In due course a preliminary expedition left Mex-ico in 1539 under the supervision of Fray Marcos de Niza. He was accompanied by a number of Mexican Indians and a Moor named Esteban, who acted as a sort of master guide.[11] The Niza group set out with Esteban preceding the main party as part of an ad-vance patrol, and as they crossed into what is now New Mexico, reports of a settlement reached the main group. The Moor headed toward the villages, convinced of his own invulnerability prompted by his successful escapes from life-threatening situa-tions during his prior journey of survival. The Indi-ans, knowing nothing of his supposed invincibil-ity, proved hostile and dispatched him summarily. His patrol fled, countering its original report of a golden city with news of the skirmish and Esteban's death.

Marcos de Niza approached the village with trepidation and maintained his distance from the settlement. His report to the Spanish authorities confirmed the existence and richness of the Seven Cities of Gold, although he did not specifically write that he had seen them up close. "It appears to be a very beautiful city, the houses are . . . all of stone, with their stories and terraces, and it seemed to me from a hill whence I could view it."[12] The Franciscan's report has prompted much subsequent discussion, particularly because it was instrumental in encouraging the exploration and eventual settle-ment of New Mexico. Had the friar lied? Had he seen buildings of mud and stone—now generally ascertained to have been part of Zuñi pueblo—at sunset and, so wishing to be convinced of their rich-ness, misconstrued mud for gold? Had the desire for a successful outcome biased his judgment, or had he just been mistaken? The friar had been cho-sen for his education, reputed powers of observa-tion, and trustworthiness, traits rare among soldiers and colonists. In spite of these precautions, the authorities were misinformed.

Quite possibly, the government had anticipated the content of Fray Marcos de Niza's report, and the image of the cities of Cíbola—now actually seen—fueled the fire of exploration. As a result, a full-fledged expedition set forth during 1540–1542 under the leadership of Francisco Vásquez de Coronado, whose group is credited with the first European sightings of many major features of the American Southwest. Fray Marcos accompanied him. The expedition approximated Niza's prior route in moving north, reaching today's United States–Mexico border near the New Mexico–Arizona state line. Forcing entry into Cíbola, the Spanish found, much to their dismay, nothing to confirm their expectations. In place of gold they found mud; in place of riches, a small agricultural community sus-taining its existence with a limited supply of water. The Indians tired quickly of their intrusive guests and enticed the Spanish to move on by telling them of other sightings of the cities of gold, a tactic they would repeatedly use.

The expedition moved past Acoma eastward to-ward the Rio Grande, where it headed north along the river after stopping in the Galisteo basin on the edge of the Salinas district. Near Sandia pueblo the party established camp, evicting the rightful inhab-itants, commandeering their supplies and foodstuffs, and making fitful attempts at religious conversions. With better weather the Spanish headed north once again—always in search of Quivira, the other leg-endary city of gold—and finally east, entering the plains of what is now southwestern Kansas. Each time the explorers wore out their welcome, and each time they listened to tales of gold further on, just out of sight, just out of grasp. But Coronado's men had reached their limit. Their lot was miserable; their material gains, nonexistent. Beaten by hardship, the barrenness of the desert, and the extent of the Plains, they retraced their steps, rejoined a splinter group that had explored as far as the Grand Canyon, and headed back to Mexico.

Given the dismal outcome of Coronado's expedition, only a few subsequent attempts were mounted in the following years. In 1581 the joint civil-religious Chamuscado-Rodríguez expedition set out; it added to knowledge of New Mexico but made no major economic or social discoveries. The following year an expedition led by Antonio de Espejo achieved similar results and found slain the two friars left behind by Coronado to proselytize among the Indians. Not until the expedition of Don Juan de Oñate several decades later were serious plans for the settlement of New Mexico entertained.

COLONIZATION

Only in the 1580s was interest in the colonization of New Mexico revived as profitable silver mining in northern Mexico suggested that long-term efforts, rather than quick gains, in New Mexico might prove financially rewarding. In addition was the prospect of thousands of Indians waiting for conversion: people whose existence had been confirmed. As a result, a royal decree of 1583 delegated the viceroy of New Spain to organize the settlement of New Mexico. Considered a politically attractive and potentially lucrative post, the governorship of the new province was actively solicited. The appointment was finally awarded to Don Juan de Oñate of Zacatecas, who provided most of the financial support for the expedition himself and spent three years assembling the necessary supplies, settlers, stock, and permissions.

Even though the lands of the New World were the property of the king, in matters of their administration he was advised by the Council of the Indies, a group composed of humanists, politicians, and religious figures. Articles, later formalized as the Royal Ordinances on Colonization and commonly referred to as the Laws of the Indies, specified in great detail who could and should found colonies, where towns should be sited, where certain buildings should be placed, and so forth. The native peoples were seen as a resource to be protected and educated until ready to enter European culture. In principle the articles, for their time, treated the natives remarkably fairly, proscribing their exploitation or genocide. Article 5, for example, exhorted colonists to "look carefully at the places and ports where it might be possible to build Spanish settlements without damage to the Indian population."[13] Although the articles were imbued with the humanism of the times, they were overly optimistic in their conception of human nature, and their actual implementation often fell short of the spirit that created them.

Royal approval for Oñate's expedition was finally issued in 1598, and he set out accompanied by five Franciscans who had been granted the religious jurisdiction of the new province. New Mexico had been deemed a *nullius*, a land without the benefit of a bishop or regular clergy, and had been assigned to Franciscan jurisdiction. Oñate more than met the requirements of Article 89 of the revised Laws of the Indies, which governed the requisite numbers of settlers, livestock, and clergy to accompany an expedition. Burdened with thousands of head of cattle and sheep; 400 men, of whom 130 had families;[14] 200 soldiers; and 5 priests in eighty-three wagons, the expedition moved slowly.

Military protection was a necessity not only for the journey but also for the founding of missions. Two to six soldiers were assigned to maintain the religious enterprise, although the friars were often more fearful of the poor example the soldiers might set than of danger from the Indians. Centuries later the problem remained unchanged. Fray Romualdo Vartagena, guardian of the College of Santa Cruz de Querétaro, wrote in a manuscript dated 1772:

> What gives these missions their permanency is the aid which they receive from the Catholic arms. Without them pueblos are frequently abandoned, and ministers are murdered by the barbarians. It is seen everyday that in missions where there are not soldiers there is no success, for the Indians, being children of fear, are more strongly appealed to by the glistening of the sword than by the voice of five missionaries. Soldiers are necessary to defend the Indians from the enemy, and to keep an eye on the mission Indians, now to encourage, now to carry news to the nearest *presidio* [fort] in case of trouble.[15]

That both the presidios and missions were financed from the same source, the War Fund, suggests the basically hostile nature of colonization.

Oñate's expedition followed the most logical highway, the Rio Grande, and entered New Mexico through El Paso del Norte (The Pass to the North, or El Paso, now part of Texas). This route was more direct than the one taken by earlier expeditions;

without the benefit of real roads, travel followed the river valleys, which provided the benefit of a defined path and an assured source of water. From central Mexico northward there were two primary routes separated by hundreds of miles of desert: the Rio Grande drainage in New Mexico and the Gila River drainage in Arizona. Mission systems were founded along both rivers, but contact between these geographic areas was negligible until the arrival of the railroad in the nineteenth century. Like the lands between the two river systems, the Indians who dwelled in them were groups apart.[16] Acoma occupied a fringe of the Rio Grande missions, and pueblos like Zuñi and Hopi were difficult to administer because they lay too far from either jurisdiction. Zuñi, as a result, suffered its lapses of missionary presence, and Hopi was never convincingly brought within the Catholic circle.

As the Oñate group traveled north, it nominally pacified the Pueblo Indians with whom it came in contact and extorted an oath of allegiance to guarantee future obedience. The natives were to acknowledge that there was one God and one king, the former residing in heaven, the latter in Spain. After nearly half a year, the expedition reached what became its destination: the town of Ohke, rechristened San Juan de los Caballeros by the settlers, near the present-day town of Española. Because winter was rapidly approaching and insufficient time remained to build shelter, the Spanish commandeered a segment of the pueblo in which to live. As time and weather permitted, they set about constructing their own dwellings and a crude chapel to serve the entire colony and undertook rudimentary farming. The first church was dedicated in September 1598, although the structure was still incomplete. The Indian residents of San Juan were apparently calm—probably more out of fear than generosity—in tolerating the Spanish incursion.

In late fall 1598, Oñate dispatched a survey expedition of soldiers to explore certain lands to the west, including Acoma. The Spanish were brutally attacked and decimated by the Acoma warriors. In retaliation, Oñate ordered a party headed by Vicente de Zaldívar to avenge these deaths. Zaldívar's men fought their way to the top of the mesa and eventually took the battle, but the bloodshed did not end there. Oñate decreed that all "men over 25 were to have one foot cut off and spend 20 years in personal servitude; young men between the ages of twelve and 25, 20 years of personal servitude; women over twelve, 20 years of personal servitude; 60 young girls to be sent to Mexico City for service in convents, never to see their homeland again."[17]

Today this chronicle, although probably exaggerated, still seems particularly severe despite the fact that its perpetrators were desperate to establish a precedent for obedience and control of the native peoples.

Having secured military control of the territory, the Spanish turned to its administration. The *encomienda* was a central aspect of settlement policy in both Mexico and New Mexico and served as the basis for religious and economic administration when the northern province was colonized.[18] Under the encomienda system, all land was ultimately held by the king, but tracts could be granted in his name to individuals by the royal representative. Together with the land, settlers, friars, or churches could also be assigned as "trustees" (*encomenderos*) for one or more Indians. A trustee was "strictly charged by the sovereign, as a condition of his grant, to provide for the protection, the conversion, and the civilization of the natives. In return, he was empowered to exploit their labor, sharing profits with the king."[19] The Spanish thereby encouraged the education of native peoples to the ways of European religion, civilization, and technology but in turn taxed them for the privilege. The encomienda served a military purpose as well. Because the governor was responsible for the protection of the colony, it was to the common good to create a civil militia to augment the scant complement of regular troops. No funds were earmarked for this purpose, but the encomendero could be paid in tribute goods by the Indians he protected. The law specified that goods, not labor, be used as currency, but this was often not the case. In New Mexico "heads of Indian households were required to pay a yearly tribute in corn and blankets to the Spaniards. That put affairs on an orderly basis, since the Pueblo peoples now knew exactly what their obligation was, but it made the burden no more palatable."[20]

The Franciscan, as religious leader, oversaw the spiritual welfare of his charges through the catechism, baptism, and mass. Policy dictated that after conversion individuals could not depart from the church or, once settled in a village, had to remain in residence until the period of encomienda was terminated or the mission was secularized. In some parts of the Spanish New World the encomienda could be hereditary through at least two generations.[21] In others ten years was assumed to be sufficient for the completion of the missionary's work and elevation of the native. But oftentimes ten years was not "sufficient," and the terms were usually extended. His charge seemed not to learn as fast as he should, a colonist might report—not surpris-

1–6

1–6
TAOS PUEBLO
The northern residential block.
[1986]

14 ing given that Hispanic settlers often exploited the Pueblo peoples mercilessly and treated them as little more than slaves. The imposition of unreasonable burdens left the natives little time to work their own fields, and when the yield was meager, there was hardly enough for the taxes, much less to live on. Attempts to repeal the system in 1542 provoked such a strong reaction by the colonists that modifications were enforced only minimally.

Friction intensified as differences among the various Spanish factions and Governor Oñate solidified. Soldiers and colonists alike were dissatisfied by the limits of Indian productivity and the stringent conditions under which Spanish settlers were forced to live:

> They accused the governor of all kinds of crimes and malfeasance. They charged cruelty in sacking Pueblo villages without reason; that he had prevented the raising of corn necessary for the garrison and people and thereby brought on a famine and caused the people to subsist on wild seeds; and insisted that the colony could not possibly succeed unless Oñate was removed. On his part, the governor wrote to the viceroy and the king, charging the friars with various delinquencies and general inefficiency.[22]

To bolster his sagging prestige, Oñate set out in 1604 on an expedition lasting six months; his goal, to find precious metals. In his absence, Oñate's enemies in Mexico increased their advantage. News of the punishment he had meted out, reports of desertion, and the general condition of the colony reflected unfavorably on Oñate in spite of his military accomplishments. His efforts to secure riches for Spain were fruitless. He was ultimately suspended from office in 1607 and subsequently stood trial for indiscretions committed during his tenure.[23]

CONVERSION EFFORTS

Eight additional friars arrived in New Mexico in 1600, but within a year two-thirds of them had departed disheartened by the poverty of the land, leaving only a handful of Franciscans to tend the province. The mission effort was tottering in 1608, but at the eleventh hour a report reached Mexico that there were now seven thousand converts, not four hundred, as had been previously reported. The missionary project would continue, and additional Franciscans were dispatched north. Eight years later the churches numbered eleven, with fourteen thousand Indian converts.[24] Although a quota of sixty-six priests had been established for the efforts in New Mexico, it was rarely filled because negative factors usually outweighed religious zeal.

In 1617 Fray Estevan de Perea was chosen as the first *custos* of the Conversion of Saint Paul;[25] as such, he headed the missionary program in New Mexico. The province was divided into a series of governances, each of which might include several pueblos, and was placed in the custody of friars. They were charged to bring the word of the Catholic God to the heathen, to build a fitting church, and to civilize and improve the material lot of the Indians. Their concerns mixed religious and humanitarian intentions, seen as coincident in Franciscan doctrine.

At the close of the 1620s major church structures were being built in the southeastern part of the Salinas district skirting the Manzano Mountains: Abo, Las Humanas (Gran Quivira), and Quarai [Plate 4]. Fray Francisco de Acevedo assumed direction of missionary work in 1629, and the pueblos and their missions were thriving on the edge of the arid plains. Although serving as the first administrative center for this mission group, Pecos proved too distant for effective governance; Salinas was reorganized as its own jurisdiction with Abo as its headquarters.

No less impressive than the structures of the Salinas group was the church of San José de Giusewa in the Jemez Mountains west of Santa Fe, a major stone structure built and abandoned by the 1630s. At Acoma to the west, Fray Jerónimo de Zárate Salmerón assumed his post in 1623; within twenty years a voluminous stone structure had been substantially completed on the most difficult of sites. Along the Rio Grande itself a string of mud-built mission churches of varying sizes and sophistication arose bearing witness to the dedication and determination of the Franciscans. By 1630, according to estimates, twenty-five missions had been sent to ninety pueblos containing sixty thousand Indians.[26]

The friars' efforts were not unqualified successes, however, as they confronted constant resistance to conversion paired with frequent backsliding. Whipping, head shaving, and intimidation by the missionaries undermined their attempts to convert the Indians, and the rotation of the friars precluded any substantive bonds with converts, potential or otherwise.[27] Caught between civilian exploitation of the native peoples and their own religious duties, the Franciscans made no accommodation to the native religion, destroying masks, fetishes, and kivas and forbidding dances. All this in spite of Saint Francis's admonition: "Devotion to an ideal can never be had by repression and reprisal."[28]

From Spain's point of view, the New Mexican enterprise seemed to progress satisfactorily notwithstanding the difficulties and its distance from central Mexican administration. The standard of living was marginal, but the colony managed to survive. Reports of mass conversions, which often arrived just as the mission program was on the brink of collapse, strengthened flagging interest in this land that offered so little and required so much. When Zárate Salmerón recorded his visit to the province in 1626, he listed all the missions, ranking them as "ordinary," "fair," "good," "very good," "excellent" or "splendid," "handsome," and "most handsome." Acoma was most handsome; Isleta, very fine; and Jemez, splendid.

Four years later, Fray Alonso de Benavides of the Order of Saint Francis, Commissary General of the Indies, provided a description of the mission program that would be a worthy competitor for the claims made by modern advertising:

> [The Pueblos] have a notable affection for them [the Franciscans] and for the things of the church which they attend with notable love and devotion. As all the churches and monasteries they have made fully testify. Of all the which it will seem an enchantment to state that sumptuous and beautiful as they are, they were built solely by the women and by the boys and girls of the curacy.[29]

Despite these favorable descriptions of the missions, problems escalated during the 1630s: a governor was murdered although not by Indians, clergy and civil authorities argued over Indian labor, and soldiers at one point occupied Santo Domingo, charging that the pueblo had become a fortress against the governor and the king. The clergy, fearful for their lives, stayed close to the pueblo that served as administrative center for the mission program.

Problems reached crisis proportions. At Jemez Springs the San José de Giusewa mission had to be abandoned around 1630. Pestilence, drought, famine, and attacks by Plains Indians on the eastern pueblos severely undermined their survival. European communicable diseases continually plagued the densely settled pueblos, doubly frightful as an enemy that could neither be seen nor resisted. In 1640 alone, three thousand Indians died of smallpox, 10 percent of the entire population.[30] The Salinas missions, which had been tottering on the edge of disaster since their inception, buckled under various economic and medical pressures and attacks by the Apache and Comanche, who had been granted added mobility by the Spanish importation of the horse. By the end of the 1670s all these missions lay deserted.

Although conditions deteriorated rapidly, the Spanish continued to apply new means to extort production from the Indians. Any fairness that might have been intended under the encomienda system was rarely practiced. The chafing relations between the native peoples and the Europeans increased, as conflicts between the military and the clergy demonstrated to the Pueblo peoples that little unanimity joined the various Spanish factions.

THE PUEBLO REBELLION

Traditionally, the Pueblo tribes had lived as independent units governed by their own councils. Even among groups that shared the same language, mutual tolerance, rather than political union, was the general practice. But resistance to the Spanish had been building. The colonists' demand for additional fields and pastures at times forced the Indians to relocate, often to land less convenient or less fertile. Late in the 1670s, under the instigation of Popé from San Juan and several other influential leaders from the northern pueblos, the resentment that had been smoldering for a century finally ignited. A native informant recalled:

> Popé came down to the pueblo of San Felipe, accompanied by many captains from the pueblos and by other Indians, and ordered the churches burned and holy images broken up and burned. They took possession of everything in the sacristy pertaining to divine worship, and said that they were weary of putting in order, sweeping, heating, and adorning the church; and that they proclaimed both in the said pueblo and in the others that he who should utter the name of Jesus would be killed immediately; and that thereupon they could live contentedly, happy in their freedom, living according to the ancient customs.[31]

On August 10, 1680, the rebellion flared; the Spanish were either killed or forced to flee south to El Paso. Twenty-one Franciscan friars died in or near their churches; four hundred colonists were slaughtered. The Indian victory was swift and complete: the first loss of a Spanish province in the New World.

Life without the Spanish did not prove easy, however, nor was the confederation of pueblos an administrative success. "Scarcely a Pueblo alive in 1680 could remember how affairs had stood before the Spaniards had brought them cattle and sheep, exotic vegetables and grains, iron hardware, and a new religion."[32]

For twelve years the Indians retained control of the country. In 1691 a preliminary expedition attempted to reclaim the province, but this effort proved premature. Finally, however, under the

1–7

1–8

1–7
PLAZA DEL CERRO
Chimayo
The best preserved of the fortified plaza
town plan.
[Dick Kent, mid-1960s]

1–8
ORTEGA CHAPEL
Plaza del Cerro, Chimayo
Only the small wooden belfry identifies
this particular cell as serving a religious
function.
[1984]

leadership of Diego de Vargas, New Mexico was retaken during the campaigns of 1692–1693. Given the hostilities of 1680, the Reconquest was swiftly accomplished. Vargas retook the capital in 1693, and Spanish rule was reinstated at the same Palace of the Governors from which the Spanish had fled twelve years before. Relations between the military and the clergy were still strained. In one case, the military purposely provoked the clergy by saying the kachina images (of Pueblo deities) were harmless and allowing the Pueblos to maintain possession of them. This taunting was a familiar practice with a long history. In 1661, for example, one priest recorded "that once when there was a great deal of snow the *catazinas* (i.e., kachina) Indians went up to the flat roof of the very church and began to perform their superstitious dance very noisily."[33]

During the insurrection, the Indians had in most cases simply torched the roofs of the churches, as if this act alone were enough to deconsecrate these buildings and remove them from the Christian province. Laying adobe walls was time consuming, and if they were still standing, why not use them to good purpose: as a corral, for example? With the Spanish return, the church walls were repaired or rebuilt, and new roofs were constructed. The Pueblo Revolt marked a turning point in the history of virtually every existing church structure in New Mexico, thereby making problematic questions of origins, dating, and formal evolution.

In 1696 a second revolt flared but was quickly quelled. For the most part the colony—both Spanish and Indian alike—settled thereafter into maintaining its existence. Bishop Pedro Tamarón y Romeral undertook an inspection in 1760 and was appalled at the state of both clergy and religion in the province. Sixteen years later, Fray Francisco Atanasio Domínguez and Silvestre Vélez de Escalante made a two-thousand-mile voyage of exploration and investigation. As an official *visitor*, Domínguez left an excruciatingly detailed description of mission architecture and native ethnography; his inventory of even the smallest object suggests the paucity of the missionary program in general and church holdings in particular. Domínguez's *Description of New Mexico* provides an invaluable document for examining the state and use of the churches of the province at the end of the eighteenth century.

Almost from the very beginning, the regular church had continually attempted to wrest control of the New Mexican religious project from the Franciscans, who had been granted its jurisdiction. Finally in 1797, under renewed pressure from the bishop of Durango, the towns of Santa Fe, Santa Cruz, and Albuquerque were secularized, which placed the churches under the direction of parish priests rather than Franciscan missionaries.

SPANISH TOWN PLANNING

At the time of the initial Spanish *entrada* into New Mexico, the Pueblo Indians already occupied most of the rich river drainage lands, such as the Rio Grande and the basins of the Chama, Pecos, and Galisteo rivers, which were fertile with organic matter eroded by the rivers near their origins and redeposited along their banks. The rivers also guaranteed the steady supply of water necessary to make the land viable. Because the Europeans shared with the Pueblo Indians a need for productive soil, Spanish colonies often overlaid native settlements, forcing the indigenous peoples to shift location by pushing them on or by circumscribing the lands surrounding the pueblos. Although a proscription against this kind of incursion was included in the Royal Ordinances on Colonization (the king declared his concern for the well-being of *all* his citizens, including those of non-Hispanic origin), disputes arose constantly as the fight over arable land continued without conclusive resolution.

Defense against a mutual enemy, the Plains Indians, encouraged an uneasy alliance between the Spanish and the Pueblo tribes. Unlike the Pueblo peoples, Hispanic settlers displayed a distinct preference for living next to their fields in scattered ranches, even though this left them particularly vulnerable to Apache, Comanche, or Navajo attack. When danger threatened, they were forced to flee or to live within the pueblo until the threat subsided. While uncomfortable with the alien presence, the Pueblo peoples were at least grudgingly grateful for the security offered by European arms. In any event, they were offered very little choice in the matter.

To withstand the hit-and-run tactics of Indian incursions, settlements were developed on the model of the *plaza*, a word that can be loosely translated in English as "fortified village."[34] Consisting of a continuous perimeter of thick-walled adobe buildings, the plaza presented an almost unbroken exterior surface. At Las Trampas and Ranchos de Taos, vestiges of the plaza remain and suggest that the church was built pragmatically as a part of the circumferential wall to reduce the total volume of construction. The best-preserved example of the type is found at the Plaza del Cerro at Chimayo (founded about 1730, heavily restored in this century) northeast of Española. Here the structures for dwelling

18

1–9

1–9
CENTRAL SANTA FE
The plaza occupies the area in the center of the photo; the Cathedral of Saint Francis is above and to the left; the Palace of the Governors lies to the lower left.
[Paul Logsdon, 1980s]

and utility adjoin along the perimeter, and almost all of them, even today, expose few openings to the countryside. The enclosed land offered limited areas for gardening and grazing, a problem aggravated by the limited availability of water to those who sought refuge within the walls of the plaza during times of threat. The plan of the plaza as a whole was more important than any single building, and there was little adjustment of building form for any particular use. (On the west side of the plaza, for example, the small private Ortega chapel of San Buenaventura is distinguished from the houses and utility structures of the plaza only by a cross and a small wooden turret on its roof.) The plaza was a more generic and less formally conceived type of town layout. The only true architecturally planned communities in New Mexico were the *villas*, or chartered municipalities, the foremost settlements in the territory.

In 1599–1600 the Spanish moved into the town of Yunque (also Yungue or Yunge) on the bank of the Rio Grande and established the first de facto capital of New Mexico at San Gabriel.[35] Lying far to the north, San Gabriel was soon deemed to be an ineffective administrative center because the Rio Grande pueblos extended from Taos in the north to near Socorro in the south, with spurs to the southeastern Salinas district and westward to Acoma and Zuñi. The capital was relocated for expediency in 1610 to what is now Santa Fe. Although not directly on the Rio Grande—which was a distinct disadvantage for agriculture—the site was otherwise well suited for settlement. Its average rainfall far exceeded that of the lower elevations, and the new site was more centrally located in relation to the string of native communities along the river.

As early as 1513 various ordinances governing a wide range of details regarding colonization had been issued; these were formalized by Philip II in 1573 as the Laws of the Indies. Although they were intended to cover virtually every aspect of colonization, the impact of these directives diminished with distance from Mexico City, and in New Mexico their dicta were often only weakly applied. Santa Fe, however, remains one of the few cities in the United States that clearly bear the stamp of these codes even today. The city, as envisioned in the Laws of the Indies, was to be rational in design and yet possess and express symbolic and ceremonial attributes. The conception of urban form embodied in the articles was derived from Renaissance humanism and was a response to the medieval city's dual problems of crowding and civil strife, both the results of uncontrolled and convoluted incremental growth. To some degree the prescribed city plans were based on cross-axial grids similar to those of the Roman city, with its *cardo* (north-south) and *decumanus* (east-west) streets. Each subsequent revision of the planning ordinances after 1513 more closely emulated the rectilinearity, if not the precise layout, of the Roman model.[36] Also, the reintroduction of the grid in Spanish Renaissance thought probably revealed the influence of the architect and theorist Leon Battista Alberti's noted architectural treatise *De re aedificatoria* (Ten Books on Architecture, 1485 or 1486), which circulated widely in learned circles. Alberti, in turn, had drawn on the Roman Vitruvius, an architect who also influenced sixteenth-century Mexican architecture, as a major source of information and inspiration.[37]

Although Renaissance humanism is usually identified as the motivating force for the use of the grid plan throughout Spanish America, a direct connection with European practice has been lacking, even though the bastides of southern France and siege towns in Spain were both planned on the grid system and resembled settlements built in accord with the Laws of the Indies. George Kubler recently demonstrated, however, that towns constructed in France between Grasse and Nice to repopulate the countryside during the early sixteenth century were just such a connection. Previously abandoned during the plague years of the fourteenth century, new towns such as Valbonne (1509) and Vallauris (1501)—both of which were developed by the Benedictine abbey of Saint Honorat of Lérins—were planned without walls but with contiguous dwellings forming a defined perimeter. Valbonne in particular resembles an enlarged version of a New Mexican fortified village such as Chimayo, subdivided using an orthogonal geometry with the plaza near its center.[38]

The Laws of the Indies also prescribed the location and site of the town by, for example, specifying on which shore of a river the city should be built for defense or commerce and how to ascertain the quality of the land:

> The health of the area which will be known from the abundance of old men or of young men of good complexion, natural fitness and color, and without illness; and in the abundance of healthy animals of sufficient size, and of healthy fruits and fields where no toxic and noxious things are grown, but that it be of good climate, the sky clear and benign, the air pure and soft, without impediment or alterations and of good temperature, without excessive heat or cold, and having to decide, it is better that it be cold.[39]

Colonists were urged to settle "in fertile areas with

1–10

1–10
EAST PALACE STREET
Santa Fe
The arcades of Sena Plaza and the Palace of the Governors suggest the character of the capital's streets during the late nineteenth century.
[1981]

an abundance of fruits and fields, of good land to plant and harvest, of grasslands to grow livestock, of mountains and forests of wood and building materials for homes and edifices, and of good and plentiful water supply for drinking and irrigation."[40]

The ceremonial heart of the town was the *plaza mayor*, the principal open space. Less a square or a promenade than a *campus martius* on which the military could train and parade, the main plaza was "to be the starting point for the town. . . . The Plaza should be square or rectangular, in which case it should have at least one and one half times its width for length inasmuch as this shape is best for fiestas in which horses are used and for any other fiesta that should be held."[41] Moreover, "the size of the plaza shall be proportioned to the number of inhabitants. [The plaza] shall be not less than two hundred feet wide and three hundred feet long and five hundred and thirty-two feet wide. A good proportion is six hundred feet long and four hundred wide."[42] Fronting the north side of the plaza was the Palacio Real, or Palace of the Governors, a site the building still occupies in Santa Fe.[43]

Curiously, the principal religious edifice was to be built, not squarely on the main plaza, but to one side—apparently to provide greater prominence. "The temple in inland places shall not be placed on the square but at a distance and shall be separated from any other building or from adjoining buildings; and ought to be seen from all sides so it can be decorated better, thus acquiring more authority."[44] "For temples of the principal church, parish, or monastery, there shall be assigned specific lots. . . . These shall be a complete block so as to avoid having other buildings nearby."[45] The predecessor of today's Cathedral of Saint Francis in Santa Fe, the Parroquia (parish church) occupied a site in accord with this directive. It should be noted, however, that the plaza originally encompassed twice its current area and that the block today bounded by East Palace Avenue, Federal Drive, and East San Francisco Street was originally part of the plaza before it was displaced by commercial construction during the nineteenth century.[46]

The cathedral thus originally occupied a position of only secondary importance on one corner of the plaza. Prominence and centrality were instead granted to the Palace of the Governors, the administrative center and residence of the king's representative in the colony. Although the relative position of church and state on the plaza of Santa Fe might strike us today as curious, the urban form embodied implicit attitudes about their respective positions in the provincial capital. In spite of the tone and intermittent specificity of the planning ordinances, they were ultimately ambiguous and open to interpretation, and their literal application was only very rarely the case in New Mexico.

Extending from the political, social, and commercial heart of the town were streets arranged in a rectangular grid. Article 114 proclaimed that "from the plaza shall begin four principal streets," and Article 115 announced that "around the plaza as well as along the four principal streets which begin there, there shall be arcades, for these are of considerable convenience to the merchants who generally gather there." Indeed, native merchants continue to trade in the arcade of the Palace of the Governors in Santa Fe today. The Laws of the Indies also described other characteristics of the ideal city and warned that unhealthy but necessary services, such as fisheries, slaughterhouses, and tanneries, should be positioned so "that the filth can be easily disposed of."[47] The town should have a commons, and sites for houses and shops were to be distributed by lottery, although no lots on the plaza were to be given to "private individuals."[48] Once assigned, the inhabitants were admonished that "each house in particular shall be built that they may keep therein their horses and work animals, and shall have yards and corrals as large as possible for health and cleanliness."[49] In spite of the careful planning of the city and in spite of its status as provincial capital, Santa Fe was characterized in the late eighteenth century by Domínguez as "lack[ing] everything. . . . The Villa of Santa Fe (for the most part) consists of many scattered ranchos at various distances from one another, with no plan to their location."[50]

After the Reconquest of 1692–1693, Governor Vargas was forced to find new land to accommodate sixty-six families that had recently emigrated to northern New Mexico. One must assume, however, that the limited tracts of arable land surrounding the capital, rather than any actual dearth of building sites, caused the founding or refounding of the second villa, Santa Cruz. Reduced today to a dusty field of intersecting roads, Santa Cruz retains even less of its original plaza than does Santa Fe. Perhaps buildings never fully enclosed the space, although an 1848 sketch plan suggests a dense, contiguous architectural fabric. The definition of the plaza in an architectonic sense is minimal, and to the great bulk of the church of Santa Cruz falls the task of marking the center of a densely built town that no longer exists.

The third of the charted municipalities, Albuquerque, was founded in 1706 and still possesses a neat plaza whose style, like that of the church of

1–11

1–11
SEVERINO MARTÍNEZ HOUSE
Taos, circa 1804
The house as protection from the
enemy and the elements, with stout
adobe walls, few openings, and internal
courtyards.
[1986]

1–12

1–12
FARMHOUSE FROM MORA
Reerected at Las Golondrinas Folk
Museum, La Cienaga
The interior of the house was developed
as a linear arrangement of rooms; the
pedimented doorways and painted wall
decoration are characteristic of northern
New Mexico.
[1984]

San Felipe Neri on its north side, was anglicized
late in the nineteenth century. The vast expansion
of the city in the postwar years and the unfortunate
development of Old Town Albuquerque as a tourist
attraction during the last decade or two have undermined the calm dignity amid dust that characterized
the earlier plazas. Beneath the surface, however,
the skeleton of the original plaza and the diluted
directives of the Laws of the Indies can still be
ascertained.

THE HISPANIC DWELLING

The idea of a rectangular space enclosed by walls
or buildings pervaded Spanish colonial construction
from house to church to city. In settlements the idea
manifested as the fortified plaza town or the plaza
mayor of the city. In the house or on the ranch, the
placita, or "courtyard," was the configuration basic
to all but the simplest dwellings, and it shared certain affinities with the *convento* of the church and
the church building itself. In their construction and
plan the house and the church complex displayed a
common sensibility, if a somewhat different form.
Thus, an examination of both Spanish and native
dwellings provides a foundation for understanding
the planning of the more monumental religious
architecture of New Mexico.

The Hispanic New Mexican house, as Bainbridge
Bunting showed, shared formal similarities with
native dwellings, although it sometimes differed in
configuration or detail.[51] The house was usually
of simple construction: rooms of rectangular mud
blocks with a few window openings and a door.
Joined in a linear fashion, rooms extended along
the longitudinal axis of the house; the width of the
house—like the nave of the church—was often
determined by the length of the trees available to
make the beams. The layout could take landform
and use into account, bending where necessary to
better accommodate the builder's wishes or the topography. When land was plentiful the house remained a single story; only in the later nineteenth
century did the pressures of limited land availability in cities encourage multistory structures. This
building pattern of single-story dispersed housing
stood in marked contrast to the stacked blocks of
Indian pueblos, such as those at Pecos, Zuñi, and
Taos, built before contact with the Spanish.[52]

Thick-walled structures address the hot and dry
climate of the desert by storing or delaying the
transmission of heat (a property known as thermal
mass). Heat transfer works this way: the thick walls
cool during the night. Throughout the day the

1–13

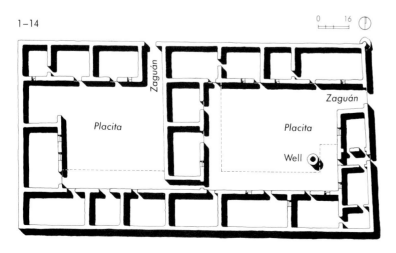

1–13
SEVERINO MARTÍNEZ HOUSE,
THE WEST COURTYARD
[1986]

1–14
SEVERINO MARTÍNEZ HOUSE, PLAN
An example of the double courtyard
plan: one for human dwelling and one
for work, storage, and animals.
[Source: Plan by Jerome Milord, 1985]

walls, particularly those facing south and west, receive considerable radiant heat from sunlight, which is absorbed by the adobe. But some time is required for this heat to penetrate through the wall mass. All throughout the cool night the heat in the walls radiates into the room, keeping it warm, until by morning the heat has dissipated and the cycle begins anew, with the room remaining cool throughout the day. The system, of course, never works perfectly, but it explains the performance of thick-walled buildings in a hot and dry climate and the thermal characteristics of the interior spaces of houses, churches, and conventos.

In time the thermal advantages of thick walls were augmented by the addition of arcades, which shielded the south and west walls from solar heat buildup. The function of the *portal*, or arcade, in Hispanic architecture thus roughly paralleled the stick frameworks, or *ramadas*, of Pueblo building: shaded, ventilated areas under which the Indians sat or worked and on which they dried vegetables, fruits, and grains. In fact, the Pueblo tribes lived out of doors much of the time, on the roof terraces of the stacked dwellings or on the ground. Their architecture also revealed an understanding of thermal performance. Dwellings constructed in compact units, with only narrow pathways between adjacent structures, shaded the opposite building, thereby reducing the direct heat gain. Conversely, stepping the pueblo's form toward the south guaranteed greater solar collection during the winter months. Although many of the pueblos illustrated both these general tendencies, certain aspects of this climate management might have been circumstantial, rather than intentional, and in any event were not the sole parameters directing building.[53]

The linear bar, growing by accretion to accommodate the family's needs, was also a common residential configuration. As the dwelling grew, the string of rooms bent around an enclosed placita, thereby limiting the exterior openings to one or a few while increasing the structure's defensibility. The dwelling spaces and perhaps storage or work areas occupied one side of the courtyard, which shared the intimate internal orientation of Muslim domestic architecture. A covered passage, called a *zaguán*, permitted entry to the interior courtyard, and depending on its size, the zaguán could double as a wagon entrance, a breezeway, or a work area.[54] Larger ranches might also include a chapel, a barn for the animals, and even a *torreón* (fortified tower), a defensive stronghold and observation point. Built of adobe or stone, the upper floor was used for reconnaissance and shooting, the lower to store water

and provisions and house women and children during attack.[55] When necessary, the court itself could serve as a corral.

More complex building groups could be organized on the double courtyard configuration, which separated the inhabitants from the animals by providing one human and one agricultural court. This planning arrangement was also used in building the convento, or friary, that accompanied each mission. As a plan type, the convento was more a farm or ranch abutting a church than a monastic cloister. Its concerns were more functional than ceremonial or spiritual; its form was secular, not sacred, although the nave of the church itself often contributed one side to the square court.

Unlike the later California missions, which were almost always formed in a quadrangle, the New Mexican church complex was more haphazard in its planning and more ad hoc in its adjustment to prevailing conditions. The New Mexican church also frequently served less of an economic role in the community than did the mission among the seminomadic Indians of the West Coast. In New Mexico the religious institution was forced to acknowledge the society and buildings of a sedentary culture and to adapt to the existing structure of the pueblos, rather than to create a new town, as was the case in California.

The ornamental courtyard garden of the California mission never developed in New Mexico: water was too precious for purely ornamental purposes, and most priests had enough difficulty raising their own food, much less time to pursue the decorative. If there were ornamental plants, they were probably grown in ceramic pots.[56] Because the pueblos in New Mexico were scattered and priests were few in number, friars usually lived alone. The pattern of the cloister or monastery was thus inappropriate—although there was always a lingering image of what the Franciscan monastic home in Mexico had been. And a century and a half separated the evangelical campaigns of Franciscan New Mexico and California. By the late eighteenth century the purposes and models of conversion had been significantly altered by the impact of Jesuit thought, instigating a consequent shift in architectural response.[57]

CHURCH PATTERNS

When the missionaries began evangelical work in Mexico in the early 1500s, they carried with them the architectural prototypes of the churches of Spain. The centuries of Moorish occupation had precipitated there the development of fortified religious architecture, particularly in those areas of southern Spain in proximity to the lands of the "infidels." Even though the traditions of Spanish Romanesque and Gothic architecture continued in the New World, military uncertainty caused their modification. Walls were thick, penetrated by few openings, and buttressed by masonry piers. According to George Kubler and Martin Soria:

> The massing of mid-century [sixteenth] churches suggests military architecture. The bare surfaces of massive walls were a necessary result of untrained labor and of amateur design. Furthermore the friars needed a refuge, both for themselves, as outnumbered strangers surrounded by potentially hostile Indians, and for their villagers, who were exposed, especially on the western and northern frontiers, to the attacks of nomad Chichimec tribes after 1550.[58]

In their simplicity, their single nave, and the relation of the convento to the church, the monastic churches neatly presaged the later religious sanctuaries erected in New Mexico.

Vestiges of these prior concerns remained in Mexican church architecture into the seventeenth century, but their prominence was undermined by an expenditure of accumulating wealth and the exuberance of the baroque attitude toward form and space that countered the Protestant Reformation. Splendor and light became the foremost vehicles for reasserting the power of the church, and an enthusiasm for architecture paralleled religious ecstasy. The single-naved church, perhaps extended by transepts, served as the basic form in Andalusia and later in the New World; but with the development of a facility in central Mexico for working stone, an elaboration in both size and complexity followed suit.

Early builders restricted areas of ornamentation to the facade, doors, and window surrounds. With the ultrabaroque, however, the ornamental field exploded.[59] Decoration focused the celebrants' attention on the facade and the altar. At the extreme, the building's mass merged with its ornamentation and virtually dissolved in luminous illusion. The physical limits of the space admitted no visual bounds, and the light that flooded through cupolas and lanterns dramatically illuminated the theater of belief. In some New World colonies, this extremity of architectural expression waited for decades, if not centuries, to achieve a near parity with the churches of the homeland. In certain Mexican churches, in contrast, the architectural exuberance at times surpassed that of contemporary Spain. In New Mexico, to the contrary, exuberance never really arrived.

The native building technology of the sixteenth century was limited primarily to stone implements; the vast majority of tools and ironware needed to construct the new churches was imported by Europeans. At first churches were small, particularly the rural missions set in the mountain country or jungles of Mexico.[60]

As late as the close of the sixteenth century, decades after the Conquest of Mexico, these outlying churches remained simple affairs: single rectangular halls with neither the transepts nor side aisles common to the Romanesque or Gothic religious architecture of Spain. Built of stone, mud, or a combination of the two, the churches employed wooden beams, rather than masonry vaults, to support the roof.

Even in the most isolated areas the church grew correspondingly with the size of the community, and for these rural missions the church and the village were nearly synonymous. Building came under the priest's supervision, and he no doubt based his plans on memories of Spanish or central Mexican ecclesiastical prototypes. Military engineers or civilian builders probably contributed critical construction expertise. In one documented instance, Padre Nicolás Durán brought to Lima a scale architectural model of the Casa Professa in Rome to serve as an object lesson for Peruvian religious architecture.[61] Few records of such formalized transmission of architectural ideas as this one remain, however, and by the mid-sixteenth century Mexico was producing noteworthy architecture by resident designers.[62] The sophistication of an architectural idea and its methods of realization varied with the period and the place in which the church was built.

In Peruvian towns, architecture developed from the beamed, single-nave structure of the vaulted form more reminiscent of the Iberian Peninsula. At times the vaults were more ornamental than structural, built of plaster over wooden lath rather than carefully fitted stone. In the hinterland, however, in mountain districts such as those around Lake Titicaca, vestiges of the primitive church remained, the closest parallel forms to those of the religious architecture of early New Mexico. And like the New Mexican churches, these buildings were tempered by necessity in their isolated locations; their fabrics avoided the elaborate formal play of urban religious architecture and more directly addressed the exigencies of their sites and religious programs.

The combination of the *reducción* and the tremendous number of rapid conversions exerted insistent pressures on both the clergy and the physical fabric of their churches. As a result, hundreds or perhaps even thousands of new or would-be Chris-

26

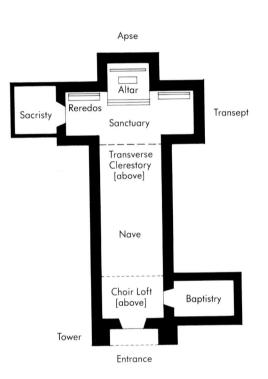

Apse

Altar

Reredos

Sacristy

Sanctuary

Transept

Transverse
Clerestory
[above]

Nave

Choir Loft
[above]

Baptistry

Tower

Entrance

1–15
HYPOTHETICAL PLAN OF A NEW
MEXICAN CHURCH WITH TRANSEPTS

tians waiting to receive conversion required religious accommodation. Because the diminutive church structures allowed by rural construction methods could not embrace all these converts, a new form of open-air chapel known as the *atrio* was developed to serve this purpose.

Even though it was common practice to enter the Hispanic church through a walled burial ground called the *campo santo,* the conversion of this enclosed but unroofed space to ceremonial use was a Mexican contribution. This development was not wholly without precedent, however. Faced with similar programmatic demands, the churches of early Christiandom and many of the great pilgrimage churches of Europe had included an outdoor altar from which mass could be celebrated. But the adaptation of the sanctuary's form to strengthen the prominence of the entry and the slight reorientation of the focus of the church toward the atrio represented a development of historical precedent.

Although permitted to enter the cemetery, Indians were forbidden to enter the church until they had successfully completed catechism. Certain devotions were performed by the priests on the front steps of the church, however, the congregation having gathered within the walled enclosure of the campo santo. In time a rudimentary chapel directed toward the exterior was integrated into the front or side of the church to accommodate these new uses.[63]

CHURCH TYPES

In seventeenth-century New Mexico the mission answered both liturgical and propagandistic callings. The building served as a sanctified house that signified the Christian presence in the "wilderness." At the same time, architecture itself served as an instrument of conversion, a structure of scale and splendor sufficient to create an appropriate sense of awe and respect for Catholic doctrine.

While bound to pledges of poverty for themselves, the mendicant orders were relatively unrestrained in their creation of places of worship. In Mexico the Dominicans, the Augustinians, and even the Jesuits were criticized for the lavishness of their constructions, which were at times drastically overbuilt for the small hamlets in which they were located. By the beginning of the 1700s baroque architecture had penetrated Mexico with concepts of free space and undulating form, the exuberant curve, planes of elaborate decoration, and, perhaps most important, a sense of light. The missionaries who served in New Mexico, however, were unable to implement the elaborate styles of the already wide-

1–16

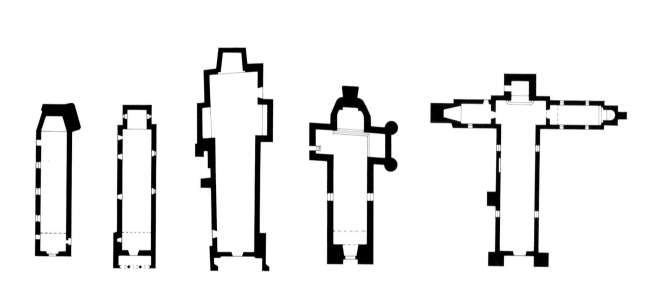

IA
Single Nave,
Battered Apse

IB
Single Nave,
Square Apse

II
Shallow
Transepts

III
Developed
Transepts

IV
Extended
Transepts
Forming
Chapels

28 spread Mexican baroque, hampered as they were by
two mitigating factors. As Franciscans, they were
bound to vows of poverty, chastity, and obedience,
the inherent simplicity of which extended to expres-
sions in architecture. More important, much of the
new architecture of central Mexico was simply impossible to duplicate concurrently in New Mexico
given the state of the building technology in the
colony, the building skills of the native laborers, and
the local materials. Nevertheless, the churches of
the early seventeenth century were the largest ever
to be built in New Mexico. They were erected when
religious fervor ran high and the Pueblo peoples
had not yet been decimated by famine, raids by Plains
Indians, or European diseases; and they expressed a
religious institution that intended to remain.

The first church type constructed for the specific
purpose of Catholic religious services was a relatively modest, single-nave structure measuring
about twenty-five by seventy-five feet, its apse articulated as a smaller rectangle. Representative of
this early type is the chapel at Gran Quivira dedicated to San Ysidro (1629–1632?), the patron saint
of agriculture. Built of a gray-yellow limestone, the
chapel's walls were mud plastered inside and out
according to the normal Indian and European practice. The roof, of wooden beams on which were laid
smaller ceiling pieces and a thick layer of earth, suggested Indian methods dating from Anasazi times.
The Europeans provided the architectural design
for the church, but the Indians provided the physical labor and practical building knowledge derived
from centuries of construction experience. If San
Ysidro was ever completed, it was soon outgrown or
found wanting, and its stones were probably reused
in the more ambitious structure, San Buenaventura,
that succeeded it.

A church consisted primarily of a nave to shelter
the congregation and an altar at which the priest
could celebrate the mass. The scale of the church
was circumscribed by need. Walls of mud could
only be practically piled to a height of about thirty
feet, stone to perhaps fifteen feet higher. The width
of the nave was fixed by the length of the beams
available in the relative vicinity. There were no
aisles to widen the nave, and thus the length of the
church was the principal variable. Modifications
to the archetypal building plan developed as a response to the particularities of the site, the availability of building material, and the desired height
of the walls. The altarpiece, usually a later addition
to church furnishings and often imported, typically
reflected contemporary Mexican taste far better
than did the church structure itself, which remained

1–17

1–17
FACADE TYPES: THE PLANAR AND THE
TWIN-TOWERED

a relatively consistent form for nearly three centuries. Thus, the Indian mission and the Spanish colonial church employed the same basic architectural competence—that is, the same vocabulary of building form—up to the Anglo influx of the mid-nineteenth century.[64] The Santuario at Chimayo, built as late as 1816, used roughly the same construction and architectural form as had churches from the early sixteenth century, and the same building techniques continue in use even today.

Larger or more complex church structures (labeled as Types II, III, and IV in Figure 1–16) sometimes extended their naves with partially or fully stated transepts, and in some instances, such as San José de Giusewa or Quarai, these churches also had secondary altars for devotions other than the high mass. The main altar occupied the sanctuary (chancel or choir). This part of the structure, particularly in early-seventeenth-century churches such as Abo and Quarai, was battered in plan to a considerable degree, perhaps nostalgically recalling the true hemispherical apse of the Continental prototypes. The pronounced form of the angled apse became a prominent feature of New Mexican mission architecture and is well represented by San Miguel in Santa Fe. These almost prosaic features—the thick-walled nave, the flat roof, the articulated apse, and the basic long and low profile wedded to the ground—combined to create the distinctive form of the Spanish sanctuaries of the colonial period.

SITING

Just as there were good reasons for founding villages in certain locations, so there were good reasons for siting churches in particular places. In the latter case, however, the logic of the choice was quite simple: parish churches were established as the centers of their communities; mission churches were built where conditions allowed. Site selection was always a compromise, the missionary trying to balance his hope for an imposing site against the realities of the topography and the pueblo's values.

Once the missionary had secured a foothold in the community, he usually tried to acquire permission to build the church and convento on a physically suitable and prestigious site. A central location was conceptually ideal, but acceptable sites were difficult to locate. For pueblos located along the Rio Grande, flat land in proximity to the community was relatively easy to find. This was less the case, however, in villages located on rising land or in the mountains. Where suitably level terrain was in limited supply, friars were forced to accept sites that

were far less than ideal. The series of churches built at Pecos, for example, occupied a narrow slice of the *mesilla* remaining after the construction of the two segments of the pueblo itself.[65] The first church at Pecos was erected well outside the pueblo proper, and all four churches built there had to add fill to the ridge so as to level the floor of the nave. Concepción at Quarai rose on the ruins of a prior pueblo. More spectacular was the case of Acoma, where the inhospitability of the rock necessitated the importation of thousands of baskets of earth to level the site and fill the campo santo held within its stone retaining walls, a process that took several decades to complete.

In the Spanish villages the church's position on the (often fortified) plaza was nearly standard; but most missions evidenced little consistency in their placement. In the pueblos several factors mitigated against a single, idealized siting or orientation that would guarantee prominence to the religious edifice. For one, the church arrived in the pueblo long after the physical structure of the village had been determined, and the Indian dance plaza hardly matched the more regularized architectural statement of its Spanish counterpart. The native space represented or suggested instead a locus, rather than an absolute center, and was rarely constructed as a clearly defined architectural entity. Typically, it was already surrounded, however irregularly, with dwellings and kivas by the time the Franciscans arrived. In truth, the native populations probably had little desire to admit the church, which would become the largest structure in the village, into the center of its community. Thus, most churches remained resolutely on the periphery of the pueblo.

Basically, the church occupied whatever site its builder could find where land was sufficient and where the missionary was allowed to build. Although sufficiently elevated to become a focal point for the community when seen from a distance, San José at Laguna stands on a site well behind the plaza. Zia turns its low, massive back on the pueblo and becomes a quiet neighbor. San Esteban at Acoma dominates the village's architecture; its height and mass are almost antagonistic to the adjacent rows of dwellings. Only at Tesuque, Isleta, and the rebuilt San Jerónimo at Taos pueblo do the churches rest squarely on the plaza; and even in these instances, they lack the same sense of conviction about siting displayed by a church in a Spanish town. Kubler offered four possible reasons the separation of church and pueblo might have been desirable: the pueblo's hostility to friars, the friars' mistrust of the pueblo, the function of churches as forts, and the need for

ample land for mission buildings, fields, and corrals.[66] Of these, only the last seems plausible because the "separation" of these churches from the pueblo rarely exceeded fifty yards and because settlers on occasion took refuge within the pueblo from Apache or Comanche attacks. The relegation of the religious sanctuary to land beyond the pueblo and the chronic problems it might occasion were well illustrated by the situation at Picuris. During the late eighteenth century Comanche raids wreaked havoc on the church, ultimately necessitating its removal and reconstruction within the pueblo walls, with Spanish and Pueblo brought together against a common enemy.[67]

In theory, churches would have followed an east-west orientation, with the principal facade facing west. But the realities of frontier construction mitigated against a consistent orientation, and New Mexican churches faced in virtually all directions, thereby confounding attempts to utilize the transverse clerestory to its best advantage. Even in Mexico City by the turn of the nineteenth century, the religious reasons for an east-west orientation had been for the most part lost to the building tradesmen. "I have heard it said," the anonymous author of a treatise roughly translated as *Architectural Practice in Mexico City* confessed, "that a church should be oriented in such a way that the principal door looks toward the west, to satisfy some rite of the church that I do not understand. Where there are no other buildings to obstruct the site one should orient it as prescribed, but if buildings prohibit this, one builds where he can."[68] Although written fully two centuries after the founding of the Catholic enterprise in New Mexico, this admission of relativity applied almost universally to religious construction in the northern province.

LAYOUT

How much of the building project was designed prior to its realization is not precisely known, although the complex spatial programs of the church and convento, compounded by the particularities of each site, suggest that considerable deliberation preceded construction. Possibly the friar used a charcoal stick or ink to mark design studies on a board, hide, or paper, if supplies of the latter were still available.[69] The definitive layout, with adjustments for the site constraints, was necessarily made directly on the ground.

To lay out the church, the friar had several options, all of them quite basic measuring techniques. In Mexico proper, lime was used to mark out the plan of the building on the site.[70] A free expenditure of valuable lime in such a manner would have been wasteful in the frontier conditions of New Mexico, so colored soils or sands could have served as worthy substitutes. A simple lightweight cord—easy to use and revise and easy to transport—was probably the principal means for marking the plan of the building on the ground. In conjunction with stakes for locating the corners, wall intersections, and principal building points, this medium was typically used in surveying and was readily applied to building construction.[71]

Most useful to the religious builder would have been an understanding of geometry, in particular the three/four/five relationship of the right, or Pythagorean, triangle. Measurement was based on the *vara*, roughly thirty-three inches, although minor variations did exist. Using strings as measuring tapes, the builder could lay out with relative precision the edifice and its rooms. Alignment was ascertained with the compass and solar or celestial sightings, all of which were known to the military and presumably to the educated Franciscans. These instruments could have been employed in combination, with one used as a means to confirm the other. While relative accuracy could be attained, construction with massive stone or mud walls allowed for relative imprecision, as the thicknesses varied depending on the moisture in the adobe and the wall's state of preservation.

Each friar brought tools to found the church, including shovels and hoes for digging foundations and mixing adobe; axes, adzes, saws, chisels, and augurs for working the timber; and nails, tacks, and hinges for fitting the pieces together.[72] Given that construction was undertaken by a sizable team of native labor organized in gangs under the supervision of a foreman, these tools would have been the minimum needed unless some domestic means was used to reproduce them. Fortunately, making adobe blocks required little formwork; and stone was used as it was found in situ.

SITEWORK

With the plan of the church laid out on the ground, excavation for the stone foundation began. Whether the church was built of masonry or adobe, the first step in construction was to secure a solid foundation. Large stones were placed in foundation trenches excavated along the perimeter of the building to provide a structurally stable base for the mud or stone walls. The stones also retarded capillary action and provided better drainage than the earth

alone would have allowed. Drainage was a critical factor in earthen construction. (The present-day use of cement stucco instead of mud plaster has interrupted the natural evaporation patterns from the ground through the wall to the air, thereby undermining more than one church.) If the site was neither level nor gently sloping upward toward the altar, earth removal or terracing was necessary. The nave of the church at Jemez Springs was cut into the steep hillside, and the excavated material was used to fill the downhill side until a relatively level floor was finally devised. Even the altar was stepped up several feet to take advantage of the topography—a sensible strategy given that bedrock could not be reformed. The slope and the interruption of the natural drainage pattern are the probable reasons for the church's double floor: two layers of earth separated by a layer of burnt wood or charcoal, the latter intended to absorb the ground seepage and desiccate the upper earthen layer.

Jemez Springs was an instance of extremely inhospitable topographic conditions, but it was certainly not the only instance. Consider the uneven surface of the Acoma mesa, where even the land for the campo santo was imported in baskets, or the limited strip of buildable land at Pecos, or the contoured hilltop at Laguna. All these sites required goodly amounts of labor just to establish workable footings and erect a suitable platform for construction. At Acoma, about eighteen inches of earth were used to fill and level the surface of the mesa to create a suitable floor.

The floors were finished as tamped, compacted earth, packed to almost rock hardness over the years. In residential construction animal blood was sometimes used as a sealant, and the practice may also have been used in the churches. Women swept floors weekly and in some churches repacked the surface each year with new mud and straw.[73] In the case of Abo, stone flags completed the interior floor surface, but this was common practice only at the Salinas missions.

Allowing the floor to remain earthen also served a practical need because the more noted personages of the parish would be buried inside the church as space allowed. Presumably for health reasons, a royal decree banning burials within the church was issued in 1748, although it took more than a year to reach Santa Fe. The practice remained desirable, however, in light of frontier conditions, fear of native deprecations, and the pious impulse to lay at rest near the altar. Higher fees for interment within the nave made the custom more attractive for the clergy as well as the congregation. In 1822, 1826,

32

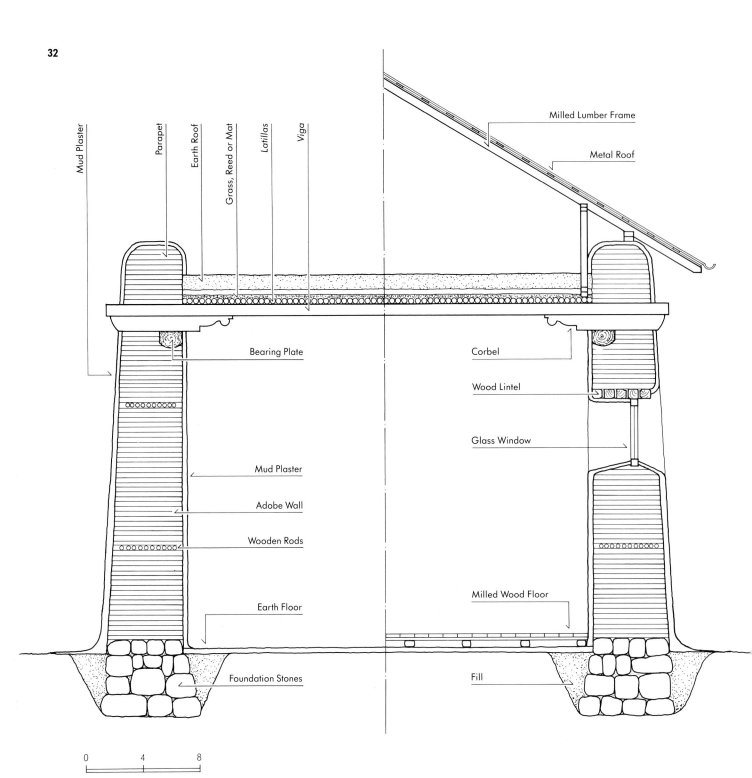

Mud Plaster

Parapet

Earth Roof

Grass, Reed or Mat

Latillas

Viga

Milled Lumber Frame

Metal Roof

Bearing Plate

Corbel

Wood Lintel

Glass Window

Mud Plaster

Adobe Wall

Wooden Rods

Milled Wood Floor

Earth Floor

Foundation Stones

Fill

0   4   8

1–18
GENERIC CONSTRUCTION SECTION
OF WALL
The pitched metal roof, a common
addition during the late nineteenth
century, is shown in the right half
of the drawing.
[Source: Sketch by Robert Nestor,
1989]

and again in 1833, the Mexican government renewed the proscription, probably with the same
ineffectual result.[74]

WALLS

Upon the stone foundation, which rose about eighteen inches above the ground, the walls were laid,
their progress checked vertically by plumb bob and
horizontally by a wooden leveling device. A triangle
of wood, this mason's level relied on a plumb to mark
the midpoint of the horizontal stringer along the
hypotenuse of the frame. An effective tool, easily
replicable, the level could be used horizontally to
check for true right angles as well as vertically to
ensure that walls and doors were plumb. As the walls
of the church rose, scaffolding was erected, sunk
into the ground, lashed with rawhide, and fixed to
the wall as necessary for stability.

Contrary to European practice, and much to the
shock of the missionaries, the construction of walls
was the women's province: "Among these nations,"
Benevides told us, "it is the custom for the women
to build the walls and the men to spin and weave
their mantas, and to go to war and the chase; if we
try to oblige some man to build a wall, he runs away
from it and the women laugh. And with this work
of women there have been built more than fifty
churches, with roofs, with very beautiful carvings
and fretwork and the walls very well painted."[75]
This practice probably derived from traditions in
Pueblo prehistory, not surprising because real property—the house and its contents—belonged to the
wife and was passed through matrilineal inheritance.

Without exception, New Mexican churches employed a type of construction known as bearing
wall; that is, a structural system in which the roof
was directly and continuously supported by the
walls rather than by columns or piers arranged in
series. Given the economic and technical conditions
in which the churches were built, the width of the
naves was relatively large and the weight of the roof
substantial. Design was to some extent based on
trial and rule of thumb, and walls tended to be massive. The resultant thick wall, whether of stone or
adobe, imparted the particular character of architectural solidity to these religious structures.

One structural device notably absent in New
Mexico was the arch, which one hundred fifty years
later was to become a hallmark of California mission architecture. Few instances of the arch are
known to have existed in New Mexico, the one remaining, although structurally impure, example being the arched opening in the chancel at Pecos. A

lack of advanced building knowledge, dressed stone,
and wood for the formwork used during construction precluded an architecture based on the vault or
dome. The colony was restricted to churches using
bearing walls spanned by heavy beams, an architectural method that traced back through Spanish history to Asia Minor and that by the end of the seventeenth century was somewhat archaic in central
Mexico. Indeed, bearing wall construction also precluded the development of a church with side aisles,
as the construction of columns or piers proved
structurally impractical when built of adobe or unworked stone.

Stone construction methods drew on centuries-
old Pueblo practices; in look and technique they
possessed only a passing resemblance to all but the
most elementary European masonry. Rock was used
as it was found, neatly fissured into usable pieces in
hillsides and exposed cuts; it was not finished in any
way. (An eroded bank by the stream approaching
Abo provides a clear example of the readily available
sources for stone. So evenly are the stones fractured
there that they give the appearance of having been
quarried with tools.) Pieces commonly measured
about one foot square and four inches thick. Normally laid up without mortar, stone fragments were
sometimes inserted in the gaps to increase stability.
In other instances an adobe mortar was packed
around the stones; having no chemical binding
power, this bond was noticeably weaker than the
stones it joined.

Five of the major churches included in this book
were constructed of stone: Quarai, built of a rich,
red sandstone; Abo, quite similar in texture but not
as intense in color; Gran Quivira, a gray-yellow
limestone [Plate 5]; San José de Giusewa, a yellow
limestone; and Acoma, actually a composite structure of stone and mud.

A masonry wall, deriving its strength from mass,
was piled to nearly six feet in thickness (a rubble
core filled with a more finished surface) to attain
the height of fifty feet the early church builders
sought. There was a pronounced battering to the
walls, reducing their thickness as the walls rose and
producing a section resembling an elongated version of a truncated pyramid. At Quarai the walls of
the nave were considerably splayed in plan, adding
some stability to the basic quadrilateral form, although its effect must have been minimal in comparison to the dead weight of the wall itself. In sum,
these stone churches derived their structural capacity from the straightforward laying of stone on
stone, which thickened the wall as required to allow
it to reach the level of the roof beams.

1–19

1–19
MAKING ADOBE BRICKS
during the reconstruction and stabilization of the Pecos churches, circa 1915
[Museum of New Mexico]

Abo was one exception to this general pattern; there the thickness of the walls was reduced, and the walls were stiffened instead by buttresses—extra masses, like columns, attached or "engaged" to the walls themselves. This practice, which may have had its origins in the fortress churches of Spain, provided additional bearing surface just below the beams where the weight was concentrated, thereby helping transmit the load to the ground. At the crossing—the intersection of the nave and transepts—the wall was considerably thickened to accommodate the sizably increased load and to support the bell tower. In comparison to Quarai or Gran Quivira, Abo's walls were light and elegant, although hardly thin when compared with modern construction in wood or steel. Nevertheless, neighboring churches in the Salinas area avoided the risk the builders at Abo took when contriving its more sophisticated structural system.

The Spanish did not introduce mud construction into New Mexico; they merely rationalized its production. Although stone was a building material at Mesa Verde and Chaco Canyon, it was used in conjunction with mud, which functioned as a mortar and finishing material. Exactly when the transition to a mostly mud or purely mud wall construction took place has not been ascertained, but the transference of the mesa top or cave villages to the river valleys made obvious the superseding of stone construction.

Continuing an attitude that perhaps derived from ceramic production, New Mexican builders did not use mud as a unit material, although blocks shaped like loaves of bread and called turtle backs were used to build the Casa Grande in Arizona.[76] The Indians built their pueblos on the basis of puddled construction: with or without a form, they piled up heaps of mud in layers to make walls. Piled up one or two feet at a time, walls were raised in a manner that paralleled the construction of pottery using rolled coils of clay. From a central point, these coils spiraled outward and upward and were ultimately smoothed over inside and out to remove traces of rough construction and lend unity to the surfaces. This technique enabled construction to proceed without formwork and with no time spent in the production of units. But extensive time was needed for each layer of the walls to season properly, drying slowly to retard cracking.

Mud bricks had existed in New Mexico prior to European contact, but their use was not widespread. The Spanish introduced the idea of unit construction in large numbers—in this case the manufacture of the basic mud brick and its use in a manner simi-

1–20

1–20
SAN AGUSTÍN
Isleta Pueblo
The problems created by applying hard
plaster to adobe walls are evident in the
cracks and peeling paint.
[1981]

lar to stone. This common unfired mud brick was
called adobe.

The word adobe derives from the Arabic *atob*,
which suggests a Moorish, rather than a Spanish,
origin.[77] Indeed, the earthen constructions of North
Africa provided a centuries-old proving ground for
this remarkably practical building system. Adobe is
also related to the English daub, which formed one
part of the wattle and daub construction of medieval
England: applying (daubing) mud over a wooden
framework.

Therefore, use of the word mud in this context
is an oversimplification. Mud for adobe is not *any*
form of wet earth; it is a carefully balanced product
of clay, soil, and a binder such as straw, all blended
in proper proportion. Although the straw does not
increase the tensile properties of the brick, during
drying it helps modulate evaporation in different
parts of the block. Too much clay in the mix causes
the bricks to shrink and crack while drying; too
much sand causes them to become brittle and fall
apart. An ideal composition is required, a balanced
mixture derived in any locality only through a process of trial and error.

Wooden frames, with neither tops nor bottoms,
form a number of bricks at a time. The mud is
mixed in batches, and the form is filled while lying
flat on the ground. A short time later, after the mud
has set, the mold is lifted off, leaving a neat field of
wet adobes each measuring roughly ten by fourteen
by four inches. When the bricks are sufficiently dry,
they are turned over and eventually stacked diagonally or on edge to complete the drying process.
Unlike brick, adobe is not fired to high temperature in a kiln; being nonvitrified, the blocks are always susceptible to deterioration by moisture and
wind. Traditionally, a layer of mud plaster applied
over the adobe wall has been its primary means of
protection against the elements. The absorption of
moisture from the ground or the air or evaporation
can cause a marked change in the size of the bricks,
a movement that renders the use of the more stable
cement plaster coatings impractical.

When the adobe matured, construction could begin. The builders laid up each course of blocks in an
adobe mortar that rendered the construction homogeneous. Timbers imbedded horizontally within the
wall at vertical intervals of up to four feet served to
lessen cracking between bricks as the adobe or mortar dried or settled or could be used to reinforce the
joint between new walls and old construction. After
a few vertical feet of construction, the entirety was
left to dry. Moisture permanently trapped in the
walls could ultimately lead to the structural failure

36

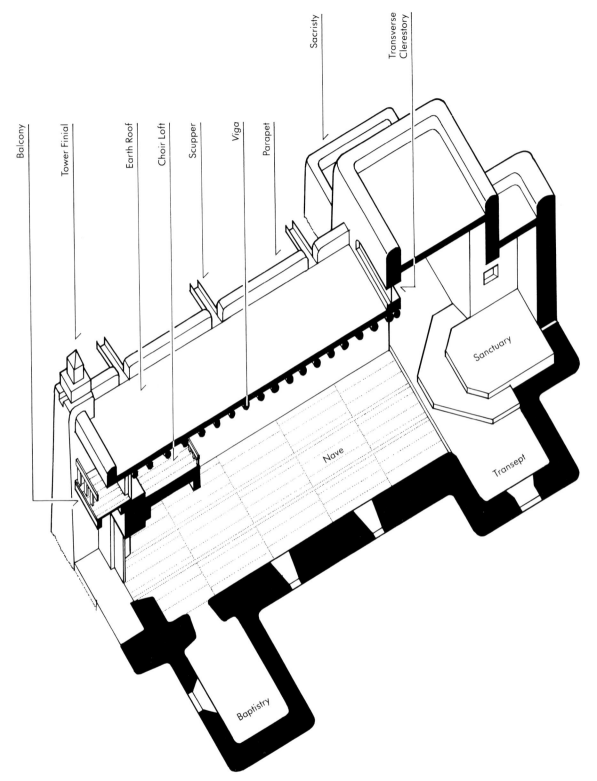

Balcony

Tower Finial

Earth Roof

Choir Loft

Scupper

Viga

Parapet

Sacristy

Transverse
Clerestory

Sanctuary

Nave

Transept

Baptistry

1–21

1–21
THE ARCHITECTONIC ELEMENTS
OF THE CHURCH
[Source: Sketch by Robert Nestor,
1989]

of that section, or of the entire church, so judiciousness was the rule. Obviously this concern for moisture restricted construction to those periods of the year when rain was not a threat, a practice that compounded the extensive time periods required to build a church, often at least five to six years during the early periods. At difficult sites such as Acoma the construction activity extended over decades.

Adobe provides excellent bearing strength in compression and, in sufficient thickness, thermal mass [Plate 6]. The unbaked brick, however, is quite vulnerable to erosion by water and wind. During normal exposure certain portions of the external surface of a wall abrade, while other sections dissolve in rain, contributing to the subtly curving contour of an adobe structure. Wind erodes the top parapet, tapering the upper wall backward, while eroded earth is deposited at the base of the wall, giving it a pronounced bulge. Although in most cases walls are constructed as truly vertical or cleanly slanting, they acquire a sculptured profile that is never quite the same in any two places.

Erosion is both a natural and an unforgiving process, and church builders were forced to consider its effects when devising construction techniques. If the buildings are not replastered at regular intervals, weathering will eventually deteriorate the structural portions of adobe walls. One problem is known as coving. As water drains off the wall, or pours from the drains, it splashes on the ground and decays the base of the wall. Poor drainage compounds the effects of the problem, although a stone foundation can lessen it. Unless the water sources are checked, however, the wall will become seriously undermined, or coved, which can ultimately lead to the collapse of the structure.

The parapet remained another chronic problem area. Because this section of the wall extends past the roof level, it is exposed to weathering on three surfaces and is thus three times as susceptible to erosion. In many instances the parapet is the first part of the wall to deteriorate, furthering pronounced dissipation on the tops of the walls, destroying the roof and beams, and eventually leading to ruin. Perhaps in no other method of construction is the adage that an ounce of prevention is worth a pound of cure so true. And even though there have been many attempts to eliminate the required upkeep, such as a pitched roof to cover the tops of walls, bricks or concrete blocks used for the parapets (now a common practice), a hybrid adobe made of mud mixed with cement or oil, and the more usual—although technically unsuccessful—application of cement stucco, nothing is as techno-logically and aesthetically triumphant as the time-consuming application of mud plaster [Plate 14]. (See Ranchos de Taos for a discussion of stucco plastering and a restoration story with a happy ending.)

The walls of stone or adobe were plastered on both inside and outside to appear monolithic and to suggest the more finished wall surfaces of the advanced religious architecture of Mexico or Spain. On the exterior the mud plaster served not only to integrate the separate bricks (because a chemical bond was formed) but also to add an inch or more of protective surface as a first line of defense against the elements. At Quarai and Jemez Springs traces of plastering and even painted decoration were discovered during excavation, indicating that the *perceived* surface was ultimately the architectural concern and that the vehicle of construction, stone or mud brick, was only the means to that end.

Building and plastering the walls of the church were women's work performed during the initial construction and then every second year for maintenance. As in ceramic production, the final coat of mud plaster was smoothed or burnished with sheepskin, deerskin, or small, round stones.[78] The technique was most often employed when interiors were plastered with *yeso* (or *yesso*), a baked gypsum mixed with wheat flour and water to form a thick paste. Yeso walls were typical of Moorish interiors and created a surface much harder and more durable than mud, but this technique was less widespread than coating a wall with whitewash.[79]

ROOFS

The builders constructed the corners of the church first; the intersection of the walls helped stiffen the structure as it rose. The remainder of each wall was then laid between the corners until it reached to the height of the plate line of the roof. Large beams, called *vigas*, provided the standard roof structure (the vault was not used in New Mexican church architecture). The beams were cut during the winter months from the extensive conifer forests that blanketed the mountains. Winter was the desirable time for forestry both for the internal consistency of the wood and the relative ease with which the logs could be hauled the ten to thirty miles to the building site. In addition, agricultural fields were dormant and required less care, thus allowing time to work on building projects. Although the wheel and the cart were available, their use in construction was probably limited. It is conceivable, of course, that wheels from supply wagons could have been used to

1–22

1–22
SAN AGUSTÍN
Isleta pueblo
Typical roof construction: round vigas
(main rafters) supported by corbels inserted in the adobe wall. The ceiling
boards, however, are milled lumber.
[1981]

1–23
SAN GREGORIO
Abo
Construction drawing showing sets of
six squared vigas grouped to form a
composite beam.
[Adapted from Toulouse, *The Mission of
San Gregorio*]

1–24
EL SANTUARIO
Chimayo
Detail of the pivot joint—here made of
wood—which preceded or substituted
for true metal hinges.
[New Mexico Tourism and Travel
Division, no date]

haul vigas if conditions allowed. During the winter, logs were either dragged on the ground or carried on sledges if snow was sufficient.

Although the Spanish brought iron axes, saws, and adzes with them as part of their basic church-building supplies, the task of cutting the required timber remained formidable. As in Indian construc-tion, beams were cut over the required length; the excess increment was accepted and allowed to ex-tend through the completed adobe or stone wall. Cutting the beams too short was regarded as a mi-nor disaster. For example, when the beams at Zia were found to be of insufficient length, the builders constructed a second wall inside the first rather than wait a year to recut the timber. Most commonly, the beams were left round, with only the bark and branches removed. Rotting continually plagued roof construction because the beams were packed in the adobe wall, which freely conducted moisture and ensured its continued contact with the wood beams. Deterioration of this sort seems to have been regarded as a normal part of the construction process; only in the twentieth century were alter-nate methods used in restoration work. During the 1923 rebuilding of the church roof at Zia, for ex-ample, the ends of the beams were surrounded by stones to prevent their coming into direct contact with the adobe while allowing a freer passage of air.[80] Today beams are dipped in creosote or some other wood preservative to forestall deterioration.

At times vigas in churches sat directly on the stone or adobe walls, but more commonly they were set on corbels, wooden support pads, or cush-ions between the viga and the wall material, which in turn was supported by a wooden plate. This practice produced a minimal support benefit, how-ever, and the use of corbels was primarily a decora-tive practice. Indeed, the rows of corbels in some churches are the principal ornamentation [Plate 8]. Isleta, San Miguel, and Laguna all feature splen-didly carved wood corbel blocks, their decorative effect heightened by the contrast of their intricate designs to the rudely shaped vigas above them. In some instances a wooden molding ran continuously around the interior of the nave just below the level of the corbels, a purely aesthetic practice said to have been the architectural rendering of the Fran-ciscan waist cord.

An average viga measured about fifteen inches in diameter and spanned just under thirty feet, limits fixed by the maximum height and caliper of the available trees. In response to the length of the span and the weight of the roof above, the beams were spaced quite closely. If a large congregation required a sizable church, the length of the nave was elongated to provide the necessary volume. At its extreme this practice produced tubelike spaces almost 130 feet long as, for example, at San Felipe. Except in the earlier Salinas churches, heights, like widths, rarely exceeded thirty feet and were often less than the width of the nave. Fray Domínguez, visiting the old Santa Clara church, commented that its interior reminded him of nothing so much as the inside of a cannon.[81] Kubler also noted that in many churches one longitudinal wall was noticeably thicker than the other,[82] suggesting that the thicker wall served as a working platform when the vigas were raised into place. This remark was only speculative, however, because James Ivey noted that hoisting tackle was used on Spanish ships and, presumably, for building and military purposes as well. Church builders should have had access to this equipment when lifting the vigas into place either from the roof or from the ground with wooden tripods.

Not all roof beams were left round, however. In the early Salinas missions it was not uncommon for builders to saw or adze the beams into a square section and stack them together in bundles of six. Not only did grouping the finished timber contribute to an overall level of craft rare in the province, but also the additional depth provided by the composite stack augmented the carrying capacity of each individual beam. Square and bundled beams, however, died out rather early, supplanted by the round viga as the common form. Of pine or spruce, the round vigas were mounted so that their undersides and the plane of the ceiling were horizontal, thereby utilizing the natural tapering of the tree trunks to slope the roof for drainage.

Although the vigas provided the primary structure, they were too widely spaced to support the roofing materials directly. A secondary layer of smaller poles of peeled juniper, cottonwood, or aspen, perhaps four inches in diameter and known as *latillas*, were positioned perpendicularly across the beams or set obliquely in a herringbone pattern, a design best represented by the underside of the choir loft at Laguna [Plate 9]. An alternate system used split cedar logs called *rajas* or *savinos*—if riven from native juniper—installed with their flat side down to form a roughly textured ceiling. A third, more polite alternative was the adzed board, or *tabla*, usually reserved for the finest room of the home. The choice of one system over another was decided on the basis of availability of wood types, tools and skilled labor, and the aesthetic preferences of the makers.[83]

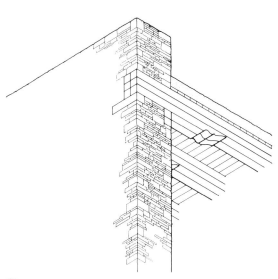

1–23

1–24

40

A layer of cedar twigs, grass, plant fibers, reed, or even fabric was placed on the latillas, and on top of that a foot or more of earth and adobe was packed. Builders hoped that in times of rain, water would seep and diffuse within the thick earthen mat before it penetrated to the interior of the nave—a hope that could only be called naive when measured against experience. A flat roof and parapet, even if minimally sloped to drain through holes in the parapet provided with scuppers called *canales*, was a poor system at best. The expansion and contraction of the roof's structure caused fissures between roof and walls, and once water gained entrance, the situation deteriorated at an ever-increasing rate. Only vigilance and continual maintenance could turn the tables on the elements and postpone the inevitable collapse of the walls.

And even in the face of these constant efforts, roofs leaked continuously: reports of ceilings dripping, floors eroding, and inside walls washing away were numerous. As late as the beginning of the twentieth century priests bemoaned the lack of waterfastness of the nave of the Cochiti church and rationalized the need for a metal roof to combat the elements.[84] In spite of the radical aesthetic consequences, the pitched metal roof gained widespread popularity in the nineteenth century because it *covered* the parapet and protected the upper part of the wall, sealing it off from the intrusion of water and wind. For the late-eighteenth-century missions along the more humid coast of California broad tile roofs were ubiquitous, extending outward to form arcades that sheltered both the wall and the strolling friar. Nevertheless, the New Mexican church, like the Pueblo Indian dwellings before it, relied on the flat earthen roof, although it was a far from perfect solution.

APERTURES

Openings in masonry structures have always presented a challenge because stone, brick, and especially mud are weak in relation to tensile forces. In more advanced structural applications the arch was used to support the section of the wall above the aperture; in New Mexico this role was assigned to a lintel. Wooden pieces, usually squared, although sometimes left round, were placed one against another above an opening throughout the entire thickness of the wall. Where the wall continued over the top of a window or door, the wooden lintel was embedded in the adobe or stone and subsequently carried the weight of the wall above it. In some churches these lintels have been plastered

1–25

1–25
SELENITE "WINDOW"
Acoma Pueblo
[1984]

over; in others they remain in view. At Ranchos de Taos, for example, the timbers that span the openings above the arched windows are painted white, clearly visible against the adobe into which they have been set.

Although the Franciscans brought iron hinges to the colony along with tools and locks, such as those noted by Joseph Toulouse at Abo, most doors were made to pivot on wooden pins.[85] Chimayo clearly illustrates this technique and demonstrates that the practice continued well into the nineteenth century. The doors themselves were assembled of multiple pieces of wood joined, nailed, or fastened together with metal brought by the missionaries. Wherever possible, the doors were fitted with locks. Domínguez was careful to comment on the existence not only of locks on the main doors to the church but also of locks on various chests and furnishings. A somewhat typical note was found in the description of Zuñi: "At the head there is a beautiful wooden table which the priest uses for vesting. It has two drawers, one above the other, *with a key to the top one*. . . . The following are in the drawer *which has a lock*" (italics added).[86]

ILLUMINATION

New Mexican architecture is an architecture of both mass and light: the structure itself is little without the radiance that imparts visual life to the inert soil. As Charles Lummis wrote of New Mexico's light, "One cannot focus upon sunlight and silence; and yet without them adobe is a clod."[87]

Today we find beauty in these structures' simple volumes, striking profiles, soft textures, and vital, if rudimentary, ornamentation. But in the creation of a sense of sanctity and significance within the church, light was the critical ingredient. If the vault and the dome were nonexistent in New Mexico, and if elaborate, gilded decoration was impossible to procure, then brilliance and sparkle had to be created by other means. Pueblo rooms were dark [Plate 17]. Lacking glass, the Indians made small eyelike windows of flaked mica stone called selenite, at least one example of which still remains at Acoma. The Spanish brought glass in small pieces into the province, but glass was a precious commodity because it had to be transported overland from Durango or Chihuahua. Hence its use was not widespread. More commonly Spanish church builders used oiled hides or adapted the native practice, creating windows of translucent selenite set in wooden grills that admitted a soft and diffused light.[88] The individual units rarely exceeded five inches square,

however. Even with the opening of trade in American goods during the Mexican period, the size of the panes remained limited. Shipping invoices that served as customs declarations for a shipment of products from St. Louis in 1854 listed glass of only eight by ten inches and ten by twelve inches. Presumably, only smaller panes could be economically produced and transported by wagon.[89]

George Kubler, in his pioneering work *The Religious Architecture of Early New Mexico*, asserted that the transverse clerestory was the most characteristic invention of the New Mexican church.[90] He suggested that the clerestory was a vestige of the Mexican cupola, a form unattainable with New Mexico's limited technology and materials. The light quality and configuration of the church's cross-section, however, recalled more closely the stepped roofs of Moorish construction, such as the mosque at Córdoba, Spain, begun in 785 and converted into a Catholic church in the thirteenth century at the time of the Reconquest. The mosque's space comprised a seemingly infinite number of bays spanned by horseshoe arches that disappeared into the murky distance. A series of linear clerestories provided strips of diffused illumination running nearly the full length of the mosque. Its soft and indistinct lighting and the strength of its structure were recalled in the New Mexican nave.

Raising the ceiling height between the nave and the choir area in the New Mexican church introduced a slit of light that, with care and luck, would fall directly on the altar. The effect of this device can be stunning and is best witnessed today at San Agustín at Isleta and San Ildefonso [Plate 16]. Unfortunately, other factors governed the selection of church sites within the pueblo so that the nave was not consistently oriented toward the south, which would have guaranteed continued light throughout the day, or the east, which would have secured light during the morning mass. Santo Domingo, for example, faces roughly west, while the sequence of Pecos churches actually reversed orientation in subsequent reconstructions.

The theatrical impact of the clerestory doubles when one enters the church after crossing a bright, sandy plaza, as the eyes require some minutes to accustom to the darkness. Then at the end of the nave is revealed the striking presence of light flung across the crucifix and altar, a radiance enhanced by the basic darkness of the interior.

Windows in the early churches were precious commodities, and Domínguez provided detailed descriptions of them in his report. But at that time windows were fewer than those seen in churches

1-26

1–26
SAN JOSÉ
Las Trampas
The longitudinal profile of the church
reveals the raised chancel roof necessary
to create a transverse clerestory.
[1981]

1–27
SAN AGUSTÍN
Isleta pueblo
As a result of the 1960 renovation and
the removal of the pitched roof, the
clerestory was restored to working
order—a striking use of dramatic
illumination.
[1981]

1–28

1–28
SAN MIGUEL
La Bajada
The single nave and battered apse are
characteristic of the basic church.
[1984]

today and were almost certainly of smaller dimensions. Often restricted to a single side of the nave, such as the south at Acoma or the west at Isleta, these apertures high in the wall provided accents of light rather than a principal source of illumination—that role was granted to the transverse clerestory. Only with the large-scale importation of glass made possible by the railroads in the late nineteenth century could the size of windows be feasibly increased or new ones cut [Plate 13]. With their enlargement came a rather significant modification in the quality of light within the church. Even more severe was the effect of changes wrought by the pitched metal roof that accompanied American jurisdiction. While protecting the adobe walls from deterioration by water, the roof completely sealed off the clerestory, making the windows the sole source of light. Only at Santa Cruz, where a south-facing window lights the *reredos* (altarpiece) and altar, has a qualitative equal to the clerestory been found.

ARCHITECTURAL EFFECTS

The two long walls of the naves in New Mexican churches are rarely perfectly parallel, and in some instances they converge slightly toward the chancel end of the church. Architectural historians have long sought an explanation for this tendency, but no completely satisfactory explanations have been offered to date. Kubler proposed a theory of optical illusion, suggesting that converging walls "forced" the sense of perspective and made the nave seem longer.[91] Although this might have been the case, a narrowing of the nave would have contributed little to this impression. In relation to the overall length of the nave, the disparity was so minimal as to appear unintentional. In addition, the degree of convergence was by no means consistent, which suggests that it was not the result of a systematically applied body of missionary knowledge. Nor does it appear probable that a friar could have discovered this perspective property and disseminated it among his fellows; given the height of the church—nearly fifty feet—the overall reading and perspective trick would have been all but impossible to detect.

A second argument against optical adjustments derives from the light level of the church itself. Churches were rather dark, so the wall surfaces could hardly have been discerned; small windows, often high up in the walls, created pinpoint conditions of severe glare and silhouetted the wall planes. The full effect of forced perspective would have required some system of bays that modulated the lat-

1–29

1–29
SAN JOSÉ
Laguna pueblo
The interior of the nave, looking toward the entrance, with the choir loft above.
[1981]

eral *depth* as well as the width of the nave. But the transverse clerestory, which illuminated the sanctuary, drew the eye directly to the altar and effectively mitigated the impact of any adjustments for perceptual modulation.

But what of the heightened sense of depth produced by the very pronounced, battered form of the apse [Plate 11]? Here it is a question of proportions. These splayed ends are so abrupt in their angling, so small in relation to the length of the nave, and so interrupted by the reredos that they could hardly have been created for optical effects. In some instances they are merely inset to distinguish the chancel, for example at San Buenaventura at Cochiti. A more reasonable explanation for the tapered apse might be that the making of truly curved walls was too troublesome or was even completely precluded by construction in adobe. Although the hemispherical apse might have been the architectural precedent and aspiration, the splayed form of the apse was accepted as a reasonable compromise. Admittedly the native kivas were round, and thus curved construction in stone was possible. Perhaps the friars hesitated because the church, unlike the kiva, would be entirely above ground, thus requiring the building of *high* curved walls. Or perhaps the additional effort required for the more sophisticated architectural form was not deemed worthwhile.

Immediately inside the church was the choir loft, which often extended through the facade wall to form a balcony on the exterior of the church. Typically a window, centralized in the main facade and vaguely recalling the rose window of the Gothic cathedral, illuminated the loft. When bracketed by two towers, this balcony also created a basic narthex that served as a loose transition to the sanctuary proper and might also have been used on occasion for outdoor ceremonies. So characteristic was this arrangement that Domínguez at times simplified his descriptions and referred to a choir loft "in its usual place." Although the choir loft was consistently at the rear of the nave, access to the platform was not necessarily logical. In most instances access to the loft was by ladder or even rope, and in the case of Isleta the only manner of entry was a warrenlike path that led over the roof of the adjacent convento. Domínguez betrayed his mild exasperation while visiting at Isleta: "Although this convent is square, the plan is so intricate that if I describe it, I shall only cause confusion. It has upper and lower stories so badly arranged and planned that in proof of the poor arrangement I reveal that the entrance to it all is by a stairway which gives on the corral."[92]

The choir loft was built with the same techniques

1–30

1–30
SAN BUENAVENTURA
Gran Quivira
The two courtyards of the convento of the second church at Gran Quivira are seen in this aerial photograph. The ruins of the pueblo are to the right.
[Paul Logsdon, 1980s]

used to construct the roofs and ceilings of the church. Like the ceiling vigas, beams extended across the nave and were embedded in the walls at both ends. In some churches a post on either side of the center aisle reduced the span and helped support the loft and its human cargo. The floor of the choir loft was built exactly like the roof, including earth as the finished floor. The railings of the balconies, like the corbels supporting the beams, could be plain or elaborately worked, and at times they were carved with intricate geometric patterns.

With the nave, its transepts, and its apse, two other rooms completed the church program. The first was the baptistry, usually built as a rather small rectangular room near the entry to the church, if one existed at all. The baptistry at San José at Las Trampas provides a clear illustration of this type; located just east of the main doors, it still has a dirt floor on which the baptismal font, a simple affair, stands fixed. The same adobe of which the church walls were made, as Domínguez reported, often supported the fonts. The sacristy at Ranchos de Taos exemplifies the minimal features of these rooms, although a wooden floor was added in the last century. During the colonial period goods were stored in wooden chests, each provided with a sturdy lock brought from Mexico.[93] This completed the religious portion of the mission, but the priest also required quarters in which to live and work.

THE CONVENTO

Lodging was located as close to the church as conditions would allow, and if the friar was to be resident at the pueblo, these quarters, called the convento, were more extensive. Translation of the word convento is a bit problematic because the English word convent, a direct rendering of the cognate, is associated with a community of nuns, which was not the case in New Mexico. Neither is the word friary entirely accurate—although it has been used in the past—because strictly speaking priests usually lived alone or in pairs. "Priest's quarters" is perhaps the best English rendering for convento, although the term must be taken to include not only the domestic rooms but also the support spaces, such as storage rooms, workshops, and buildings for livestock.

Architectonically, the convento comprised a block of low buildings that acted as visual anchor for the larger volume of the church. The contrast in scale between these domestic and auxiliary spaces and the nave only served to increase the apparent dimension of the church structure itself. At Pecos, for example, the pueblo and convento read almost as a lower platform on which the church was raised, a condition also present at Quarai, Gran Quivira, Laguna, and Acoma, where the contrast is perhaps the strongest.

In place of monetary tithes, the Indians were to provide labor and "first fruits," which allowed the priest to live and continue his efforts on their behalf.[94] As Domínguez noted, in more than one instance the friar was forced to fend for himself, tending his garden and perhaps even his stock or augmenting his scanty income through trading, although this practice was frowned upon by the authorities. Ornamental gardens were rare, but at Acoma there were "some little peach trees . . . watered by hand" that served decorative and functional needs. "When it is necessary to water the little trees mentioned above, the girls who come to catechism go with the weekly fiscal and bring a great deal all at once, even more than enough."[95]

The convento in almost all cases took the form of the placita and was attached directly to the long side of the church or separated from it by a narrow corridor. The great mass of the church served as wind or weather break when the convento was sited to its south or to the most desirable sheltered side.[96] Where sufficient level terrain was not available, as at San José de Giusewa, the irregular topography forced a juggling of the spaces and a somewhat random layout. Where the premises and the needs were large enough, the convento grew to two courtyards, paralleling the layout of the more prosperous ranchos. The living chambers, porter's lodge, office, and storerooms opened onto the first enclosed court, while the second served as a more secure, internalized corral for the animals as well as storage for their maintenance and perhaps for firewood. The convento at Acoma provides a good example of the single court type, while the ruined San Buenaventura at Gran Quivira exemplifies that of the double courtyard.

Hardly less important than the habitable structures were those for storage. Since supply convoys were dispatched or arrived only every third year, the life of the mission depended on systems and spaces for handling goods, foodstuffs, and even live animals. Provisions had to be made for both directions of the flow. When a missionary arrived with his allotment of supplies for initiating religious and construction activities, he required rooms in which to keep them. Supplies both quotidian and exotic that arrived from Mexico needed to be kept safe from rot, vermin, and theft since several years would elapse before any losses could be replaced.

48   Meanwhile, the annual harvests of agricultural, animal, and woven produce had to be stored until they could be shipped south to Mexico to trade for necessities not available at the edge of the empire. In the Salinas missions during the 1660s, for example, when drought brought famine and Apache raids, food and supplies were provided to the less fortunate by those conventos with an increment. There would have been no surplus without sufficient storage; indeed, new, more secure storerooms were constructed to meet the increased threat of theft fanned by desperation. Thus, these meager, undistinguished, and architecturally undifferentiated storage cells are better thought of as critical financial institutions rather than as mere rooms without windows.

Rarely were the conventos maintained in anywhere near excellent conditions; often they were only marginally habitable. Although their layouts might have been carefully planned, with time the nature and function of the spaces could change. Domínguez's pages were filled with negative judgments on the design or state of the friar's facilities. He frequently commented on the warrenlike configurations of rooms. Even at the Parroquia of Santa Fe, which should have been the flagship of the New Mexican system, the friar reported, "All these rooms are large with good windows, and everything was well designed when it was first built, but the neglect by those who should have taken care of it has left it in such a state that it has been necessary for some careful friars to repair what others have torn down."[97] At Tesuque the ambivalent state of the ministry left the convento in limbo. For the most part the pueblo was cared for by a priest from Santa Fe, and as a *visita* the convento was not maintained. "And when there was perhaps a resident missionary, it was for a short time, so that even if he was willing to undertake repairs, he could not do so."[98]

Yet perhaps these quarters, however dilapidated, were preferable to living in the pueblo itself—a common practice before the convento was built. At least living quarters placed some distance between the Franciscan and the pueblo and raised no question of jurisdiction. But construction of a convento was not the last word. At the close of the eighteenth century at Picuris the missionary there was forced to live in the pueblo's "community house" and celebrate the mass in one of its three rooms while a new church was being built. "It is kept with great cleanliness, care, and neatness," Domínguez wrote approvingly, "but it is very inadequate and poverty-stricken."[99]

1–31

1–31
FUNERAL
Cochiti Pueblo
In some pueblos the campo santo—like the church—was divided along a central axis, with women to one side and men to the other.
[Museum of the American Indian, Heye Foundation, Frederick Starr Collection, 1894–1910]

Fronting virtually every church was the campo santo. Enclosed by a wall about five feet high, it distinguished the church zone from the wilderness or the remainder of the village and acted as a transition between the secular world and the consecrated church. Burial within the campo santo was the normal practice, although in many churches today only one cross, more or less centrally positioned, serves as a collective remembrance of those interred. At Laguna and Picuris the ruddy background renders the single white cross a powerful icon but only hints at its role as a grave marker. The remainder of the ground is earthen, swept clean. The actual burial ground at Las Trampas lies to the right of the church and occupies only a small part of the sanctified zone within the outer walls and those of the church of San José. The importance granted the campo santo is most clearly illustrated by Acoma, where the density of the rock permitted no burials. A massive retaining wall of stone was required, and constructing and filling the burial ground itself took decades. The multitude of simply marked graves within the walls today attests to the spirit and determination of the congregation.

Charles Lange reported that by the late 1960s the original campo santo at Cochiti had been filled, and a new burial ground was opened west of the church. Unlike the original campo santo, where "the sexes were segregated, with the males south of the midline and the females north, duplicating their normal division within the church during Mass," no segregation of sexes characterized the new century, although the graves continued to be arranged in north-south rows.[100]

The sedentary nature of the Pueblo communities—in contrast to the scattered or seminomadic peoples of central Mexico—permitted a more accurate census by the Spanish and a church structure more in accord with the size and stability of the settlement. As a result, the use of the atrio, designed to accommodate fluctuating populations and sudden conversions, was probably not widespread in New Mexico. In several churches, however, parts of the mission complex were assigned only hypothetical functions because of the generic nature of colonial construction and lack of documentation. Whether these open rooms adjacent to or near the entrance of the church were used as a porter's lodge or as a site for exterior religious services is still open to question. An early photograph of San Ildefonso showed one of these covered shelters, which Kubler suggested might have served as a chapel.[101] John

McAndrew thought otherwise:

> Echoes have been seen in the eighteenth century porterías of the missions of New Mexico, a recently converted frontier region in some ways equivalent to the frontiers of the time of the Great Conversion; but inasmuch as most of these porterías have a doorway in the middle of the back wall where the altar would have to be and a built-in adobe bench all around the walls, and as there are no notices of altars or of any use of chapels, it seems unjustified to accept them as chapels.[102]

Joseph Toulouse, however, was certain that a "small shrine" on the south side of the Abo church was a chapel: "This is undoubtedly a posa or courtyard chapel which is found in Mexican sixteenth-century churches." He was basing his opinion only on subsurface archeological evidence rather than on an extant structure, however.[103]

FURNISHINGS AND DECORATION

Hispanic colonial buildings had no closets. In fact, spaces for storage were not included within the house except in rooms used for agricultural reserves or wares related to the farm. Domestic goods were stored in wooden or rawhide chests, which were either horizontal with hinged tops flat or arched or upright with hinged doors. Furniture of this sort—first imported as traveling trunks but later domestically produced—offered surfaces for carved or painted decoration. In certain instances, particularly for domestic purposes, the chest might double as a table: ornament and show, not comfortable sitting, were the main considerations.[104]

In these chests everything was deposited. Dominguez commented on the need to secure all the church possessions, poor as they were. His recordings of the holy vessels as well as all the furniture and furnishings only pointed out how barren and destitute the churches actually were at the time. Had they been repositories of ecclesiastical treasure, a comprehensive list of the contents would have been a formidable task, or an abridged inventory might have sufficed. But the friar did list the *complete* stock of the church, and in the end, the list was not long. Although the floors were of earth and Indians stood in their churches throughout the service, Herbert Bolton reported that to increase the prestige of the governor, alcalde, and council, "Separate benches were placed in the churches" for them, implying that seats did exist in the Spanish churches.[105]

Just as the possessions of the church were meager, so were its decorations. Missing were the extensive ornamental programs of central Mexican church interiors. On the plastered surfaces of the walls decorative patterns were brushed. At the ruins of Jemez Springs as well as at Abo excavated fragments of red and black paintings suggested an intention to ornament church interiors from the earliest construction period. But the first decoration, if it can be called that, was probably whitewash applied to the interior of the church or to the facade or all the exterior. And in a landscape of earth tones, the power of the color white is considerable. Prior to its recent collapse, the facade of Picuris, for example, palpitated visibly, so striking was its contrast with the remainder of the earth-red church and its surroundings [Plate 12]. Laguna and Zia—the former stark white, the latter a rusty golden cream—are dazzling counterpoints to the rubicund surrounding landscape. And the orange-brown and white vertical stripes of San Jerónimo at Taos pueblo further the elaboration, although the color scheme is from this century and is executed with commercial paints.

Beyond this basic chromatic tinting, facade decorations included geometric or animal motifs, two outstanding examples of which are the churches of Santo Domingo and San Felipe. In both instances animated images of horses appear above the serrated wainscot with brilliantly colored geometric designs that recall the ornamentation of ceramic vessels. Although these paintings are of recent execution, their images stem from and continue a centuries-old iconographic tradition.

Decoration also finished the naves of many churches. Early builders applied to the walls a lightly colored wainscot of whitewash prepared by baking limestone, plastering with a white sandy soil known as *tierra blanca* or with a yellow *tierra amarilla* that sparkled with mica flakes. The sanctuary of San Ildefonso in the late eighteenth century was "painted blue and yellow from top to bottom like a tapestry." [106] Upon these painted surfaces geometric patterns might be added, such as those at Acoma, whose designs recalled the motifs used on the pueblo's noted pottery. Floral and animal motifs were also common. The painted wainscot not only addressed the functional problems of wear; it also provided a visual base of reference against which the apparent scale of the nave increased.

In addition to the simple and delicate pink-tinted wainscot paintings at Acoma, the boldly painted interior decoration of San José at Laguna is also noteworthy. The white walls of the nave host painted abstract and animal images in red, green, and black; when taken together as a progression, these images

1–32
SAN JOSÉ
Laguna pueblo
The ornamental program is executed in red and black paint on the whitewashed surface of the walls.
[1986]

1–32

1–33

1–33
SAN JOSÉ
Las Trampas
The main altarpiece, attributed to
José Gonzáles.
[1981]

provide a rhythm that binds the entrance to the altar. The ceiling latillas are turned obliquely to the vigas, forming a herringbone pattern emphasized by selective painting in red, white, and black. And in its totality the Laguna church comes the closest of any mission in the state to possessing a unified decorative program, which extends beyond its wall paintings and ceiling to a fine altarpiece and paintings. The choir loft of Santa Clara is also lavishly painted in bright colors, but the size and intensity of the designs are not in complete sympathy with the intimate scale of the nave. As a result, the interior lacks the unity and harmony of pictorial devices found at Laguna and Acoma.

The ritual focus of the church was the high altar, which was centered in the nave and marked the sanctuary area. Although the altar could be made of as simple a material as adobe, or more politely in stone, its surface was always intended to be covered by a cloth. Linens and other fine fabrics accompanied the missionaries from Mexico or might have been shipped on subsequent supply trains or borrowed from other churches when a new mission was founded. Native weavings could grace the interiors; parishioners might have donated examples of their own crafts as acts of devotion or social display.

Upon these cloths rested the regalia of the sacred service, and here at least was one surface able to rise above the roughness imposed by frontier conditions. Or perhaps there were *two* surfaces. Although the altar was the heart of the church, the altarpiece, or reredos, provided a suitable backdrop to the divine rite. [Plate 7] The reredos was a didactic instrument, narrating in images the stories of the saints, illustrating vignettes from their lives, and depicting their portraits, attributes, and, perhaps, martyrdom. Rather than a single, large painting, the altarpiece comprised a series of separate panels joined together in an architecturally treated frame with the images in each panel painted, usually in tempera, on gessoed wood. In later periods the framework containing the paintings was elaborately worked and colored and rivaled the painted images themselves in intricacy and beauty. The iconography of the reredos derived from European and Mexican precedents, although those painted in the severely constrained conditions of New Mexico were of necessity relatively fundamental and naive. Frequently a dark contour line outlined the image, suggesting its derivation from printed sources such as engravings, woodcuts, or books on biblical subjects. The wooden engraving, for example, relied on a style of rendering that used thick outlines to retard deterioration by continuous impressions. Early *santeros*, the makers of sacred images, employed similar techniques that relied on line rather than on the elaborate modeling of form.

In many areas beyond those generating primary cultural and artistic change, the portable book provided the principal source for images. Since the woodblock and, later, the engraving were the dominant modes of graphic reproduction, their characteristics necessarily influenced artists who sought inspiration from them. This reliance on line, rather than on modeling, considerably simplified the act of painting by enabling a two-stage execution: the first stage determined the form; the second, its rendering. Although complementary, the two stages did not have to be absolutely congruent, as would have been the case without use of the outline. A simplification in tone and intention paralleled the shift from modeling to line.[107]

Of course, exceptions to this approach did occur, most notably in the work of the so-called Laguna Santero credited with the altarpiece of that church (c. 1803—1809).[108] The Laguna altarpiece is a splendid and exuberant work that combines the secular imagery of the moon and sun on a panel inclined above the principal reredos with religious images of San José, the patron of the church, Santa Bárbara, and others [Plate 10]. Because depictions are conveniently ambiguous, these celestial subjects could derive from the Laguna religion, or they could just as easily relate to Saint Francis's Brother Sun and Sister Moon. Although the nave is dark and without the benefit of a clerestory, the colors of the paintings display an intensity that conveys gripping conviction: to a member of the congregation the reredos must have had an almost hypnotic effect, rendering the presence of the saints almost tangible.

Usually a reredos stood in each transept facing toward the nave, whereas in single-nave churches secondary screens were mounted on the walls just before the sanctuary. In the church of San José at Las Trampas, however, there are five separate reredoses: one behind the high altar, two at subsidiary altars in the transepts on either side, and two more now within the nave itself. Each supersedes the previous one in size and lavishness. These paintings date to the late eighteenth century and include images of the more popular Franciscan saints as well as Santiago (Saint James the Greater), a military figure who led battles against the Muslims and whose spiritual presence would have aided in the battles in the New World against hostile Indians. At Santa Cruz, Fray Andrés García worked from 1747 to 1779 carving and painting pulpits, altar rails and

1–34

1–34
GOD THE FATHER
Rafael Aragón
The painting of religious images during the nineteenth century was characterized by a simple outlining that resembled prints produced from woodblocks. Expression derived from linework and gesture rather than from careful modeling or accurate resemblance.
[Taylor Museum, Colorado Springs Fine Arts Center]

screens, and religious images.[109] Other exemplary paintings can be found at Chimayo, Acoma, and Ranchos de Taos.

More basic were paintings executed on animal hides, used throughout New Spain when wood and canvas were not available. Buffalo, elk, and deer provided the most common surfaces, the images being rendered in vegetal dyes or water soluble paints.[110] E. Boyd underscored the role of Mexican precedents for this genre, particularly in years following the Reconquest, when the hide paintings bore a distinct resemblance to wall paintings: "The Franciscans who then came to New Mexico had been stationed at one or more of the 16th century churches built in New Spain, such as those at Acolman, Actopan, Cholula, and Huejotzingo. These had extensive frescoes in their convents and churches in the Renaissance manner and must have been the sources used from memory by New Mexican missionaries."[111]

Although Domínguez was critical of many aspects of the church furnishings, he appeared remarkably open-minded in estimating the worth of paintings on hide. In the inventories of most churches he merely recorded that the paintings used animal skins, rather than canvas or wood, for their substrate and even conceded that the sacristy of San Ildefonso had "a white buffalo skin painted with flowers and very pretty."[112] Juan Bautista de Guevara (whose visitation extended from 1817 to 1820) was hardly as accepting: "The painting of Santa Barbara on elkskin (at the parroquia in Santa Fe) must be removed and done away with completely as it is improper as an object of veneration and devotion of the altars."[113] His condemnation was reinforced by Jean-Baptiste Lamy, the bishop who arrived in the mid-nineteenth century.

As an expression of faith these paintings could not be faulted, but the nature of their ground, the hides of animals, was deemed "indecent" and unacceptable. In the field missionaries maintained a pragmatic flexibility necessary for survival under frontier conditions. Official visitors, however, gauged the appropriateness of the paintings against an absolute standard and found them wanting.

The earthen floor of the nave was at times covered with rugs, usually of Indian manufacture. The sanctuary of Laguna still contains weavings of various designs that, when grouped with altar cloth and reredos, form a decorative ensemble of considerable richness and complexity.

Being imported, worked metal was scarce in New Mexico, although ore was later found in some distant parts of the state. Early explorers were uninter-

1–35
SAN JOSÉ
Laguna Pueblo
Detail of the principal altarpiece with its mixture of Christian and possibly native iconography.
[1986]

56 ested in those minerals whose monetary return was not immediate. Although silver mines rewarded their investors with considerable profit, their portion of the state's history was played out mostly in the nineteenth century. Iron was used and reused for functional purposes; decorative metalwork remained relatively rare. Where possible, connections utilized alternate means, such as wooden pins or rawhide ties, to substitute for iron.[114] Early on the Franciscans taught smithing to the Indians and were so successful that during the Reconquest the Spanish found an operating blacksmith shop at Sandia pueblo. New Mexican blacksmiths produced a full variety of iron products from military supplies to construction and household articles that included lances, awls, hinges, latches, and ploughs. That the mission under Fray Estevan de Perea had acquired much of the imported iron was verified by a complaint to the viceroy by the municipality of Santa Fe. The missions had received so much of the available iron that scarcely enough remained for civilian needs, such as agricultural tools and horseshoes.[115]

At its founding, a mission was endowed with a standardized list of construction products such as locks and fittings, furnishings, and devices for mass. France Scholes provided a list of these supplies, from which the following has been excerpted and from which we can derive a sense of the inventory of the early missions:

> For each new mission: cloths; 1 bell; iron framework for bell; oil painting of saint; cupboard for chalice; rug for altar steps; crucifix; for every five friars, iron for making wafers; and a set of trumpets. For each friar for building his church: 10 axes; 3 adzes; 3 spits; 10 hoes; 1 medium saw; 1 chisel; 1 latch for the church door; 2 augurs; 1 plane; 10 lbs of steel; 600 tinned nails for church doors; 4000 assorted nails; 800 tacks; 2 small locks; 1 dozen hinges for doors and windows; 1 dozen hook and eye latches; 1 pair braces for the two doors.[116]

Although intended as minimum provisions for a consecrated church, the list more commonly remained incomplete. Too many factors intervened to prevent fulfillment, from the staging of the goods in Mexico City to the long overland route threatened by humans and nature. Since supplies in the northern province were always at a premium, continued consultation and borrowing among the missionaries were the normal course, and competition was kept to a minimum, especially when compared to the competition among church, military, and civilian authorities. On the whole all metal, even iron, was treated as a precious substance. The eighteenth- or early-nineteenth-century hinges, straps, and grills

extant demonstrate the settlers' ability to produce high-quality goods even when the availability of metal and the methods for working it seemed to preclude doing so. The church remained to the end a structure primarily of earth and wood, however.

The most noted fragment of metal in the church's fabric was neither of iron nor of silver but of bronze. This was, of course, the mission's bell, which in time became the symbol of the church. The bell, with the drum, brought the Indian to catechism or worship and was most often fabricated in Mexico or Spain and brought to New Mexico on supply caravans. Even a military expedition, like those of early exploration, carried a small bell among its supplies so that its Franciscan chaplain could celebrate mass en route. In certain inventories a bell was described as "a gift from the king," a reference to the practice of paying for the bells from Royal Fisc funds provided for the continuance of the missionary program. Domínguez, in his fastidious fashion, noted the existence or nonexistence of the bells in the churches he visited, assigning to the bell cultural qualities beyond the economics involved.

In the simpler structures the bell was tied with rawhide to the wooden lintel of a small opening within the pediment crowning the facade. In the churches with twin towers, one or both of the towers could be used as belfries. A more unusual arrangement is that of San Miguel, where one much-altered tower is centered in the facade above the main entrance. At the turn of the century doors or louvers were installed in the tower, thereby partially screening the bells from view but allowing their sound to resonate.

Bells, their mountings, and their soundings continued to be problematic. Since bells were often cast without clappers, a rock was used as a substitute. Striking the bell required the sacristan or his assistant to mount the roof of the church or belfry, which was rarely an easy task given the uncoordinated planning of the church and convento circulation. Even the bells of Santa Fe's principal religious structure, the Parroquia, could be reached only by ladder. The motion of a swinging bell held in place by rawhide also took a toll on its adobe supports. Even if the lintel or arch was strong enough to withstand the forces of bell ringing, the forces of nature still held sway; rawhide ties wore, rotted, or snapped. Photographs illustrate that towers and bell arches, at San Felipe or Santa Clara, for example, were always the first part of the building to suffer erosion by wind and rain. As a result, some churches resorted to methods first used before churches were

1–36

RITUAL

"Every day at sunrise the bells call the Indians to Mass." Although this remark was contained in a late-eighteenth-century report by Fray Joaquín de Jesús Ruiz, a missionary at Jemez, the picture he painted of mission life had probably been typical for at least several decades. His text, which is worth quoting at length for its wealth of details, suggested that mass held little of the solemnity for the Indians that it did for the Spanish and that attendance was highly regulated.

The bell is rung at sunrise. The married men enter, each one with his wife, and they kneel together in a row on each side of the nave of the church. Each couple has its own place designated in accordance with the census list. When there are many, the married couples make two rows on each side, the two men in the middle and the women at the sides. This may seem a superficial matter, but it is not, for experience has taught me that when these women are together they spend all the time dedicated to prayer and Mass in gossip, showing one another their glass beads, ribbons, medals, etc., telling who gave them to them or how they obtained them, and other mischief. Therefore the religious who has charge of the administration must have a care in this regard. After all, it is a house of prayer, not of chitchat.

The widows and widowers form another row, the widows on the Gospel side and the widowers on the Epistle side,[118] leaving the passage from the altar to the door of the church free for the ceremonies of Asperges and [nuptial] veiling.

From the pulpit to the altar on the Epistle side are seated in order the boys receiving instructions in doctrine, as I shall explain below. The girls are on the Gospel side. Beside them are the two fiscales mayores and their subordinates, six in number, so that they may not permit them to play games and laugh (which they do even under this regime) or play pranks or fall asleep or draw unseemly things upon the wall.

The petty governor and his lieutenant have their places at the door so that the people may not leave during the hour prayer and Mass.

When all are in their places, the fiscal mayor notifies the father, who comes down with his census lists and takes attendance to see whether everyone is there, whether they are in their proper places, and whether their hair is unbound. If anyone is missing, the petty governor goes to fetch him. If he is not in the pueblo, it is indicated by the thong and he is punished on the following Sunday or holy day of obligation. If the truant is a woman, her husband is sent to fetch her.

1–36
SAN ESTEBAN
Acoma Pueblo
The drummer calls the congregation to prayer.
[George H. Pepper, 1903; courtesy Museum of the American Indian, Heye Foundation]

58　Even those in positions of trust were not above suspicion: "Do not entrust the key of the baptistry to the sacristans. Take great care lest they steal the holy oils and the consecrated water for their suspicions."

Frontier conditions presented difficulties little dreamed of in larger cities: "Remove the water from the font in winter so that the bowl may not be damaged by ice. Keep your cloth vestments in your cell, for even if the chest in the sacristy is good there are many mice."

Religious instruction was rigidly disciplined, although Fray Joaquín continually cited incidents of mischief to substantiate the necessity for such treatments:

> In the morning the bell is rung at the same hour as for Mass, and in the evening before sunset. All the unmarried people come, even if they are old, and some young married women who have not yet borne children or who were married (for urgent reasons) before they knew the Christian doctrine well, and all the children over six years of age. In the summer they gather at the north portal; in the winter, in the cemetery. Some will say that it is unsuitable to have them come here to these places because the church is intended for this purpose and these functions are held in the church in all the missions. Moreover, they will say that it is cold in winter, the cemetery is full of snow, and it is an unkind thing. With my father's permission I shall say that when I came to this mission and went down to the church at the hour for devotions, I saw youths and girls romping, laughing, and pulling one another around by the fringe of their buckskins or blankets, and the women by their girdles, and, during a certain prayer, a nude fiscal with his private parts uncovered performing many obscene acts. So if one has compassion, they do not pray; and since they only behave this way when there is comfort, let him not grieve for them.[119]

To the friar resident at a pueblo with only his charge and some meager supplies, the attainment of even such a limited routine alone was a significant accomplishment.

MUSIC

Music played a prominent role in the mission program; indeed all means possible were used to "enlighten" the native inhabitants and draw them into the church. Where practical, the Indians were educated in musical technique in fourteen of the missions,[120] and a small orchestra and choir were included as part of religious celebrations. Listing the material goods at San Ildefonso, for example, Domínguez noted "two old breviaries, which, along with introits, etc., written in musical notes, are for

the use of the choir singers."[121] At the least a drum announced the mass. The Abo congregation raised sufficient capital from salt exports to purchase an organ, an impressive feat in light of the cost and difficulties of importation. Several other missions also possessed small organs for the divine service. That music continued as a part of religious ceremony well into the nineteenth century was verified by John Gregory Bourke's reports in 1881. An unskilled performance at Santa Cruz amused, rather than touched, the lieutenant: "Two guitars and a violin, each of domestic make and each in the last stages of decrepitude, furnished the music for a choir of voices, also of domestic manufacture and also in the last stage of decrepitude. To somewhat complicate the matter, the musicians (I use the term for want of a better), played different tunes and the singers pitched their voices in different keys."[122]

While skeptical of the merit of the performance at Isleta, Bourke was moved by the quality of the indigenous ceremony and the symbiotic relationship of the rite to its architectural settings:

> At the moment of our entrance, an organ in the choir was playing a soft prelude. (This was one of the very few church organs I heard in New Mexico.) Shortly afterwards, a woman struck up, in a voice crackled and feeble, a chant, the purport of which I could not make out; the antiphone to this was rendered in a murmur of gentle music by the chorus kneeling figures about her.
>
> There is something peculiar about the church-music of the Río Grande valley: the solos are stridulous and strained, but the choruses have in them something weird, soft, and tender, not to be described.[123]

ARCHITECTURAL SOURCES

Although the process of construction for the New Mexican church can be traced with relative precision, an exact understanding of its design has been elusive. Parallel architectural and cultural conditions in Mexico and Florida, however, shed some light on what might have been the practice in New Mexico. Certain documents postdate New Mexican construction by up to two centuries. But both the institution and its architecture were essentially conservative in the distant province, and a church constructed around 1800 shared more similarities than differences with its seventeenth-century predecessors.

Like so many aspects of serving in the outermost provinces of New Spain, church construction was a trying activity, requiring more perseverance than precise building knowledge or skill. During the construction period, which usually extended over periods counted in half decades, the missionary might be the sole European worker or one of two religious companions; at best he was a member of a small group that included an experienced civilian builder or military engineer. Whatever the Franciscan motivation, the church constructions were formidable accomplishments. Whether it was a fear of Spanish retribution, a genuine love or fear of God, or the challenge that prompted the Indians to build, the missionaries themselves must also be credited with both religious zeal and organizational talents.

The sources of architectural knowledge available to the missionaries were usually limited to what they could remember. Their experiences in Spain, Mexico, or other New World colonies might have provided models for construction in New Mexico, but the construction materials and techniques at their disposal were primitive compared to what had become normal architectural methods in central Mexico. They may also have acquired some building knowledge from actual work on construction projects, although they could certainly have learned by observing or directing as well. Kubler cited one Fray Juan de Gaona, who "labored as a hod-carrier and ditch-digger among the Indian" workers at Xochimilco, Mexico, before 1550.[124]

European architectural treatises had arrived in New Spain by the close of the sixteenth century, creating a momentum for stylistic change and development.[125] A document intended for master builders/architects, *Architectural Practice in Mexico City* (tentatively dated between 1794 and 1813) suggested parallel, if not specifically coincident, building practices in New Mexico.[126] As a document it balanced prosaic listings of materials and their costs with fragments of ideas and resources. The anonymous author admonished the architect to have a compass; a perfectly smooth, preferably bronze drafting table; and a "well-made level of wood with a plumb."[127] For design and construction knowledge, he suggested Serrano's *Universal Astronomy* for basic geometry and the writings of Fray Lorenzo.

Fray Lorenzo de Nicolás, born in Madrid in the 1590s, published the first part of his *Arte y uso de la arquitectura* (Art and Use of Architecture) in 1633. Following the Renaissance canon, he included a description of the architectural orders and summarized the work of leading theorists such as Sebastiano Serlio, Andrea Palladio, Giacomo Barozzi da Vignola, and Ottavio Bertutti Scamozzi. The 1667 edition also included an explication of the teachings of Euclid. "A working architect as well as theoretician," Fray Lorenzo aimed his writings at the mason and builder as well as the designer.[128]

But if the Franciscans had ever had access to these studies while in Mexico, once in New Mexico they could resort only to memory or notes in the field. For the most part any idealized vision of the church had to be tempered by the constraints imposed by the site.

The Pueblo Indians provided experience as well as knowledge of techniques and construction materials. But although the Indians had centuries of experience with multistoried buildings, their construction had been limited to small cells. Bearing walls in the pueblos rarely continued for more than a single story and were built upon the roof of the floor below. Even in pueblos such as Zuñi, where the wooden post replaced the bearing wall, the dimensions of the spaces were only a fraction of those of a church nave. A building of the size and complexity of a church was not within the compass of native knowledge. Structural considerations compounded at increased scale, especially problems caused by high unbraced walls and the concentrated loads of roof beams.

Another source of knowledge, although rarely recognized, was the civilian builder or military engineer. By the middle of the sixteenth century, trained master builders–cum–architects were practicing in Mexico City, although knowledge of their existence in New Mexico is more limited. The ranks of the military included those who had built fortifications, dwellings, and/or storage buildings. During the 1700s in Saint Augustine, Florida, for example, these consultants played an active role in constructing the city: "Quite likely the government also furnished [the settlers] technical help in the person of one or more construction experts. These could range from royal engineer or construction superintendent to master builders in the various trades."[129]

Some civilian settlers must also have possessed substantial knowledge because each was responsible for erecting his own house and farm buildings as well as contributing to the raising of the church. Even on Pueblo lands these master builders were employed to consult, inspect, supervise, and undertake church construction. As late as 1819 at Cochiti, for example, a Spanish mason from Santa Cruz was ordered to appear at the pueblo to finish topping off the church's walls so that they could receive a roof.[130] The architectural idea remained nearly constant from the time of settlement to the turn of this century. But with the change in governance and the consequent demographic shift from Indian and Hispanic to Anglo, a modification of building form followed suit.

1-37

1-38

1-37
A REPLICA OF A MORADA
The Las Golondrinas Folk Museum,
La Cienaga
The structure is divided into two spaces:
a service room and a chapel.
[1984]

1-38
SOUTH MORADA, PLAN
Abiquiu
[Source: Ahlborn: *The Penitente Moradas of Abiquiú*]

The early nineteenth century witnessed two major events in the secular and sacral governance of New Mexico. Mexico's independence from Spain in 1821 brought New Mexico under Mexican hegemony, and in 1834 the government secularized the mission system as a whole, transferring the jurisdiction of the churches to the bishop of Durango and local parish priests. The shift in rule from Spain to Mexico had only minor political consequences, but the religious effects in New Mexico were much greater.

In 1788 thirty Franciscans were serving in New Mexico; by 1826 only nine remained, aided by five secular priests.[131] In 1797 the first six of the New Mexican parishes, including the three villas, were removed from Franciscan jurisdiction. When secular priests from Mexico journeyed north to the borderland settlements, they found the living conditions so unappealing that they shortly returned south. Historically, the quota of missionaries needed in New Mexico had rarely been filled, but the disparity between the number assigned and the number actually practicing the vocation increased during the 1800s. This was partly the fault of the order and the church in New Spain. Native Americans and those of mixed blood were not accepted into the order, and the tensions between friars born in Spain and those born in the New World plagued the enterprise from the start. From 1600 to 1800 there were only two known instances of native-born clergy in New Mexico.[132] After the secularization of the missions, some Franciscans remained as parish priests, but by 1840 no Franciscans were working in New Mexico.

As early as 1813 a separate bishopric and collegiate seminar had been authorized for Santa Fe and a suitable visit of inspection undertaken. Neither the Santa Fe Parroquia nor its convento received a favorable evaluation as the site of a potential cathedral.[133] Nor was the state of the province more hopeful. In 1820, on his return to Durango after an official visit to New Mexico, Juan Bautista de Guevara wrote of his experience: "Of 35,500 and more souls, one thousand Spanish and mixed know the Christian doctrine. Thirty of these read and write with some orthography. But the Indians of all missions except Senecu barely know any more of God than do the Gentiles. . . . From so much irreligion comes the indecent state of the churches, lack of ornaments, the fatal desolation of the House of God."[134]

This vacuum was filled to some degree by the conflation of the lay Third Order and the Brotherhood of Light, or Penitentes, whose religious practices, although often frowned upon by the church, provided a rudimentary substitute for those churches without an ordained priest.[135] The Brotherhood of Light also contributed the *morada*—a simple, private chapel and meeting space—to New Mexico's religious architecture. The founding of the order is usually assigned to 1835, and the earliest documented moradas date from the second quarter of the nineteenth century.[136]

The morada shared the basic profile of the single-nave church, although its interior commonly consisted of only two rooms. The first room served as a chapel for worship during holy week and on saint's days and was furnished with an altarpiece, painted or carved images, and candles. The second room was used by the chapter for eating and dressing. Morada architecture was never codified, and siting, building configurations, and sizes varied widely. The degree of interior finish, for example, reflected the beliefs and material resources of the confraternity. Two common distinguishing features were the large wooden cross used during Holy Week and the belfry atop the walls of the chapel. The morada is inwardly focused; from the exterior, the structure appears almost monolithic, with few apertures for light or egress. And yet in its simplicity of mass and profile—so characteristic of New Mexican architecture—lies its beauty.[137]

Simultaneously, the creation of *santos*, painted or sculptured religious images, flowered in the middle of the nineteenth century. Rough and yet highly expressive, these wooden figures (*bultos*) were often created by families of carvers, much like those still living in villages such as Cordova.[138] These sculptures exhibit a power and directness that recall the Gothic art traditions of medieval Europe, in which gesture and exaggeration substituted for polish and detail. A noteworthy example of the bulto tradition is the *Santo Entierro*, or deposed Christ. A late-eighteenth-century work credited to Fray Andrés García, it still lies within a niche in the south wall of the Santa Cruz church. The rendering and modeling are explicit, the expression direct and realistic, although cast in heightened intensity. On the morning of Good Friday it was carried in procession, with the followers holding banners and singing dirges.[139] The santo carving tradition declined after the mid-nineteenth century when it was superseded by the increased importation of inexpensive, commercially produced, plaster figures made readily available by the use of rail transport.

The removal of the missions from Franciscan administration created a void in the religious activity

1-39

1-39
SAN MIGUEL ARCANGEL
Carved wooden figure, 14″ high
[Taylor Museum, Colorado Springs
Fine Arts Center]

of New Mexico that continued until the arrival of Bishop Jean-Baptiste Lamy in 1851. Until then, jurisdiction had remained with the bishop of Durango, who was far removed from the parishes under his control. Many congregations were left without clergy, which further weakened the ties between the people and the church.

There were simply not enough ordained priests to minister the churches, and jurisdictions were consolidated as a result. By 1895 San Ildefonso had come under the jurisdiction of a priest based at Peña Blanca. Acoma became a visita of the more easily accessible Laguna after an outbreak of smallpox late in the eighteenth century. Tesuque had been ministered from Santa Fe almost from its founding, but by the end of the 1700s a priest from Nambe celebrated mass there only periodically. The results of these efforts were only partially successful. Bishop José Antonio Zubiría made the arduous journey from Durango to New Mexico on a visitation in 1845 and was saddened by the results. He found that many Hispanic parishioners had wandered from the path and that the natives were faring much worse, lacking, as they did, priests to tend the missions. "Church and missions were in disrepair, and the bishop lacked the financial resources to remedy the deficiencies."[140]

Location had always played a critical role in the creation and maintenance of New Mexican settlements, but it became even more important during the 1800s. The architecture of the churches in these villages remained constant and conservative, and until the Anglo influx following the opening of the railroad in the 1880s, the population remained primarily Catholic.

The model for the typical village church of the nineteenth century followed the same lines established through centuries of building practice in New Mexico. The plans and architectural types were the same: single-nave structures with bearing walls of adobe, beams, and ceilings of wood. The facades could be flat and planar or graced with one or a pair of towers. Domínguez would have recognized the building type, with the sacristy appended to the nave, although the choir loft had become less frequent as the size of the buildings was reduced.

Two changes in the pattern were readily discernible, however, becoming more pronounced as the century progressed. The first affected the town plan; the second, the mass and profile of the structure. The church on one side of the plaza—the typical siting—was replaced by a church in the middle of the plaza, its role shifting from a central, social, open space accommodating commerce as

1-41

1-40
SENA
Typical of many small village churches, the Sena structure has a single nave, simple facade and bell structure, handsome and well maintained.
[1986]

1-41
SAN JOSÉ
In nineteenth-century towns the church was often sited in the center of the plaza instead of on its periphery.
[1986]

1–42

1–42
SAN VICENTE DE PAUL
Punta de Agua
1838.
[1986]

well as public display to one used for training and exercise.[141] Visually this arrangement more closely paralleled the Anglo model of the county courthouse set in the middle of the square than the central plaza prescribed by the Laws of the Indies.

Although occupying an unusual geographic position, San Miguel del Bado illustrates a somewhat typical pattern for village churches in the nineteenth century [Plate 20]. Like Truchas and Las Trampas in the mountains to the north, the town was established primarily to provide a defensive buffer between Spanish settlements along the Rio Grande and Plains Indians marauders. Founded in 1746, the inhabitants of the village consisted of *genízaros*, or Catholic Indians who served as a militia as well as farmers or ranchers. A small plaza was established not far from the banks of the Pecos River near a spot where the velocity and depth of the water were sufficiently reduced to permit fording.

The church of San Miguel del Bado (Saint Michael of the Ford) was under construction on the plaza in 1805, following traditional lines.[142] Its facade lacked ornamentation except for a door and perhaps a window to the choir loft cut into its adobe walls. To secure the structure against floods, the site was filled to create a platform raised above the high water mark.

With the opening of the Santa Fe Trail in 1822, the village thrived. Two days distant from the territorial capital of Santa Fe, San Miguel del Bado became a resting place for outward-bound convoys and a haven from the Plains Indians for those arriving from St. Louis. The bustling economy funded major repairs to the church in 1866, including the addition of the twin towers still extant. But the advent of the railroad ruined the town's role as a prosperous way station and rapidly reduced San Miguel del Bado to the status of a backwater.

The evolving village plan is illustrated by communities such as Sena and San Jose in the upper Pecos valley. Although the size of the plazas differ, their respective churches occupy the center of the open space. Houses, barns, and other structures ring the perimeter of the plaza, although at Sena the enclosure provided by the surrounding hillsides overrides that offered by the masses of houses and shops. In the type regulated by the Laws of the Indies, the center of the town was a void, the principal edifices occupying the edge of the space, lending it composure and dignity. The model that developed during the nineteenth century, on the other hand, reflected the centrality of the church in the social order.

Architecturally the strongest visible difference between the old and new manner of building was the pitched roof. In more mountainous areas, like those of the upper Pecos, where rain and snowfall were greater than on the plains, pitched roofs of split shakes or vertically oriented boards were typical. Where precipitation was lower, the flat roof of mud over wooden beams sufficed, however imperfectly.[143] As with the larger religious structures, the use of the pitched roof became more widespread with time and the greater availability of corrugated and sheet metal roofing. Architectural form changed correspondingly.

The old church at Truchas, in use by 1852 and given a new roof in 1878, could well serve as a generic model. The churches at Villanueva, San Vicente de Paul at Punta de Agua, San Ysidro at Agua Fria, and Tecolote all represent a type that today includes hundreds of structures. As the population grew, churches were built—in spite of the declining number of clergy to care for them—and construction peaked around the turn of the twentieth century.

Even today the remarkable consistency of the building type remains impressive. The single nave, the pitched roof, the central belfry riding the roof or attached to the nave wall, the basic proportions and measure—all reflect a history of more than three and a half centuries. Of course, there are divergences in style. The Anglo importation of the new Gothic style affected many of the structures to at least a minor degree: the detail of window trim or a small wooden belfry set on the roof, for example. Windows grew larger as railroads and later trucks provided smoother and more inexpensive means of transport. Regional and community preferences also affected the style, materials, and color of the churches to some extent. A taut metal roof and light belfry cap the heavy base of the church at Algodones; San Ysidro shows signs of a more conscious effort to bring the building in accord with the popular image of a colonial period church. But these variations appear superficial when tested against the basic, nearly homogeneous architectural pattern. Consistency dominates modification, even in churches whose history may be less than a century, in a land where time and change both have passed remarkably slowly.

Recent surveys have revealed more than three hundred village churches in the northeastern portion of the state alone.[144] Some of these were larger than the early missions; many were smaller. Today they stand in various states of repair: some thriving, some used only on feast days or once or twice a month to celebrate mass, some removed from use,

66 some tottering on the brink of collapse or threat of destruction for economic reasons.

In 1846 the Americans entered Santa Fe under the command of Colonel Stephen Kearny, who was moving west to California to claim Spanish territory for the United States. This forceful acquisition of alien territory was a spinoff of the Spanish-American War coupled with the belief in Manifest Destiny. Notices were posted in the towns announcing that the inhabitants were now citizens of the United States, not Mexico, and that all rights and legal land claims would be respected by the new government. In time this attitude precipitated immense legal problems because Spanish land grants were neither registered nor staked according to American methods. The majority of New Mexico's inhabitants did not immediately apprehend the scope of the change and the upheaval it caused. Except for the Taos insurrection, which concluded with the destruction of the San Jerónimo church at the pueblo, the transference in governance was primarily nominal.

Land claims, legal and linguistic problems, and noticeable differences in religion and culture all created sources of friction between the Anglos entering the territory and the settled Hispanic population. Little social integration bonded these two culturally distinctive peoples. But the increase in commerce that accompanied the Anglo influx was certainly welcomed. To strengthen the trade monopoly of the Chihuahua merchants who supplied trade caravans after 1805, the Spanish crown had prohibited trade with the United States. Under Mexican rule the enforcement of mercantile isolation was more lax, but only with the advent of American governance did a flood of new products and styles pour into New Mexico and ultimately shift the cultural axis from north-south to east-west. Trade on the Santa Fe Trail between the capital and St. Louis gradually increased, and by the 1840s a serious commercial rivalry between the merchants of Missouri and Chihuahua had developed. The Yankee trader in his prairie schooner filled with trade goods was a familiar sight in Santa Fe notwithstanding the long haul and the continued threat of Indian attacks. The new goods influenced a change of styles not only in domestic habits but also in religious architecture.

One additional and overwhelming factor also influenced a departure from the almost static pattern of Hispanic church building. Although ownership of the territory of New Mexico was transferred to Washington, the bishop under whose jurisdiction New Mexico fell was still seated in Durango. Pressure was exerted to positive effect, and in time Santa Fe became its own archdiocese. In 1851 Jean-Baptiste Lamy became the first bishop of Santa Fe.

Lamy was a Frenchman, born in Lempdes, Poyde-Dom, a district rich in Romanesque church architecture. In 1839 he came to the United States at the age of twenty-five, serving in southern Ohio and Kentucky until he was elevated to the rank of archbishop. No doubt because he was French and New Mexico was Spanish, someone thought he would be the ideal archbishop for Santa Fe; and in many ways he was. Lamy was indefatigable; he regarded his charge as bishop as a holy campaign and seemed to share the zeal of the early missionaries. Troubled by the low level of literacy in New Mexico, he immediately established schools to raise the standard of education. His emphasis on funding for education left only limited resources for church construction. In 1859, for example, he sold the derelict Castrense chapel on the plaza to raise money and land for a school planned southeast of the cathedral.

If education was Lamy's main concern, a cathedral worthy of the name for Santa Fe ran a close second. The existing Parroquia had been gothicized to some degree, a by-product of the American occupation, but it nevertheless retained the original Conquistadora chapel that had been preserved since at least the eighteenth century. The new cathedral subsumed them all, the chapel becoming an adjunct to the north transept (it is the only adobe portion of the complex left today). In its place rose a church of cut stone in the French Romanesque style, a style without precedent in New Mexico; a church of arches and vaults, columns with carved capitals, a rose window, and the never-realized aspiration for two soaring spires. Architects Antoine and Projectus Molny were also French, imported by the bishop expressly for this purpose. The plan was grandiose, ambitious, and never completed. Despite repeated renovations, or because of them, the cathedral today remains an architectural anomaly amid the Pueblo/Spanish Colonial styles of Santa Fe.

But the writing was on the wall. Lamy displayed little sympathy for the rudimentary or histrionic side of New Mexican Catholicism. In place of unity and harmony of parts, materials, and emotion, the archbishop saw structures crying to become acceptable houses of worship. When funds allowed, the churches were remodeled and "modernized." To deter the infiltration of water or the erosion of the interiors, many churches were capped with pitched metal roofs. Santa Cruz, with its broken-back hulking silhouette, is an excellent example of the new

1–43

1–43
FEDERAL BUILDING
Santa Fe, Louis A. Simon, 1921
The building's design comprises a
romantic assemblage of elements from
a number of missions.
[1984]

form, as was turn-of-the-century Isleta. At last the
leakage was solved; at last the clergy overcame the
continual problem of the parapet/roof intersection
that plagued a roof made only of earth. Technologi-
cal progress and success must have been equated
with beauty, or beauty was not regarded as a worthy
concern. When a pitched roof was added to the traditional architectural form, two problems arose: the
clerestory was lost, and a facade gable was required
to cover the ends of the roof. Both factors forced
changes in the architectural expression of the
churches.

If the trade on the Santa Fe Trail produced notable changes in domestic architectural styles, its
effect was minimal when compared to that of the
railroad. Entering New Mexico in 1879 and binding
the territory along two transcontinental routes, the
railroad rendered traditional building techniques
passé or obsolete. Proximity to the railroad overcame the strictures of tradition, and Albuquerque
and Las Vegas eclipsed Santa Fe as the rails bypassed
the capital. Milled lumber was readily available,
facilitated by the construction of local sawmills;
brick and glass became available as well. In, too,
came religious items, pattern books, and new styles
in the Gothic mode: a style fitting and proper for
religious architecture. A. W. N. Pugin has been
instrumental in establishing the supremacy of the
style in England in the early nineteenth century,
regarding the Gothic as the only proper vehicle for
Christian architectural expression. The Romanesque drew on the architectural idioms of Greece
and Rome, both pagan. Gothic, in contrast, recalled
the religious fervor of the Middle Ages, when piety
had built the true cathedrals. How Pugin would
have viewed New Mexico's architecture, the product of its own religious fervor, is open to question.

Church faces and facades changed drastically. At
Isleta, for example, the plain and very simple facade
became a wonderfully impossible concoction of
wooden Gothic belfries and gables. San Felipe
Neri in Albuquerque was only slightly less so, with
gothicized towers and entries and a nave veneered
with pressed metal and articulated in bays by
wooden arches and columns [Plates 18, 19]. In the
four decades between 1880 and 1920 the appearance of the churches underwent more transformation than they had in the previous two and one-half
centuries.

Pitched roofs, gables, turrets, enlarged windows,
wooden floors, milled lumber, metal stoves for
heating, mass produced plaster statuary, and printed
art all drastically modified the look and essence of
New Mexican religious architecture. The new look

1—44

1—44
SAN AGUSTÍN
Isleta Pueblo
After renovations in the early part of
this century, the Anglo pitched roof and
turrets sit uneasily upon the Hispanic–
Native American adobe base.
[New Mexico Tourism and Travel
Division, no date]

1–45

1–45
SAN AGUSTÍN
Isleta Pueblo
The church after the 1960 renovations.
[1981]

70 also caused the collapse of at least one church: Santa Clara was felled by the thrust caused when a pitched metal roof was being installed. Cochiti took a spire and a three-arch portico more typical of California than New Mexico, and by the end of 1923 Isleta had become an absolute Gothic fantasyland. Even Santa Cruz passed through an ornamented phase that was decoratively complex, quaint, and hopeless in terms of the endurance of the adobe in which the ornamented parapets were executed. Some churches endured more than one stylistic transfiguration. Nuestra Señora de Guadalupe in Santa Fe was first rendered as a New England Gothic church but later wore a more respectable, although not exactly New Mexican, mission style. Although the remodelings were incongruous, clumsy and, in instances like Isleta, even architecturally bizarre, they represented the cultural trends of the times as clearly as a diagram. The Anglo-French influence was a gloss, a topping applied to the solid, established Hispanic base. Beneath the visual changes were those traditional attitudes and cultural values that withstood changes of political administration and the importation of new stylistic trends.

RESTORATION

The evolving styles of architecture and construction methods normally reflect social change, a process that continues perpetually. Our current regard for historical verity is only a recent occurrence, which has arisen in response to the threat of the complete destruction of building. During the 1960s interest in the restoration of the missions swelled to the extent that several structures underwent remodeling or rebuilding. Restoration is not an easy process, either in terms of intellectual conceptualization or actual construction. In many cases restoration actually raises more questions than it answers, and even when an answer announces itself, it does not satisfy all involved parties or stand as a simple conclusion.

Only when a number of the missions had lost their historical features to Neo-Gothic or more modern styles in the early twentieth century, did certain parties become sufficiently concerned to take action. In some respects this interest was prompted by the attention lavished on the California missions by Charles Lummis, the editor of the southern California auto club magazine. The citizens of New Mexico also raised their banner. Compounding the ranks of the proponents for the preservation and restoration of the missions was a group of artists and architects possessing a romantic attachment to Indian and Hispanic cultures. It was a period of stylistic and romantic revivals mixed with a searching for roots. In the 1920s the search led to an appreciation of the simple, geometric qualities of the pueblos, which shared certain qualities with the exotic sources of cubism and European modernism. The best known among the architects, John Gaw Meem, often worked in a style sympathetic to the colonial period. He was also an important figure in the preservation of the missions, playing a pivotal role working on various committees and raising funds for repairs and restoration. Built to Meem's traditional designs in 1939, Cristo Rey is the largest adobe church in the state.[145]

Among the artists, the group of painters known as Los Cinco Pintores occupied the foremost position in mission restoration work.[146] Of these, Carlos Vierra was the most prolific polemicist on the subject of New Mexican architecture; his series of "restored" mission portraits served for a number of years as the accepted versions of past building form in several publications.[147] Although he was knowledgeable about the look and history of missions, his paintings were more fanciful than factual, although the flavor of many of them rang true. When the Committee for the Preservation and Restoration of New Mexico Mission Churches was founded in the 1920s, artists were among those involved in restoration projects, often in an active role as consultant. The Museum of New Mexico served as the primary state agency for restoration, and on one early project at Zia Jozef G. Bakos worked as a consultant with Odd S. Halseth of the museum staff. The committee also provided funding for Acoma at a point when further delay might have meant the total loss of the building. The policy at that time was to restore according to archaeological and documented evidence; only in rare instances did work extend beyond that needed to assure the continued existence of the structure.

Ironically, the Depression provided an enormous boost to the acquisition of knowledge about the missions. The lack of building money and design projects drove many artists and architects to seek employment in government-sponsored projects, such as the excavation work on churches at Quarai and Jemez Springs and the measurement and documentation of buildings under the sponsorship of the Historic American Buildings Survey (HABS). A number of churches, including Acoma, Ranchos de Taos, and San Miguel, were recorded at that time in drawings that remain notable for their excellent delineation and completeness of information.[148] More recently Perry Borchers, working with a team of

1–46

1–46
ORATORIO OF SAN YSIDRO
Las Golindrinas Folk Museum,
La Cienaga
The basic single-cell chapel.
[1981]

students and relatives, has photogrammetrically recorded several of the pueblos and their religious structures. Unlike the HABS documents, however, certain of these drawings are not in the public domain, but they exist for the future nonetheless.

Concerned groups fueled by a combination of local pride, threats of change or destruction to historic structures, and sufficient affluence have come to regard building style as an important cultural issue. In 1957 the city of Santa Fe passed an ordinance dictating that all buildings undergoing repair or construction in the central district would have to adopt the "Old or New Santa Fe Style." The "styles," of course, are not accurate historical recreations but a romanticized conglomerate of the way things never had been. Restoring those buildings that had acquired an Anglo patina to their prior Pueblo or Hispanic idioms makes some sense, but legislation that decrees the creation of new architecture in an old form with little regard for the urban pattern itself may not be viable. The 1957 ordinance remains in force, but public planning agencies have subsequently sought and demonstrated a more substantial understanding of New Mexico's traditional architecture and of urban patterns in subsequent studies and legislative proposals.[149]

The traditional battle between the "scrapers," who want to remove all the layers of acquired modifications and restore buildings to their original form, and the "antiscrapers," who want to leave buildings as they are, dates to the last century and still lacks resolution. The former group argues that a building is the product of a certain period in time and that it should represent that period in its pristine state.[150] The latter replies that a building acquires its own history and that consequently any modifications to its fabric are as real and meaningful as the original construction. A church scheduled to become a museum or monument, such as Guadalupe or Abo, is a problem more easily resolved since the people involved as a governing body are relatively few. But what of churches such as Santa Cruz or Ranchos de Taos that exist as *churches* and whose current form—whether historical or not, in "bad taste" or cluttered—exhibits just those layers of history that are the most meaningful to the congregation? Should these be removed just to provide "historical accuracy" for the preservationist?

Certainly there is no single answer to these questions, and one can only hope that in each major restoration project a balance will be struck between what is lost and what is gained. In some cases, such as at Las Trampas, restoration and preservation efforts were almost in contradiction with the aspirations of the congregation.[151] In others, such as Isleta, where remodeling stemmed from the congregation's wishes, the church today appears architecturally a bit bald, although of a decidedly more "mission" style.[152]

In the earliest photo of Isleta, dating from 1870, the church sports a flat facade capped by a simple pediment and a bell. To its right is the two-story, slightly out of whack rectory, with some of the few adobe arches known to have existed in the state. The character of the facade is simple, plain, even grave. By 1900 the post-Lamy influence coupled with the need to maintain the adobe had produced two simple wooden towers of a delicately Gothic flavor. The arrival of Father Antonine Docher at the pueblo, however, produced further and stylistically cataclysmic alterations: a thick base added at either side of the door supported a porch enclosed by an intricate railing. The two towers became more mannered, complex, highly worked constructions of sawn wood paired with a new gable. Certain elements of this architectural fuzziness had disappeared by the 1950s, although the curious polarity of Anglo wood to Hispanic adobe still existed. Here then was a direct rendering of social evolution. Although curious and hybrid, change was transparent in the architectural expression of the church.

In the 1960s all this Neo-Gothic and stylistically uncharacterizable detail was removed. The church was "restored" to the romanticized Spanish colonial style characteristic of those years [Plate 15]. The reinstitution of the clerestory was a positive move, but the removal of so many layers of history was certainly a social loss and a visual disappointment.[153] Perhaps this fantastical restoration of Isleta will be seen in the future as an entirely fitting and proper undertaking that was indicative of *our* time.

The fate of the missions, like all architecture, parallels the life cycles of biological organisms: they are created, made to grow, reach fruition, deteriorate, and, in some instances, pass away. The process can be retarded, but it cannot be stopped. Most of these structures, which have existed in some form or another for almost three centuries, today seem to be in good health.[154] Although nature and society will always take their toll, great architecture accepts the tribulations of both as part of its evolution and integrates these forces in its form. In New Mexico the course has been no different.

1–47

1–47
PROCESSION WITH SAINT'S IMAGE
Santa Clara
[George H. Pepper, 1903. Courtesy of
the Museum of the American Indian,
Heye Foundation]

And what of the state of churches in New Mexico today? Certainly the Hispanic American communities, even small communities such as San Ysidro or Sena, display a sincerity of belief and a care for their church that are deep-rooted and pervasive. But these communities must still face the deterioration of the body of the church, isolation, and, more recently, a lack of clergy.

In 1916 Father Jerome Hesse, in describing Christmas at Santo Domingo, said that the pueblo's was certainly Catholicism but Catholicism in a different form: "The inhabitants of this Pueblo are Catholic, and wish to be Catholic, but according to their own fashion."[155] John Bourke had been less gracious in 1881, commenting, "The Pueblos became hypocrites, they never became Catholics." And he added, "Coercion never yet made a convert."[156]

The native Pueblo religions have been a continuous presence in New Mexico since the beginning of habitation. Even today the situation does not seem to have changed. Edward Dozier offered this explanation:

> The new religion [Catholicism] provided no institutions for the relief from [the] immediate and pressing anxieties of daily life. Instead the new religion dwelt on incomprehensible rewards or punishments in the life after death. In Pueblo belief, conduct in the temporary world did not determine the kind of existence one might have in the hereafter. There was no concept of heaven or hell; one lived on after death but no rules existed here and now for improving or worsening one's position in the next world. Life was difficult enough in this world. Let the future take care of itself. So loyalty in the native beliefs and its rites persisted. The Pueblo Indian accommodated himself to the external practices of the new religion for the simple expedient of survival, but his own indigenous religion was not abandoned.[157]

Lummis added, "The nine thousand Pueblo Indians—peaceful, fixed, house-dwelling and home-loving tillers of the soil; good Catholics in the churches, they have build with a patience infinite as that of the pyramids; good pagans everywhere else."[158]

One hot day in August 1981 when I began working on this book, I traveled to one of the Rio Grande pueblos to take a careful look at the church and village because the community permitted no photography or note taking. As it was a Sunday morning, I thought I might be able to attend mass and thus gain access to the interior of the church, which had remained locked on several previous vis-

its. Arriving about ten o'clock, I found the gates to the campo santo securely locked. Peeking through the gate, I noticed that the doors of the church were also firmly closed to entry.

Rejoining a friend, I walked over to the plaza where the sound of drumming attracted our attention. In the plaza were a group of *koshare*, clowns or "delight makers," as Adolph Bandelier called them,[159] indicating that a dance was in progress. Our initial panic as the only two Caucasians in the area was dispelled when several members of the community courteously told us that we were welcome to remain and watch the dance, although it had not been announced to the general public. Shortly thereafter the dancers filed into the dance plaza. Their intricate steps to the rhythm of the drum and the shifting of columns continued for several hours. Like the feeling I encountered in the Hispanic villages, the dancers' sincerity was without question, although the Koshares' comic antics displayed none of the staid solemnity of ritual in the Western church.

What should one make of this? A tentative explanation might suggest that each of the two religions has governed certain aspects of human existence and that after centuries of Western contact the native religion, the religion of the ancestors, still remains a strong presence in the lives of the people. D. W. Meinig put it more strongly: "Although the Catholic Church was a prominent part of the visible scene, it was rarely centered either in location of allegiance, in some villages nominally accepted, in others largely ignored, in all at most no more than co-existing with the *kiva* and the ancient rituals."[160] The Catholic church still stood, but it was locked. Its presence has been tolerated and at times even venerated. The church has lived in New Mexico for three centuries, a long period of time in terms of European presence in the Western Hemisphere but only a short period of time in the Pueblo sense of existence. Place, not a particular structure, remains sacred in New Mexico; the spirit, not the stone.

1–48

1–48
*PROCESSION OF THE SAINT,
SANTO DOMINGO*
Alexandre Hogue, 1928
In this painting the saint belongs to the
people, although the priest's attention
appears to be directed elsewhere.
[Sheldon Memorial Art Gallery, Uni-
versity of Nebraska, Lincoln, Nebraska
Art Association, Nelle Cochrane Woods
Collection]

1
Enchanted Mesa seen from the Acoma
peñol.
[1986]

2
The green-gray landscape of the High
Sonoran Desert ecological zone: grasses,
chamiso, mesa, and distant storm.
[1986]

3
Thunderstorm over the Rio Grande
at sunset.
[1981]

4
NUESTRA SEÑORA DE LA PURÍSMA
CONCEPCIÓN
Quarai, circa 1630
The partially restored mass of the red
sandstone church.
[1986]

5
SAN BUENAVENTURA
Gran Quivira, circa 1660
Detail showing the yellow-gray
limestone walls.
[1981]

NUESTRA SEÑORA DE LOS ANGELES
Pecos pueblo, 1620–1705
View from the altar, westward over
the valley.
[1986]

7
EL SANTUARIO
Chimayo, 1816
The rapidly tapering nave converges on
the brilliant hues of the altar screen.
[1981]

8
SAN JOSÉ
Las Trampas, circa 1760
Detail of the carved wooden beam and
entrance doors.
[1978]

9
SAN JOSÉ
Laguna pueblo, circa 1700
These latillas—among the most elabo-
rate and most beautiful of the New
Mexican churches—are set diagonally
to form a herringbone pattern.
[1978]

10
SAN JOSÉ
Laguna pueblo, circa 1700
The altar and altar screen.
[1986]

11
SAN MIGUEL
La Bajada, post-1831
Within this small chapel are all the basic
elements of the New Mexican church:
heavy walls of adobe, a roof structure of
exposed wooden beams, earthen floor,
and the collective presence of the members of the congregation.
[1981]

12
SAN LORENZO
Picuris pueblo, circa 1770
Later additions, such as the stepped
pediment and end "wings" executed in
hard plaster, gave the church a sharp
profile against the sky or mountains.
[1978]

13
SAN FRANCISCO DE ASÍS
Ranchos de Taos, circa 1780
The windows were enlarged at the end
of the nineteenth century, and rounded
tops were added within the traditional
lintel openings.
[1981]

14
SAN FRANCISCO DE ASÍS
Ranchos de Taos, circa 1780
The two buttresses have been stabilized,
and the freshly plastered church faces
the morning sun.
[1981]

15
SAN AGUSTÍN
Isleta pueblo, pre-1629+
In this view from the apse of the church,
the brittle quality of hard stucco contrasts markedly with the worked and
mutable masses of mud walls.
[1981]

16
SAN AGUSTÍN
Isleta pueblo, pre-1619+
The strategic and dramatic play of light
from the transverse clerestory upon the
sanctuary.
[1978]

17
KIVA INTERIOR
Pecos pueblo (reconstructed)
The illumination from the transverse
clerestories of the Spanish churches
recalls the light falling through the
kiva's single roof opening.
[1980]

18
SAN FELIPE NERI

Albuquerque, 1706+
The interior still displays the Victorian
architectural overlay that added a
rhythm of bays to the longitudinal
movement of the nave. The ladder to
the pulpit has been removed.
[1986]

19
SAN FELIPE NERI
Albuquerque, 1706 +
The church has remained relatively true
to its late-nineteenth-century renovation.
The rockwork around the entrance, how-
ever, is a recent addition.
[1986]

20
SAN MIGUEL DEL BADO
1806, 1886
Elevated on an earthen plinth to
counter flooding by the nearby river,
the church stood at the end of the Santa
Fe Trail as the entry to the capital.
[1982]

PART II

THE CHURCHES

SANTA FE

SAN MIGUEL

pre-1628; 1693–1710

As a member of the family of New Mexican churches, the chapel of San Miguel is an anomaly in several respects. Its primary congregation was neither the Europeans of Santa Fe nor the Pueblo Indians, but the Indian servants who accompanied the Spanish as they pushed colonization and Christianization north into New Mexico. As a physical form the church today is unique, being capped by a single tower in contrast to the more typical flat-faced and twin-tower arrangements. Only in its interior arrangement does the chapel follow the common mold characterized by a single nave, tapered sanctuary, transverse clerestory, and choir loft.

The first mention of the ermita of San Miguel appeared in a document dated July 28, 1628, in which Governor Felipe de Sotelo Ossorio was charged with "impious conduct during the mass."[1] Hence by that date a chapel already existed, constructed sometime after the provincial capital was transferred to Santa Fe south from San Gabriel in 1610. The site for the chapel lay on the opposite bank of the Santa Fe River apart from the formally planned and plotted part of Santa Fe. The Barrio Analco, as the district was known, was a piece of land settled by the Indians who had accompanied the Spanish as allies and intermediaries. The site shows signs of Indian occupation from the fourteenth century, as evidenced by remains found during excavations under the chapel in 1955 by Stanley Stubbs and Bruce Ellis.[2]

Tradition has it (although without documentary evidence) that a portion of the barrio's residents were Tlascalan Indians from Mexico who had been granted special dispensation by the king because they had allied with the forces of Hernán Cortés in the Spanish battles against the powerful Mezo-American tribes. As a result, they were exempted from paying certain taxes and were allowed to bear European arms. The Spanish also used them as colonial liaisons: to undertake negotiations on behalf of the Europeans and to set an example in farming and mining techniques. They worked, Marc Simmons noted, as colonists, miners, soldiers, and assistants to Spanish explorers and missionaries going north.[3] Although the Pueblos conformed more closely to the Spanish concept of civilization and thus had less need of models, some Tlascalan Indians might have accompanied Oñate's expeditionary forces in 1598. It is believed that at least one Franciscan in the party brought with him a Tlascalan assistant.[4]

Although relatively highly regarded by the Spanish, these Indians were not considered as equals and worked as menial help for the Spanish settlers of

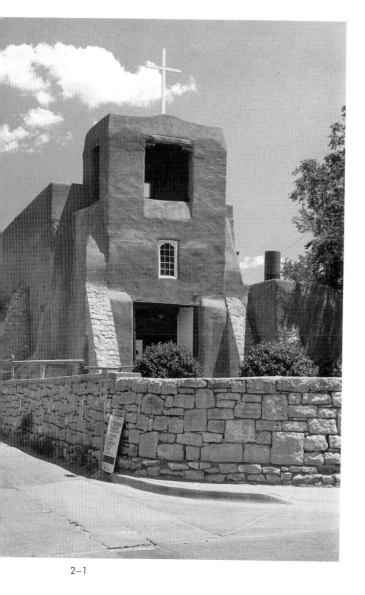

2–1

2–2

2–1
SAN MIGUEL
The church in its current form, a curious mixture of stone buttresses, a single tower, and an oversized void.
[1984]

2–2
SAN MIGUEL
1872–1873
Late in the nineteenth century the five-level tower grew from a solid earthen base.
[Timothy O'Sullivan, Museum of New Mexico]

Santa Fe. Consequently they settled the land *analco*, a Nahuatl (language of the Tlascalans) word meaning "across the water" or "on the other side of the river." Whether the barrio's original inhabitants were specifically Tlascalan or were simply other peoples from Mexico has been the subject of some debate. In either case, by 1640 the Barrio Analco was considered a viable community by the Spanish, as evidenced by a document in the General Archives of the Indies. Benavides wrote that "it [the villa] lacked the principal thing, which was the church; that which they had being a poor 'jacal'; because the Friars first gave their attention to building churches for the Indians whom they converted, and among whom they lived and labored; and therefore as soon as I became Custodian, I began to construct the church and convento to the honor and glory of God."[5] One may infer from this statement that the ermita de San Miguel was the first religious structure constructed by the Spanish in Santa Fe, a rather curious occurrence considering the attention given to the formal planning of the town. The construction of the first parroquia followed the completion of the Indian chapel across the river. The 1628 document that cited the governor's misconduct indicated that the Spanish were still using the chapel as their parish church through the late 1620s and early 1630s.

Little is known of the first edifice that occupied the site. Excavations in 1955 by Bruce Ellis and Stanley Stubbs revealed several layers of construction beneath the floor of the current church. The older chapel, believed to have been built sometime before the Reconquest and possibly before the pre-1640 church, was smaller than the present-day building, with a narrow, rectangular apse in place of the current angled walls and a sanctuary raised two steps above the nave. The facade was probably planar, with neither towers nor buttresses.

Relations among the civil authorities, the military, and the clergy were frequently stormy, and in the late 1630s, with the governorship of Luis de Rosas, the trouble was brought to a head. Attempts to resolve the problems had been in vain. When Fray Bartolomé Romero and Fray Francisco Núñez were sent to Santa Fe in 1640 to meet with the governor and attempt a reconciliation, he verbally abused them, beat them with a stick, and had them imprisoned. The friars were later released, but the church was closed and its bells removed.

The culmination of the disputes between church and state was the razing of San Miguel in 1640, the adobes presumably taken down with the vigas and reused in other construction. The drama did not end with demolition, however. Late one night Ni-

2–3

2–3
SAN MIGUEL
circa 1880
The chapel in derelict condition, the upper stages of its stepped tower had vanished. Note the embedded timber used to reinforce the adobe construction.
[F. A. Nims, Museum of New Mexico]

2–4

2–4
SAN MIGUEL
circa 1884
A single, more massive tower has replaced its staged predecessor; stone buttresses strengthen the facade.
[Dana B. Chase, Museum of New Mexico]

colás Ortiz discovered his wife in Governor Rosas' house, which precipitated a turmoil that resulted in the murder of the excommunicated former governor some weeks later. Rosas was absolved of his activities against the religious by a priest named Juan de Vidania, who was arrested later by the Inquisition but escaped while en route to Mexico. This complex, fascinating, and bizarre chapter in New Mexican history brought into high contrast the chronic antagonisms within the civil administration and the church as well as those between church and state.[6]

Although the church was subsequently reconstructed, the new structure did not last long. Burned during the Pueblo Revolt in 1680, its shell remained unused for the next twelve years. The report issued by Diego de Vargas on his return to Santa Fe made no mention of a need for new wall materials, so it is assumed that only the wooden superstructure required replacement. Vargas, on inspecting the burned church, instructed the people "to roof said walls and to whitewash and repair its skylight in a manner that shall be the quickest, easiest, briefest and least laborious to said natives."[7] In December 1693 men went to the mountains to cut vigas but turned back after several days because of the extreme cold.

The poor condition of the chapel must have upset some members of the congregation, not the least or least noble of whom was Alférez (which corresponds to second lieutenant) Agustín Flores Vergara. In a request to the custos, Flores wrote, "I beseech and entreat his reverence to grant me permission to go about in this city and in other territories of this kingdom, with the holy image, to make a collection of alms which will be of assistance in the execution of the chapel, in order to locate the image therein."[8] He presented this to the custodian, who, Kubler told us, "instantly grant[ed] his request." The history of San Miguel from that time on, at least in terms of politics and ownership, was much calmer.

The repair or major renovation of San Miguel is discussed in great detail in George Kubler's *Rebuilding of the Chapel of San Miguel*. Ensign Flores had raised the funds for the repairs and had hired fifteen workers to execute the work, although none seems to have been Indian.[9] By calculating the number of adobes needed to repair the walls, Kubler figured their height at about seven feet, although archaeological investigations in 1955 were unable to ascertain whether this estimate was correct. It is believed that the change from the rectangular to angled apse dates from this period, as do the two niches in the

2-5

2-5
SAN MIGUEL
circa 1881
The apse end of the structure eroded,
its mud plaster covering all but gone,
the church's adobes are clearly visible.
Note also the crenellated top courses.
[Museum of New Mexico]

rear wall of the apse currently covered by the reredos. Because no Indian names appeared on the register of workers, there might have been two periods of repair: the first a more cursory effort following Vargas's instructions to get the church back in shape for consecration and the second, carried out in 1710, to glorify its body and raise its aesthetic level. By the end of 1710 the work was finished and a new roof was in place.

The carved beam of the choir loft, which was completely remade at the time, read, "The Marquis de la Peñuela erected this building, The Royal Ensign [sic] Don Agustín Flores Vergara, his servant. The year 1710." [10] The credit for construction is usually assigned to Vergara, however, Peñuela's name being required by courtesy because he was governor at the time.

Except for the modified form of the apse, the church was probably built on the same foundations and to the same layout as before. What it looked like, however, remains problematic. A work report noted a carpenter's being paid for four small doors "para las torres" (for the towers), although what the towers referred to remains a mystery. Perhaps the plural "towers" could refer to the tapering stepped tower seen in late-nineteenth-century photographs. But in 1776 Domínguez made no reference to such towers. He may have inadvertently omitted mentioning them, and there is some question as to the accuracy of his report, which placed the sacristy on the north side of the church when archaeological evidence shows that it should have been to the south with the remainder of the convento. A tower scheme might have evolved by the mid-eighteenth century, although this, too, is conjectural. Tamarón, in 1760, was more impressed by the spaciousness of the "principal church" and the promise of the "very fine church dedicated to the Most Holy Mother of Light being built." San Miguel received his visit, if not his enthusiasm; "It is fairly decent; at that time they were repairing the roof." [11]

Domínguez also noted that there were only three windows in the chapel, two in the south wall and one in the west lighting the choir loft. [12] Juan Agustín de Morfi observed that the "section of Analco" was in part regular and that most of it was "without order." He mentioned San Miguel only as "a little church . . . where mass is said to them [genízaros] living in the district on feast days." [13] Bishop Juan Bautista de Guevara's 1818 inventory noted a "little adobe tower without bells," hardly the massive construction that accompanies the crenellations visible in photographs from the 1870s. These may date from an 1830 rebuilding under the sponsorship of Don Simón Delgado or from a slightly later period.[14]

By the time of the American occupation some century and a half after the refounding of the chapel, the nature of the barrio had changed significantly. Some of the Indian residents had followed the Spanish south during the revolt, others had just left, and perhaps others had stayed to merge with the pueblos. Through intermarriage and resettlement, the composition of the district changed, as did the demands placed on the structure. By the mid-nineteenth century only two formal masses each year were being conducted in the church: on St. Michael's Day, May 8, and on September 29.

With annexation to the United States came increased pressure for universal education to the new Anglo way of life, and with Bishop Lamy's prompting, the Brothers of Christian Schools founded Saint Michael's School on the land just south of the chapel. The brothers bought the church from the diocese on July 31, 1881, and used it as a school chapel, holding services on a daily basis. "In this church," wrote Bourke in 1881, "are paintings hundreds of years old, black with the dust and decay of time, which were brought from Spain by the early missionaries." He recorded the beam carving that credited the builder of the church, but he could not make out its date. "With a feeling of awe we left a chapel whose walls had re-echoed the prayers of men who perhaps had looked into the faces of Cortés and Montezuma or listened to the gentle teachings of Las Casas."[15]

The chapel suffered additional physical vicissitudes, this time as the result of natural forces. The roof had been a perennial problem and had been replaced or repaired in 1730 and 1760. The four-tiered tower was toppled by either a wind storm, as some say, or the undermining of the lower walls. In 1887 the lower part of the tower, which formed a narthex to the chapel, was stabilized and capped with a neat pitched metal roof. The round arches of the bell loft had a decidedly non–New Mexican flavor, and in general the result of the 1887–1888 reconstruction was to anglicize the entrance to the church. At this time a disparity already existed between the architectural characters of the front and rear portions of the building. To reinforce the lower walls of the tower for structural purposes, stone buttresses flanked the entrance. Three similar buttresses on the north wall presumably date from this same period. In 1955, the time of the last restoration, all the elements of the 1887–1888 rebuilding were maintained intact except the stone buttresses on the west facade, which were thickened

2–6

2–6
SAN MIGUEL
The church seen from its eastern, apse end.
[1981]

and plastered to bond them visually with the front of the church. The pitched roof was removed, and the Victorian wooden louvers, still in place for the 1934 HABS drawings, were eliminated to create a simpler void in the belfry. The improvements were considerable. In 1978 church authorities requested the Santa Fe architectural firm of Johnson-Nestor to prepare a "Historic Structure Report and Master Plan" to include a comprehensive history of the chapel as well as projected schemes for restoration and maintenance.[16]

What is the church like today? From the exterior the chapel of San Miguel still appears somewhat uneasy to any eye that has visited several of the mission churches. Its single tower is unlike any others, and the large void in the belfry displays rather awkward proportions for mud-bearing walls. The flanking buttresses appear too thin for adobe construction, and indeed they are made of stone, although stuccoed to conceal that fact. A comparison to those of San Francisco at Ranchos de Taos makes clear the difference in construction materials. And yet in its clumsiness the church does display considerable charm, particularly in its setting in the Barrio Analco, now a historical district that claims the "Oldest House in the United States" just across the street.[17]

If the exterior is awkward, the church interior appears all the more elegant in comparison. The nave is well proportioned and virtually serene, and with the exception of disturbing recorded messages that play almost incessantly, this is an excellent space in which to consider the history of Spanish architecture in New Mexico. The chapel's shape is classic, with its single nave roughly twenty-four feet wide and seventy feet long and tapering decisively toward the east. The years upon years of replastering have added to the mass of the walls, whose textures indicate the accumulation of time like the steady movement of a clock. In the afternoon when the sun is right, the light sliding through the clerestory is quite striking, evoking a sense of the beauty and drama of light and its role in creating religious presence. With the north windows blocked and the south windows high in their wall, only artificial light detracts from the total effect.

The majority of the vigas, in fact all but two, date from rebuildings in the nineteenth century, and only the two square ceiling beams in the chancel survive from earlier times. The balcony support beams and all the corbels are beautifully carved and lend an air of elegance and polish to the simple interiors. In the course of subsequent renovations, including the work of 1798, the floor was raised two feet with adobe; thus the distinction between the sanctuary and the nave was lessened. In 1853 Bishop Lamy built a stone altar, followed in 1862 by a new communion railing. The wooden floor dates from 1927, and the pews, the most recent addition, were not installed until 1950.

The full-height reredos, which fills the front of the sanctuary, is said to be the oldest in New Mexico. In the center is the small figure of Saint Michael the Archangel. In one hand he holds a sword drawn to conquer Satan; his jeweled crown symbolizes victory. Dating from 1709 and brought from Mexico, the reredos has resided at San Miguel since at least 1776, as evidenced by its inclusion in Domínguez's inventory.

The chapel of San Miguel has had its judgments and suffered its destructions and rebirths. Now protected by law and operated by the Christian Brothers, it is more secure than it has ever been in three hundred–odd years of existence.

2-7

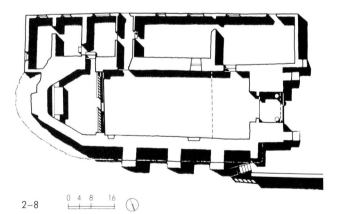

2-8   0 4 8 16   (N)

2-7
SAN MIGUEL
The church interior in the late nineteenth century. Compare the state of
the reredos with its contemporary
condition.
[Museum of New Mexico]

2-8
SAN MIGUEL, PLAN
[Source: Kubler, *The Religious Architec-
ture*, 1940; and field observations, 1986]

2–9

2–9
SAN MIGUEL
The reredos with the figure of San Miguel occupying the central niche. [1981]

2–10
SAN MIGUEL
With its narrow section, heavy vigas, and battered chancel, the nave is a classic representative of New Mexican colonial religious architecture. [1981]

SANTA FE

LA PARROQUIA

1610?; 1626–1639; 1713–17; 1796–1806

THE CATHEDRAL OF SAINT FRANCIS

1869–1895; 1966; 1986
Architects: Antoine and Projectus Molny;
François Mallet

When the location of the provincial capital at San Gabriel proved to be impractical, it was moved south to Santa Fe, where it has remained since its establishment in 1610. The city complied only roughly with the ordinances for founding new cities. These regulations dictated that the "principal church" was not to occupy the central position on the plaza mayor, which was reserved for the most important civil structures of authority. The plaza was to be the center of the municipality and would be augmented by "smaller plazas of good proportion . . . where the temples associated with the principal church, the parish churches, and the monasteries can be built." More specifically, "the temple [principal church] shall not be placed on the square but at a distance and shall be separated from any other nearby buildings, or from adjoining buildings, and ought to be seen from all sides so that it can be decorated better, thus acquiring more authority."[1] "Decoration" was a long time coming to the church in Santa Fe, and in spite of the ordinances, the Parroquia was tucked on the southeast corner of the plaza.

Like the city itself, the church—today the cathedral—still occupies the same site, although the location of the church itself has shifted slightly over the years. The identification of the original structures is made more difficult by the construction of commercial structures in the nineteenth century, which eradicated the entire eastern half of the plaza. The Parroquia as such no longer exists: the building was subsumed by the stone cathedral, substantially completed in the 1880s, that succeeded it.[2]

The parish church was not the first major religious structure in the capital. That honor fell to the chapel of San Miguel across the Santa Fe River in the Barrio Analco (see San Miguel). An appropriate parish church was a necessity, however.

According to Kubler, a rudimentary chapel existed on the site of the Parroquia as early as 1610 and was probably the product of Fray Alonso de Peinado's first efforts.[3] It possessed neither commodity nor architectural quality and was later referred to by Benavides as a mere plastered pole structure (jacal).[4] Appreciated or not, this original church was dedicated to Nuestra Señora de la Asunción (Our Lady of the Assumption).

By 1626, when Benavides took office, or by 1630, when his first report was published, about two hundred fifty Spaniards lived in the city and roughly three times that many Indians were affiliated with them, most of them serving in menial positions. The town was lacking a suitable parish church, Benavides related, "as their first one had col-

3–1

3–1
CATHEDRAL OF SAINT FRANCIS
The spireless principal (south) facade,
based on a design by Antoine and
Projectus Molny, executed in a style
recalling the Romanesque religious
structures of their native France.
[1986]

lapsed. . . . I built a very fine church for them, at which they, their wives and children, personally aided me considerably by carrying the materials and helping to build the walls with their own hands, to the honor and glory of God," and not incidentally to the glory of the friar himself.[5] The institution seemed to progress satisfactorily: "We have them well instructed, and they set a good example. The most important Spanish women pride themselves on coming to sweep the church and wash the altar linen, caring for it with great neatness, cleanliness, and devotion, and very often they come to partake of the holy sacraments."[6]

While the second parroquia was under construction, San Miguel served as the parish church. Chavez believed that construction of the convento might have preceded or progressed more rapidly than the church itself because the convento was probably in use by 1631. Construction of the church was completed by 1639. The dedication of the church possibly changed, as in 1661 there were references to a church of the immaculate conception.[7] Fronting the church and extending westward toward the plaza was the cemetery. The convento lay south of the nave, which was oriented east-west. A report from the 1640s recorded that the capital of the territory was also the seat of the custodia and that it had "a very good church in which is kept the Blessed Sacrament; everything pertaining to public worship is very complete and well arranged; it has a fair convento, and there are 200 Indians under its administration who are capable of receiving the sacraments."[8]

Unlike nearby San Miguel, the Parroquia was destroyed during the Pueblo Revolt, and although Vargas vowed to rebuild the ruined structure in 1693, he in fact never did. What remained of the pre-1680 structure was rebuilt as the existing Conquistadora chapel and was refurbished to house the statue of the Virgin that had accompanied the Vargas expedition of Reconquest (see El Rosario). The population of the city had grown, increasing pressure for the erection of a religious edifice of more appropriate stature. The convento for the Franciscans, however, had been maintained through the auspices of Governor Cubero, who took office in 1697. Within fifty days of his arrival, repair work was "for the most part" completed.[9]

A chapel in the east torreón of the Palace of the Governors still stood at the time of the Vargas entry into Santa Fe. During the years of native occupation the chapel had been converted to serve as a kiva. Necessity seems to have triumphed over desecration, as the chapel was reconsecrated and served as a center of worship until the construction of the

3–2

3–2
LOOKING NORTH ON SAN FRANCISCO STREET
Circa 1878
The Parroquia stands at the end of the street.
[U.S. Signal Corps, Museum of New Mexico]

new parroquia almost two decades later.[10]

The new church, shifted on its original site, was under construction in 1713, as evidenced by two documents referring to building activity. One, dated 1713, referred to "the church which is now being built in Santa Fe"; the second described a house "on the main street which goes from the Plaza to the new church now being built."[11] The structure was probably completed by 1717, and from then until the end of the eighteenth century, the building suffered continual decay. Tamarón noted its existence in his report of 1760 but had little to say either in praise or condemnation: "On May 25 [1760], which was Whitsunday, the visitation was made with all possible solemnity in the principal church, which serves as the parish church. It is large, with a spacious nave and a transept adorned by altar and altarscreens."[12] Tamarón appeared more caught up with the excitement of building the chapel of Nuestra Señora de la Luz (Our Lady of the Light) on the south side of the plaza.

"Surely when one hears or reads Villa of Santa Fe, along with the particulars that it is the capital of the kingdom, the seat of political and military government with a royal presidio, and other details that have come before one's eyes in the perusal of the foregoing," wrote Domínguez in 1776, "such a vivid and forceful notion or idea must be suggested in the imagination that reasons will seize upon it to form judgments and opinions that it must at least be fairly presentable, if not good." Alas, the city did not live up to those expectations. In all, he had little that was positive to say about the villa other than to remark its splendid site: "Its appearance, design, arrangement, and plan do not correspond to its status as a villa nor to the very beautiful plain on which it lies, for it is like a rough stone set in fine metal."[13]

The Parroquia, in his estimation, fared a little better. He noted that it was built of adobe, that its doors faced west, and that its "regular transept" was raised three steps up from the rest of the nave. He gave no hint that the walls of the church converged slightly toward the transept. "Across the mouth of the nave a clerestory rises to light the transept and the sanctuary," while three windows in the south wall lit the nave. "The church has a choir loft in the usual place which occupies the full width and projects 5 varas into the nave. . . . The entrance is below it near a corner, like a trap door, reached by a ladder inside the church. Its furniture, or adornment, is the entire absence of any, for there is not even a bench for the singers. The floor is bare earth packed down like mud."[14] The effort of making the building registered favorably on the visitor, perhaps

more than the actual structure. He conscientiously recorded what was there: the cemetery, the floor of wooden planks, the governor's throne in the transept, and the wooden altar screen. In addition to the two altars in the chancel, four more flanked the nave, two on either side. The beams in the ceiling were new, suggesting a recent renovation. The baptistry stood to the right, adjacent to the convento to the south, and was entered under the choir. Protecting the image of the Conquistadora, the Rosario chapel extended the north transept and was built in the typical manner, although it lacked a clerestory. Domínguez's judgment was mild: "Its interior may not be cheerful, but it is not gloomy either."[15] Whereas the Benavides church may have borne only a plain facade, the eighteenth-century church featured two tower buttresses spanned by a balcony from which "all the view the villa has to offer to the north, south, and west can be easily surveyed."[16]

Before 1797 portions of the church had dangerously deteriorated and had subsequently been rebuilt. The inevitable processes of entropy and erosion were only temporarily halted, however, as the church was again in ruinous condition or had even collapsed by 1799.

In 1804, by which time the walls had been substantially completed, disaster called: just before the roof beams were scheduled to be installed, the church was struck by lightning and the new construction was destroyed. The sponsorship of the rebuilding is credited to Don Antonio José Ortiz, who also funded improvements to San Miguel about the same time.

> After it [the parish church in this city] had fallen down, six years ago, I undertook by myself to reconstruct the same, and in fact I [prepared it] for the vigas last year. [O]wing to the damage of lightning which struck, I was obliged to tear it down again and enlarge it ten varas. From the foundation up I extended it 8 varas and reconstructed its walls and have it now ready nearly up to the placing of the vigas, there missing four rows of adobes in order to be able to roof it.[17]

Ortiz paid to lengthen the church toward the west and to erect a chapel dedicated to San José that extended the south transept. The church thus filled out a cross-shaped plan configuration, while the Conquistadora chapel and chancel were recast into the characteristic battered form.[18] Renewed efforts completed the structure in 1808.

The church form at that time displayed certain properties still observable in the earliest photographs of the Parroquia since it was described in a report by Agustín Fernández, vicar general of the

3–3

3–4

3–3
LA PARROQUIA
The church in 1846 as sketched by
J. W. Abert.
[Museum of New Mexico]

3–4
LA PARROQUIA
circa 1867
Within a decade of Lamy's arrival in
New Mexico, the Parroquia was pol-
ished with a mild Gothic trim.
[Nicholas Brown, Museum of New
Mexico]

3–5
LA PARROQUIA
1880
In this illustration by Charles Graham,
probably based on a photograph by Ben
Wittick, a wooden arch distinguishes
the central nave from the sanctuary.
[Museum of New Mexico]

archdiocese of Durango, as having two small towers and measuring about 29 feet by 162 feet—a relatively long and narrow space.[19] The elongation of the nave in subsequent rebuildings reduced the dimensions of the campo santo, thereby bringing the facade closer to the plaza.

When the Americans entered the city in 1846, they found the church, made of adobe, little changed in architectural style from the previous century. Typically, the mass of the church and the manner of the pious stood foremost in the eyes of observer Lieutenant J. W. Abert.

> October 4, 1846. We were early awakened with the ringing of the campanetas, summoning the good citizens of Santa Fe to morning mass at the parroquia, or parish church. I had a great desire to see the interior of this church, which with the "Capilla de los Soldados," are said to be the two oldest churches in the place, and were doubtless those alluded to by Pike, when he says, "there are two churches, the magnificence of whose steeples form a striking contrast to the miserable appearance of the houses." . . . The body of the building is long and narrow; the roof lofty; the ground plan of the form of a cross. Near the altar were two wax [wooden] figures the size of life, representing hooded friars, with shaved heads, except a crown of short hair that encircled the head like a wreath. One was dressed in blue and the other in white; their garments long and flowing, with knotted girdles around the waist. The wall back of the altar was covered with innumerable mirrors, oil paintings, and bright colored tapestry. From a high window a flood of crimson light, tinged by the curtain it passed through, poured down upon the altar. The incense smoke curled about in the rays, and, in graceful curves ascending, lent much beauty to the group around the priests, who were all habited in rich garments. There were many wax tapers burning, and wild music, from unseen musicians, fell pleasantly upon the ear, and was frequently mingled with the sound of the tinkling bell. . . .
>
> In the evening [of October 5] I made a sketch of the parroquia, although mud walls are not generally remarkable; still, the great size of the building, compared with those around, produces an imposing effect.[20]

Like Abert, Lieutenant William Hemsley Emory was taken by the activity more than the space:

> August 30. This was on a Sunday.
>
> Today we went to church in great state. The governor's seat, a large, well-stuffed chair, covered with crimson, was occupied by the commanding officer. The church was crowded with an attentive audience of men and women, but not a word was uttered from the pulpit by the priest, who kept his back to the congregation the whole time, repeating prayers and

3–5

94

3–6

3–6
CATHEDRAL OF SAINT FRANCIS
1880
Taking advantage of some clever planning strategy on the part of the architects, the builders used the roof of the
Parroquia as a work platform for the
new stone structure rising around it.
[Museum of New Mexico]

incantations. The band, the identical one used at the fandango, and strumming the same tunes, played without intermission. Except the governor's seat and one row of benches, there were no seats in the church.

The interior of the church was decorated with some fifty crosses, a great number of the most miserable paintings and wax figures, and looking glasses trimmed with pieces of tinsel.[21]

Five years later when Jean-Baptiste Lamy arrived in New Mexico, he set to putting his house in order. Although he might have harbored no love of the native architecture, aesthetics was not the major issue. "The trouble with the native tradition as Bishop Jean-Baptiste Lamy and his French priests saw it was that New Mexican Catholicism of the times too closely resembled its crumbling churches," wrote Bruce Ellis in a recent monograph on the cathedral.[22] As a cathedral, rather than a parish church, the building demanded a greater expression: "No adobe-walled, viga-spanned structure could be as high or as wide as proper cathedral dignity required; to permit its consecration in strict accordance with canon law the building must be of solid masonry throughout."[23] Yet another factor was the chronic repair demanded by adobe construction: why not build a masonry structure that required less maintenance? Nor was there popular support for the existing structure on the basis of its historical significance—such appreciation would have to wait another century to flourish. For the moment modernity and progress held sway over sentiment. "When finished," a newspaper editor wrote in 1873, "the edifice will be a credit and an ornament to the city and territory. . . . That old mud church [the Parroquia] has stood for years looming up dingy, gloomy, and awkward, like an adobe brick-kiln—an eyesore to every man of taste and a disgrace to the city."[24]

After saving and repairing the Castrense chapel, Lamy sold it in 1859 to raise money for the Parroquia and to acquire a piece of land upon which to erect a school. But he also had bigger plans in mind, and they had little to do with traditional Spanish colonial building types. The parroquia had become his cathedral, and the bishop sought a church building that would objectify the church's newly elevated status. Neither adobe nor local builders could produce what he envisioned, and for stylistic expression he looked, not to the land around him or its parent country of Spain, but back to his mother country of France.

Lamy's search had numerous precedents in the history of ecclesiastical architecture. Early in the

1840s Greek and Roman revivals had been used to reinvigorate the spirit of the American republic, however farfetched and muddled the stylistic associations were. Among the Catholic and Episcopal faiths Gothicism became the predominant religious architectural style, mostly through the original instigation of A. W. N. Pugin, who looked back to the medieval era in Europe as the most fervent—and truest—expression of Christian religion. The impact of medievalism was felt as far afield as New Mexico, where many of the simple adobe churches received at least minor Gothic redressing. Early photos of the Parroquia show that it, too, was modified under this influence, with crenellations added to the parapets and pointed arches to the belfries.

It was not the Gothic style, but the Romanesque, in which the cathedral of Santa Fe was finally built. Lamy came from southern France, where the Romanesque churches of the eleventh and twelfth centuries remained the major monuments—the Gothic cathedrals were mostly built farther north in the Isle-de-France or further east. In spite of years of living and working abroad, even in the relative wilderness of Kentucky, Lamy retained his early stylistic preferences. But the Frenchman encountered problems in realizing his vision: lack of a building tradition that used the vault and the arch was one; lack of money was another. The new bishop overcame them both. He imported the architects Antoine and Projectus Molny from France as well as certain craftsmen who worked with local crews. Molny probably prepared his drawings while still in France and sent them to Santa Fe "in or just before 1860." [25]

As in any project of this size, complications arose. At the start the work was given to an American contractor who either was "dishonest" or "did not understand the work." [26] In 1869 work commenced; the cornerstone was laid on October 10—and *stolen* within a week! "Some heathen with infamous hands tore up the cornerstone of the new cathedral which had been laid by Bishop Lamy only the Sabbath preceding . . . and everything of any value, silver and gold coins, etc., etc., were [*sic*] carried off." [27]

The strategy for erecting the new cathedral was rather ingenious. Because the Parroquia would be in use during the period of construction, the new structure would be built over and around it. The width of the existing church would determine the width of the central nave, which would be flanked on either side by an aisle. The roof of the Parroquia would serve as a useful platform for the construction of the vaults of the masonry structure.

A red native stone was chosen for the walls and a

3–7

3–7
CATHEDRAL OF SAINT FRANCIS
An engraving of the revisions proposed by Francois Mallet to the Molny scheme, including completion of the spires left as stubs.
[From *Aztlan*, by William G. Ritch, 1885; Museum of New Mexico]

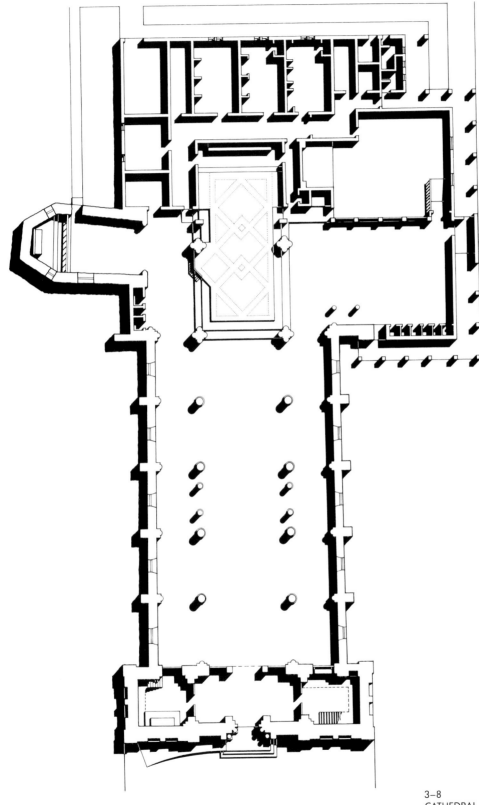

3–8
CATHEDRAL OF SAINT FRANCIS, PLAN
[Sources: Architects' drawings by
McHugh Loyd Associates; and field
observations, 1990]

3–8

volcanic tufa for the ceiling, which established a prototype for succeeding religious architecture in New Mexico—although few, if any, builders followed it. Modifications were made en route: the width of the proposed facade was reduced and rotated slightly to align it with the streets. Work stopped for about four years beginning in 1874, and a new architect, François Mallet—French, living in San Francisco—replaced Antoine Molny, who had returned, blind, to France in 1874. Mallet prepared documents and an estimate for completing construction, including the two spires that were never built.[28] When the centering for the vaults was removed, cracks appeared, prompting the insertion of triple arches between the pillars.[29] The arrival of the railroad facilitated the movement of some materials, although stone was still transported to Santa Fe from Lamy by teams. European workmen arrived in 1883, lending their stone-carving skills to the project.[30] A year later construction had reached a point sufficient to permit the final demise of the adobe Parroquia, its earth used to fill the streets of the city: "Its adobes and rocks are now doing other public work," said Father James Defouri.[31]

In time the cathedral rose, with its new stone walls surrounding the venerable adobe church it was to supersede in majesty and style. John Bourke, writing in 1881, observed the construction process and its results:

> I went to the Cathedral of San Francisco, a grand edifice of cut stone, not more than half completed and enclosing within its walls the old church of adobe. As I purpose, at a late date, giving a more detailed account of this old building and others equally venerable in Santa Fe, as well as a sketch of the town itself, I will content myself now with saying that the town has been transformed by the trick of some magic wand during the past 12 years. . . .
>
> The old church in itself is a study of great interest; it is cruciform in shape, with walls of adobe, bent slightly out of the perpendicular. Along these walls, at regular intervals, are arranged rows of candles in tin sconces with tin reflectors. The roof is sustained by bare beams, resting upon quaint corbells. The stuccoing and plaster work of the interior evince a barbaric taste, but have much in them worthy of admiration. The ceilings are blocked out in square panels tinted in green, while two of the walls are laid off in pink and two in light brown. The pictures are, with scarcely an exception, tawdry in execution, loud colors predominating, no doubt with good effect upon the minds of the Indians. The stucco and fresco work back of the main altar includes a number of figures of life size, of saints I could not identify and of Our Lady. In one place, a picture of the Madonna and Child represents them both with gaudy

3–9

3–9
CATHEDRAL OF SAINT FRANCIS
The unusual configuration of arches and columns reflects revisions made to ensure structural stability.
[1981]

crowns of gold and red velvet. The vestments of Archbishop Lamy and the attendant priests were gorgeous fabrics of golden damask.[32]

By 1886 the church was substantially completed, but a construction hiatus in 1895 left the eastern end of the church in adobe until 1966. Structural and economic problems continued to haunt the structure. During the 1930s cracks again appeared in the vaults and north wall, belying the problematic soil of the old burial ground and the poorly laid foundations. With John Gaw Meem as consultant, the foundations were reinforced in an attempt to stabilize the settlement.[33]

What was left after the removal of the Parroquia was a competent Neo-Romanesque church with two side aisles, round arches, a great rose window, and the stubs of two eighty-five-foot towers that would never receive their spires. At the time it must have appeared as a very impressive structure unlike anything ever seen in the territory. Today it is a handsome church with little of particular aesthetic note. If there is a lesson to the venture, it might be that a provincial version of an international style is often of less interest and emotion than a superb example of a local tradition. Nevertheless, the traditional style was unable to produce a structure of a cathedral's desired scale and magnificence. A recent renovation, executed in 1966–1967, demolished the remaining adobe structures except for the Conquistadora chapel and introduced a south chapel dedicated to the blessed sacrament that also serves daily as the entrance to the cathedral.[34] A grand skylight floods the altar with light. In the mid-1980s renovations designed by McHugh Lloyd and Associates, Santa Fe, were again in progress, flooring the crossing and the sanctuary in a pattern of light and dark wood.

Recent revisions in ecclesiastical doctrine resulting from the Vatican II accord have brought about the modification of many traditional church interiors, and this last renovation is one such project. Liturgy will always determine church architecture; the process is inevitable. Unfortunately, the new lighting lacks the orchestration characteristic of traditional church architecture. The ambient nature of the cathedral's light has reduced the light quality from a source of inspiration or wonder to a source of illumination. The miniature Conquistadora chapel, however, remains the cathedral's north transept and retains the character of its predecessors, a reminder of the humble beginnings of the city and its "principal church."

3–10

3–10
CATHEDRAL OF SAINT FRANCIS
circa 1948
The church during services.
[Robert H. Martin, Museum of New Mexico]

3–11
CATHEDRAL OF SAINT FRANCIS
The altar area was opened during the renovations begun in 1986. Although the sanctuary is bathed in light, the unorchestrated quality of the illumination is foreign to the choreographed play of lighting in the traditional New Mexican church.
[1986]

3–11

SANTA FE

EL ROSARIO

(1693?); 1808–1818; 1914

Don Diego de Vargas paused, tradition has it, on a hill outside Santa Fe, which today is graced by a shopping center named in his honor, and declared that if he were successful in retaking the city, he would erect a chapel on the site as a token of his gratitude. His prayer seems to have been answered, although not immediately. His attack was repelled. He prayed again to the Virgin and set out: this second time he was successful.

On their journey north from El Paso, the Spanish were accompanied by a small Mexican wooden image of the Virgin, with which they had fled in 1680. The image had originally been brought to New Mexico by Benavides in 1625 and was taken south on the retreat from the Pueblo Rebellion in 1680. The Reconquest was enacted in her name—hence the title "La Conquistadora"—and the statue is currently housed in the north chapel of that name in the Cathedral of Saint Francis.[1] There is an alternate legend as well: that the statue became so heavy when carried past that spot that it was regarded as an omen for the construction of a chapel.

A small wayfarer's chapel might have been erected on the site, although the exact date of construction is unknown, as is whether it was actually built under Vargas's instigation. There is, in fact, no documented evidence that the tale is true since the usual sources, such as Tamarón and Domínguez, made no mention of the chapel. If there had been an earlier structure, it was so deteriorated by the turn of the nineteenth century that a new one was built between 1808 and 1818, most probably 1806–1807 because the license was issued in 1806. The Ortiz family, which had underwritten repairs at San Miguel and the Parroquia, commissioned Pedro Fresquís to paint the altarpiece and supported construction of the chapel as well. The reredos served primarily as a frame for the statue of the Conquistadora and was executed in the characteristic, somewhat scrappy and rough style of Fresquís.[2] The chapel fits the typical New Mexican pattern, with a single nave, battered apse, flat roof with clerestory, and choir loft at the south-facing entry. The land has become a national cemetery, and about 1915 an addition that greatly diminished the presence of the older chapel was constructed. The new wing, which now makes up two-thirds of the current structure, lacks particular architectural distinction. It is more a neutral building turned perpendicularly to the axis of the original church. Thus serving as the chancel and transepts to the current structure, the historic chapel with its altar and reredos has been reduced to a subsidiary role.

4–1

4–2

4–1
EL ROSARIO CHAPEL
The twentieth-century expansion re-
configured the original chapel as the
transepts and sanctuary of the new
structure.
[1986]

4–2
EL ROSARIO CHAPEL
1911
In spite of the rows of fired brick used
both to stabilize the parapet and add a
touch of Territorial ornamentation, the
old chapel is in need of repair. Large
areas of plaster have spalled from their
adobe base.
[Jesse L. Nusbaum, Museum of New
Mexico]

4–3

4–4

4–3
EL ROSARIO CHAPEL
The apse of the old structure, today the eastern transept, shows the original reredos, although it lacks religious images.
[1986]

4–4
EL ROSARIO CHAPEL
The adobe chapel was reduced to the status of an appendage to the new nave when the building became part of a national cemetery.
[Paul Logsdon, 1980s]

4–5
EL ROSARIO CHAPEL, PLAN
[Sources: Field measurements by Marc Treib and Dorothée Imbert, 1987; and Susan Lopez, 1986]

4–6
EL ROSARIO CHAPEL
The early-nineteenth-century chapel now serves as the sanctuary and transepts of the renovated structure. The windows were probably cut around 1914 to address the new axis created at the time of renovation.
[1986]

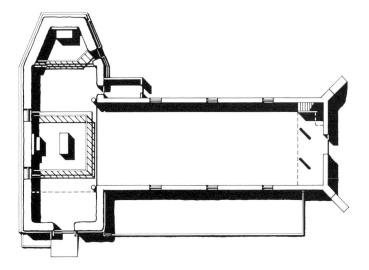

4–5

4–6

SANTA FE

**NUESTRA SEÑORA
DE GUADALUPE**

1795?; 1808?–1821

Nuestra Señora de Guadalupe is one of those adobe churches that has changed so radically over time that recognizing it in uncaptioned photographs would be difficult. The church appears neither on the 1766 map by José de Urrutia nor in the Domínguez report of about the same time. The exact date of its origin remains a bit of a mystery, although it was probably built at the very end of the eighteenth or early in the nineteenth century because a license was issued for its construction in 1795.[1] The map of the city by Jeremy Francis Gilmar drawn in 1846 shows the plan of a cross-shaped church and campo santo on the site, but no tower. (The Castrense chapel is also shown without towers, however, suggesting that the church was rendered symbolically rather than literally.)

Father James H. Defouri, who administered the parish in the later nineteenth century, may have been the source for Ralph Twitchell's claim that the church dates from before the Pueblo Revolt: "[In 1680] Guadalupe being somewhat out of town fared better for a while, but was sacked the following year."[2] Except for these undocumented assertions, there is no recorded evidence of the church's existence or description until 1821, as Kubler noted, when it was visited by Agustín Fernández after Mexican independence. Having been omitted in Pereyro's inventory of 1808, Kubler ascribed its construction to the period between 1808 and 1821.[3] From then on the church suffered the normal pattern of ups and downs.

When the Americans took control of the city in 1846, the year of the Gilmar map, the church was sadly dilapidated, although Abert reported that it had been in use until as late as 1832.[4] An 1886 map now in the Museum of New Mexico illustrated the church in a vignette with typical New Mexican massing, stepped up at the choir and transepts to admit a transverse clerestory, and, of course, made of adobe. There was a three-stage tower similar to the old bell tower at San Miguel that was destroyed in the 1880s, but it was placed off center, to the east of the main door. Lieutenant Bourke confirmed the church's ruinous condition in 1881:

> It shows great age in its present condition quite as much as in the archaic style of its construction. The exterior is dilapidated and time-worn; but the interior is kept clean and in good order and in very much the condition it must have shown generations ago. The pictures are nearly all venerable daubs, with few pretensions to artistic merit. At present, I am not informed upon this point and cannot speak with assurance, but I am strongly suspect that most of them were the work of priests connected with the early

5–1

5–1
NUESTRA SEÑORA DE GUADALUPE
The renovations of the 1970s converted
the church into a performing arts center
and gallery, although there were no
attempts at a precise historical
restoration.
[1981]

5–2

5–2
NUESTRA SEÑORA DE GUADALUPE
1881
The single tower, with its massive base,
cast the church into asymmetry; its
stepped profile resembled the old
San Miguel chapel.
[W. H. Jackson, Museum of New
Mexico]

missions of Mexico. Many of the frames are tin. The arrangement for lighting this chapel are the old-time tapers in tin sconces referred to in the description of San Francisco and San Miguel. The beams and timber exposed to sight have been chopped out with axes or adses, which would seem to indicate that this sacred edifice was completed or at least commenced before the work of colonization had made much progress.[5]

At that time its only official services were held on December 12 at the annual festival of Our Lady of Guadalupe.[6] The church also seems to have been used for Protestant services in the 1880s under pressure from Anglo immigrants.

The growth of mining in northern New Mexico at that time also brought an influx of Catholics who, although centered around Cerrillos, petitioned for an English-speaking congregation in Santa Fe. About 1881 Reverend James H. Defouri was placed in charge, and like Saint Francis centuries before, Defouri energetically went about putting God's house in order. L. Bradford Prince noted that new windows, made available by the railroad, were installed and that a typical, although light-smothering, pitched roof of shingles was added. Capping the new incarnation was "a wooden spire of the strictest New England meeting house pattern in the place of the venerable tower."[7] Pews graced the new wooden floor. The transformation was so complete that had it been worked on a child, even its mother would not have recognized it—which was, no doubt, the intention.

A fire in 1922 destroyed the roof timbers of the sanctuary and transepts as well as the alien steeple. By then the popularity of the California Mission style had begun to work its romantic magic on the populace, and Guadalupe was accordingly rebuilt with curved shoulders supporting a two-staged tower with proper arched openings. Although not accurate in terms of historical precedent—as was clearly visible in the sloped tile roof—the new form fit better into the architecture of Santa Fe than had its dilute Gothic predecessor. On the interior a single arch spanned across the altar, somewhat elevating the character of the historic adobe structure.

5-3

5-3
NUESTRA SEÑORA DE GUADALUPE
April 1881
Like the exterior of the church, the interior underwent extensive changes at the end of the nineteenth century. In this early photo the accretions and clutter of votive offerings are apparent. [Ben Wittick, Museum of New Mexico, School of American Research Collections]

Guadalupe became an auxiliary of the cathedral parish in 1918, but its status as a separate congregation was restored in 1931. A new church was constructed south of the original structure in a sympathetic, if not historicist, style. What was to become of the old building? For some time it functioned as a chapel. Through the initiative of Archbishop Robert Sánchez, however, the old church was restored for use as a museum of Spanish Colonial art and, when appropriate, as a performance center for chamber music and recitals. The Santa Fe architectural firm Johnson-Nestor directed the restoration, which was undertaken during the years 1976–1978.

The building has not been restored but has been significantly remodeled; the tile pitched roof still conceals the clerestory. The tower has been revised to a more severe form, with square openings using wooden lintels to replace the former arches. Throughout the interior and exterior the inappropriate aspects of the 1920s rebuilding have been removed and the architectural entirety simplified. A small watercourse leads toward the river as a tentative gesture toward establishing a link between the old church and downtown. While this remodeling is neither complete nor accurate in an archaeological sense, the current state could best be termed sympathetic and successful in feeling, if not in form.

5–4

5–5

5–4
NUESTRA SEÑORA DE GUADALUPE
circa 1887
At the end of the 1880s the new pitched
roof and belfry gave the church the look
of a New England schoolhouse.
[F. A. Nims, Museum of New Mexico]

5–5
NUESTRA SEÑORA DE GUADALUPE
circa 1920–1925
By the late 1920s a central belltower
had replaced the Anglo belfry, and a
California Mission style had glazed the
church.
[T. Harmon Parkhurst, Museum of
New Mexico]

5–6
NUESTRA SEÑORA DE GUADALUPE,
PLAN
[Sources: Plan by Johnson-Nestor,
Architects; and measurements by
Susan Lopez, 1987]

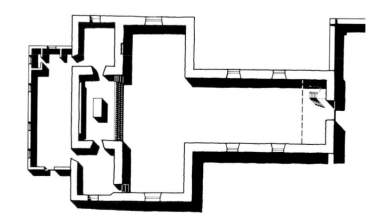

5–6

110

5-7

SANTA FE

NUESTRA SEÑORA DE LA LUZ
[LA CASTRENSE]

1754(?)–1761; deconsecrated c. 1859

CRISTO REY

1940
Architect: John Gaw Meem

Although the Laws of the Indies did not specify that a church be built prominently on the plaza, neither did they proscribe its construction. And because the plaza was originally conceived primarily as a military space, it is not surprising that the chapel of the military confraternity should be built directly fronting the parade ground. It took some time, however —about a century to be more precise—before a chapel was built on the site.

During his term as governor (1754–1760), Francisco Antonio Marín del Valle purchased a lot on the south side of the plaza, facing the Palace of the Governors "between two houses of settlers."[1] He raised a chapel there for the sum of 8,000 pesos. Captain as well as governor, he had an interest in the project that probably exceeded piety. On this site a structure was erected with its facade toward the plaza, following the configuration of nave and transepts common to the Spanish towns of northern New Mexico.

As early as the 1620s Benavides had reported the paucity of church buildings in Santa Fe because the size of the population was small: "The Spaniards . . . may number up to 250. Most of them are married to Spanish or Indian women or to their descendants. With their servants they number almost 1,000 persons. They lacked a church, as their first one had collapsed." To rectify the problem, he had "built a very fine church for them, at which they, their wives and children, personally aided me by carrying the materials and helping to build the walls with their own hands."[2]

By the time of Bishop Tamarón's visit a century and a half later, the population had increased by about one-half: "I have confirmed 1,532 persons in the said villa, [but] I am convinced that the census they gave me is very much on the low side, and I do not doubt that the number of persons must be at least twice that given in the census."[3] Public worship was limited to the nearby Parroquia and the chapel of San Miguel across the river. Construction of the Castrense chapel was well under way, although building would not be completed for another year. Unlike the majority of churches in New Mexico at the time, this chapel would be highly embellished, receiving praises even from critical Mexican visitors. Tamarón witnessed the event:

> In the plaza, a very fine church dedicated to the Most Holy Mother of Light was being built. It is thirty varas long and nine wide, with a transept. . . . The chief founder of this church was the governor himself, Don Francisco Marín del Valle, who simultaneously arranged for the founding of a confraternity which was established while I was there. I attended the meeting and approved everything.[4]

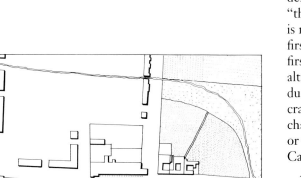

6–1

6–1
LA CASTRENSE CHAPEL
This redrawn detail based on the Gil-
mer map of 1846, shows the Castrense
chapel just south of the plaza. The
Parroquia (today the Cathedral of Saint
Francis) lies to the right of the original
plaza, already filled in with private
buildings.

Written by Marín del Valle himself, the organization's constitution was approved by Bishop Tamarón during his visit, indicating that the founding of
the confraternity postdated the chapel already under construction. Given what Domínguez termed
"the fervent and glowing order of his devotion," it
is no surprise that Marín del Valle was elected the
first "Hermano Mayor," or "as we should now say,
first president of the Society."[5] Work on both the
altar screen and the body of the chapel continued
during Tamarón's visit and were officially consecrated on May 24, 1761. Although officially the
chapel was dedicated to Nuestra Señora de la Luz,
or Our Lady of Light, it was usually known as La
Castrense in reference to the military confraternity.

A considerable sum was to have been expended
on the chapel interior, although the exterior remained the simple mud-plastered adobe common to
the province. Most notable among the furnishings
was the elaborate altar screen that filled the rear
wall of the chapel. Under Marín del Valle's patron-
age, Mexican stone carvers, perhaps from Zacatecas,
were imported to handle its crafting. "Eight leagues
from there," Tamarón recorded, "a vein of very
white stone had been discovered, and the amount
necessary for the altar screen large enough to fill a
third [of the wall] of the high altar was brought to
this place. This then was carved."[6]

Domínguez, exceptionally, was just as impressed
during his visit of 1776. His description noted that
the structure "has walls about a vara thick. Its door
faces north, and a little above it is a white stone me-
dallion with Our Lady of Light in half relief. At the
very top of the flat roof are three arches, a large one
in the center with a good middle-sized bell, and a
small one on either side without anything." A clerestory and a choir loft, both supported by "wrought
beams" on corbels, were typical, although the carving was more elaborate than usual. Three windows
faced east. Unlike the more normal wood-fronted
steps into the chancel of most churches, however,
"the ascent to the sanctuary consists of four octagonal stairs of white stone. The whole sanctuary is
tiled with said stone, and there are three sepulchers
in it."[7] The sacristy adjoined the east transept, its
window to the south.

The focus of the interior was the altarpiece that
dominated the rear wall.

> The altar screen is all of white stone . . . very easy to
> carve. It consists of three sections. In the center of
> the first, as if enthroned, is an ordinary painting on
> white canvas with a painted frame of Our Lady of
> Light, which was brought from Mexico at the afore-
> said Governor Marín's expense. . . . On the right side

of this image is St. Ignatius of Loyola, and on the left St. Francis Solano. Toward the middle of the second section is St. James the Apostle, and beside him, St. Joseph on the right and St. John Nepomuk on the left. The third section has only Our Lady of Valvanera, and the Eternal Father at the top.[8]

Originally, the entirety was polychromed in the tradition of the wooden altarpiece, and the architectural framework of the screen was filled out with Arabesque columns and entablatures. The effect, Domínguez noted, was that the altar screen "resembles a copy of the facades which are now used in famous Mexico."[9] Two altars of stone, like the altar screen, stood in the transept. "Its interior is very attractive," Domínguez said in summation.[10] Given that his opinion of the villa of Santa Fe was that it "lacks everything," this was no mean compliment.[11] The effect of the altarpiece was never equaled in colonial New Mexico, although its design served as the basis of many painted altar screens thereafter.[12]

The chapel was set back from the south limit of the plaza, fronted by a campo santo apparent in the simple Urrutia map of 1768. Six years later de Morfi provided fewer details but showed a bit more respect for the villa: "The plaza," for one, "was square and beautiful. A chapel consecrated to Maria Santisima de la Luz [Most Holy Mary of the Light] also adorns it [the plaza], where was established the parish of the military which a religious served since 1779, the year [of its erection and other private buildings]."[13] As the chapel was completed in 1761, this was either an error or a reference to a renovation, possibly the construction that added the two towers and balcony to the north facade, commented on by nineteenth-century observers.

By the end of the century the walls and roof had badly deteriorated, and in 1805 Fray Francisco de Hozio requested funds to make "repairs necessary for the decency of the divine worship."[14] The official visitor, Juan Bautista de Guevara, in a lengthy report, was "deeply saddened by the 'ruinous and lamentable state' to which the confraternity had sunk." His document, however, did record that "across its entire facade looking toward the plaza there is a gallery of six sections with columns and a wooden roof; two small adobe towers with wooden tops, all old and falling down."[15]

Services were well attended and treated with some degree of pomp. "During the first government of Manuel Armijo (1827–29), he went regularly with the whole garrison force of Santa Fe in full uniform to attend services there."[16] Although the chapel remained intact through the 1830s, this was to be the last period during which most of its

6–2

6–2
LA CASTRENSE CHAPEL
The upper portion of the stone reredos sponsored by Antonio Marín del Valle, now in the church of Cristo Rey.
[1986]

6–3
LA CASTRENSE CHAPEL
In this photo taken around 1877 the old chapel has been converted into a store, with a latticed terrace addition at the second-floor level. The beam ends still protrude through the adobe wall, and the new cathedral is rising at the end of San Francisco Street.
[Benjamin H. Gurnsey, Museum of New Mexico]

previous glory remained. When the new republic of Mexico withdrew stipends for military chaplains, the Castrense lost its congregation.[17]

James J. Webb, a trader visiting Santa Fe in 1844, wrote that the "old church about the centre of the block on the south side of the plaza . . . has not been occupied as a place of worship for many years."[18] The chapel was not to have a quiet end, however—at least not yet. The military continued to support its upkeep with occasional repairs, however sporadic. At the time of the American entry shortly thereafter, the building was in derelict condition. Lieutenant Abert described the interior as having been

> the richest church in Santa Fe. . . . There is some handsome carved work behind the altar, showing a much higher order of taste than now exists. . . . One finds the bones of many persons scattered about the church. These belong to wealthy individuals who could afford to purchase the privilege of being beneath the floor where so many prayers were offered up; but they have not found as quiet a resting place as the poor despised publicans. The roof of this church fell in a few years ago and it has not been used since.[19]

The United States Army acquired the use of the church, repairing the roof and using it for storage until 1851, when Justice Grafton Baker sought a suitable location to conduct due process. He eyed the property and began the process of adapting the storage buildings as a court of law. Surprisingly, given the dilapidated state of the chapel, he met with considerable resentment from the citizens, who cited the burials within the building as reasons not to use the chapel for civil purposes. Baker held his ground and the controversy grew. After one judicial session, however, an agreement was struck that passed the chapel back to the diocese. Bishop Lamy, after receiving the keys to the building, called for a subscription to repair the chapel. His efforts were successful, and the building was at least partially restored during the next few years.

Lamy had problems of his own. As an avid supporter of education he had formulated a rigorous program of instruction and school building. He had also set his mind on the construction of a stone structure to replace the adobe Parroquia that was now his cathedral. Both programs required money. In an effort to raise the necessary capital for the repairs and land for a school, he sold the Castrense in 1859 to Don Simón Delgado, who built a house on the site. In turn Lamy was given $2,000 by Delgado and a plot of land for Saint Michael's College.[20] Parts of the structure remained until 1955, when

6–3

demolition of the chapel was complete.[21]

The noted stone altarpiece of Nuestra Señora de la Luz was moved first to the cathedral, where it was kept until the church of Cristo Rey was built in the late 1930s. There it remains, but with only traces of its original polychromy, its force partially diminished by the much larger scale of the new structure.

Three factors contributed to the construction of the new church. The first was the interest of the Committee for the Preservation and Restoration of New Mexico Mission Churches in finding a new home for the stone altar screen from the Castrense. Since the 1860s the screen had been "stored" in a space behind the altar of the cathedral in a state of benign neglect. Second, when Reverend Rudolf Gerken became archbishop of Santa Fe in 1933, he found the need for an additional parish on the city's east side. A site was purchased on upper Canyon Road, John Gaw Meem's firm receiving the commission for design in 1939. The third factor was the four hundredth anniversary of Coronado's expedition through the Southwest. At a dinner in the cathedral rectory on April 6, 1939, Archbishop Gerken announced the commencement of the project: "We shall build a memorial to the Coronado Centennial in the form of the most beautiful church in the Southwest. This memorial will become a new parish."[22] For a project of this size, the design process must have proceeded rapidly, although there never seemed to have been any question as to the style of the structure.

The appearance of the church is traditional, but its form somewhat belies its construction. Although Cristo Rey is principally an adobe structure—with the number of bricks estimated at between one hundred fifty and one hundred eighty thousand—it is not a pure bearing-wall building. In response to the loads that the walls had to carry and the span of the nave, the adobe structure was augmented by a structural steel frame that not only reinforced the walls but also carried a portion of the vigas of which the roof was made.

The craft is of the highest order throughout. The corbels supporting the vigas are finely carved, and the split juniper logs, or *cedros*, that form the ceiling are carefully fitted. The exterior departs from the rigid symmetry of the interior composition, freely utilizing inspiration or forms from a number of historical structures. As Bainbridge Bunting noted, "It has the grand scale and at least one tower of Acoma, the balconied facade of Trampas, the transepts of the old Parroquia of Santa Fe, and the effective transverse clerestory of Santa Ana."[23] The totality escapes the level of pastiche, however, and evidences a coherent architectural idea executed with understanding and skill. The church received the archbishop's blessing on January 1, 1940, and was formally dedicated later that year on June 27.

When judged against the ideal, the church as the home for the Castrense altarpiece has two shortcomings. The first is the size of Cristo Rey, which is of a grander order than the historical chapel. The effect of the reredos seen from the distance, surrounded by larger walls, is just not the same, being diminished by the size of the space. The second is the greater level of illumination, which from windows as well as skylights at times undermines the drama created when only a clerestory transmits light. Despite these minor criticisms, the fine Castrense reredos is again accessible to the public, and it lives once more within a church, not a museum.

6–4

6–4
CRISTO REY
In spite of the large scale of the church,
the effect of the clerestory light falling
upon the reredos remains effective and
dramatic.
[1986]

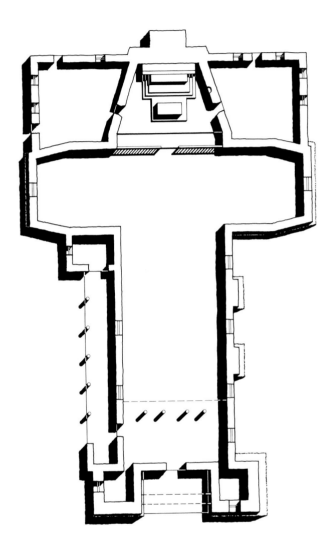

6–5

6–5
CRISTO REY, PLAN
[Sources: sketch plan by John Gaw Meem,
University of New Mexico Library
Special Collections; and measurements
by Dorothée Imbert and Marc Treib,
1986]

6–6
CRISTO REY
May 1942
Shown three years after its completion,
the church displays far greater subtlety
in its mud plaster modeling than in
today's hard stucco.
[New Mexico Tourism and Travel
Division]

NORTH OF SANTA FE

TESUQUE PUEBLO

SAN DIEGO

(1620s?); 1706; c. 1914

Tesuque, the first of the pueblos north of Santa Fe, is one of the smallest of the Tewa group: its population was listed as 281 people in 1973. In contrast to the larger agglomerations of living units, such as the multitiered blocks at Taos or the more rambling configurations at Isleta, Tesuque's form is unequivocal and centralized. Constantly deteriorating, although continually being restored, the pueblo is a simple and singular statement of collective building. Federal housing policy enacted in the mid-1960s produced single-family detached houses planned in patterns at odds with the traditional collective forms. The results are seen on the periphery of the pueblo.

The plaza, at the center, is laid out east-west, which prompted one set of authors to associate orientation with the configuration of the land.[1] Ralph Knowles claimed that this alignment, which creates a southern solar exposure, was a fine-tuning of the architecture to exploit the thermal properties of adobe mass.[2] There is probably at least an element of truth in both explanations, although in many cultures the east-west axial plan also objectifies the rising and setting of the sun and its movement across the skies.

Tesuque pueblo exhibits one of the tightest architectonic compositions, more or less a single rectangle with parts of its eastern block stacked in two stories. Archeological evidence has established occupation on the site as early as A.D. 1200. According to Bertha Dutton, the pattern of this "prehistoric" community bears a recognizable architectural relation to earlier settlements such as those at Mesa Verde.[3]

Tesuque is also unique in that its church, dedicated to San Diego, sits directly on the plaza. This may not have always been the case, however. Frederick Hodge believed that the current village is sited three miles east of its pre–Pueblo Revolt location,[4] which would suggest that the pueblo either occupied a site that had been inhabited in the distant past or established a new pueblo and mission after the Reconquest.

The original church was dedicated to San Lorenzo, and its founding is credited to the indefatigable Benavides in the late 1620s. But "on August 10, 1680, the feast of San Lorenzo," Paul Walter narrated, "the day of the Pueblo uprising and martyrdom of the Franciscan missionaries, Fray Tomas [at Tesuque] was killed and the church burned."[5] Perhaps negative associations with the saint or the saint's day led to the reattribution to San Diego when the church was reestablished in 1695, construction having been supervised by Fray José Díez. Substantially deteriorated by 1745, it was rebuilt under the guid-

7–1

7–1
SAN DIEGO
The hard plaster is cracked and peeling,
spiting repairs made to maintain its
integrity. A small bush reclaims the
summit of the facade.
[1981]

ance of Fray Francisco de la Concepción, who was often at odds with the colonial government. Typically, the disputes regarded the use of Indian labor.[6] The mission remained a visita of Santa Fe into the eighteenth century.

Kubler believed that the new church was built prior to 1706—a common dating—and that this was probably the church de Morfi described in 1782 by saying, "The religious of Santa Fe have a church there and an adequate dwelling place . . . although of adobe and very poor."[7] Bishop Tamarón left a sociological, rather than a physical, picture of the mission. Writing in 1760, he described the church as a visita of Santa Fe and bestowed a blessing of sorts by saying that "these Indians are more civilized (than the Comanche to whom they are compared), but he was troubled by their lack of confessions.[8] Unfortunately, he added little else except that there were thirty-one families with 232 people. The 1750 census tallied a population of forty-four households with 171 people.[9]

By the time of the Domínguez visit in 1776, the population stood at forty-five families with 194 persons.[10] Domínguez wrote that since 1769 the church had been served by a priest from Nambe, although in a note Adams and Chavez indicated that church records listed a *resident* priest at the pueblo between 1729 and 1772.[11] Catechism was delegated to the *fiscal mayor*, an Indian appointed to assist the priest and in this case act as his surrogate, but Domínguez seemed pleased to report that "on Saturdays and feast days the whole pueblo gathers in the church at the peal of the bell to recite the rosary."[12] The priest from Nambe, however, came to hold services at Tesuque on feast days and sometimes heard confession. On other occasions the Tesuque congregants traveled to Nambe for mass.

At that time the disposition of the pueblo differed from what we see today. The church was not directly on the plaza but was separated from it by a block of buildings that intervened between the church/convento and the plaza. Perhaps at that time the church was still not completely accepted into the community. "The planting for the father is entrusted to the pueblo up to the harvest, and since stealing and carelessness prevail, it goes ill for the priest," Domínguez revealed. The congregation seemed to have had a different agenda. After a description of the pueblo blocks, Domínguez noted, "It is obvious from the foregoing that the church is outside this little plaza, and this is true. Yet it stands at the end of a blind alley, for there are some small new houses a little farther down facing the back of the aforesaid tenement."[13] Apparently the form of

7–2

7–2
TESUQUE PUEBLO
The pueblo from the air. The church of San Diego is in the upper center, one of the few pueblo churches located directly on the main plaza.
[Dick Kent, 1960s]

the plaza as a defined rectangle was not regarded as sacrosanct; its presence was more often suggested than physically defined in the European tradition.

The church Domínguez visited and described in the late 1770s was not the church that occupies the site today. The older church was a larger structure, although even in the late eighteenth century, it stood in a somewhat dilapidated condition. It measured about eighty-five feet long by twenty feet wide with a ceiling height of twenty-two feet. There was no choir loft, indicating a lack of musical development at the pueblo, limited resources, or little interest in a foreign religion. The natives' casual regard for the priest suggested a certain informality on their part, as did Domínguez's comment that "the ceiling consists of thirty beams with a little carving which rest on small corbels (three of them are ready to fall down)."[14]

The nave had an earthen floor and a transverse clerestory; the convento in the courtyard plan was to the church's southeast. The facade was bolstered by "two buttresses from the front corner (like those I described at the Santa Fe church). On each there is a little tower with four arches but no grating." It was a basic building, for which the priest showed little enthusiasm: "Essentially this church looks like the great granary of an hacienda."[15] No matter how extended his sojourn or how many churches he visited in New Mexico, Domínguez remained a product of Mexico and willingly shouldered the burden of that archetypical image of what a church should be. In all probability, then, the composite image of the church, except for its location and size, was somewhat similar to the way the church at San Felipe pueblo appears today. The 1870s photo published here shows the remnants of this structure in rather poor condition, although the overall impression is considerably grander than Domínguez's description implied. Shortly thereafter the church was replaced by a new structure, although in all likelihood a simple adobe cell served as the interim church until the construction was completed. Edgar Hewett probably referred to this building when he wrote that the sacristy had been remodeled into a chapel. Walter, however, asserted that part of the older structure "is incorporated into the much smaller structure in the village."[16]

Prince published an image of the church in 1915 or just before, that showed only the flat facade and single nave seen today.[17] Curiously, a very flat pediment in the Territorial Style over the entry door indicated that Anglo architectural details shaped by the influence of sawmills and the American notion of progress had already infiltrated the bastion of

7–3

7–3
SAN DIEGO
circa 1870
The old church shown in this photograph collapsed in 1880.
[National Anthropological Archives, Smithsonian Institution]

7–4

7–5

7–4
SAN DIEGO
Taken by Carlos Vierra during a dance, this photograph shows a church with a crisp white facade and Territorial Style doorway.
[Carlos Vierra, University of New Mexico Special Collections]

7–5
SAN DIEGO
circa 1916
Framed, printed religious images over-lay and complement the rear panel, dated 1886, which provides the focal point for this rare interior photograph.
[*Franciscan Missions of the Southwest*]

7–6
SAN DIEGO, PLAN
[Source: Plan by Johnson-Nestor, Architects, late 1970s]

7–7
SAN DIEGO
The battered end of the apse and the small graveyard.
[1981]

Spanish religious architecture. Perry Borchers, on the basis of the photogrammetric study his group undertook at the pueblo, claimed that the church seen today shares the same wall positions as those shown in Adam Clark Vroman's 1900 photo.[18] The clearest explanation is provided by John Kessell, who ascertained that the church had fallen into such disrepair that for a period prior to 1880, an adjacent domestic building served the religious purpose. The current church was rebuilt on the foundation of the old and completed sometime late in the decade.[19]

Today the church of San Diego, like so many of the buildings around the plaza, is rarely in pristine condition. The door to the church is kept locked, and the condition of the interior and its contents is unknown. The simple facade and the exterior have been stuccoed with gray cement, and the result is a texture quite antithetical to the feeling of the church, if not the feeling of the pueblo. Nature—or God—seems to be having the final revenge, or reward, however. On the pediment that tops the main facade, the stucco has cracked from the temperature differential or from the movement of the adobe as its moisture content changes. There at the peak a small plant has found its roots in the adobe of the sanctuary, thereby seeming to reclaim the Indian land that the Catholic church had once claimed as its own.

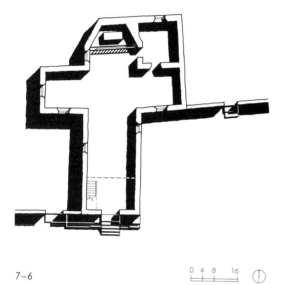

7–6

0 4 8 16

7–7

SAN ILDEFONSO PUEBLO

SAN ILDEFONSO

(1617); 1711 (new site); 1905;
1969 (new structure)

Architects: McHugh and Hooker;
Bradley P. Kidder and Associates

Some twenty miles north and west of Santa Fe, at the foot of the mountains, lies the pueblo of San Ildefonso. The architectural disposition of the pueblo and its plaza orients toward Black Mesa, which rises behind the community. San Ildefonso was little known as anything other than another pueblo until the rediscovery of the beauty of its pottery. Maria Martínez, who died some years ago, was the best known of the pueblo's potters, but she was only one of a number of makers of the elegant black, highly burnished, unglazed San Ildefonso ware.

Originally the pueblo featured two plazas divided by a block of dwelling units that were still visible in Stubbs' aerial view of the pueblo published in 1950.[1] The settlement of a dispute between the tribe's factions led to the block's removal, and the result today is a single plaza cut by the road leading to the church sited just off the northwest corner of the space. The freestanding kiva—one of the most beautiful of any pueblo—is still mud-plastered and blessed with a magnificently strong staircase that blends the pure geometry of its stepped profile with the softening influence of time on adobe.

Hewett dated the founding of the mission of San Ildefonso prior to 1601, although Walter was less specific and suggested that it was established some time before 1617.[2] Kubler listed no date for the founding of the first missions, giving only the 1680 date of its destruction during the Pueblo Revolt.[3] Whatever the exact date of its construction, the church was in place by 1629, the year of the Benavides visit. Although Benavides was generous in his evaluation of the Spanish efforts, church and convento still warranted the rating of "very spacious and beautiful"; Benavides also noted the positive influence of the irrigation water added by Fray Andrés Bautista.[4]

The church must have been in relatively decent condition at the time of the Reconquest, or it was rebuilt; there remained enough of it to be burned in the incidents of 1696 during which two priests were killed. The insurrection was rapidly quelled, but it was only in 1706, according to Kubler, or 1717–1722, according to Walters, that the church was reconstructed on a site just north of the original location.[5] This edifice seems to have weathered the remainder of the eighteenth century and most of the nineteenth rather well, until its deterioration in the latter part of that century. Tamarón mentioned little of the physical structure in the record of his 1760 travels. He did note, however, that there were ninety Indian families with 484 persons and "four families of citizens, with 30 persons."[6] The Domínguez description of San Ildefonso in 1776 reads al-

8–1

8–1
SAN ILDEFONSO
The new church replicates the form, if
not the exact feeling, of its predecessor.
[1981]

130

8–2

8–2
SAN ILDEFONSO
The plaza with the church to the
rear left.
[1981]

most as a generic description of New Mexican religious architecture of that period. Built of adobe and wooden roof construction, the church took the form of a single nave. Notwithstanding the clerestory and two "ill-made" windows that faced east, the friar noted that "this church is dark."[7] The structure faced south, with the baptistry extending to the east and entered under the choir loft, which extended across the south end of the nave. Curiously, the "whole wall around the sanctuary is painted blue and yellow from top to bottom like a tapestry, and not too badly."[8] Coloring an entire wall, rather than a wainscot, was rare in mission interiors and was probably intended to add a celestial and regal touch to the backdrop of the high altar, itself made only of adobe. Two additional altars faced into the nave at its sanctuary end.

The convento, situated to the west of the nave, took the form of a rough, enclosed square with a cloister "very pretty and cheerful, for it is square and open, with adobe pillars at the four corners and others in between in regular intervals, but of wood, carved with corbels above to imitate arches."[9] Much of these facilities, however, were in poor repair. At the time San Ildefonso contained 111 families with 387 people.

Domínguez credited Father Juan de Tagle with instigating and funding the improvements to the church's fabric. Fray Juan de Tagle "built and founded" the church and convento, its dedication taking place on June 3, 1711. Arriving at San Ildefonso in 1701, he remained there almost 25 years, "a most singular record in post-Revolt New Mexico, where missionaries, like the swallows, transferred almost with the seasons."[10]

By 1881 the church stood in poor condition. Bourke observed that the "church is very dilapidated and the rain runs through the roof in a perfect stream."[11] The traditional problem of water leakage through a flat, earthen roof with parapet was inescapable, and the temptation to sheathe the structure with a pitched metal roof must have been strong. Kubler recorded that the church was pulled down in 1905 and that a new church was built, possibly on the original seventeenth-century site adjacent to the dance plaza.

Writing in 1915, Prince told us that the church had been reconstructed after the 1696 difficulties and that it had continued in its rebuilt form "until a few years ago."[12] Three years later Walter concurred, although he might have used Prince as a reference, and assumed that "it was practically destroyed by alterations and mutilated by the construction of an ugly tin roof a few years ago."[13] Despite their con-

8–3

8–3
SAN ILDEFONSO
1899
The old church with its weathered belfry and immense buttress used to support a sagging wall. The remains of the structure to the left, probably a porter's lodge, may also have served as an atrio. [Adam C. Vroman, Museum of New Mexico]

8–4

8–5

fusion about the nature of the new construction, both writers were troubled by the "more practical" form in which the church was built.

Whatever the exact date and whether it was a new church or not, Walter and Prince both expressed regret at the new construction, illustrating once again the continuing conflict between expedience and romance. The church in its 1905 form was a modern building and may have been the reason Kubler wrote nothing about the church in the text of his book but relegated it to a small mention in the chronological table. Kessell provided the definitive word on the history of the building by explaining the construction of a simplified structure in 1905 that replaced the badly deteriorated fabric of the old church, which was sustained primarily by the bulk of its eroding mass: "The 1711, 1905, and 1968 churches have all stood on the same site at San Ildefonso."[14]

One notable element in the church (visible in an 1880s photograph) was the "porter's lodge" that might have served at one time as an open-air chapel. Kubler mentioned that the chapel was placed perpendicularly to the main axis of the church, although Domínguez's descriptions referred to the appendage as a porter's lodge. Open-air chapels may have taken a modified form in New Mexico, but they continued a tradition that developed in sixteenth-century Mexico when the number of converts was extreme and the available space within religious structures severely limited. In theory, only Christians should enter the church for prayer. In the atrio, an enclosed courtyard that doubled as a campo santo, a small chapel was built as part of, or adjacent to, the main church. From this location services could be held, catechism could be directed, and a greater number of celebrants could be accommodated. The atrio represented a compromise between pragmatism and idealism; the courtyard was set off and defined as sanctified ground, although the full power and religiosity of an interior space were absent. An 1899 photograph of the San Ildefonso structure shows a simple three-bay construction of wood and adobe, which may have served a religious purpose, although this remains conjectural.

In the mid-1950s the question arose as to how repairs to the church should be carried out. Apparently the elements had so seriously undermined its physical condition that a major reconstruction was considered necessary. The simple tin-roofed building, so indicative of the practical, yet insensitive remodeling or constructions of the late 1880s through 1920s, possessed little character and little relation

8–6

8–4
SAN ILDEFONSO
1899
The apse end of the church shows the buttresses bracing the west wall.
[Adam C. Vroman, Smithsonian Institution, National Anthropological Archives]

8–5
SAN ILDEFONSO
The apse end of the rebuilt structure.
[1981]

8–6
SAN ILDEFONSO
after 1920
The remodeled church, closer in feeling and form to a New England schoolhouse than to a New Mexican church.
[Museum of New Mexico]

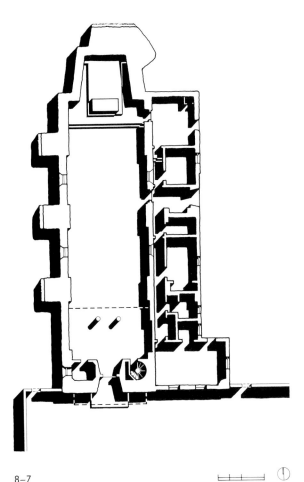

8–7

8–8

8–9

8–7
SAN ILDEFONSO, PLAN
[Source: Plan by John McHugh and
Associates, Architects]

8–8
SAN ILDEFONSO
The ceiling, looking toward the altar.
The herringbone pattern of latillas
recalls the church of San José at
Laguna.
[1981]

8–9
SAN ILDEFONSO, NAVE
Despite the windows on both sides of
the nave, the transverse clerestory provides the dramatic lighting characteristic of the New Mexican church.
[1981]

to the adjacent pueblo. The ultimate solution was to construct a new church in the form of the old one documented in early photographs. Of course, this approach raised questions of authenticity and intention. Would it be possible to recreate the aura of an old building without the original materials or the passage of time? Should the building replicate its predecessor or merely incorporate enough of the old features within a believable framework? Or should there be a new church built "in the spirit of tradition" but without slavishly imitating the old forms? All three approaches were problematic, particularly when the talent of the architect—and possibly the financial resources of the client—were limited. In the case of San Ildefonso, however, the story had a relatively happy ending.

Certainly there is no way to duplicate the feeling of adobe and mud plaster using cement stucco. The smoothness and imperviousness of hard stucco do not catch light or reflect time in the same way and to the same degree that soft mud plaster mixed with straw does. The purpose of stucco is to thwart time; it acquires the mark of history only through spalling and cracking. Mud, however, disintegrates unevenly, although more rapidly. There is a hardness to the look of stucco, and that it weathers evenly, rather than unevenly, ensures that the form of a church will not change drastically over the years. These properties are illustrated here in two photographs taken some eighty years apart. The softness and sensitive texture of mud are missing in the new structure. The towers and facade of the new church and the arch with its bell will never feel as comfortable and organic as the old structure; its edges will remain relatively precise, unlike the softened corners of adobe. Nevertheless, the merits and the suitability of the 1969 church, designed by McHugh and Hooker, Bradley P. Kidder and Associates, can cautiously be deemed a success.

The interior of the church is more convincing, however, because the vigas and the latillas that make up the roofing *do* continue the historic building tradition. The single nave and the prominent presence of the transverse clerestory return to the congregation some of the character lost in the 1905 rebuilding. The nave tapers in the apse end, visually extending its length, while the clear light falling on the altar creates the appropriate visual focus. The church faces roughly south, which guarantees a continual source of light from the clerestory throughout the day. To the east are a small convento and sacristy, and a campo santo fronts the church with its single cross.

The church of San Ildefonso lies in the northwest segment of the pueblo, neighboring the two plazas that have now become one. Traditionally dancers emerged from the darkness of ceremonial spaces, such as the handsome kiva at the south end of the plaza. Yet on saints' days, in the blending of Catholic ritual and native religions, the church was integrated into the dance. At Isleta, for example, the Christmas dance began in the church and was completed out-of-doors. Prince published one image of a dance at San Ildefonso in which the entry portal of the campo santo was clearly present in the photograph, demonstrating how the plaza space before the church was used for the dance. The presence of the church as the dominant structure in the community was unquestionable, yet the kiva remained more central ceremonially to the built fabric of the pueblo.

SANTA CLARA PUEBLO

SANTA CLARA

1626–1629; c. 1758; 1905 (collapse);
c. 1914; late 1960s

Santa Clara is a small Tewa pueblo on the western bank of the Rio Grande not far from Española.[1] Today, although difficult to discern, the formal layout of the pueblo is organized on a loosely defined double-plaza plan. To the north of the pueblo, and quite distinct from it, is the diminutive church of Santa Clara. The structure that stands today exhibits few of the qualities of the older building that collapsed early in this century and certainly none of its cautious grandeur.

Evangelization earnestly began in 1598, the first mission at Santa Clara being established by Fray Alonso de Benavides somewhere between 1626 and 1629. A church was built at this time, although its dimensions and form are not known. A 1664 report stated that "the pueblo of Santa Clara has a very good church, whatever is necessary for public worship, a choir and organ, a fair *convento*, and a *visita* in the pueblo of San Juan. . . . It has 993 souls under its administration."[2] If we judge by the amount of increased effort needed to rebuild the ruined church after the Reconquest, its dimensions could not have been impressive. Having no resident friar, Santa Clara witnessed no martyrdom at the hands of the Indians during the revolt, although Spaniards in the vicinity were killed. The mission thereafter remained a visita of San Ildefonso, continuing its religious program when Bishop Tamarón visited the province in 1760. He noted that a missionary resided at the village and that the Indian population of 157 persons almost equaled that of the "citizens," who totaled 277 souls.[3] Domínguez surpassed his usual thoroughness by offering the complete story of the then-extant church.

> Because the old church had fallen down, beginning in the year 1758 Father Fray Mariano Rodríguez de la Torre started to build the present one and finished it. . . . Although the Indians and settlers of the mission assisted in this project, no levy was made for the purpose, since most of it was at the father's expense, as is shown by the fact that he supplied twenty yoke of oxen to cart the timbers and he fed the laborers gratis.
>
> When the roof of the nave was finished, the Indians and the settlers left the rest up to the father alone and to his industry. Therefore, what was necessary to roof the transept and sanctuary was taken from alms, and with this he roofed it. The carpenters, in addition to being well paid, ate, drank, and lived in the convent at the father's expense for a period of two months in the winter, when the days are short in this region. And since these workmen are very gluttonous and spoiled (in this land, when there is work to be done in the convents, the workers want a thousand delicacies, and in their homes they eat filth; the gravy

9–1

9–1
SANTA CLARA
The single tower of the smaller and
simplified church was added between
1962 and 1978.
[1981]

cost the father more than the meat (as the saying goes). That is to say, they ate and were paid more than they worked.[4]

While the church was under construction, mass was said in a small chapel or other convenient place. The former chapel found a new use on completion of the new church: "And the reward which has been given to the said shrine for its holy service is that it serves as a stable for dumb beasts that gather in it of their own accord."[5] The new church, Domínguez continued, was built of adobe with thick walls and a main door facing the east. But its proportions were more exaggerated than the common church; in fact, Santa Clara at the time exceeded all other missions in narrowness. The reason, he explained, was that large vigas were more difficult to transport down the rough terrain of the canyons of the west side of the river than from the mountains to the east.

The resulting nave reminded him of a cannon, so long (more than one hundred fifteen feet) and narrow (merely fourteen feet wide) was the nave. There was no choir loft—the good Franciscan even expended a mild joke on that fact. There were transepts, each with a window at the end, and two additional windows on the south side to provide continued light for the nave. The roof contained an unusually high number of vigas, forty-seven he counted; they were of limited diameter and were installed at short intervals to achieve the strength necessary to support the heavy earthen roof. The floor was of earth in the nave, the baptistry, and, naturally, the cemetery.

Over the entry was a small arch with a bell. "There is a sacristy joining the church on the south as did the convento built by Fray Mariano in the form of a square cloister."[6] Although the rooms were commodious and seemed to impress the usually nonimpressionable Domínguez, their layout was hardly functional in terms of direct circulation. "One must ride from this passage [in the convento next to the kitchen] on a hobbyhorse, because the stable, strawloft, oven and hencoop are not connected with the convent and church." The population counted sixty-seven families with 229 persons, a slight decline from the 1760 figure.[7] The church's prize possession was an altarpiece painted by Fray Ramón Antonio González in 1782, the same year he painted two screens for the side altars.[8]

Photographs from the 1880s taken from the side of the church show its incredible length. The nave appears as a prone figure, almost like a Gulliver tied down by Lilliputians, so elongated and grotesque is it in relation to the surrounding pueblo structures. The nave actually gives the impression that in ear-

9–2

9–3

lier times it had once been both shorter and wider and that some supernatural hand had stripped its entry facade and stretched it across the dry earth. It stood that way into the twentieth century.

Lieutenant John Bourke, in 1881, noted in his journal:

> My guides were anxious to show me the ruined church of "Santa Clara" and under their care, I made a brief examination. . . . The ceiling is formed of pine vigas with a flooring of rough split pine slabs, upon which is laid the earthen roof. In one arm of the transept, were a collection of sacred statues, dolls, crosses, and other appurtenances of the church. The altarpiece, though much decayed, is greatly above the average of church paintings to be found in New Mexico. It is a panel picture, with an ordinary daub of Santiago in the top compartment and a very excellent drawing of Santa Clara in the principal place. The drawing, coloring, and expression of countenance are unusually good and I don't blame the Indians for being so proud of their Patroness. A confessional and pulpit occupy opposite sides of the nave.[9]

Before 1903 it was decided that the chronically leaking flat roof should be covered by a metal pitched roof, which would solve the water problems once and for all, while the eastern facade would be trimmed with a crisp gable. The results, however, were not fortuitous. Earle Forrest told the sad tale:

> This great building was so massive that no one ever dreamed it would not stand for all time to come; and some twenty years ago [1909] when the destructive hand of the modern spirit reached Santa Clara, the work of remodeling the ancient edifice was started. The old roof was removed with its supporting timbers, and during a terrific storm the walls fell, the same as at Nambe, and this historic landmark was utterly destroyed.[10]

Prince's version of the events was more emphatic: "So the old timbers were removed and a modern roof placed on the adobe walls and alas! when the storm came, the great building which had withstood the vicissitudes of centuries fell with a great crash."[11]

The pueblo lived without a church for about nine years, and when a new building was erected, it "replicated" the old structure. That is to say, although possessing none of the extreme dimensions or proportions, it had roughly the same facial characteristics as its predecessor: flat, with two peaks at its corners and a small bell arch in the center of the pediment. The new church was built with transepts but without a pitched roof. Walter was heartened by the process, noting that we can "rejoice that the Pueblo at Santa Clara are rebuilding in the old way."[12] By 1962, in a photo published in a new edition of Prince, the hard cement stucco was shown badly peeling,

9–4

9–2
SANTA CLARA
1899
At the turn of the nineteenth century Santa Clara looked much like Laguna does today: a single bell arch, a flat facade, and two spikes at the corners. [Adam C. Vroman, Museum of New Mexico]

9–3
SANTA CLARA
1904
The church uncomfortably wears the pitched roof that will cause its collapse. [Museum of the American Indian, Heye Foundation, Churchill Collection]

9–4
SANTA CLARA
circa 1910
Collapsing under forces exerted by the added pitched roof, the church was in ruins.
[Museum of the American Indian, Heye Foundation, Fred Harvey Collection]

9–5

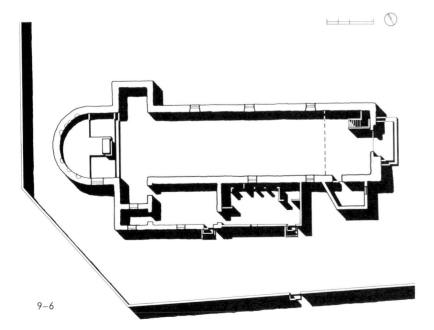

9–6

9–5
SANTA CLARA
The new structure, although a much-
reduced version of the church that
preceded it, sprawls along the earth.

9–6
SANTA CLARA, PLAN
[Source: Plan by John McHugh and
Associates, 1978]

9–7
SANTA CLARA
The contemporary interior is low and
long, enlivened by bright paintings but
no clerestory.
[1981]

indicating that although the church was made of adobe, the fatal mistake of hard plastering had been made.[13] Sometime thereafter the church was re-modeled. The single tower in the southeast corner of the facade seems to date from this time, as it is missing from the aerial photo of the pueblo published in Stubbs in 1950.[14] At least minor changes occurred between September 1976 and summer 1981: a pediment was added to the facade, and a window cut was added to light the choir loft.[15]

The present church appears somewhat forlorn, set off as it is from the remainder of the pueblo. Gray beige in color and surrounded by an earthen cemetery, only clusters of artificial flowers provide points of bright colors. The interior is just the contrast: long and low, perhaps in the old manner, it is now illuminated mostly by windows with milled window frames. Painted decorations line the walls, rendered a brilliant pink color (1981) in the sanctuary area. Sadly, there is no clerestory or increased elevation to the ceiling of vigas over the chancel areas. The feeling is low and heavy. But perhaps the composite feeling—low and oppressive—unwittingly recalls that of the "cannon" church on which Domínguez commented two centuries ago.

9–7

SAN JUAN PUEBLO

SAN JUAN BAUTISTA

1913

OUR LADY OF LOURDES

1890

Two noticeable bumps interrupt the view over San Juan pueblo: the church of San Juan Bautista and the chapel of Our Lady of Lourdes. In contrast to the mostly single-story texture of the pueblo, the chapel and church stand more than two stories high. Built of stone and brick, rather than of native adobe, their Neo-Gothic style contrasts distinctly with the prismatic earthen masses of the low-lying native dwellings. There appears to be no existing common ground between these buildings of two cultures, and the inevitable conclusion is that it is the Christian structures that remain foreign to the site.

As early as 1915—just two years after the construction of the present church—L. Bradford Prince lamented the passing of the earlier adobe sanctuary it replaced, although he added that "no one can fail to revere the devotion which has thus laid its gifts upon the altar, and has made this little Indian pueblo a center of ecclesiastical artistic beauty."[1] His reference was to the generosity of Father Camille Seux, who tended San Juan for more than half a century and was responsible for the building of the church. And while the aesthetic merits and appropriateness of the structure's style might be questioned, they serve as excellent examples of Catholic building at the turn of the twentieth century—illustrating the overlay of alien styles on the traditional foundation of Hispanic-Native architecture.

San Juan Pueblo lies some twenty-eight miles north of Santa Fe on the eastern bank of the Rio Grande. Situated between two forks of the river system—near the confluence of the Rio Grande and the Chama River—the pueblo's rich alluvial plains have provided excellent and continued yields. The distant mountains, considered sacred by the people, provide a dramatic backdrop for the village. San Juan is currently the largest of the Tewa pueblos and for centuries has served as a commercial and religious center, its importance having been diminished only with the impact of automobile transportation.[2]

A branch of the Coronado expedition reached the pueblo of Ohke, or Yunque (Yunqe in Tewa), in 1541, but news of the expedition's summary manner of dealing with other pueblos had preceded its arrival, causing the people to flee to four fortified villages nearby.[3] A half century later Oñate determined that the pueblo would be an excellent center of operations and colonization, and he settled in for the winter. The inhabitants are said to have willingly allowed the Spanish to occupy their village, although, as Ortiz commented, the pueblo's side of the story has not been passed down to us. In return for the gracious manner in which they acted, to Oñate's name "San Juan Bautista" (after Saint John

10–1

10–2

10–1
SAN JUAN PUEBLO
Above the flat plane of the pueblo roofs
rises the Gothic form of the chapel of
Our Lady of Lourdes.
[Smithsonian Institution, National
Anthropological Archives]

10–2
SAN JUAN PUEBLO
circa 1905
The steeple of the renovated old church
punctuates the horizontal pueblo
landscape.
[Edward S. Curtis, Museum of New
Mexico]

10–3

SAN JUAN PUEBLO
Aerial view of the pueblo showing the
church of San Juan Bautista in the
center and the chapel of Our Lady of
Lourdes to its left across the road.
[National Park Service Remote Sensing,
1979]

the Baptist) was appended "de los Caballeros" ("of
the gentlemen") by his captain, Gaspar Pérez de
Villagra. This anecdote was probably a nineteenth-
century fabrication.[4] The qualifying phrase more
likely referred to the Knights of Malta, whose patron saint was John the Baptist.[5]

Some decades later Benavides provided his own
creation myth: the pueblo converted to Christianity because a miraculous rain alleviated the impact
of a serious drought. The inhabitants called on the
blessed father to intervene on their behalf: "It was
remarkable, for, while the sky was as clear as a dia-
mond, exactly 24 hours after the outcry had gone
up, it rained throughout the land so abundantly that
the crops recovered in good condition."[6] In the following years pragmatic irrigation, according to Benavides the work of Fray Andrés Bautista, replaced
divine intervention and allowed the community to
prosper.

Habitation was one aspect of living; relations
with God were another. Soon after the arrival of
the complete party on August 18, 1598, work commenced. On September 8 the chapel was dedicated,
although its fabric remained unfinished. The ceremonies, including sports of both Spanish and Indian
varieties, continued for an entire week.[7] With the
colony established, the religious enterprise began:
Fray Cristóbal de Salazar, with two lay brothers,
assumed the jurisdiction of the Tewa pueblos that
included San Ildefonso, Santa Clara, and San Juan.[8]
During 1599 or 1600 the Spanish established San
Gabriel within the pueblo precinct on the opposite
bank of the river, a colony that subsisted but did
not prosper. Finally, in 1610 the capitol was reestablished in Santa Fe. Although records do not provide
a description of the early church, it is believed that
the San Juan enterprise included a church, a convento, and the "necessary (auxiliary) facilities for
missionary work."[9]

Relations between the pueblo and the Spanish
were hardly amiable. As was characteristic of so
many New Mexican pueblo stories, the first mutual
antagonisms were fanned by the Spanish persecu-
tion of native religions and exploitation of Indian
labor and resources. A 1664 report, which France
Scholes believed to be a supplement to the *Relación*
of Fray Jerónimo de Zárate Salmerón, stated that
San Juan at this time was treated as a visita of Santa
Clara.[10] In a document concerning the mission program needs for the years 1663–1666, however, San
Juan was listed as under the jurisdiction of San Ildefonso: "In the *convento* of San Ildefonso there serves
and will serve one friar-priest, who will administer
pueblo and six estancias, and because of the lack of

10–4

10–5

10–4
SAN JUAN BAUTISTA
October 1881
The old church with its distinctive
bell arch.
[William H. Rau, Museum of New
Mexico]

10–5
SAN JUAN BAUTISTA
circa 1912
Viewed laterally, the historical church is
barely visible under its pitched roof
disguise.
[Carlos Vierra, Museum of New
Mexico]

friars he visits the *convento* of Santa Clara of the Te-was, and that of San Juan of the same nation, distinct and separate pueblos; and at least three friars are needed, two priests, and one lay brother."[11]

In 1675, forty-seven Indians were brought to trial in Santa Fe for witchcraft or more likely for the practice of the native religion. Efforts to intercede on their behalf by a medicine man named Popé were unsuccessful. This incident is often cited as contributing to the Pueblo Revolt, in which Popé played a major role.

At the time of the Spanish resettlement in 1693, little or nothing remained of the prerebellion church. In 1706 a new church was under construction.[12] Domínguez credited Fray Juan José Pérez de Mirabal with the "construction" of the church, although this could have meant substantial repairs, not a completely new building.[13] This eighteenth-century structure probably followed the normal pattern of a nave and raised sanctuary and possibly possessed transepts and transverse clerestory.

Bishop Tamarón included San Juan on his 1760 tour of inspection but had more to say about the surrounding countryside than the church building itself. The Indian population stood at fifty families with 316 persons.[14] The 1750 census report of Custodian Andrés Varo, however, had listed the number of Indians as 500.[15] In 1776 Domínguez included San Juan on his survey of the Franciscan project in New Mexico and was little impressed by what he saw. "Poor," "hideous," and "ugly" were the adjectives he used to describe San Juan.

The nave was more than four times as long as it was wide, was about square in section, and gave the appearance of a "gallery," or corridor.[16] The convento was a bit rude, enclosing a courtyard south of the church.[17] There was a choir loft but no access to it within the church; indeed, it could be reached only "from the flat roof of the convent."[18] Over the entry was a single adobe arch supporting two bells without clappers, which people rung by striking them with stones! The floor was bare: "The only dais and carpet are the earth floor."[19] The picture was not a happy one, although Domínguez, perhaps with a sigh of relief, noted that because of the richness of the soils, the land was "sufficient to maintain the friar."[20]

Paintings on buffalo hide, the type that so upset Bourke a century later, included one image of San José and one of San Juan Bautista. Two adobe tables nearby, however, Domínguez termed "hideous."

In 1776 the population stood at sixty-one families with 201 people,[21] a figure that, if accurate, recorded the village's continuing decline. An attack of small-

10–6

10–7

10–6
SAN JUAN BAUTISTA
circa 1912
The facade was surfaced with plaster
carefully scored to resemble cut stone;
with its steeple and architectural trim,
the church created the aura of a proper
Anglo church.
[Museum of New Mexico]

10–7
SAN JUAN BAUTISTA
circa 1903
The interior of the old church.
[George H. Pepper, Museum of the
American Indian, Heye Foundation]

10–8
LOURDES CHAPEL
The rusticated Romanesque stone
facade more closely recalls memories
of Europe than the mud buildings of
the adjacent pueblo—a typical practice
at the close of the nineteenth century.
[1981]

10–9
LOURDES CHAPEL, PLAN
[Source: Measured plan by Pat McMur-
ray and Bob Wicks, 1967; John Gaw
Meem Collection, University of New
Mexico]

pox in 1781 reduced the remaining population by one-third. The late eighteenth and early nineteenth centuries were relatively uneventful at San Juan, with religious and domestic life maintaining a sleepy pace. The relations between the Spanish and the pueblo communities appear to have been less strained than in earlier times, and the secularization of the missions in the first decades of the nineteenth century went almost unnoticed.

Reports dating from 1818 and 1826 described the church as in good repair, with a "renovated baptistry, a new pulpit and confessional, and the cemetery with a deadhouse, *depósito de difuntos*, for corpses until burial."[22] The 1846 U.S. Army reconnaissance party, of which Lieutenant W. H. Emory was a part, bypassed the Rio Grande pueblos on its way to Santa Fe and California as the territory quietly joined the dominions of the United States.

Of far greater impact on the church institution was the establishment of the new diocese in Santa Fe in 1853. With the installation of Jean-Baptiste Lamy as bishop, the traditional simple mud church structures underwent considerable modification. Lamy brought a new view to New Mexico: the church should raise the educational and aesthetic standards of the parishes. To achieve the second, existing structures were substantially renovated, at times to the point of unrecognizability.

A number of Lamy's priests came from France, like the bishop himself. They seemed intent on exchanging the look of the "primitive" church for that of a "contemporary" (i.e., "polite") institution. The parish church in Santa Fe became the new cathedral, a considerable stone structure in a Romanesque style. Isleta, under Father Etienne Parisis, assumed a Neo-Gothic guise that was curious at best and bizarre at worst, a wooden Gothic crown on an adobe base. San Juan underwent a similar transformation.

The architectural developments of these years, as several authors have noted, must be seen as congruent with the generosity of Fray Camille Seux. Seux, known in a more familiar Spanish form as Padre Camilo, was born in Lyons, France, in 1838 and issued from a family of means. He arrived in the United States in 1865 and served at Taos, Santa Fe, Pecos, and Albuquerque before being assigned to San Juan in 1868.[23] San Juan changed under his hand; during his tenure at the pueblo he had built and paid for a church, a chapel, a statue, and a rectory.

Up to that time the historic form of the church— the "corridor" church of Domínguez's report—had been preserved. In 1881 Bourke found the church

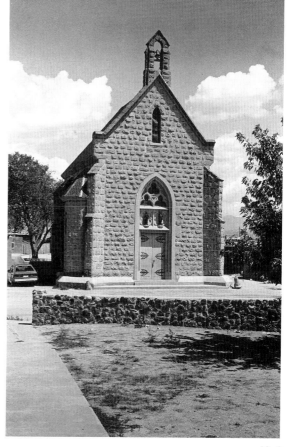

10–8

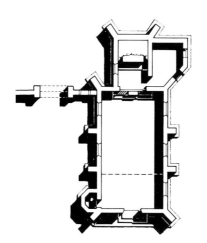

10–9

to be a "much better structure than at Santa Clara" and remarked that the rear wall of the structure had been washed out by heavy rains the previous summer but that the church had "to all appearances, been restored quite recently, whitewashed and provided with a new altar-piece."[24] First, the existing church was inundated by a Gothic tide. Perhaps closest in appearance to Santa Fe's Nuestra Señora de Guadalupe in a similar state of remodeling, its exterior walls were not covered in wood but in a hard plaster scored to resemble masonry.[25] A single bell tower rested on the facade—in all a successful effort at dressing up an adobe structure to look like a polite masonry edifice.

Father Camilo did not stop here. When a statue of the Virgin, a full-size copy of the one at Lourdes, attracted a flock of pious visitors, he built a chapel to accommodate them. The chapel of Our Lady of Lourdes, built in 1890, was seen by certain contemporaries as a landmark in northern New Mexico, what Prince termed "an architectural jewel set down on the edge of a desert."[26] The single-nave chapel, constructed of red stone with characteristic angular apse and buttresses, was a decent essay in the style, although foreign to the local architectural tradition. Padre Camilo was buried within the chapel in 1922.

During the early part of the twentieth century the church of San Juan Bautista no doubt suffered the ravages of time and the elements. The new pitched roof helped retard water leakage, but the walls beneath it were still adobe and were therefore prone to the extensive expansion and contraction that cause cracking. The hard plaster covering created additional problems by trapping water behind its surface and preventing evaporation. Padre Camilo also saw a new church as his ultimate gift to San Juan Pueblo and the surrounding peoples. The old building fell; the new one rose on the same site.

This new church, consecrated in 1913, once again took the Neo-Gothic style popular at the time, although this was a version of the Gothic quite foreign to France. Built of brick, its design was not particularly distinguished, but with the Lourdes chapel across the street, the church created a suitable backdrop for the statue of the Virgin.

That these two structures abut the traditional field of the pueblo may cause some consternation to the visitor. They are without question imports, sharing neither the soil nor the profile of the traditional buildings. Even Forrest was troubled by it. In 1929 he wrote:

> While it [the new church] is a fine, substantial building and would be a credit to any New England town or some other eastern village, the style of architecture is very incongruous out there in the sun-baked desert, surrounded by adobe Indian houses centuries old. It is so strangely out-of-keeping with its surroundings in a land where everything is Spanish that it strikes a harsh, discordant note, and leaves an unpleasant thought of what would otherwise be an ideal visit to old San Juan.[27]

The contemporary critic with less of a romantic streak might find curiosity instead of harsh discord. The distance between the look of vernacular building and that of the church and chapel lucidly depicts the relationship between the architectural and ecclesiastical views of the modern clergy and the tastes of the people. The eighty years that have elapsed since the construction of the two sanctuaries have done little to soften the basic disparity, except by adding the ruddy dust that inevitably coats all buildings in the area. The lesson seems obvious: architecture is a statement of the values behind its construction. The congruence and disparities between two value systems remain clear, even decades later.

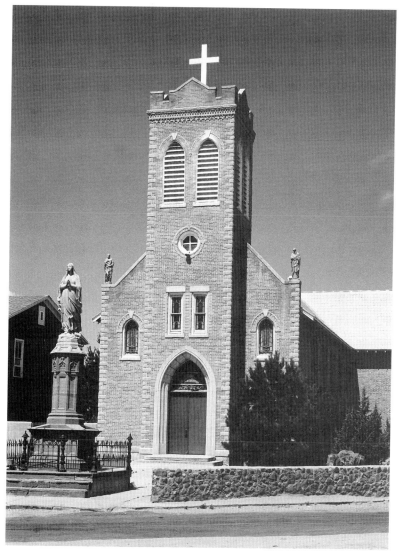

10–10

10–11

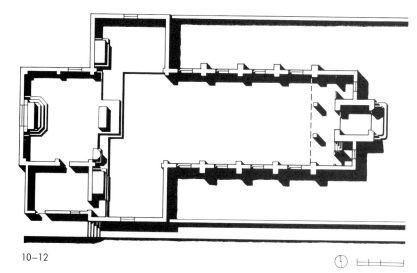

10–12

10–10
SAN JUAN BAUTISTA
The new church: brick, Neo-Gothic, and a stranger to the earthen structures of the pueblo.
[1984]

10–11
SAN JUAN BAUTISTA
The smooth plastered surfaces of the nave contrast with the textured brick exterior.
[1990]

10–12
SAN JUAN BAUTISTA, PLAN
[Sources: Measurements by Susan Lopez and Thomas Cordova, 1986; and Dorothée Imbert and Marc Treib, 1990]

SANTA CRUZ

SANTA CRUZ

1695–1706; 1748; 1870s; 1974

Given the vast amount of land in New Mexico that is untenanted even today, it seems strange that there has been concern with overpopulation as far back as the colonial period. In actuality, the problem was not high population but a lack of water and arable ground. When Santa Fe was resettled after the successful return of the Spanish under the leadership of Diego de Vargas in 1693, the town could support only a limited number of people. Also in question were the yield and distribution of the surrounding lands. The founding of Santa Cruz was intended to alleviate the problem, at least for a specific group of settlers.

Santa Cruz occupies the north side of a fertile valley watered by the Santa Cruz River about twenty miles north of Santa Fe. Prior to the Pueblo Revolt there were some scattered ranchos and haciendas on the gentle slopes loosely confederated as La Cañada. On August 11, 1680, they attempted in vain to fortify themselves at Santa Cruz; but their efforts were unsuccessful, and they were forced to flee. During the twelve-year Spanish absence, a mixture of Tano Indians from Galisteo, San Cristobal, and San Lazaro, experiencing difficulties once again with their traditional rivals, the Pecos Indians, moved into the valley, in time forming what Prince termed "quite a large community."[1]

When Vargas retook Santa Fe and set up domestic and political housekeeping, he was faced with a land shortage. The problem was further escalated when a group of colonists from Zacatecas, Mexico, arrived in 1694 and requested land on which to establish homesteads. The governor looked north and decided on the valley of La Cañada, basing his claims to the land on settlement by the Spanish prior to the revolt. Vargas urged the Indians to move farther up the valley and in a gesture of good faith postponed the actual date of removal until the following year. When his order was not heeded, the Indians were forcibly removed. The new colony was to be called "La Villa Nueva de Santa Cruz de Los Españoles Mejicanos del Rey Nuestro Señor Carlos Segundo" (The New Town of Holy Cross of the Spanish Mexicans of the King Our Master Carlos II), a cumbersome name in either language for such a small town. Records usually refer to it more simply as La Villa Nueva de Santa Cruz de la Cañada (The New Town of Holy Cross of the Gentle Valley).[2] The "new" in the title refers to a small community existing before the floundering in 1680 and the subsequent establishment of the new one. Today it is simply Santa Cruz.

The town began by proclamation. On April 19, 1695, Vargas informed the settlers that they were to

11–1

11–1
SANTA CRUZ
The church after its most recent
restoration.
[1981]

11–2

leave Santa Fe on the following Thursday at ten in the morning. "And I will then have in the plaza of the city the pack-mules I now have and will furnish some horses to mount in part those who may need them, and I will aid them in all things, assuring them a ration of beef and corn shall not be wanting as well as half a *fanega* of corn to each family for planting."[3] Fray Antonio Moreno was to accompany the settlers to comfort them in this troublesome time, minister to their spiritual needs, and help them build a church.

The Spanish first settled on the south bank of the river, probably occupying to some degree the structures vacated by the Indians. The Spanish might even have built a small chapel. By 1707 they had begun to erect a church. Before construction began, however, the entire town was reestablished on higher ground removed from the threat of the floods that had been bothersome in the past. A widow, one Antonia Serna, donated "the necessary land for the church which had already been started, since it was for the religious, and that for their protection and that of the church, she was giving sufficient land in order that in all four directions the citizens might build the houses they liked in the form of streets, with the church in the middle."[4]

The size of the structure was probably meager, and it was noticeably lacking in either construction expertise or maintenance. If "by 1706 they had a small church and a bell," the building had declined in aspect to a rather dilapidated condition by 1732.[5] After a careful examination Governor Servasio Cruzat y Góngora declared the building to be "beyond repair and in danger of collapsing."[6] In response to a petition from the parish for a new structure, the governor then granted the parishioners the right to rebuild the church "at their own cost, the present one being in ruins."[7] About a week later, on June 21, 1733, the news was proclaimed in the plaza at Santa Cruz.

The widow Serna's intentions would take some time to reach fruition, however. Bishop Tamarón visited La Cañada in 1760. Although more concerned with the manner of confession than the state of the books, he noted that "the church is rather large but has little adornment." The Nueva Villa impressed him even less: "There is no semblance of a town."[8]

Although the exact population at the time is not known, the church project was certainly ambitious, and even today Santa Cruz is the largest colonial period church in the state. The 1750 census listed 197 families with 1,303 persons, already twice the size of most contemporary pueblos.[9] Santa Fe, with

11–3

11–4

11–2
SANTA CRUZ
The church and the town plaza. The assemblage of roofs covering the nave and transepts illustrates the changes brought with the late-nineteenth-century renovations.
[Dick Kent, 1960s]

11–3
SANTA CRUZ
circa 1935
The interior of the church more than fifty years ago looks very much as it does today. Note the Santo Entierro in the niche on the left.
[T. Harmon Parkhurst, Museum of New Mexico]

11–4
SANTA CRUZ, THE SOUTH ALTAR
[Jesse L. Nusbaum, Museum of New Mexico, 1911]

an additional eighty-five years of on-and-off heritage, contained between fifteen hundred and seventeen hundred total souls, including some natives and persons of mixed blood. Albuquerque, the youngest of the three new villas, however, equaled Santa Cruz in population, although it was ten years or so younger in age.

"As late as 1744," Kessell noted, "a Franciscan superior declared that the resident minister at Santa Cruz, probably Fray Antonio Gabaldón, 'is now building a sumptuous church by order of my prelates, without its costing his Majesty half a *real* for its materials or building.'"[10] Kubler added that J. A. Villaseñor y Sánchez recorded the construction as finished in 1748, the date now ascribed to the church's completion.[11]

At least a partial remedy to the lack of adornment was the arrival of Fray Andrés José García de la Concepción, who seems to have possessed an equal love for compulsive labor and wood carving as well as a tremendous zeal for improving the church interior. During his three or so years at Santa Cruz, he completed an altar rail and an altar screen and carved santos of various sorts. His strongly emotional and evocative image of the dead Christ, the Santo Entierro, still occupies a niche in the south wall and records the efforts of one of New Mexico's first santeros.

Enter Fray Francisco Atanasio Domínguez on his tour of the missions in 1776. In his fastidious fashion Domínguez recorded that the church was built of adobe, faced east to its plaza, contained a clerestory, and had the typical steps up to the sanctuary. But alas the choir could not sing in its usual place, he noted, because there was no choir loft. There were four windows with wooden gratings, one in each wall of the transept on the Gospel (south) side, two in the nave on the south wall, and another over the main door. The roof construction, however, was unusual: "The roof of this church is arranged differently from the usual, for there are five cross timbers consisting of three strong beams at regular intervals as far as the mouth of the transept. They are wrought and have multiple corbels. In each of the five spaces between these cross timbers there are twelve wrought beams running lengthwise of the church." The sanctuary also contained "a vaulted arch made of boards."[12] Domínguez then credited Captain Juan Esteban García as the builder of the ceilings and Fray Andrés José García with the remainder of its construction. There was but one tower at the time.

Domínguez, usually critical of New Mexican church ornaments, had mild praise for the García altar screen: "The altar screen is of the kind of wood common in the kingdom, and it is exquisitely made, for it is painted with white earth and consists of two sections that look like the boxes of a bull ring, for the niches are squared and, except for the chief one, all have little balustrades below as is customary in the aforesaid boxes."[13] Less appealing to the friar's Mexican taste was the pulpit: "The pulpit is in the usual position and is a horror."[14] Period. The altar for the Third Order occupied the Gospel side of the chancel, although the Carmel chapel extended to the north. The latter *was* blessed with a choir loft, however, as the nave was not. At the head of the transept was a sacristy. The convento, built mostly by Gabaldón, abutted the church to the south. Its furnishings were scant.

Like Tamarón, Domínguez was not impressed with the disposition of the town. "In view of the fact that the Villa of Santa Fe," Domínguez noted wryly,

> is not as golden as the glitter of its name, in spite of the circumstances mentioned that it is the capital, etc., it will be apparent that this Villa of La Cañada, which does not have such an ostentatious aspect, is probably tinsel. . . . The church, then, is in the place I described with eight small houses like ranchos to keep it company. The rest of the villa is nothing more than ranchos located at a distance.[15]

The church had ministration of Chimayo, Quemado, and Truchas further up the valley. The population comprised 125 families with 1,389 persons, suggesting that the land supported just about as many colonists as it could.[16]

Just seven years after Domínguez's visit, Fray Sebastián Fernández had to replace some of the roof beams that had rotted. To balance the chapel of Our Lady of Carmel to the north, the south transept was rebuilt as the Third Order chapel some time between 1784 and 1789, underwritten by the financial resources of Fray José Carral.[17]

Change, whether constructive or destructive, was chronic in the lives of New Mexican churches. By 1796 considerable work had been expended on the body of Santa Cruz. The church "is very spacious," wrote Fray José Mariano Rosete, "of good adobe construction, with new roof having large pine *vigas* and lumber of the same. . . . The Church and Chapels contain their new pulpits; throughout there are four excellent confessionals." The single tower remained, but "there is a choir loft with its railings and its ladder, all new."[18]

Santa Cruz church, a massive structure dwarfing the few residential structures that might have surrounded it, must have appeared extremely im-

11–5

11–5
SANTA CRUZ
Although the clerestory is blocked by
the metal roof, a south-facing window
approximates the light quality of a
clerestory on the altarpiece.
[1981]

11–6

11–7

11–6
SANTA CRUZ
circa 1883
Late in the nineteenth century the
church was ornamented with elaborately
decorated parapets.
[W. H. Jackson, Museum of New
Mexico]

11–7
SANTA CRUZ
June 1897
By the end of the last century attempts
to decorate the mud church had dis-
solved in the rain and wind. The painted
lower part of the facade concentrates
attention on the entry.
[Philip E. Harroun, Museum of New
Mexico]

pressive for its day; perhaps more as the image of a fortress of God than as a welcoming shelter. The elements of God and nature, however, in conjunction with the passage of time never ceased their effect on adobe construction.

Visitors to Santa Cruz were continually impressed by the size of the church, but never by its quality of finish. Fray José Benito Pereyro's 1808 report found the church "[is] materially reasonable and has, although very old but serviceable, the necessary ornaments." The convento, however, "is almost totally unserviceable, and was built at the expense of Fray Ramón Antonio Gonzáles, consisting of seven rooms, upper and lower levels." [19] Don Juan Bautista de Guevara, paying the villa a visit in 1818, had little except critical comments for the expressive imagery used on the hide paintings that decorated the church, although he noted that the chapel of Our Lady of Carmel had a wooden floor. Tamarón condemned its bareness; Domínguez and Guevara cared little for the aesthetics of its painting, with the exception of the altar screen. "The cemetery is thirty-one varas square, with its entrance, which is without the wooden door because it is broken. . . . In each corner is a little chapel (*ermita*). One of them has fallen but the wood to rebuild it is at hand. . . . In each of said chapels there is a platform-like table, and these serve as stations during the procession on the day of Corpus Christi." [20]

With 1826 came the visit of Don Agustín Fernández San Vicente, who also described Santa Cruz: "The door of the church looks to the east and is of two leaves. . . . Above there is an adobe tower with two small stories and its spire (*capitel*) and a cross of wood. . . . The church yard or cemetery is thirty varas square with a gallery all around having wooden pillars and a good roof but without drain spouts, and with its main gate. In the center is a wooden cross on a flat-topped pedestal." [21]

Santa Cruz remained a sleepy town during the first half of the nineteenth century, although it was a battle site in the revolution of 1837. During the insurrection of 1847 the villa witnessed another key shootout, which ultimately led to the destruction, by cannon and fire, of the Taos pueblo church of San Jerónimo. Father Juan de Jesús Trujillo left a report in 1867 that credited his own efforts for changes and repairs to the church. "[Of] two towers of earth and rock, the one on the south [was] constructed during my time. . . . There is a choir loft, a glass window with its screen. The choir loft and window screen were installed during my tenure. There is another choir loft at the door of the church held by supports added during my tenure." [22]

French taste arrived with Archbishop Lamy in the 1860s and reached Santa Cruz shortly thereafter. Kessell credited either Reverend Jean Baptiste Courbon, who lived at Santa Cruz from 1869 to 1874, or Reverend Lucien Remuzon, in residence from 1875 to 1880, with the incredible transformation of the exterior of the church at that time. [23] The bulk of adobe bricks piled one on the other in walls five feet thick remained in evidence, but its mass was disguised beneath an ornamental treatment that could have rivaled pastry decoration. The walls were left unplastered, or at least the brick units were exposed, and each wall was capped with decorative spun finials. Little arches running along the length of each of the chapels graced the parapets. The towers now supported chapeaux of wood; and each of them—and the pediment—was crowned by a decorative, florid iron cross.

Most prominent in the early photographs from the 1870s is the high (twelve- to fourteen-foot) wall that surrounded the entrance court and that was pierced by a gate on axis with the main doors of the church. Two tiny arches capped the pediment, forming a transition between the towers and the slope of the pediment. The entirety was aesthetically provocative—some evocative conjuring of an exotic conglomerate style that seems to rate the name of Primitive-Moorish-African-French or any combination of these in any order. It could not last. Decorations of that sort exposed to natural forces too much surface area for their mass, a property that hastened the disintegration of unfired earthen material. No doubt, the lovely and charming French efforts began to melt almost as soon as they were completed, if not before.

At this time, however, additional windows had been added to the church, the sole source of lighting having been the clerestory and the window that illuminated the choir. In a William Henry Jackson interior photo of 1881 the handsomely proportioned interior, with its rough whitened walls, heavy vigas and corbels, and gently rising packed earth floor, appears sparse, yet focused. The Santo Entierro still occupies its niche in the south wall, and the old altarpiece is now mounted on the north wall of the nave. A baldachin covers the altar extending into the nave, and the pulpit to which Domínguez so strongly objected is not to be seen. The walls around the entrance court, however, have not fared so well. Another of Jackson's photos, this one an exterior, shows the walls melted down to three feet, fragments of the parapet decoration of the north chapel still remaining and one iron cross on the north tower sadly askew. As a positive gesture the area immediately around the main door has been whitewashed: the efforts toward maintenance are still present but are limited.

About this time Lieutenant John Bourke passed through Santa Cruz and waxed sufficiently romantic to use the sublime aspects of the church as a counterpoint for the "horrors" of its iconography:

> Within there is a choir in a very rickety condition, and a long narrow nave with a flat roof of peeled pine "vigas" covered with riven planks and dirt; on one side, there is a niche containing life-size statues of our Savior, Blessed Virgin, and one or two Saints; all of them, as might be expected, barbarous in execution. Facing this niche is a large wall painting, divided into panels, each devoted to some conventional Roman Catholic picture, which in spite of the ignorance of the artist could be recognized.[24]

Although Bourke took issue with the aesthetics of the images, he seemed at least somewhat touched by the quality of the church as a religious setting:

> Tallow candles in tin sconces, affixed to the whitewashed walls, lit up the nave and transept with a flicker that in the language of piety might be styled a "dim religious light," but in the plain, matter-of-fact language of every day life would be called dim only. Full atonement for the comparative obscurity of the parts of the sacred edifice occupied by the Congregation was made in the illumination of the chancel which blazed in the golden glory of a hundred tallow candles. A dozen or more cedar branches, souvenirs of last Christmas, held to their positions of prominence with a sere [sic] and yellow persistence much like that of maidenly wall-flowers in their tenth season.
>
> Upon the floor of flagging and bare earth, a small congregation was devoutly kneeling . . . without a seat or bench upon to rest at any moment during the long service.
>
> Ridiculous as some of these proceedings were, it was impossible not to be deeply impressed by the fervent and unaffected piety of all the congregation.[25]

By the turn of the century the church had been protected by a wooden pitched roof, shortly thereafter superseded by one of metal. The sloped caps on the towers were probably contemporary. Four windows in the nave, two on the north wall, two on the south wall, were cut in 1918 by Anastacio Luján, who is also credited with plastering the exterior.[26] The wall around the campo santo eroded further and in time was reduced to a wire and pole fence. A transom was installed over the main entrance, and the earthen floor was replaced by a level wooden floor set on sleepers. The enlarged windows were to some degree a necessity because the clerestory had been lost when the pitched roof was added. One window, however, high on the south wall in the sanctuary, effectively replaced the directional clerestory light that had fallen on the altarpiece.

In 1974 the Santa Cruz church was designated a National Historic Site. Shortly thereafter the church council requested architect Nathaniel Owings to prepare a master plan for the church's restoration, which was undertaken in association with Johnson-Nestor, Architects, of Santa Fe. Its report reviewed the history of the church as well as its current context and condition. The findings recommended that the transom over the door be removed to improve the scale of the building and that a high wall be reinstated around the campo santo to create a more significant transition to the plaza, which had been reduced over time to a traffic crossroads. The plaster on the towers should be removed to expose the stone construction; in fact, all cement plaster should be replaced by mud plaster, the report stated. Repairs should be made to the wooden floor where necessary, and in the transepts and in other areas of low use, earthen floors should replace the concrete, tying the church back into its past. The report also recommended the reinstallation of the baldachin, the pulpit (Pace Domínguez!), and the choir loft in the north chapel.

More radically, the architects suggested that the north windows be sealed and that the size of the south windows be reduced to recreate more of the feeling of the original illumination in the nave. The metal roof should remain, the recommendation said, meaning that the clerestory itself could not be freed; the reasoning here suggested that the high metal roof was now common in the architectural vernacular of the New Mexican mountains and that with it the church had acquired a certain familiarity. Certainly the hulking roof had become almost as much the image of the church as the adobe beneath it. It was a curious and unique form, derived from its leaping over the clerestories in each of the transepts.

Not all the work was carried out. In the late 1970s priority was given to the restoration of the artworks, some of which were in a precarious state of preservation. The cement plaster in the interior was stripped and replaced with mud plaster covered with tierra blanca. Certain portions of the exterior walls were stabilized, and some attempts at landscaping the campo santo were undertaken. Much remains to be done.

Santa Cruz is still a large church for New Mexico, and the visitor coming upon it on the High Road to Taos is always surprised; the church's bulk is so much greater than any structure in the immediate

11–8

11–8
SANTA CRUZ
The pitched roof covers the irregular
profile of the adobe forms like a metal
carpet.
[1986]

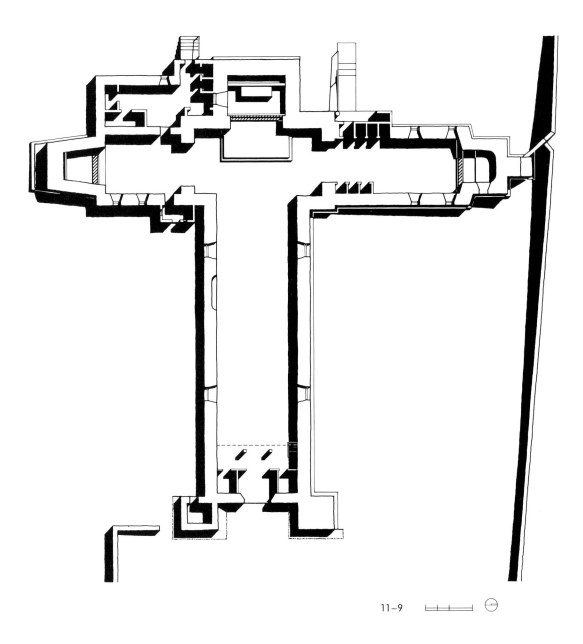

11–9

11–9
SANTA CRUZ, PLAN
[Sources: Kubler, *The Religious Architecture*, 1940, based on HABS; and plan by
Johnson-Nestor, Architects, 1978]

11–10
SANTA CRUZ
The wood appliqué entrance doors to
the nave.
[1981]

vicinity. The grounds of the church and the plaza it fronts are almost always dusty, which can either be annoying or atmospheric, depending on the visitor's mood. The two-leaved doors, although eroded by exposure to the elements, are still beautiful, with graceful, yet simple carvings applied to the panels. In 1981 the transom above the door was blocked: not in adobe as prescribed by the restoration report but with a piece of plywood covering the broken glass. Inside, the newly restored altar screen glows yellow with the brilliant light from the south sanctuary window. The art in the church is splendid and includes several works by Rafael Aragón, a noted mid-nineteenth-century santero who is buried in the church. The parish seems to thrive, with 1,400 families registered, according to a 1980 article, and is committed to restoring and maintaining the structure and its art.[27]

In 1920 the administration of the church was turned over to the Congregation of the Sons of the Holy Family from Barcelona, Spain, in whose care it remains today. There is a solidity to the church anchored to the earth by its eastern facade: the two squat towers sitting on their portly bases. From a distance the structure appears almost toylike; from closer the toy is transformed into powerful bulk. Notwithstanding his dislike of the more gory aspects of Hispanic colonial art, Bourke could still wax poetic about Santa Cruz. Sleeping out in the plaza in 1881, he awoke: "The rising sun threw against the sapphire sky the angles and the outline of the old church, bringing out with fine effect its quaint construction and excellent proportions. The waning moon in mid-sky shed a pale, wan light that grew fainter and fainter as the orb of day climbed above the horizon;—back of all rose the massive, deep-blue spurs of the Sierra de Chama."[28] Today, at sunset as well as sunrise, the effect remains poetic.

11–10

CHIMAYO

EL SANTUARIO

1816; 1920s

L. Bradford Prince, writing in 1915, had only good things to say about the Chimayo valley; truly he found it the Land of Enchantment:

> It would be difficult to find a population more entirely cut off from the vices and frivolities of the world, as well as from its newer conveniences and luxuries, than of Chimayo. The people are contented to live almost entirely on the products of their own valley. Money is little needed where requirements for happiness are so few; and the community illustrates the philosophy of content, which proclaims that happiness is not attained by the multiplication of possessions, but by the satisfaction of a few real wants of man, and the absence of desire for anything that is unattained.[1]

The twentieth century has entered the town and valley forcefully, particularly in the postwar period with the impact of television and the automobile, but certain traditional aspects of the place still linger. These include a noted restaurant that draws diners from all around the state, the continuation of the Ortega family's long tradition of Chimayo blankets, the growing of small apples and apricots, and the Santuario de Chimayo, which has attracted pilgrims from an extremely large area for almost two centuries.

With the Reconquest of 1693 came a steady influx of Spanish and Mexican settlers into northern New Mexico. Santa Fe already contained its fill and could provide land for neither shelter nor agriculture. To the south the land was less fertile, much of it already occupied by the sedentary pueblos, and so Diego de Vargas, seeking a solution, looked north. Colonizing San Gabriel had provided a familiarity with the mountain valley lands between Santa Fe and Taos (the zone that runs along what is now known as the High Road to Taos). Vargas's first effort was to relocate the Tano Indians who had been living in the Galisteo basin to the Chimayo valley farther north and east, vacating the lands for the "reinstituted" settlement of Santa Cruz. The Indians had little time to establish thriving farms because hardly a year later increased pressure for land by the Spanish forced them to move once again. The Spanish incessantly spread out, usually moving north into the Chimayo valley, occupying and farming the fertile, protected valleys irrigated more or less automatically by mountain streams.

The land, however, was hardly quiet or free of danger, and the Indians did not always accept their displacement willingly or without a fight. In 1696 there was a minor insurrection, quickly suppressed, which like the revolt of 1680 originated in the northern pueblos. The continual shifting of homelands

12–1

12–1
EL SANTUARIO, A PROCESSION
circa 1917
The Santuario in its prior form, with
flat roof and without wooden caps to the
towers.
[Museum of New Mexico]

may have been an important factor contributing to this flare-up. Following the directives of the crown and the viceroy (the king's agent in the New World), the town of Chimayo, formalized about 1695, was arranged in the form of a fortified plaza (known as the Plaza del Cerro). The walls of the dwellings and animal structures were made contiguous, with only small doors and gates of heavy wooden construction admitting passage. Inside the ring of structures were limited pasture lands for cattle and sheep in the event of siege or attack by the natives. Today the plaza at Chimayo is the best preserved (although much restored) of these arrangements and provides an excellent picture of the town type that also served as the basis for planning at Las Trampas and Ranchos de Taos farther north. The small Oratorio de San Buenaventura remains on the west side of the plaza under the care of the Ortega family.

The families that originally settled the Chimayo valley came from the valley of Mexico and were part of the group that settled Santa Cruz. Among them, as Stephen de Borhegyi reported in an excellent study of the shrine, was one Diego de Veitia.[2] The name has changed within the family over the centuries, and from the original spelling and pronunciation it was modified to de Beyta when he moved to Santa Cruz and became Abeyta at Chimayo.

Against the hardships of winter and the native population but with the blessing of fertile soils and sufficient water, the small settlement managed to thrive and grow. Prince credited Abeyta with particular abundance, the reasons for which he thanked the Lord by building a chapel on his land.[3] On November 15, 1813, Bernardo Abeyta, representing nineteen families, petitioned the Very Reverend Álvarez, who forwarded the request for construction to the vicar general of the diocese, stating that "the miraculous Image of our Lord of Esquípulas has been already honored for three years in the *hermita*, a small chapel next to Bernardo Abeyta who built it."[4] The petition recorded the first mention of the curious connection between the Santuario of Chimayo and its predecessor in Guatemala.

During the conquest of Central America the Spanish were aided in several instances by allied Indian groups. The Tlascalan Indians, for example, were granted special favors in response to their alliance and possibly served as laborers and model settlers as the Spanish pushed settlements further north (see San Miguel). The Guatemalan chief Esquípulas also saw the futility, one assumes, of fighting against superior arms and supplies and was astute enough to surrender his town to avoid loss of life. In his honor the Spanish named the town Santiago de Esquípulas, which combined the name of the chief with that of the holy military patron Santiago, who had inspired the Christian forces against the Muslims. The town soon became a local trading center, and the consequent accumulation of wealth and resources was expressed in religious images.

One example of this art was an image of Christ made from balsam and orange wood by local woodcarver Quirio Catano. The color of the natural grain of the wood endowed the statue with the facial skin tones of the Indians. The carving soon became famous for its curative power. Among the sufferers who were cured through the intervention of this Christ of Esquípulas was the bishop of Guatemala, Pedro Pardo de Figueroa, the victim of "contagious disease." He began construction of a chapel to house the image, but it was not completed until after his death. His body was interred there, along with the Christ figure, in 1758, and the site became a venerated destination.

Part of the ritual of pilgrimage was the consumption of clay (a practice known as geophagy) pressed into small tablets. This custom had parallels in certain practices of the Pueblo Indians in the American Southwest. Among the Hispanic settlements there was only one recorded instance of the practice: at the Santuario de Chimayo. Here the clay, or *tierra bendita* (blessed earth), was found in a pit in the chamber to the west of the sanctuary. Prayer, pilgrimage, and ingestion of a small amount of this substance were supposed to cure the afflicted of "pains, rheumatism, sore throat, paralysis and childbirth."[5]

Into the early twentieth century, Prince told us, there was a daily stream of visitors to the shrine:

> Every day throughout the year, men, women, and children from all directions, from Colorado on the north to Chihuahua and Sonora on the south, may be seen approaching the shrine, in carriages, in wagons, on horses, on burros, or on foot; but all inspired with full faith in the supernatural remedial power that is here manifested, and high hopes that a good Providence will vouchsafe life and health to the suffering pilgrim.[6]

The pilgrimage continues to this day.

According to legend, the Indian name for Chimayo, Tsimmayo, suggested the site of healing spirits, possibly in the form of warm or sulphurous springs. The valley was first inhabited some time between 1100 and 1400, which coincided with the migration of the Chaco Canyon and Mesa Verde peoples. Thus, once again there is a coincidence of Indian and Hispanic cultures, in this case the overlaying of a source of healing with a legend originating in Guatemala, applied to a site traditionally

12–2

12–2
EL SANTUARIO
circa 1935
The addition of the pitched roof closed
the nave to clerestory lighting and necessitated a gable on the facade. The
building was trimmed in wood and
topped by two roofs.
[T. Harmon Parkhurst, Museum of
New Mexico]

regarded by the Indians as ameliorative prior to European contact.

The chapel was originally annexed to the Abeyta farmstead. In a letter Reverend Álvarez wrote that "the most decent and appropriate spot on the said plaza fortified village, or Rancho de Potrero, is called El Santuario de Esquípulas, where they can worship the lord."[7] Thus, the current structure replaced a smaller preexisting chapel that was deemed too meager or too private. The application for a new structure was approved at the bishopric in Durango in a letter dated February 8, 1814. The letter reached the custos, Fray Francisco de Otacio, and in April 1815 he granted permission to the faithful Bernardo Abeyta. Sponsored by Abeyta, the chapel was built with the help of the parish.

Although the chapel was built in 1816, its plan type and form match those of missions dating from centuries earlier. With single nave, tapering apse, and twin towers, the building resembles a smaller version of early seventeenth-century churches such as San Esteban at Acoma or San Agustín at Isleta. Built of adobe and plastered with mud, the chapel is roofed by vigas and latíllas covered by a foot or so of packed earth. Fronting the Santuario is a campo santo with a single cross, once again in the traditional pattern. Unusual, however, is its siting, now overgrown with mature cottonwood trees watered by the adjacent creek. The Santuario sits separately from the houses around it, which, unlike those in the rigid rectangle of the plaza nearby, display no conformity to geometric design. By 1816 the threat of attack had become marginal, and the need for a defensive structure was all but negated for an inland settlement such as Chimayo with sufficient elevation from the plains to the east.

Early photographs show the flat-roofed church with towers unadorned by the wooden finials that cap them today. We can assume that during the 1920s the pitched metal roof was added to the chapel, thereby forcing the addition of the pediment between the two towers. The folded wooden hats on the towers were most likely added at this time, given the consistency of the style. These were added for protection against deterioration of the plaster (noticeable in photos from about 1915), which could have led to erosion of the structural adobe bricks. There seems to be some affinity between this remodeling and that of San Augustín at Isleta dating from 1923, where elaborate wooden turrets, pediment, and balcony were added to the solid and stolid adobe base. One enters the Santuario through a zaguán formed by two uncharacteristic storage rooms and an exterior balcony. Early

12–3

lists of goods stored there suggest that sales of commodities donated to the Santuario were used to maintain and administer the site.[8]

As an act of humility, praise, and faith, the interior of the chapel was highly ornamented—to a degree unacceptable to the Reverend Agustín Fernández de San Vicente. In a letter dated August 29, 1826, he instructed the resident priest of Santa Cruz, who had jurisdiction over the Santuario, to remove all the saints' images painted on animal hides or rough boards.[9] De Borhegyi credited the reredos to José Aragón and the east wall to Miguel Aragón of nearby Cordova, where even today a wonderful tradition of santos wood carvings thrives.[10] The principal reredos are attributed to Molleno, called "the Chile painter."

Today the lavishness of the paintings rivets one's attention forward from the moment of entry into the nave [Plate 7]. The pitched roof blocks the clerestory, a common malady in church remodelings, and the incandescent floodlights that illuminate the reredos only suggest the true power of the directed clerestory lighting once present in the chapel. Nonetheless, one is moved by the sanctity of this small edifice and of the adjacent rooms covered with votive offerings with gratitude for miracles rendered to the afflicted faithful.

Some time between 1850 and 1860, apparently prompted by jealousy of the trade generated by the Santuario, a neighbor built a second chapel, this one dedicated to the Santo Niño de Atocha. Its popularity drained the revenue of the Santuario's owners, who ultimately acquired a Santo Niño of their own—although they selected by mistake an image of the Holy Child of Prague. The statue currently rests in the room with the pit of sacred earth.[11]

Possession of the chapel passed to Abeyta's daughter, who maintained it, as he did, with access to all. She was troubled by an overzealous clergy, who perhaps believed that the possession of the chapel should rest with the archdiocese in Santa Fe. Apparently various threats failed to gain their intended object, and the daughter steadfastly held on to her inheritance. In time the conflict became known to church authorities and the matter was settled.[12] In 1929 title was transferred to the archdiocese of Santa Fe through the generosity of an anonymous donor, "a Roman Catholic graduate of Yale."[13]

Because the chapel and site have a collective history that predates the arrival of the Spanish, there are a series of legends associated with the place. De Borhegyi explained that most of these stories deal with apparition and disappearance in groups of three and with the taking and return of some

12–4

12–3
EL SANTUARIO
The entrance and courtyard seen from the creek.
[1986]

12–4
EL SANTUARIO, PLAN
[Sources: Kubler, *The Religious Architecture*, 1940, based on HABS; and measurements by Susan Lopez, 1987]

12–5

12–6

12–6
EL SANTUARIO
Artificial illumination today replaces the
original clerestory and window lighting
in the nave.
[1981]

12–7

object.[14] For example, Bernardo Abeyta saw a bright light one day and found the crucifix of Our Lord of Esquípulas. Abeyta placed it in the main altar of his chapel, but the next morning, to his surprise, found that it was missing. This happened three times. Realizing that this must be a sign, he later constructed the chapel over the hole where the crucifix had been found. A similar story was told of a Picuris shepherd who found an image of Saint Istipula and put it under his pillow.

> At Chimayo, the traditional home of the Tewa immigrants to the Hopi, there is preserved in a room of the church a hole in the ground of which clay has in the Indian opinion potent medicinal value, "good for pains in the body, and for being sad," said my Isletan informant. Twice he had visited the "santuario" or Shamno, as it is called from the man of Picuris (Shamnoag) who first found the saint. He was out herding sheep. With his crook he was tapping some rocks and there by a big rock he found the saint, Saint Istipula. He was made of clay. The old herder took the image and placed it overnight by his pillow. In the morning the saint had disappeared; he had gone back to his rock where the herder sought him and found him. But from there, too, the morning after, the saint disappeared. The herder returned to the rock and there was the saint. So the herder thought there was no use in carrying the saint away and on that spot he built a shade for him. Later in some way Mexicans got possession of this place.[15]

Among the best-known images in the Santuario is a rather small statue of Santiago. This figure has traditionally been decorated with crafted flowers and candles and even pictures of the pilgrims offering thanks for the healing properties of this representative of the saint. In earlier times, E. Boyd noted, the figure received tiny boots, sombreros, and even bridles in thanks for children cured.[16] The figure has been painted many times during its history, but it was restored in 1955 by Alan Vedder of the Spanish Colonial Department of the Museum of New Mexico.

Veneration for the Santuario of Chimayo continues to this day. Marc Simmons reported that in response to the extremely high losses suffered by New Mexicans in the early part of the Pacific War, including the infamous Bataan death march, "some of the survivors, keeping a vow made during that harrowing time, later undertook a pilgrimage on foot to the rustic adobe Santuario de Chimayo."[17] Sanctity lies embedded in this place.

12–8

12–7
EL SANTUARIO
Detail of the vigas, carved wooden
corbels, and milled ceiling boards.
[1982]

12–8·
EL SANTUARIO
Detail of the restored reredos.
[1981]

172

LAS TRAMPAS

SAN JOSÉ DE GRACIA DE LAS TRAMPAS

c. 1760

In the original license that authorized the construction of a church and chapel at Las Trampas, Bishop Tamarón admonished the parishioners to construct a religious edifice that would be appropriate and proper. "We charge the citizens of the place to try to maintain the aforesaid chapel with all possible seemliness and cleanliness so that the devotion of the faithful may thus be aroused to frequent it and the spiritual consolation which is the aim of our pastoral zeal."[1] Although the church has suffered its share of vicissitudes in its two hundred years of existence, that charge has been met.

Driving the mountain road from Santa Fe through Santa Cruz to Taos, one comes upon the church of San José de Gracia de las Trampas as an unexpected oasis. The village that surrounds it has changed with time and reflects modern building practice and a more contemporary lifestyle. But the church itself, recently restored, reflects and illustrates a devotion and a construction that in many places have long passed. To this day the church is maintained by its parishioners, and the possession of the key and the care of its interior rotate periodically within the congregation.

The vegetation changes abruptly as the plateau gives way to the Truchas peaks of the Sangre de Cristo Mountains. From the scrub juniper and piñon that dot the plains there is a marked shift to the evergreen forests that blanket the slopes. Flat land becomes a premium and water and sun a concern.

Mountain villages such as Las Trampas were settled near those few flat areas available for cultivation that could be served by irrigation. Valuable water from rivers and streams and south-facing slopes seemed to have been the primary considerations. The fields, although limited in dimension, did yield sufficient crops, including, somewhat surprisingly, fruits such as apricots and peaches.

In 1712 Sebastián Martín received a land grant for a large area including that of Las Trampas. In 1751 twelve families seeking a new place to live and farm were granted about forty-six thousand acres by Governor Tomás Vélez Cachupín, which included 180 varas of farmland for each family. In addition, plots for fifty-seven residences and dwellings were included, as was a series of one-half-vara units set aside for "droppings, enclosures, stables and other objects of that nature."[2] If this area proved insufficient, there were also 1,620 varas that could be transferred to the twelve families from the original grant. The exact fertility and conditions of the soil were undoubtedly known quantities, and this last piece was to forestall any difficulties in settling land disputes, if that proved necessary.

13–1

13–1
SAN JOSÉ
San José possesses the most poised
facade of the New Mexican churches, a
composition pitting the strong verticals
of the towers against the lighter wooden
balcony.
[1984]

Living conditions were not secure in the area, however. The mountains were distant from the plateau areas protected by the Santa Fe garrison, and as a result the settlers lived uneasily. A missionary resided at Picuris pueblo, but he could offer none of the physical security provided by military forces. Consequently, the town was formed as a fortified plaza in the manner of Chimayo and Ranchos de Taos and distinct from the dispersed ranchos of the southern Rio Grande area. Whether the plaza was ever completely encircled, however, has not been ascertained.

The settlers' spiritual needs were equal to their secular wants. With the "Indian question" far from settled and the seemingly short distance of two leagues between Las Trampas and Picuris rendered dangerous, the citizens petitioned for their own church. In 1760 Bishop Tamarón made a visitation of the New Mexican churches and responded favorably to the petition for a church. On June 15, 1760, at Picuris pueblo he granted permission to construct a "chapel and church with the title and avocation of Lord St. Joseph of Grace and of Most Holy Mary Immaculate," charging the builders to make it "seemly, clean and otherwise required."[3] Given the small number of families that made up the congregation, there would be no resident priest. Instead, the church would be treated as a visita of Picuris.

By 1776, when Domínguez made his visit, the population had grown to sixty-three families with a total of 178 people. The church, following Tamarón's direction, was built within the walled enclosure of the plaza and did not measure more than thirty varas. Domínguez seemed impressed with the nascent settlement and wrote of its setting, "It runs from southeast to northwest, with a small river with a rapid current of good crystalline water in the middle. It is not half a league long, but since it is rather wide, it has fairly good farmlands on both banks of the river. Watered by this river they yield quite reasonable crops with the exception of chile and frijol." He also told of its history: "The chapel has been built by alms from the whole kingdom, for the citizens of this place have begged throughout it. The chief promoter in this has been one Juan Argüello who is more than eighty years old."[4]

The chapel at the time was almost complete. The Franciscan noted that the choir loft still lacked a rail and that the twin towers flanking the entrance were hardly begun. This note leads one to conclude that the church was first built as a typical cross-shaped box with a flat facade, the towers added later for aesthetic and symbolic reasons rather than out

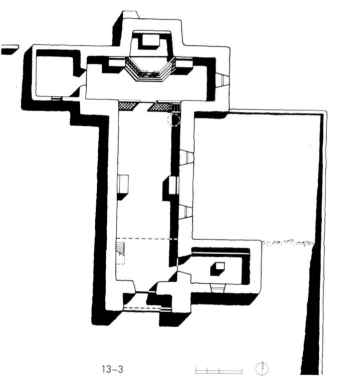

13–3

13–2
LAS TRAMPAS
The remnants of the original fortified plaza are barely discernible in this photo.
[Dick Kent, 1984]

13–3
SAN JOSÉ, PLAN
[Sources: Kubler, *The Religious Architecture*, 1940 based on HABS; and field observation, 1986]

13–4

13–4
SAN JOSÉ
circa 1935
The interior with its full complement
of santos.
[T. Harmon Parkhurst, Museum of
New Mexico]

13–5
SAN JOSÉ
San José offers a classic Spanish Colonial
church interior. Five reredoses fill the
nave, the principal altarpiece illuminated
by the characteristic transverse
clerestory.
[1981]

of structural necessity. And yet today it is just these towers and the dignity of the facade that form the gateway to the church and its ranking as the finest of the Spanish colonial religious buildings.

Following the customary pattern of building in Spanish settlements, the church was constructed with transepts. In addition, the sacristy at the Epistle (right) side filled out its profile. Windows were present by the time of Domínguez's report: he stated that there was one window on either transept end, plus two on the Epistle side near the nave. Widened over the course of time, their position has probably been the same, although the dimensions have varied from the originals.

The altar was raised by four steps fronted by wooden beams in the usual manner. Originally the floor throughout was packed earth, although today only the baptistry is so made. The wooden floor in the remainder of the church is a late-nineteenth-century addition at the earliest because milled lumber became available in the mountain villages only sometime after the American occupation.

Fortunately San José is not covered by the tin shed roofs that now protect many of the adobe churches, and as a result the light quality from the windows—however enlarged—and the clerestory reveal an interior characterized by softness and repose. The wash of light over the white plastered walls and the soft rendering of the prismatic masses create a spatial impression that complements the cubic forms of the exterior towers. The altar area is narrower than the nave, which, coupled with a decorative cut-wooden screen, distinguishes the sanctuary. The altar, now of wood, as in many of the churches, was originally of adobe, so that its base literally grew out of the earth.

Over the entry to the church and extending as a balcony on the exterior is the choir loft, with access only by ladder [Plate 8]. Its floor is also of packed earth. The baptistry is a simple rectangular room connected to the nave and found to the right immediately upon entering. Domínguez noted that the baptismal font consists of "an adobe pillar in the middle [of the room] but no font." The sacristy, which extends the southwest transept, has a simple roof with corner fireplace. Domínguez had little to say of its worthiness: "A very ordinary room without a key."[5]

At the time of the friar's visit there was little by way of religious furnishing within the church. If the building was still under construction, this would not have been too surprising. There was a "middlesized image in the round of Lord St. Joseph" and some paper prints, but little else. Today the setting is

13–5

178 quite different: there are five major reredoses, with a number of subsidiary images; all are of high quality and interest. Two flank the nave, while the remaining three—including the principal reredos—complete the sanctuary. The frames of the reredoses date from somewhere between 1776 and 1871, according to Louise Harris, and are attributed to José de Gracia Gonzáles.[6] They were probably painted in Sonora and brought by trade caravan to Las Trampas. Harris noted that they were a bit "too good" to be of New Mexican origin and not good enough to be from central Mexico—hence the attribution to Sonora.

Not all visitors have been as kindly in the evaluation of the church and its art as was Fray Domínguez. John Bourke, who visited Las Trampas on July 19, 1881, reflected the Anglo view of Hispanic Catholic iconography (a view that seemed to have been shared by Bishop Lamy). Bourke wrote, "Upon one wall hung a small drum to summon the faithful to their devotions. The paintings were of wood and were I disposed to be sarcastic I would remark that they ought to be burned up with the hideous dolls of saints to be seen in one of the niches of the transept." But his scathing condemnation is followed by a more temperate, although still condescending, attempt at accurate description:

> This criticism, in all justice, would be apt and appropriate in our own day; but we should not forget that this little chapel dates back to a period and condition of affairs when the Arts were in their infancy, so far as these people were concerned; when the difficulties of transportation compelled the priests to rely upon native talent alone. This talent supplied the fearful artistic abortions we laugh at today; yet these pictures and dolls served their purpose in object-lessons to a people unable or unwilling to comprehend abstract theology—and altho' a newer and more progressive day has dawned, one which can readily replace these productions with the works of artistic merit, the halo of antiquity has endeared these smoke blackened daubs to the simple-minded youths and maidens who gather here to recite the Rosary or chant the Creed. To the traveller, the greatest charm of New Mexico will be lost when these relics of a by-gone day shall be superseded by brighter and better pictures framed in the cheap gilding of our own time.[7]

San José has been the subject of two major restorations, one easily accomplished and the second the scene of a major social confrontation. The first took place in 1932 under the auspices of the Committee for the Preservation and Restoration of New Mexico Mission Churches. At the time the bases of the towers were repaired, new beams for the balcony were mounted, and a new turned balustrade for the

13–6

13–6
SAN JOSÉ
circa 1910?
Early in this century only one wooden turret remained, the clerestory structure was sagging, and the tops of the walls had been stripped of plaster by the elements.
[Museum of New Mexico]

13–7
SAN JOSÉ
1949
The fragile wooden turrets have disappeared and the entry arch has deteriorated since their invention and installation.
[New Mexico Tourism and Travel Division]

13–7

13–8

13–8
SAN JOSÉ
In a 1960s rehabilitation, the turrets
were remade and the church walls were
stabilized. The baptistry adjoins
the nave.
[1986]

13–9
SAN JOSÉ
The ornate wooden finials, designed by
John Gaw Meem based on historic prototypes, were installed at the time of the
last major restoration.
[1981]

balcony was installed—until that time the railing
had been lattice. During the period of the restorations the building was measured and recorded by
the HABS, which documented several New Mexican churches during the Depression.

In the 1960s the town and the church were threatened—or blessed, depending on point of view—with
the promise of a widened road. Seen as progress by
many of the citizens—connections with Taos and
Santa Fe had been tenuous because of poor road
conditions—the widening of the road would have
removed part of the churchyard, thereby causing, in
the eyes of the preservationists, irrevocable damage.
Among the leaders of the battle for the church was
architect Nathaniel Owings, who later wrote of the
saga in *New Mexico Magazine.* Apparently the towns-
folk were not united in their stand to save the church.
Although venerated, the building *was* old, and the
increased benefits of better communication could not
be disparaged. Owings recounted, "The villagers'
attitude was summed up by the comment of one that,
if their church as a historic monument was standing
in the way of *progress* as indicated by the building of
the road, they would blow up the church."[8]

Undaunted, although no doubt discouraged, the
preservationists were able to secure National Landmark status for the church in April 1967, which
granted them leverage and badly needed bargaining time. In the end a compromise was struck: the
so-called Treaty of Santa Fe, dated June 8, 1967.[9]
An alternate road design was instituted; the church
was not only saved but was also repaired. The walls
were mud plastered; there was new roofing, the first
since the 1932 restoration; and cupolas of wood for
the two towers were executed to a design by John
Gaw Meem based on old photographs.

Las Trampas today is the high point of the scenic
tour from Santa Cruz to Taos. The apse of Ranchos
de Taos, justly celebrated and publicized in the
paintings of Georgia O'Keeffe, might be better
known, and Santa Cruz might be larger, but neither
possesses the softness and quiet dignity of San José
de Gracia. The surrounding architecture reflects
modern incursions, and the architectural definition
of the plaza has seriously deteriorated, but the form
and the feel of the eighteenth-century original can
still be discerned. San José de Gracia de las Trampas, because of its handsome proportions, the
wealth of its art, its maintenance, and its refinement
in spite of crude materials and technology, remains
the finest of the Spanish colonial church interiors.

13–9

PICURIS PUEBLO

SAN LORENZO

c. 1620; 1706; 1740s; c. 1776; late 1960s; 1986+

Today the pueblo of Picuris remains relatively small and tranquil, still removed from the major settlements of the state. Yet during its history it played the role of political instigator on more than one occasion. Positioned in the mountains north of Santa Fe on the High Road to Taos, the location of the village ensured contact with the Apache and the Comanche as well as with the remainder of the Pueblo tribes that occupied the Rio Grande valley. The earliest contact with Europeans came with Gaspar Castaño de Sosa in 1581.[1] Fray Francisco de Zamora was charged with the establishment of a permanent mission at Picuris, and under his custody at least a rudimentary chapel dedicated to patron San Lorenzo was erected. In 1620 the church was under the charge of Martín de Arvide, and by the later part of the decade the religious enterprise was a going concern, serving several surrounding villages in addition to Picuris itself.

Benavides had mixed respect for Picuris: "Picuries [*sic*] pueblo; more than 2,000 baptized Indians, it has its convent and church. They have been the most indomitable and treacherous people of this whole kingdom."[2] His report implied there was a good-sized edifice with convento at Picuris; his observation was confirmed by Agustín de Vetancurt.[3] Around midcentury the pueblo was said to have "a very good church and convento . . . and 564 souls under its administration."[4] The mission was federated with that of Taos and was originally a single district under the jurisdiction of Francisco de Zamora. In the church records Picuris was continually cited for its basic lack of interest or intractability toward conversion. Tupatu of Picuris was one of the principal antagonists in the 1680 rebellion. Under his instigation the resident priest was murdered and the church burned before the party of insurrectionists marched south to join the main attack on Santa Fe.

When Vargas returned to New Mexico twelve years later, the village was deserted, perhaps out of fear of Spanish reprisals. The church lay in ruins. In his usual manner Vargas induced the inhabitants of the village to return, which they did, and probably built a new church or repaired the old one. The governor found the church "very filthy" in 1696, with Indian designs painted on the walls and the door in disrepair. Kubler questioned whether this structure and that repaired in 1706 were the same structure as the church Benavides had mentioned.[5] The village was vacated again in 1704—Forrest attributed this to superstition[6]—and its inhabitants went to live with one of the Apache groups for a two-year period. They returned in 1706, rebuilt the pueblo, and presumably rebuilt the church.

14–1

14–1
SAN LORENZO
1899
Before the start of the twentieth century San Lorenzo had a typical cross-shaped plan and a flat facade with a single bell arch.
[Adam C. Vroman, Museum of New Mexico]

14–2
SAN LORENZO
1935
Following a nearly typical pattern, the church—with its metal roof and stubby belfry—looks more like a schoolhouse than a church.
[T. Harmon Parkhurst, Museum of New Mexico]

14–2

During the decade 1740–1750 the mission was again restored. Much of the work was due, by his own admission, to the efforts of Fray Fernando Duque de Estrada, who resided in the pueblo from 1746 to 1747. He claimed to have built the sanctuary "from the foundations up," whitewashed the church, leveled and packed the dirt floor, constructed a belfry, built a crenelated parapet around the entire church, and restored the campo santo as well as providing interior furnishings. He also directed his attention toward remodeling the convento and its kitchen.[7]

Much of this was to no avail. Barely a year later his successor noted that Duque de Estrada had moved the kitchen, oven, doors, and windows to the upper floor, leaving on the first floor "nothing . . . but the ruins of what was before."[8] By 1749 there was "nothing at this mission but disrepair and misery."[9] Tamarón left no words on the church, but by the end of the 1750s Governor Antonio Marín del Valle had discovered the pueblo in ruins. The Comanche completed what nature had begun, conclusively destroying the mission in 1769 in its relatively defenseless position on the outskirts of the pueblo. Fearing another sacrilege, Governor Pedro Fermín de Mendinueta ordered that what remained of the building be leveled to the ground and a new church constructed in a more defensible location. The new church was under construction in 1776 when Domínguez arrived at Picuris to look things over and report.

The story of the new church's construction is of interest because it illustrates the presence of Hispanic building skill even in the building of churches in Indian pueblos. This may have been the principal vehicle for the introduction of the Spanish architectural tradition into that of the Indian, with the civilian builder serving as a sort of technical intermediary between the stylistic ideas of the padres and the common construction competence of the Indians. In any event a civil contract to construct the church was enacted between Fray Sebastián Ángel Fernández of Santa Cruz and Alcalde Salvador García de Noriega. It was to be a complete package, what today would be termed a turnkey project, including "transepts, door, two windows to the east, choir loft, corbels and round beams, plus a three-room dwelling, a sort of token convento."[10] The payment was to be in goods, and the amount of goods that the good friar had at his disposal seemed to wrinkle the eyebrow of Domínguez, who perhaps believed that there should be less commercial dealing and more converting. The renumeration was to be "12 cows, 12 yearling calves, 25 ewes with a stud ram,

14–3

14–3
SAN LORENZO
circa 1935
The simple spatial configuration of the church is graced by a handsome reredos and an ornate railing.
[T. Harmon Parkhurst, Museum of New Mexico]

14–4
SAN LORENZO, PLAN
[Sources: National Park Service Remote Sensing; and field observations, 1986]

a fine she-mule, 100 fanegas of maize and wheat," and for his sweet tooth "100 pounds of chocolate," enough to keep a child, and one suspects, a padre, content for years.[11] Notwithstanding the seemingly lavish payment, our first commentator, Father José Benito Pereyro, taking inventory in 1808, termed it just ordinary.[12]

Domínguez opened his report by explaining why there was neither church nor convento, that is, the problem of the Comanche raids and how the governor ordered that the defenseless church be torn down. "These raids are so daring that this father I have mentioned [Andrés Claramonte] assures me that he escaped by a miracle in the year '69, for they sacked the convent and destroyed his meager supplies; yet he considered them well spent in exchange for his life and freedom from captivity."[13] Domínguez continued by describing how the new church was in a much better position:

> This [the new location] is near one block of, but outside, one plaza of the pueblo, with the intention that the convent shall be in that block. But according to the plan, all is to be defensible as a unit, for the present space between the church and the block where the convent is to be built will be a cloister. The new church is adobe with quite thick walls, single-naved, with the outlook and main door due south. It is 24 varas long, 7 wide, and what has been built is 3 varas high.[14]

Even after a century of Christianization efforts, the friar had to fend for himself. The people remained unconvinced.

> The pueblo does part of the sowing, cultivation, and harvesting, but for the time being the present missionary bears most of the work. When I remonstrated him, citing the custom among the Indians, he replied: That since they are so lazy, even in their own affairs, they are even more inclined to let what belongs to the father be lost, and so to avoid animosities, gossip, etc., he considers it a pleasure to do it himself, even to the threshing of the wheat with six of his own animals.[15]

To live in the wilderness, the eighteenth-century Spanish missionary in New Mexico needed to be both diplomat and stoic. The census then stood at sixty-four families with 223 persons, down even from the drastically reduced 328 Indians of the Tamarón census of 1760.

The convento was at least sufficiently rebuilt in 1780 to allow habitation. Fray Francisco Martín Bueno underwrote the cost of the altar screen added in 1785–1787. In 1833 Bishop Zubiría, who had a critical eye, related that "it lacks many other things, even a legitimate altar stone, for there is none there

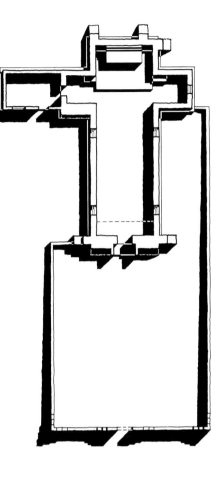

14–4

with sepulcher and relics."[16] From this point on life seemed to even out and rest quietly.

"The first building I entered was the church," reported Lieutenant John Bourke in 1881, "where I found the 'governor' of the Pueblo, Nepomuceno, who with others of his tribe was engaged in carpentry work, making a new altar and other much needed repairs."[17] About the church he said nothing more, but Bourke's sketch, like early photos, showed the building to be both simple and severe. The transepts and clerestory were clearly articulated by their additional height, fronted by a simple south facade with small arch enclosing a bell, topped by a cross. A wall of adobe six or seven feet high surrounded the campo santo, which was entered by a gate surmounted by a softened pedimented form. A ladder rested on the west wall, as it often does today. An 1899 photograph by Vroman illustrated this planar facade with its elongated bell opening and simple Territorial Style pediment above the door.

Early in this century the church received a metal pitched roof and a belfry, both of which gave it that distinctive schoolhouse look that many New Mexican churches had to suffer. The surrounding wall was lowered, and by 1935 it was barely three feet high in places—certainly none of the architectural sense of enclosure produced by the high wall remained. The stepped sky altar motif of the gateway was more pronounced, while two adobe bases appeared in a circa 1935 photograph on either side of the door. The south wall of the church was whitewashed and was strikingly distinguished from the earthen remainder.

In the late 1960s the church underwent restoration; the result producing a building of visual simplicity and interest.[18] The pitched roof was removed and the traditional flat roof reintroduced. The south, or principal, facade was extended past the side walls so that it read as a front applied to the church, a literal rendering of the word facade. Two small wings, like the old Santa Clara, flanked each side of the pediment, which was reconstructed to better proportions with a marked stepped profile. Painted white, as was the gateway, the contrast of this brilliant plane against the brown cement plaster that covered the remainder of the building was exceptionally striking on a clear autumn day [Plate 12]. Trapped between the gateway and the plane of the entry is the campo santo with its single cross. The cross on the bare earth is a fitting symbol of missionary efforts in New Mexico; one must have faith to project cultivation into the barren soil.

The collapse of a portion of the nave wall in spring of 1986 occasioned a major restoration of San Lorenzo. The reasons were familiar, the root of them being the cement stucco that covered the adobe walls. Even though the concrete "ribbon beams" helped thwart coving at the base of the wall, they could do little to alleviate the problems created by cracks in the stucco and the seepage of water into the earthen blocks of which the wall was made.[19] The work in progress is a major rebuilding, what in the eighteenth century might have been termed "a new church."

14–5

14–6

14–5
SAN LORENZO
The apse end.
[1981]

14–6
SAN LORENZO
In 1986, portions of the nave walls had given way and the church as a whole was badly deteriorated, although it was in the course of rebuilding.
[1986]

RANCHOS DE TAOS

SAN FRANCISCO DE ASÍS

c. 1815; 1967; 1981

For most Christian churches the facade is the principal architectural subject. Here is the ceremonial face of the church, its entrance, a surface to be embellished [Plate 14]. Often situated prominently on the plaza, the church occupied that zone between the mundane world of the body and the sacred world of the spirit. And although the east facade of San Francisco de Ranchos de Taos fronts the remnants of its plaza—strong, handsome, and noted in its own right—the rear of the church with its celebrated buttresses has become an icon of New Mexican religious buildings.

The notoriety of this particular apse stems primarily from the photographs of Paul Strand and Ansel Adams and the paintings of John Marin and Georgia O'Keeffe, who for many years lived and worked in nearby Abiquiu. But from the 1920s onward a host of artists, many from the northeastern United States, also gravitated to New Mexico, impressed by the area's climate and clear light. They sought the light that graced southern France, the intricacy of the native decorative motifs, or the noble people themselves as working subjects.[1] In the prismatic forms of the pueblos and adobe construction these artists found formal sympathies with the planar concerns of postimpressionism and cubism. And the nascent art deco style, popularized by the Paris Exhibition of Modern Decorative and Industrial Arts of 1925, could readily incorporate the geometric designs and colors of Indian weaving and pottery decorations.

O'Keeffe wrote, "The Ranchos de Taos Church is one of the most beautiful buildings in the United States by the Spaniards. Most of the artists who spend any time in Taos have to paint it, I suppose, just as they have to paint a self-portrait. I had to paint it—the back several times, the front once. I finally painted a part of the back thinking that with that piece of the back I said all I needed to say about the church."[2] The fragment does convey a sense of the whole: its mottled color, the texture of the earthen wall surfaces, the striking profile against the sky, and the mass of the buttresses.

Near Taos the Sangre de Cristo Mountains pull back, revealing a large and fertile plain. Watered by the Rio Grande and its tributaries, this land has been occupied as the northernmost settlement of Pueblo culture for at least seven hundred years. The Spanish followed the Indians, settling in proximity to them not only to facilitate religious conversions and provide a source of labor on their ranches but also to occupy reliable agricultural lands. One of Coronado's party, Pedro de Alvarado, "discovered" the Taos pueblo and valley in the great expedition

15–1

15–2

15–1
RANCHOS CHURCH,
TAOS, NEW MEXICO
Georgia O'Keeffe, 1930
This painting has helped make the apse
of the structure an icon of southwestern
architecture.
[Amon Carter Museum, Fort Worth,
Texas]

15–2
RANCHOS DE TAOS
The plaza loosely retains the configura-
tion of the fortified plaza.
[Dick Kent, 1960s]

15-3

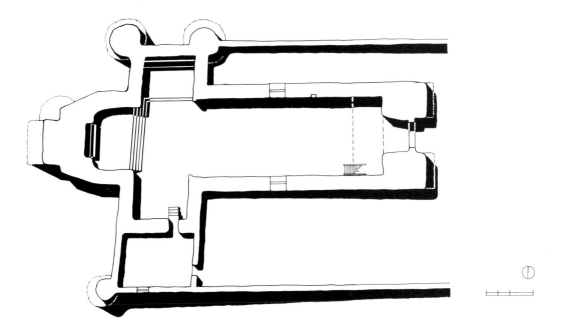

15-4

of 1540, as it moved toward the northeast in search of the legendary Quivira.

With permanent settlement in 1598, missionary activities commenced. Fray Francisco de Zamora, who accompanied the Oñate party, established the mission of San Jerónimo at Taos pueblo further north, although it lasted under his care only for several years. Not until the 1620s did the undertaking achieve greater stability. The colonists settled on the fringes of the pueblo and even a century and a half later were reported to be living inside the pueblo's walls as protection against Comanche incursions. In the 1620s New Mexico's Catholic enterprise was reformed as the Custody of the Conversion of Saint Paul, and Fray Alonso de Benavides assumed the leadership, bringing with him into New Mexico an additional twenty-seven friars.

Certain aspects of the origins of Ranchos de Taos, south of the pueblo, are not precisely ascertained. Some would like to believe that the church itself dates from as early as 1730. Kubler, citing Hackett, established that there was Spanish settlement on the land as early as 1742.[3] Bishop Tamarón, visiting in 1760, mentioned only the church and settlement at Taos pueblo and noted that there were thirty-six European families included within the parish.

Domínguez, during his 1776 visit, wrote of Trampas de Taos, the site of the present Ranchos, "The settlement consists of scattered ranchos, and their owners are the citizens who live in the pueblo."[4] The plaza apparently had not been built by this time, nor was there a church. If there had been a religious structure prior to the post-Domínguez church, it was probably a private chapel—ermita or *oratorio*—and would probably have shared the dimensions of one of the transepts of the current church rather than its nave. Parallel origins have been proposed for the Conquistadora chapel at the Cathedral of Saint Francis and the Rosario chapel, both in Santa Fe.

The peripatetic friar explained that settlers not living in the pueblo had established a small plaza (town) near its western side. They were unable to hold their own against the depredations of marauding Indians, however, and retreated within the stronger walls and more secure numbers of Taos pueblo. This arrangement would not last indefinitely,

> but only until the plaza which is being built in the cañada where their farms are is finished. This is being erected by order of the aforesaid governor . . . so that when they live together in this way, even though they are at a distance from the pueblo, they may be able to resist the attack the enemy may make. These settlers are people of all classes. Some are masters, others servants, and others are both, serving and commanding themselves. They speak the local Spanish,

15–5

15–3
RANCHOS DE TAOS
The play of curvilinear and planar forms in adobe.
[1981]

15–4
RANCHOS DE TAOS, PLAN
[Sources: Kubler, *The Religious Architecture*, 1940, based on HABS; and field observation by Susan Lopez, 1986]

15–5
RANCHOS DE TAOS
The interior in the mid-1980s.
[Vicente M. Martínez; courtesy of San Francisco, Ranchos de Taos]

and most of them speak the language of the pueblo with ease, and to a considerable extent the Comanche, Ute, and Apache languages.[5]

The population stood at sixty-seven families with 306 people.

Juan Agustín de Morfi wrote in 1780 that "the settlement forms a square plaza, very capacious. Its houses were almost finished in 1779 with towers at proportionate distances for their defense."[6] His description implies that the houses forming the plaza's peripheral construction included a number of torreones, round tower forms that served as an observation platform as well as a last bastion of defense.

Domínguez's report, and de Morfi's thereafter, served to discredit the theory of a settlement earlier in the century, that is, settlement in the form of a chartered community. Thus, it is believed that the plaza was constructed some time between 1776 and 1780, with the church following shortly after the turn of the century. Tree ring studies made by W. S. Stallings in 1937 yielded a date of 1816 plus or minus ten years. About that time Ignacio Durán petitioned the provincial custos to have Fray José Benito Pereyro minister to the community as well as Taos pueblo, to which he was assigned.[7] The Santa Fe archives contain a copy of the permission to build the church dated September 20, 1813, and Pereyro stated that in 1818 the church was completed. Vigas were alleged to have been found with the carved dates of 1710 and 1718, however. Pereyro, who left Taos in 1818, wrote that "this temple was constructed at the cost of the Reverend Father minister Fray José Benito Pereyro and the citizens of the plaza."[8] The church was substantially complete by the end of 1815, when permission was sought to permit burials within the consecrated space of the nave. The altar screen, by Molleno, appeared on one inventory from 1818 and is still found within the church.[9]

Matt Field, traveling in New Mexico around 1840 in spite of the dearth of travel arrangements, commented on the state of the community: "This town called the ranch lies at the base of a gigantic mountain and is watered by a swift stream that rushes from the ravine we have just mentioned. It contains about 300 houses, and these are built completely together, forming a wall, enclosing a large square, in the center of which stands a church."[10]

The buildings of Ranchos de Taos were constructed in the form of a fortified plaza, that is, as a ring of buildings of relatively thick adobe walls constructed contiguously. Other examples of the village type include Las Trampas and Chimayo, which still exists in a nearly perfectly preserved form. At Ran-

15–6

15–6
RANCHOS DE TAOS
circa 1916–1918
The twin towers were trimmed with wooden caps to protect them from the elements, although in spite of these precautions, the mud plaster is separating from the adobe bricks.
[Museum of New Mexico]

chos de Taos the church may have formed the western edge of the plaza—certainly its apse wall and buttresses were sufficiently thick to withstand attack.

The church of San Francisco is built in the cruciform plan type more common to the later Hispanic village churches. A good-sized church for New Mexico, it extends about one hundred eight feet in length within the nave, suggesting a significant congregation at the time of its construction. The sanctuary is elevated above the remainder of the nave by three steps, and the church fills out the normal pattern by including a choir loft ("in the usual place," as Domínguez would say) and a clerestory. The northeastern transept, which now serves as a subsidiary chapel, may continue its original use.

The walls are constructed of adobe and measure nearly six feet in average thickness. As mentioned, the enormous buttresses that prop the northeast transept and the rear of the apse have become signatures for the church. On the southeastern facade facing the plaza are two buttresses that support the tower, although these are not structurally bonded to the wall itself, which suggests that they were added at a later time. Diagonal wooden braces shoulder the main viga spanning the chancel area and recall similar braces once seen on the exterior of the Pecos church. There are two windows, one on either side of the nave, although these have been greatly enlarged. Some time after the importation of milled lumber that followed the railroad late in the nineteenth century, the window openings were enlarged. The rounded window heads, inset beneath traditional wooden lintels, appear almost Neo-Romanesque and may exemplify influence from the new cathedral in Santa Fe[11] [Plate 18].

Early photos beautifully capture the texture of the mud plaster applied to the exterior of the church. To retard the rapid erosion of the adobe belfries, wooden caps were installed on the tops of the two towers by the middle of the 1910s. At that time the posts in each of San Felipe's towers' four corners were severely eroded, resembling the earlier forms of both the Ranchos church and the Santuario at Chimayo. By 1918 the mud plaster had begun to spall, but in 1919 or thereabouts the church again sported a new coat of plaster and a protective sheathing of wooden boards over the towers. During the 1930s the church was reroofed and additional repairs were made.

Mud plaster as well as its adobe base is an unforgiving material. Once it has been neglected for an undue period of time, restoration is difficult without considerable attention and prolonged effort. Traditionally mud plaster was touched up each year

15–7

15–7
RANCHOS DE TAOS
circa 1920s
Freshly plastered, the buttresses bring the facade softly to the ground. Wooden shuttering sheathes the bell towers.
[Aaron B. Craycroft, Museum of New Mexico]

and repaired every two years. This continued maintenance represents considerable investment of time and effort and, more recently, money.

By the late 1960s the Ranchos church was again in need of plastering, and this time the church committee thought it would be better to apply hard (cement) plaster to the walls to "avoid" the problem of continued maintenance. Architect Van Dorn Hooker was asked in 1966 by the governing body to report on the church's physical condition. Working with architect George Wright, Hooker prepared a report for the archbishop that outlined the problems in the church as well as the range of possible approaches to their remedy.[12] They found not only that the walls were badly deteriorated in places but also that portions of the floor decking—and even the ends of some vigas—were severely rotted. They recommended four possible restoration strategies to the archdiocese: (1) abandon the church (and there had been some talk that the building was too small), (2) give it to the National Park Service to become a monument, (3) partially restore the structure in a piecemeal fashion, or (4) totally restore it. A complete restoration would include replacing all deteriorated wooden materials, recessing all electric wiring, installing a new heating system and confessionals, rebuilding the bell towers, and plastering with mud or stucco.

The decision was made to restore the church. In the interest of time work began almost immediately to beat the winter weather and the freezing temperatures that precluded most construction. To retard erosion, the adobe bricks in the parapets were replaced with concrete blocks, and a new balcony floor and stairs were installed. The interior was replastered and painted. On February 3, 1967, the council decided to proceed with cement plaster applied over wire mesh.

The reaction to this decision was immediate. Several architects and other interested parties strongly recommended against plaster, mostly on aesthetic grounds. The reasons they presented, however, were not sufficient to outweigh the economic savings to be derived, and the church was surfaced with cement plaster.

But hard plaster and adobe are not compatible materials. Cement plaster is a fine finish material if applied to a stable base; unfortunately adobe does not provide that base. Because the unfired mud bricks attract moisture, they expand and contract to a considerable degree. But they also permit the passage of water if they are allowed to breathe; that is, if moisture eventually finds its way to the air and evaporates. When adobe is mud plastered, fewer problems exist because the atmosphere sucks much of the moisture from the bricks. When a wall is hard plastered, however, the moisture is trapped behind the cement skin. As the adobes move, the stucco cracks, allowing moisture behind the hard plaster and subsequently behind the cement skin. In time the once-dry bricks become like mud, eventually causing wall failure.

Cracks appeared in the stucco almost immediately. In 1970–1971 a painting contractor tried to patch the cracks with fiberglass tape. Within a year the rear buttresses had a major transverse crack, and the two front buttresses appeared unstable. In 1979 the Santa Fe architectural firm of Johnson-Nestor was requested to prepare a report on the church.[13] The firm offered the following alternatives: (1) refurbish all existing exterior stucco, (2) maintain existing stucco, (3) mud plaster the facade only, or (4) return entirely to mud plaster. By that time some portions of the buttresses included adobe that was the consistency of "brownie dough."[14] The church, in an extremely difficult and sensitive decision, returned to mud plaster.

The story of the mud plastering of the church is a happy one. The return to a form of the past meant that some aspects of modern construction, and perhaps modern life, were not as valuable as an almost archaic method that had been abandoned for economic expediency. Money was short; people were many. The congregation decided it would undertake the work itself over a period of two summers beginning in 1979. The rear buttresses were taken down and completely rebuilt. Some said the church would fall when they were removed; it did not. New adobes were installed where needed, and the tedious job of removing all the stucco and chicken wire was carried out. The work was a fiesta that continued for months, with cooking and eating on the site. Not only was the church building itself being renovated but the congregation as a social institution was also undergoing the same process of renewal. In time the work was completed: a new buttress in the apse, two new buttresses supporting the towers in the front, and a complete new coating of mud plaster over the entire church. In all, twenty thousand adobe bricks were made and installed.

The restoration was an unquestionable success. In late 1981 the reredoses were also undergoing restoration, but at the hands of a professional. As the incumbent pastor of Ranchos de Taos, Father Michael O'Brien, said, "Our church 'is' human. The link and bond between an adobe church and its people are strong and require commitment; we keep the church together and the church keeps us together."[15]

15–8

15–8
RANCHOS DE TAOS
The mass, profile, and proportions of
the stubby towers provide the church
with a powerful, although somewhat
ungainly, repose.
[1986]

TAOS PUEBLO

SAN JERÓNIMO

1617; c. 1626; 1706; c. 1850? (new site)

The two tower blocks of Taos pueblo have left an indelible impression on the memory of any visitor who has ever seen them. In the direct application of adobe and mud plaster, the simple logic of structural stacking, and the symbiotic formal relationship to the surrounding mountains, the form of the pueblo can only be regarded as "appropriate." The pueblo in its multistory form is said to date to the fourteenth century, almost to the time of Anasazi emigration from areas such as Mesa Verde and Chaco Canyon. The first recorded European impressions are those of Pedro de Casteñeda, who wrote about the year 1541. He described the south and north blocks divided by the river that both binds and separates them. "In this village they do not raise cotton or breed turkeys: they wear the skins of deer and buffalo entirely. It is the most populous village in all that country: we estimate there were 15,000 souls in it."[1] Even given the usual number inflation that stems from fleeting impressions, Taos was no doubt still an expansive and impressive community. The quotation also illustrates the pivotal position the settlement occupied as the northernmost of the Rio Arriba pueblos and as a transitional community between the pueblos and the Indians of the plains.

The first mission for the Taos valley was founded at the end of the sixteenth century but floundered until the mid-1620s, when the first recorded church was built. By the time of Benavides's visit in 1629, the mission had a secure home and was thriving. "Another seven leagues farther to the north is the pueblo of Taos, belonging to the same language group as [Picuris]," Benavides wrote. "It has 2,500 baptized Indians, with its convento and church." He credited Fray Tomás Carrasco with the construction of "a good church of fine architecture" and its "marvelous choir of wonderful boy musicians."[2] From that time on settlement in the area hovered between destruction and rebuilding. In 1640 the church was razed and its friar killed. Twenty years later the restored mission was burned again.[3]

More than a century later at the time of Tamarón's visitation, the situation had not changed significantly. The church and convento still stood, and relations between the pueblos and the Comanche remained volatile. Settlements in the valley had been abandoned, and the colonists were concentrated in the pueblo. As he approached Taos pueblo, Tamarón found

> encampments of peaceful infidel Apache Indians, who have sought the protection of the Spaniards so that they might defend them from the Comanches. It is the last and most distant of the pueblos of that kingdom . . . at the foot of a very high sierra. . . .

16–1

16–1
TAOS PUEBLO
Aerial view of the pueblo, showing
north and south dwelling blocks;
San Jerónimo is center left.
[National Park Service Remote Sensing,
1979]

This pueblo has 159 families of Indians, with 505 persons. There are 36 families of Europeanized citizens, with 160 persons. There is a very decent and capacious church.[4]

The bishop was somewhat disappointed that the Indians knew the catechism and could confess only in Spanish when official policy dictated that the priest be able to confess and converse in the native language. Tamarón was also critical that the pueblo was built in several blocks. His comments, in retrospect, sound almost ludicrous: "This pueblo is divided into three many-storied tenements. It would have been better, as I told them, if they had been kept together, for one is on the other side of the river about two hundred varas away."[5] If we judge on the basis of today's Taos, his advice was neither heeded nor implemented.

Church construction in northern New Mexico shared certain parallels with native building techniques. Earlier indigenous construction applied mud using puddled or rammed earth techniques. The Spanish certainly did not introduce mud technology, but they did codify wall construction in standard units. The pueblo dwelling block comprises separate cells that have been added to and modified in the course of time. There is no formal master plan, nor is there any preordained geometric shape to which the pueblo form aspires. It is an architecture of exigency that reflects the growth and decay of the social fabric of the village. The huddling together in multistoried arrangements continues the defensive, almost fortified tradition of the settlements of the Mesa Verde and Chaco Canyon peoples. Originally without doors or windows on the ground floor, the dwellings could be reached only through the roof from the floors above. Timbers laid across the walls formed the supports for the roof, and because these were difficult to cut with the stone implements available, final adjustments to exact spans were rarely made: the beams were cut sufficiently long and allowed to extend through the walls. When walls deteriorated or were abandoned, these log beams, or vigas, could be reused, a practice that contributed to the rapid deterioration of mission ruins after their abandonment.

On top of these beams was laid roofing of smaller saplings or split logs called latillas to support the weight of the roof above. Reed or grasses constituted the succeeding layer, and on these was placed a foot or more of adobe mud. A parapet extended around the exposed sides and directed the rain water through scuppers (canales) to retard the erosion that began even before construction was complete.

Church construction in adobe differs little in principle from that of the residential and storage cells of the pueblo, the principal distinction being in the size of the unit being constructed. Indeed, that is the key distinction: the pueblo created minimal rooms for storage or human occupation as an extreme measure. For the most part life took place on the roof, in the fields, or in the spaces around the pueblo. The collective effect was that of a cellular mass.

The religious edifice, however, was not erected so much to sanctify the ground as to create a sanctified internal space. Consider, then, the Indians' regard for construction as a part of natural law, as a participant in a world of sacred space. The European tradition claims space, divorces itself from the surrounding land, and thereby creates a focus and a spiritual connection between God and human. The altar is the focus of the space, its point of transaction. The church building reflects a loosely concentric, axially arranged progression from the most to least holy: the altar, the nave, the facade, the campo santo or burial ground/entry court, and the surrounding land with the settlement in between. This hierarchy to sanctify was foreign to the native sense of religion. Indian building was the making of form and external spaces such as the dance plaza. European building in New Mexico was the creation of space through mass and light.

The first Taos church of San Jerónimo, still visible in a greatly deteriorated state, lies to the northwest of the two main pueblo blocks. Its position betrays exclusion. Grudgingly admitted into the presence of the pueblo, it was but an adjunct to Indian life. Both the pueblo and the church had similar materials, but in its forms and bulk the church was distinguished from the native structure. The church was good sized with massive walls and a tower on its south facade. At the time of its destruction in 1847, it had withstood both cannon fire and direct attack, bearing witness to its defensive capabilities.

The original mission was founded in 1617, but its position as a going entity was always tenuous. Taos was a continual hotbed of insurrection and almost always a part of any scheme to oppose the Spanish occupation forces. The first church was "suppressed there before 1626, rebuilt, but was destroyed again in 1631 or 1639."[6] Nor were the Taoseños bystanders in the great revolt of 1680: the two priests who resided there were killed, and presumably the church suffered considerable damage. How much was left of the church and in what condition it remained are not known, but in 1696 Vargas visited the site and found the church used as a stable—a common practice during the revolt. He ordered it torn down on

16–2

16–2
SAN JERÓNIMO
Twin towers added after 1939 elaborate
the facade and bear greater resemblance
to the churches at Ranchos de Taos and
Las Trampas than to earlier versions of
San Jerónimo.
[1981]

the grounds that no efforts could resurrect it. "In 1706," Kubler continued, "a new church was in construction, and it is probably the edifice of which the ruins stand west of the pueblo buildings."[7]

Domínguez, just sixteen years after Tamarón, found Taos pueblo circled by a mud wall; the pueblo was so heavily fortified that he remarked on its resemblance to "those walled cities with bastions and towers that are described to us in the Bible."[8] The uneasy relationship among Taos, Apache, Comanche, and Spanish still had not been ameliorated. Spanish settlers were living within the pueblo precincts because their safety was not assured living in their preferred scattered ranchos. At Ranchos de Taos the village being built took the form of a fortified plaza, more easily defended from Indian attack.

An inscription on the clerestory beam of the church credited the construction, completed in 1726, to Fray Juan de Mirabal, although whether this concerned a substantial renovation or completely new structure is not known. The choir loft was in its "usual place," and two "poor" windows faced east. Domínguez was less favorable in judging the extension of the church: "In the corner where this cemetery meets the church there is a hideous adobe buttress with a tower buttress rising from it and a small tower with four arches on top."[9] Ironically, it is this element that remains the ruin's most prominent feature. The interior furnishings were acceptable, if scant, and certain ornamentations, such as those on the image of the Virgin, elicited considerable description. The pulpit was "very pretty." Of course, all these evaluations were relative and must be weighed against the typical mission inventories.

The convento, in the form of a square, adjoined the church to the east and in places rose to a second story. The concern of its builder extended beyond the residential and ecclesiastical functions. "The ascent to the church and its tower is over the flat roof," Domínguez wrote. "From all this there is a good view of the Taos plain in all directions, and it is surrounded by a good railing and embrasures for defense."[10] His census reported 112 families totaling 427 persons.

There was one time of relative peace each year in the Taos area: the month of June. Strangely, but following worldwide patterns of honor amid absolute barbarity, the various parties would gather to indulge in trading, although remaining at mercilous war for the rest of the year. Tamarón discussed the fairs at length, seeming as much surprised by the ease with which they were accomplished as we might be today.

16–3

16–3
TAOS PUEBLO
The ruined walls of the earlier church, destroyed in 1846, now serve to enclose the cemetery.
[1981]

When I was in the pueblo two encampments of Ute Indians, who were friendly but infidels, had just arrived with a captive woman who had fled from the Comanches. They reported that the latter were at the Rio de las Animas preparing buffalo meat in order to come to trade. They come every year to the trading, or fairs. The governor comes to those fairs, which they call *rescates* (barter trade), every year with the majority of his garrison and people from all over the kingdom. They bring captives to sell, pieces of chamois, many buffalo skins, and, out of plunder they have obtained elsewhere, horses, muskets, shotguns, munitions, knives, meat, and various other things. Money is not current at these fairs, but exchange of one thing for another, and so these people get provisions.[11]

Unfortunately, the fairs often had subsequently unhappy endings as citizens found that horses they had purchased at the fair might be stolen several days later. Tamarón was warned: "The character of these Comanches is such that while they are peacefully trading in Taos, others of their nation make warlike attacks on some distant pueblo. And the ones who are at peace, engaged in trade, are accustomed to say to the governor, 'Don't be too trusting. Remember, there are rogues among us, just as there are among you. Hang any of them you can.'"[12] An extended description of a subsequent attack then followed.

Fray José Benito Pereyro, in an addendum to an inventory of 1815, claimed credit for the decoration and repair of the church, which ranged from a new "baptismal font and blue satin dress for the Holy Virgin" to a niche and image of Jesus. To the religious structures he added "a porter's lodge, kitchen, four doors, two windows, a balcony," a cloister, and a storage room. Three years later when Bishop Guevara visited New Mexico, he was impressed neither by Pereyro's energy nor his accomplishments and even less by his maintenance of the mission enterprise, both sacral and secular.[13] Taos became one more bit of evidence against continuing the Franciscan presence in New Mexico.

With stability gradually increasing, settlement in the valley expanded cautiously. A license to construct Nuestra Señora de Guadalupe at Fernandez de Taos was granted in 1801. The church was ministered by the priest at Taos pueblo until 1833, when its status as a parish church and the administrative center for the Taos valley was confirmed.[14]

By 1846 a new set of conflicts had arisen, this time between the Hispanic citizens and the new government of the United States territory of New Mexico. Kearny had occupied the province, taking possession for the United States, after which he continued westward to perform a similar duty in California. In his wake he left a new government in Santa Fe, with Charles Bent, from the Taos area, as the interim governor. There was sufficient antagonism against the Anglo government in the district to form the beginnings of a threatening insurrection, a group augmented by anti-Anglo sentiments from Taos pueblo. Bent died at the hands of the insurrectionists, who also killed several friends of the new government—no doubt regarded as traitors—and all the Americans in the nearby settlement of Arroyo Hondo.

Word of this substantial Mexican and Indian force reached Santa Fe, where Colonel Sterling Price, who had been left in charge of the territory, found himself in an awkward and somewhat dangerous position. Price was able to muster about three hundred troops, which marched north for battle. The rebellion had to be stopped before it appeared to be a winning proposition since those marginally allied to the Americans might join the rebellious faction. The first fight took place near Santa Cruz; the insurrectionists were forced back to Embudo and then to Taos, where they barricaded themselves in the mission church. By this time Captain John H. K. Burgwin's troops had augmented the tired American forces from Albuquerque, and Price continued the battle.

The first round of attacks proved fruitless as musket shots, and even cannon and howitzer fire, were absorbed by the church's thick walls with little more than a dull thud. The walls, three to seven feet thick, were seemingly impenetrable. Price retired his forces for some much-needed rest. The attack commenced with renewed vigor the following morning. This time the Americans were able to approach certain parts of the church that were blind to those within and began to chop away at the walls with axes. At the same time ladders were made, allowing the assailants to set the roof on fire from above. In Price's words, "In the meantime, small holes had been cut in the western wall, and shells were thrown in by hand, doing good execution."[15] The insurrectionists, undaunted, kept firing, perhaps as much in desperation as dedication, while the cannon widened the breaches that the axes had commenced. In time the holes became openings, and amid the smoke that filled the church from the smoldering wooden superstructure, the American forces stormed the building and took the insurrectionists captive. So ended the battle of Taos pueblo and the Mexican insurrection of 1847; and so ended the mission church of San Jerónimo.

Today erosion has continued what the axes and

201

16–4

16–5

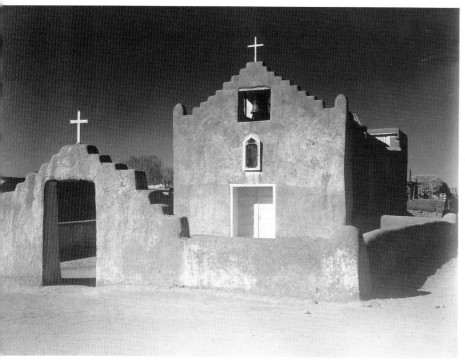

16–4
SAN JERÓNIMO
circa 1885
The church appears more typical of small village churches than the structure does today.
[George E. Mellen, Museum of New Mexico]

16–5
SAN JERÓNIMO
1939
Throughout the 1930s the church retained its flat facade, although a stepped pediment retained the look of the late nineteenth century.
[New Mexico Tourism and Travel Division]

16–6
SAN JERÓNIMO
circa 1935
The bell arch has been recast as a wooden turret.
[T. Harmon Parkhurst, Museum of New Mexico]

16–6

16–7

16–7
SAN JERÓNIMO
Seen today from the northeast, San
Jerónimo appears longer and lower
despite its painted striping in orange/
brown and white.
[1981]

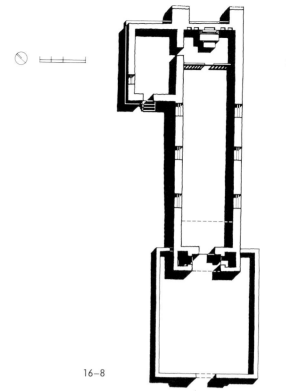

cannon began; only the melted remains of a single tower and some fragments of the nave wall remain. These demark a cemetery dotted with scores of wooden crosses with simple descriptions. Today, too, there is a new church of San Jerónimo located to the south and east, fronting the plaza south of the north tenement block.

The church was constructed some time after the 1847 destruction of the preceding church. The earliest photo of the current structure dates from about 1885 and illustrates a church rather different in form from that seen today. It is a far simpler structure, at least in its facade; it is plain, with slight shoulders that would acquire a distinct profile in the 1930s and suggest those of the nearby Picuris church of San Lorenzo. By 1900 the upper part of the facade had disappeared, leaving the bell suspended from a wooden beam. The layout of the recent church is familiar, with a single nave and a stepped profile that indicate the existence of a transverse clerestory. Two wooden posts support the choir loft over the entry. Corbels set into the adobe shoulder the round vigas.

The windows that line both walls have slight Gothic flourishes that suggest a rebuilding as early as the late nineteenth century, when Neo-Gothic elements began to affect the ecclesiastical architecture of New Mexico. Nevertheless, the modifications do not appear in photographs from the 1930s, suggesting that these revisions might have been part of building programs in the late 1950s or early 1960s. Somewhere around 1920 a single turret with a wooden cap appeared, similar to the protective devices used at Ranchos de Taos at the lower end of the valley. In photographs from the 1940s a plain facade remains on the church, and only in photos taken after 1962, or by 1962, do the twin towers found today appear. The tower scheme found its prototypes at nearby Las Trampas and in pueblos such as Santo Domingo and San Felipe. The colors of the walls, however, and their striped arrangement bear no relation to any other pueblo church structure—perhaps these are used to suggest the presence of bays in the building's form, breaking up the long thrust of the low nave.

The walled campo santo with its single cross is paved with flagstones, but some graves within the nave are still visible. The church now occupies a more prominent position in the community; no longer relegated to the back of the pueblo, San Jerónimo is now part of the main plaza. In scale, however, the building remains a subsidiary to the community, and the ambiguous position of the earliest missions is still reflected in San Jerónimo's form and siting.

16–8

16–9

16–8
SAN JERÓNIMO, PLAN
[Source: National Park Service Remote Sensing, 1979]

16–9
SAN JERÓNIMO
The church from the southwest, with the sacred mountains beyond.
[1981]

SOUTH OF SANTA FE

PECOS PUEBLO

NUESTRA SEÑORA DE
LOS ANGELES DE PORCIÚNCULA

1598?; after 1629; c. 1696; c. 1717

In 1838 the last dejected inhabitants of Pecos pueblo left their homeland forever. This remnant of a once-thriving community sought asylum with their linguistically related kin at Jemez. As a last act of devotion they deposited the sacred image of San Antonio that had graced the wall of their church with the European town nearby, instructing the new caretakers to maintain the image with appropriate care and dignity. (Each year a festival would renew the contract between the Pecos survivors and their patron saint.) So closed a long and full chapter in the history of New Mexico Indian and Hispanic relations.

A rare exception to the hundreds of miles of arid plains lying east of the Rio Grande was the Pecos River drainage. As the last outpost, the hinge between settlement and desolation, the river had supported habitation in the form of a series of Indian pueblos and later European settlements. The largest among them was the thriving Pecos cluster, which at the time of the Spanish contact was estimated at a population of about two thousand souls. During the Archaic Period (from 5500 B.C. to A.D. 700–800) the settlement was characterized by a small population living in pit houses but already engaged in agriculture.[1] After the year 900, however, no record remains of inhabitation for the next two to four centuries. Typically the architecture developed from partially subterranean to fully aboveground structures, first built in a puddled mud technique but by 1300 constructed almost entirely of sandstone from the vicinity. All the villages except Cicuye were abandoned by 1450, its population concentrated in structures stacked up to five stories in height.[2]

The village's position on the edge of Pueblo culture guaranteed an intermediary role to Pecos, in which they traded cotton stuffs, pottery, belts, and food for buffalo products, beads, and leatherwork. In time the Pecos Indians also served as the intermediary between the Plains Indians and the Spanish, as did Taos to the north and Gran Quivira to the south. As usual, the recorded story begins with Coronado's party, which moving eastward in search of riches reached Pecos in May 1540. The Spanish camped there in late April or early May on their way east to the "country of the cows" (buffalo).[3]

Coronado's chronicler, Pedro de Casteñeda, noted the configuration of the pueblo: "Cicuye is a pueblo of nearly 500 warriors, who are feared throughout the country. It is square, situated with a large court or yard in the middle containing the estufas. The houses are all alike, four stories high. . . . The village is enclosed by a low wall of stone."[4] The setting was superb: a low ridge within the valley allowed

17–1

17–2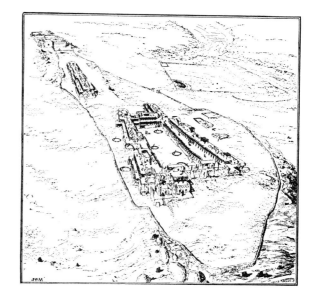

17–1
PECOS
Mission and pueblo ruins from the
southwest.
[Fred Mang, Jr., National Park Service,
no date]

17–2
PECOS PUEBLO
Restoration of the Pecos settlement
about 1700 by S. P. Moorhead. The
mission and convento are in the
upper left.
[Courtesy of the R. S. Peabody
Museum]

a clear view of the surrounding land. A spring within the pueblo's walls provided the water, as did a second spring to the east and Glorieta Creek.[5] The Pecos River helped irrigate the crops, including the cotton used for weaving. On January 1, 1591, Gaspar Castaño de Sosa, in full battle dress, took Pecos and noted in his *Memoria* that the village possessed sufficient firewood and building timber to allow each family to build more or less at will.[6]

Pecos was established in 1598 as the headquarters of the eastern division, and a church was built.[7] Kessell noted that "if even the structure was used, it must have been only briefly." It was built about a thousand feet northeast of the pueblo and measured twenty feet by thirty feet; it was built of stone, plastered inside and out, and faced south. Given the limited space available for construction on the narrow mesilla, there was no convento.[8] The threat of an Indian uprising forced the friar to leave, and the church was subsequently razed. Only in 1616 were friars once again dispatched to the pueblo.

During that year a Franciscan was assigned once again to Pecos, and a sanctuary, Nuestra Señora de los Angeles (Our Lady of the Angels), was constructed or rebuilt. Although the structure might have been scanty, with the priest still living somewhere within the south part of the pueblo itself, a dedication took place on August 2, 1617 or 1618, the feast day of the patron saint.[9] The second church arose on a site two hundred feet south of the pueblo structure, attempting to minimize its vulnerability to potential raiders. Fray Pedro de Ortega is credited with initiating the works, and by the early 1620s enough of a convento had been completed to provide him with lodging.

The uneven site required considerable fill to level its floor, similar to those problems at San Ysidro at Gran Quivira or San José de Giusewa at Jemez Springs. Its foundations, however, lay on solid bedrock. Construction continued during the jurisdiction of Fray Andrés Juárez, although how much he accomplished has been difficult to ascertain. Juárez, who had entered New Mexico in 1612 and had stayed at Santo Domingo before his assignment to Pecos, wrote to the viceroy on October 2, 1622, that

> a temple is being built in this pueblo de los Pecos de Nuestra Señora de los Angeles because it has no place to say Mass except for a jacal in which not half of the people will fit, there being two thousand souls or a few less. And then, God willing, it will be finished with his help next year. Therefore I beg Your Excellency, for the love of our Lord, please order that an altarpiece featuring the Blessed Virgin of the Angels, advocate of the pueblo, be given, as well as a

Child Jesus to place above the chapel which was built for that purpose.[10]

He continued with comments on trade between Spanish and Indian groups, noting that "many times when they come they will enter the church and when they see there the retablo and the rest there is, the Lord will enlighten them so that they want to be baptised and converted to Our Holy Catholic Faith. And in all the good that results from the altarpiece Your Excellency will share."[11] Clearly the intention behind construction of a significant edifice was not only to glorify the Lord but also to serve as a propaganda device for the divine work.

Although the claim to a church large enough to hold the whole pueblo of nearly 2,000 could have included the use of an atrio, this second church still commanded respect.[12] Benavides, visiting the territory from 1625 to 1629 to inspect the missions and encourage their development, termed Nuestra Señora de los Angeles de Porciúncula "a convent and church of peculiar construction and beauty, very spacious."[13] Alden Hayes recorded its dimensions as 133 feet long by 40 feet wide at the east entrance, about 45 feet high (almost two times the height of what is seen today), with walls up to 10 feet thick.[14] Agustín de Vetancurt called it a "magnificent temple . . . adorned with six towers, three on each side," with walls so thick "services were held in their recesses."[15] The quality of its woodwork— Pecos was noted for its fine Indian carpenters— matched the scale of the enterprise. A two-storied convento abutted the church to the west, the priest dwelling in the upper story. As the seventeenth century came to a close the mission at Pecos stood firmly established, with its structure a physical statement of the presence and importance of the church.

If Indian-religious relations appeared to be relatively stable, those between the civil authorities and the church remained volatile. Colonists usually came to New Mexico with the intention to gain. "The governor had to buy his position and neither he nor his men were paid by the Crown."[16] Obviously this prompted exploitation—either of the land or its inhabitants—to extract financial reward. Under the jurisdiction of governors like Luis de Rosas (governed 1637–1641), the situation became intolerable. Rosas was a harsh man, demanding quantities of blankets from the Pueblos and forcing Christian pueblos to work with the detested Apache and Ute under intolerable conditions. He traded knives for buffalo hides and meat with the Apache and engaged in a campaign of exploration and lucrative commerce.[17] Although an extreme example, his term of office was indicative of the typical pattern, which forced the missionary to act at times as a powerless intermediary. This pattern did little to aid evangelical efforts among the Indians. Yet an inventory, probably of 1641, stated that the mission "has a very good church, provision for public worship, organ, and choir. There are 1,189 souls under its administration."[18]

As was the case in most of the missions, the Pueblo Rebellion of 1680 brought the first chapter of its history to a close and inaugurated the second. The insurrectionists ignited piles of juniper and piñon, setting the roof of the church afire. The clerestory now served as a chimney vent, sucking in air and expelling ashes out the door.[19] Walls were pulled down, and the facade tumbled into the nave, covering the ashes of the pyre. The work of more than six decades lay buried by adobe.

With the Reconquest, plans were made to reestablish the missionary presence at Pecos and to restore or rebuild the fallen structure. Within a year Vargas turned his attention to these matters and wrote the viceroy, although his primary interests were military and strategic as well as evangelical. "At the pueblo of the Pecos, a distance of eight leagues from Santa Fe, 50 families could be settled, because it too [like Taos] is an Apache frontier and, being so surrounded by very mountainous country, suffers unavoidable ambush. Settled in this manner, and backed by the military of the villa, it will prevent the robberies and murder that follow from assured entry. It is very fertile land which responds with great abundance to all kinds of crops planted."[20] By the following year a (rebuilt) church stood on the site, but curiously it was reconstructed adjacent to the nave of the earlier structure. Utilizing the remnants of the north wall of the old convento but reversing the orientation, it measured about twenty feet by sixty to seventy feet. The structure was hastily built under the direction of Fray Diego de Zeinos, who stayed about a year at the pueblo but was ultimately removed to ease tension after accidentally shooting an Indian.[21]

Vargas visited the site in the fall of 1694 and was assured that the pueblo "would build their church in order that divine worship might be celebrated in greater decency than at present. They have provided for the construction of a chapel which they provided by showing me the beams for to roof it. . . . They had rebuilt for [the reverend] its very ample and decent convento and residence."[22] Improvements continued as part of the process of use and construction. Vargas recorded in November 1696 that they had "added to the body of the church by increasing the height of the clear story [sic], and to

the sanctuary by adding two steps to the main altar, and had walled in the sacristy and had closed the portion at the entrance to the convento with a wall."[23] Even though the walls and roof were improved periodically, the process of deterioration by the elements subverted efforts to maintain the church.

By 1705 Fray José de Arranegui had undertaken the building of a new structure, although he continued to use the makeshift chapel built on the ruins of the prerebellion church. In 1706 Fray Juan Álvarez reported that construction was under way.[24] Kessell cautioned, however, that Alvarez made a similar claim for fifteen other pueblos including Acoma, where the pre-1680 church still stood, and he may actually have been noting substantial repairs rather than truly new construction.[25] This was to be the fourth and last church at Pecos pueblo, three times the size of the Zeinos structure but not as large as the Juárez sanctuary. Thus, the last effort fit within the walls of the second church, although it maintained its reversed orientation to the west. Two bell towers flanked the main door and formed a shallow narthex. A clerestory illuminated the nave, augmented by one window high on the north wall and three facing south overlooking the convento. Construction was probably complete by 1787. The old convento was still habitable and retained more or less the same form, although probably with a nominal degree of repairs and upgrading. The raggedly profiled mound of red adobe that one sees today is primarily the ruin of this church.

The remainder of the Pecos ecclesiastical story is one of dissolution and decay. Although the pueblo occupies an excellent site within the valley, its vulnerability to Apache attack increased as the population declined. In 1694 there were 736 inhabitants, but smallpox epidemics in 1738 and 1748 reduced the population to one-fourth of that figure. Yet there were still moments of glory among those of depression, moments of pride within the confines of the vows of poverty. Fray Juan Miguel Menchero recorded in 1744 that "the construction was done through the industry and care of the Father of the mission without having spent even a half-real of His Majesty's funds." The church, he said, was "beautiful and capacious."[26]

Bishop Tamarón visited the church, but he left no specific comments or criticism; he was, however, troubled by the problems in communications between clergy and congregation. "Here the failure of the Indians to confess except at the point of death is more noticeable, because they do not know the Spanish language and the missionaries do not know those of the Indians." Perhaps this was by choice.

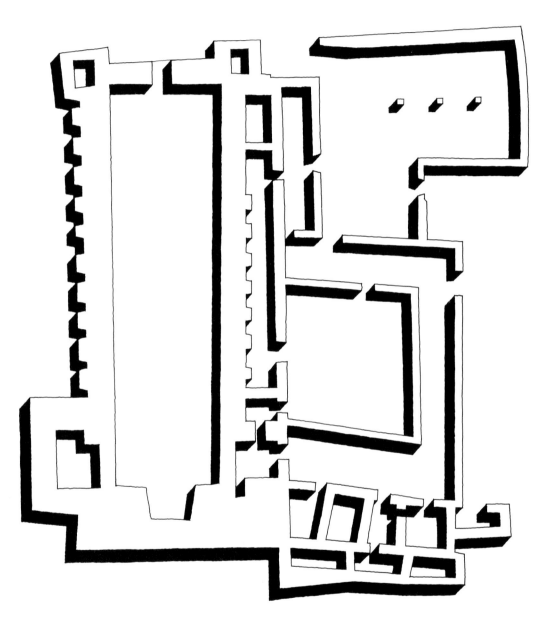

0 4 8 16

17–3

17–3
NUESTRA SEÑORA DE LOS ANGELES,
PLAN OF THE SEVENTEENTH-CENTURY
CHURCH AND CONVENTO
[Source: Hayes, *The Four Churches*]

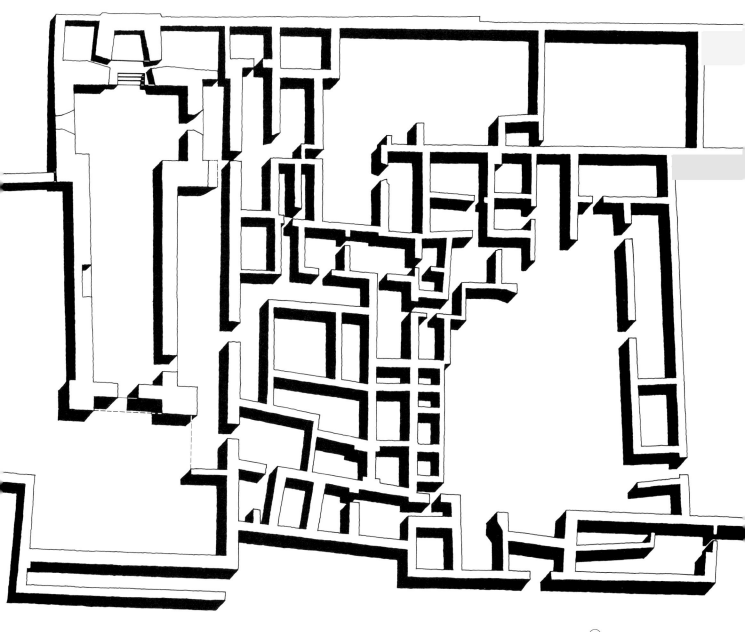

17–4
NUESTRA SEÑORA DE LOS ANGELES,
PLAN OF THE EIGHTEENTH-CENTURY
CHURCH AND CONVENTO
[Source: Hayes, *The Four Churches*]

17–4

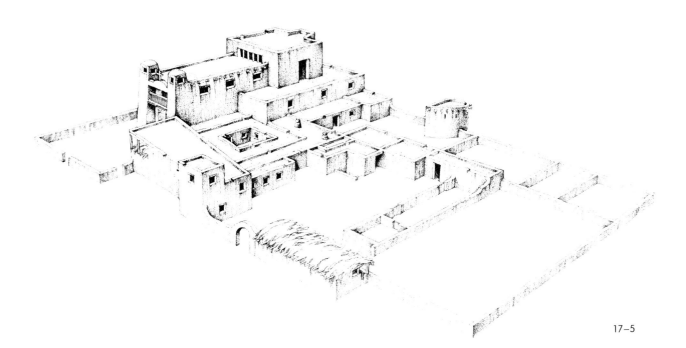

17–5

17–5
NUESTRA SEÑORA DE LOS ANGELES,
HYPOTHETICAL RESTORATION OF THE
EIGHTEENTH-CENTURY CHURCH AND
CONVENTO
[Lawrence Ormsby]

17–6
NUESTRA SEÑORA DE LOS ANGELES
The massive ruins of the eighteenth-
century church fit within the crenellated
footprint of the towers that buttressed
its predecessor, the post–Pueblo Revolt
structure.
[1981]

17–7
NUESTRA SEÑORA DE LOS ANGELES
Lithographic view of the mission ruin in
1846.
[From Calvin, *Lieutenant Emory Reports*]

"In trade and temporal business where profit is involved, the Indians and Spaniards of New Mexico understand one another completely. In such matters they are knowing and avaricious. This does not extend to the spiritual realm, with regard to which they display great tepidity and indifference." [27]

At the time of the 1776 Domínguez visit both the newer structure and the remains of the older one still stood.

> As we enter the [newer] church, on our right under the choir is the entrance to an old church outside the wall. The old building extends to the south, with the door where I said, and is joined to the convent on the Epistle side. And in order not to become involved, I state now that it is a size to fit in the nave of the one we are describing and that it is falling down. As we enter this old church, outside its wall on the left is the sacristy now in use, and the baptistry now in use is on the right, also outside the walls, and the entrance to both rooms is from the old building. [28]

Domínguez found at least two aspects of the complex worthy of comment: "All the beams in the roof are well wrought and corbeled," and the "two beautiful stables, each with a straw loft that was a part of the convento structure." [29]

De Morfi's 1782 description testified to the continuing demise of the community:

> In 1707 it had about 1,000 souls. In 1744, 125 families, in 1765, 178 . . . families, with 344 persons. Today 84 inhabit it. It suffered such a considerable decline, being the frontier for enemies who with pretext of peace frequented it and took the opportunity to wreak havoc.
>
> It has a capacious and beautiful church and a convent where two religions lived previously; today there is only one. [30]

The pueblo continued its downward spiral. Disease and raids took their respective tolls, and there was little chance of reversing the process of dissolution. After 1782 Pecos suffered the reduced status of a visita of Santa Fe and, in 1820, of San Miguel del Bado. [31] At the turn of the century "land-poor" Spanish settlers were admitted to the pueblo lands, and the independence of the village as an entity was completely undermined. By 1820 the imbalance was already apparent: the census listed 58 Pecos Indians and 735 Spanish settlers. The last entry in the church's book was recorded in 1829. Nine years later the remaining 17 to 20 Pecos Indians left for Jemez, with the Hispanic settlers agreeing to celebrate the Feast of Nuestra Señora de los Angeles each August 2. [32] This, then, was the final end of the village that Benavides had noted "of Jemez nation and languages . . . 2,000 Indians and a very fine mission." [33]

17–6

17–7

17–8

17–9

17–8
NUESTRA SEÑORA DE LOS ANGELES
Excavation and stabilization of the
church ruins in December 1940.
[W. J. Mead, Museum of New Mexico]

17–9
NUESTRA SEÑORA DE LOS ANGELES
The chancel of the eighteenth-century
church with an adobe arch, a rare
building element in New Mexico.
[1981]

Pecos today is an impressive monument, even in pieces [Plate 6]. On the narrow mesilla are the ruins of the pueblo itself, excavated by Alfred Vincent Kidder from 1915 to 1925 in the summers; these excavations figured prominently in the formulation of southwestern archaeology. Kidder believed the cellular configuration of the structure, clustered around a plaza, to be indicative of a preconceived plan built for defense. The southern group remains unexcavated but is visible as a mound between the church and the visitor center.

Today the remains of both the postrebellion church and the final, fourth church are discernible. Of the two, the younger structure is the more dominant. The western part of its construction is completely eroded, although the considerable bulk of the apse end remains. Constructed of adobe stacked to a thickness of almost six feet, the nave is articulated into two shallow transepts and steps up into the chancel, which once contained the altar. Behind the altar in the north wall is one of the rare remaining instances of the arch in New Mexico.

Like its predecessor, the fourth church boasted two towers and a balcony spanning the entrance. The structure lasted well into the nineteenth century. Emory made a record of Pecos in 1847 on his expedition for the U.S. Army, and at that time the church, although deteriorated, still bore vestiges of its earlier form. Like Domínguez, Emory was impressed by the woodwork.

> Here burned, until within seven years, the eternal fires of Montezuma, and the remains of the architecture exhibit, in a prominent manner, the engraftment of the Catholic Church upon the ancient religion of the country. At the end of the short spur forming the terminus of the promontory are the remains of the "estuffa", with all parts distinct, at the other are the remains of the Catholic church, both showing the distinctive marks and emblems of the two religions. The fires from the "estuffa" burned and sent their incense through the same altars from which was preached the doctrine of Christ. Two religions so utterly different in theory, are here, as in all Mexico, blended in harmonious practice until about a century since, when the town was sacked by a band of Indians. . . .
>
> The remains of the modern church with its crosses, its cells, its dark mysterious corners and niches, differ but little from those of the present day in New Mexico. The architecture of the Indian portion of the ruins presents peculiarities worthy of notice.
>
> Both are constructed of the same materials; the walls of sun-dried brick, the rafters of well-hewn timber, which could never have been hewn by the miserable little axes now used by the Mexicans, which

resemble, in shape and size, the wedges used by our farmers for splitting rails. The cornices and drops of the architecture in the modern church are elaborately carved with a knife.[34]

Two diagonal braces reinforced the balcony span, eliminating the need for central columns like those seen in early photographs of Cochiti and Zuñi. But the abandoned structure suffered under the forces of nature and the neighbors.

Hewett reported that as late as 1858 the roof still remained in place.[35] A widowed Mrs. Kozlowski told Adolph Bandelier that her husband had removed the timbers and used them to build or roof structures (outhouses) on his property. Bandelier visited the site in 1880 and wrote of it, "The ruins first strike his [the tourist's] view: the red walls of the church stand boldly out on the barren *mesilla*, and to the north of it there are two low brown ridges, the remnants of the Indian houses."[36]

In 1915 a significant chapter in New World archaeology was inaugurated with the beginning of excavation at Pecos by Alfred Vincent Kidder, who was followed by Jesse L. Nusbaum of the Museum of New Mexico. The site was registered as a state monument in 1935, and in 1965 it was elevated to National Monument status, administered by the National Park Service. The area of the monument was further increased in the 1970s with the donation of additional land.[37] A new interpretive center was added early in the 1980s.

The imposing red mass of the church dominates the site and the valley—an earthen lump that can be seen from miles away. Visiting the site, one will see not only the church and convento ruins and the pueblo structure but also the stabilized foundations of the second church, easily ascertained by its dentilated profile—the foundation of the "six towers" cited by Vetancurt. On the narrow mesilla at Pecos, one derives a clear picture not only of the sequencing of the four structures that occupied the land over a period of two centuries, but also of the relationship of the church to the pueblo. At first the church was separate from the pueblo; later, perhaps for defense, the church was closer or even abutting the village; but it was always a distinct entity that relied primarily on the topography of the ridge for its sense of connection.

COCHITI PUEBLO

SAN BUENAVENTURA

pre-1637; c. 1706; c. 1900; 1960s

At the bottom of the basalt flow that extends southward from Santa Fe, where the Rio Grande cuts deep into the terrain, lies the pueblo of Cochiti. Always aware of the surrounding mesas, today the community is further dwarfed by the great earthen dam that has transformed the Rio Grande behind it into a shallow lake. But the river squeezes through the sluices and then comfortably flows once again through the cottonwoods and shrubs that surround the pueblo. Earle Forrest described Cochiti in 1929 as a nearly perfect pueblo: "Cochiti contains everything that goes to make an interesting pueblo; an ancient catholic mission in charge of a priest from Peña Blanca, two large kivas where members of the Turquoise and Calabash clans still strive to keep alive the religion of their fathers in spite of the fact that most of these indians are catholic, and a picturesque plaza in the center of the village."[1] The scene, alas, is not as perfect today, nor is there a marked consistency to the buildings of the village.

The pueblo, as the northernmost of the Keresan group, claims its origins in the Tyuonyi and Frijoles canyons, where the early dwellings were enlargements of natural caves dug in the soft tufa stone (now part of Bandelier National Monument). Subsequent settlement was invested in two or three separate locations before the group eventually split in two, forming the pueblos now known as San Felipe and Cochiti. Other linguistically related Keres speakers include Santo Domingo, Zia, Santa Ana, and the western pueblos of Acoma and Laguna. Bandelier claimed that Cochiti was one of the group of eight Keresan pueblos named by Pedro de Casteñeda, the chronicler of the Coronado expedition.[2] In the fall of 1581 the Chamuscado-Rodríguez expedition was supposed to have reached the pueblo, described as having 230 houses of two and three stories and named Medina de la Torre.[3] The following year the Espejo expedition also stopped at Cochiti and described the people as being "very peaceful." They provided the Spaniards with foodstuffs such as turkey and maize and traded skins for iron goods.

The date of the mission's founding is not known, but Forrest assumed it to be early in the 1600s, the same as the nearby Nuestra Señora de la Asunción monastery associated with San Felipe Pueblo.[4] Benavides mentioned Cochiti but only as one of three churches and conventos serving the "Queres Nation."[5] Throughout the seventeenth century, Cochití remained a visita of Santo Domingo mission, although in 1637 the presence of a resident friar was noted.[6] In 1642 Cochití was said to "have a church."[7] A 1667 reference was the first to attribute the mis-

18–1

18–2

18–1
SAN BUENAVENTURA
1890s
The balcony stretching between the ex-
tended side walls was sagging noticeably
at the turn of the century.
[Smithsonian Institution, National
Anthropological Archives]

18–2
COCHITI PUEBLO
A portion of the pueblo from the air.
[Dick Kent, 1960s]

sion name to San Buenaventura, who remains the patron saint.

The early church building no doubt followed the prototype for its time and location: thick adobe walls, a single nave, a flat facade with a small arch for a bell, a beamed ceiling, and perhaps a clerestory. Although the pueblo was a "storm center" (as Prince called it) for the great revolt of 1680, no priest died there.[8] Legend has it that warned by an Indian believer, he managed to escape the pueblo. What happened to him thereafter is not known. But if the mission was a visita of Santo Domingo, there might not have been a priest in residence. In 1681 the abortive Spanish attempt to reclaim New Mexico reached Cochiti but found that the pueblo, with the warriors from San Felipe and Santa Domingo, had fled to Horn Mesa, which rises about seven hundred feet above the village. Again in 1693—the Reconquest—the Indians withdrew and fortified an adjacent hilltop but were coerced by the Spanish to peacefully return to their fields and pueblos. The peace did not last. In April 1694 Vargas returned to find the Cochiti people once again entrenched on the mesa top.[9] This time efforts toward peaceful negotiations were unsuccessful. The outcome was that the few Spanish, augmented by forces from the now pacified and allied San Felipe, Santa Ana, and Zia pueblos, stormed the summit and took the battle, large stores of food, and many captives.

The prerebellion church lay in ruins, and Vargas ordered a new church built in place of the old. How much was constructed before the subsequent revolt of 1696 is not recorded, but in 1706 the mission was still, or again, in poor condition. Fray Juan Olvarez reported, "This mission has a broken bell without a clapper. (The Indians took all the clappers away, to make lances and knives.) There is one of the ornaments which his Majesty gave. The vials are a silver one, another of tin plate. The church is being built. This mission has about five hundred and twenty Indians. . . . It is called San Buenaventura de Cochiti."[10]

Whether this meant, as it often did, that the roof was being replaced, or that work from 1694 or post-1696 continued, is not certain. Bishop Tamarón in 1760 left no description of the physical structure, although he had only mixed reactions to the parishioners: "The catechism was put, and the Indians were prepared. They do not confess and are like the rest." There was a priest in residence at the time of Tamarón's visit, and the population stood at 450 persons.[11]

A decade and a half later Domínguez summed up his remarks by calling the interior "very gloomy."

Once again he sought in vain the brilliance of the central Mexican religious interior. "The church is adobe with walls about a vara thick, single-naved, with the outlook and the main door due east."[12] Unlike today's church, the nave continued to the apse with no diminishing of width and did not include a choir loft. A clerestory and two "poor" windows facing south illuminated the interior. "There is a little belfry over (the main door) with a good middle-sized bell that the King gave."[13] "Adjacent to the church on its south side, there is a porter's lodge, which is a very pretty little portico to the east without pillars in front of it because it is very limited. The floor of this little portico is paved with small stones like those mentioned. There are adobe seats around this room, and the door is in the center of the wall."[14]

Rounding out the list of major structures was the corral, often an integral part of the religious complex. Here was kept the friar's stock as well as his means of transportation. "The corral is against the convent on the south, runs from the upper to the lower corner and is about 8 varas wide. It has a rather high adobe wall and a great two-leaved door without a lock to the east. Against the south wall in the corral are stable and strawloft, both very large rooms."[15]

The "very gloomy" church remained in eighteenth-century form until past the turn of the century, when its condition showed signs of grave deterioration. As was often the case, the neglect of the church's maintenance led to major repairs, in turn suggesting a considerable rebuilding or updating in style. Although not the resident priest, Fray Francisco de Hozio wrote to Governor Facundo Melgares in 1819 requesting that the governor aid in securing the services of a certain mason named Madrid who lived near Santa Cruz. "I have arrived here without incident and found this church in a state that caused me much sorrow since with the greatest ease it could have been finished by now. . . . I beg you therefore, by virtue of your authority, to make Madrid come and lay the adobes there are. Indeed I am of the opinion that with two days work it will be to the bed molding."[16]

The content of the letter suggests that the church was unroofed at the time, at least in sections, and that the replacement of the vigas was awaiting the final courses of adobe bricks. It seems curious that with the resources available to the Indians of the pueblo, their long experience with adobe, and the considerable sections of the church walls still remaining that the father felt it necessary to call on a Spanish or mestizo mason from fifty miles away.

18–3

18–3
SAN BUENAVENTURA
circa 1900
The interior of the church with its
raised sanctuary.
[Smithsonian Institution, National
Anthropological Archives]

221

Perhaps there had always been continual reliance on the building skills of the Spanish colonists in the construction of large edifices such as churches. Perhaps the construction was always under the supervision of a builder rather than the missionaries themselves. Or perhaps the Indians were just not interested.

In any event three days later the governor ordered the alcalde of Santa Cruz de la Cañada to send "the mason Madrid under appropriate guard to Cochiti to build up the church, on the basis that he should have done it already."[17] The work apparently was done. Kessell suggested that some major modifications to the building fabric were undertaken at this time: the narrowed chancel, the two towers, the shallow balcony, and the choir loft that had not been in its "usual place" to greet Domínguez.[18]

The remainder of the century passed uneventfully. Nevertheless, when Lieutenant John Bourke visited the church in 1881, he wrote:

The church of [San Buenaventura at] Cochiti [is] very old and dilapidated; the interior is 40 paces long to the foot of the altar by 12 broad. It is built of adobe and whitewashed on the inside—Altar pieces showing signs of age—swallows making their nests in rafters. Ceiling of riven slabs, nearly all badly rotten and those which had been nearest the altar have been replaced by pine planks covered over with Indian pictographs in colors—red, yellow, blue & black. Buffalo. Deer, Horses, Indians, Indians in front of lodges, X [cross] and other symbols. Olla used for holy water font. The cross had fallen from the front of the church and its whole appearance is strongly suggestive of decrepitude and ruin.[19]

Early photos from 1889 and 1900 by Vroman and others show the church in the condition Bourke described. The plaster has eroded, the walls look beaten, and the large beam that supports the balcony on the eastern front groans under the weight of its load. Vroman's interior photo, however, depicts a tranquil world in repose: the interior is empty, there is a bare earthen floor, and the altarpiece, flanked in symmetrical balance by two smaller paintings, fills the sanctuary. The walls, whitewashed and stained with a darker dado, support the tin candle holders Prince claimed originated in Chihuahua. The ceiling of the chancel is painted "grotesquely . . . with geometrical figures in high colors, red and yellow and black, while representations of moons, horses, etc., are interspersed without any apparent design."[20] The soft light that falls on the altar attests to the presence of the clerestory. Although the exterior is sadly deteriorated, the interior seems to be holding its own.

But then in 1900 Austrian Franciscans took custody of the church, and the strong winds of change began to blow. Of course, repairs were necessary, but the forms these repairs took were unduly severe and rather insensitive. No doubt the fathers believed that this was an opportunity not only to repair the church but also to update its style as well. If San Felipe and Santo Domingo were spared the trauma of remodeling, Cochiti, although administered by the same custody at Peña Blanca, suffered the imposition of an imported architectural style. The walls were patched and replastered, and a pitched roof of corrugated metal was erected over the entire church. Topping it in good Anglo fashion was a steeple some twenty feet high. At the front a portico of three arches replaced the open balcony/ narthex—arched forms that would have been more comfortable in California, having been almost non-existent in New Mexico. Photographs from this period portray a building so drastically revised that it would be almost impossible to match it with the form of the preceding structure. Of course, this was no doubt the intention—to create a distance between the "new" church and its predecessor. The steeple, however, caused structural problems. From the beginning its height exaggerated its wind-catching propensity and threatened to seriously crack the walls below. In short order it was lopped off to a truncated stump.

Even at the time of the remodeling in 1910, there must have been some outcry from those beginning to appreciate the rapidly deteriorating Hispanic colonial heritage in New Mexico. They were addressed directly by Father Jerome Hesse, who wrote about the remodeling in 1916 with a great sense of pride and righteousness:

> The appearance of the old, venerable church of the pueblo has been changed completely, to the chagrin of the archeologists, it is true, but to our own great pleasure and satisfaction. Some years ago the mud roof was replaced by a substantial roof of corrugated iron, and last year the interior of the church was renovated and decorated. First of all the bumpy, crooked walls had to be made as even as could be done before plastering; then the damp floor of clay had to make way for a regular wooden floor; moreover, through the inventive genius of our Ven. Brother Fidelis, the rough logs of the ceiling were hidden by a selfmade, cheap but handsome ceiling; finally the interior was tastefully decorated. . . . The whole interior of the church underwent a complete change and assumed a rather modern appearance.[21]

If there was ever a succinct statement of the conflict between Anglo and Indian or Hispanic values, this must be it.

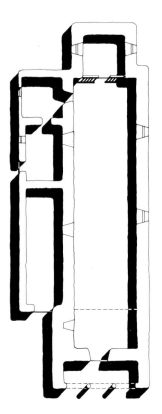

18–4

18–5

18–6

18–4
SAN BUENAVENTURA, PLAN
[Source: Kubler, *The Religious Architecture*]

18–5
SAN BUENAVENTURA
circa 1915
A three-arch porch has replaced the balcony, and the church wears a disproportionately tall steeple.
[Museum of New Mexico]

18–6
SAN BUENAVENTURA
1949
In response to the threat of structural failure, the tall steeple has been trimmed, helping return the building to the earth.
[New Mexico Tourism and Travel Division]

18–7

18–7
SAN BUENAVENTURA
A funeral pauses at the entry to the
campo santo.
[Museum of the American Indian, Heye
Foundation, F. Starr Collection,
1894–1910]

The archaeologists, and most of the writers, however, were *not* happy. In 1918 Paul Walter responded, "The beautiful Cochiti mission church . . . has been unfortunately transformed into a nondescript chapel with a huge tin roof and an arched portal, evidently an attempt to mimic the California mission style."[22] In 1929 Forrest was no kinder.

> The modern destructive spirit which has ruined several of New Mexico's ancient monuments reached out its hand to Cochiti, and a few years ago the exterior of the old edifice was so altered that it looks more like a visitor from some eastern hamlet. This is the only discordant note in an otherwise perfect Indian pueblo. The old flat roof and picturesque Franciscan belfry have been replaced by corrugated iron and a high pointed steeple. The balcony was removed and the entrance was enclosed by an adobe porch with three arches, the only attempt at ornament.[23]

To those extolling the greatness of the missions as they were, the remodeling was a sacrilege. Fray Angelico Chavez, noted authority on the missions, discussed a re-remodeling with pueblo authorities as early as the 1930s,[24] but the actual work waited until the mid-1960s when Santa Fe architect Robert Plettenberg prepared the design of the current structure based on old photographs and descriptions. Certainly the result is happier than the Victorian revisions, although new construction can hardly restore the old quality, which is the product of years. While the facade reasonably approximates the look of the church prior to 1910, elements of the bell arch and beam work are turned comments on the old. The use of a hard cement stucco is another expedient: no covering material for adobe walls produces the same properties as mud plaster, whose deterioration acquires character over time, unlike the sadness of cracked and chipped stucco. The restoration, like the reconstruction at San Ildefonso, is comforting to some extent. Perhaps as time operates on this new building, and it is patched, augmented, and eroded, even in stucco, it, too, will acquire a patina of significance.

Earle Forrest was still moved by the simplicity and the beauty of the Catholic mass at Cochiti on July 14, 1929, at the time of the annual festival:

> During the morning, mass is held in the old mission by a priest from Peña Blanca. The service is typically indian, and when you enter the church you step back across the centuries to the old Spanish days. Kneeling in the nave, which is without seats, the men on one side and the women on the other, are the indian neophytes with bowed heads listening to the black-gowned padre as in the days of old, while an indian choir sings at intervals from the gallery above.[25]

Cochiti today lacks the architectural coherence it possessed historically, even until early in this century when it was described as "the nearly perfect pueblo." The changes in the job market, the construction of federally sponsored detached houses at the periphery of the pueblo, and the impact of recreation and new development spawned by the Cochiti Dam have all taken their toll. But there is still a quality to the place, and to all pueblos, that speaks of a connection with the past and a connection to the earth.

SANTO DOMINGO PUEBLO

SANTO DOMINGO

1607; 1706; 1754?; 1895 (new site)

Many of the pueblos suffered at the hands of the Spanish or other tribes; for the churches destruction was often caused by the depredations of the Comanche or the Apache. The Salinas missions were ravaged by drought and, like many of the villages, by the communicable diseases that accompanied the Europeans. Santo Domingo, in addition to all these other problems, was also plagued by flood.

There have been four settlements in the vicinity of the current pueblo; the first, called Gipuy by Forrest, lay about two miles east of the present Santo Domingo.[1] It was here that Oñate founded the monastery of Nuestra Señora de la Asunción. This was the second pueblo of that name to exist on the site, the first, tradition has it, having been destroyed by the high waters of the Galisteo River prior to 1591. Gaspar Castaño de Sosa rechristened the village Santo Domingo when he stopped there in 1591. Both the pueblo and early efforts to found a Catholic mission there were dashed by floodwaters again in 1605. A new village, almost coincident with today's Santo Domingo, was founded shortly thereafter, moved further eastward as its western edge was lost to the river.

A new church structure arose in 1607 under the direction of Juan de Escalona, and in 1619 Santo Domingo became the ecclesiastical headquarters of the province. Relations between the religious and the Spanish civil and military authorities were not always the best during the early seventeenth century. The church precinct was apparently strengthened to such a degree that the friars were charged with constructing fortifications and storing munitions and other defensive supplies within the convento.[2]

Although Santo Domingo was not specifically named by Benavides, he attributed seven pueblos to the "Queres nation, commencing with its first pueblo, San Felipe. It contained 7,000 souls, 'all baptized,' three convents and churches, very spacious and attractive, in addition to one in each pueblo." He credited Fray Cristóbal de Quirós with conducting training in the Catholic faith but also "in the ways of civilization, such as reading, writing, and singing."[3] By midcentury Santo Domingo was said to have "a very good church . . . a choir, an organ, and many musical instruments; its convento was 'good.'"[4] Almost a century and a half later music was still a notable part of the service.

Indian vengeance struck swiftly during the 1680 Pueblo Revolt, and within two days the three priests at the pueblo were killed. Governor Antonio Otermín and his party of refugees passed through the village on their forced flight south and found the church securely locked. They broke open the fas-

19–1

19–1
SANTO DOMINGO
Seen from the air, the linear organization of the pueblo is clear. The church is in the upper left.
[Dick Kent, 1960s]

tenings and discovered a large mound of earth in the middle of the nave. Subsequent digging uncovered the bodies of the three missionaries buried in their Franciscan robes. But the physical aspects of the structure stood unmolested, and the retreating Spaniards removed the ornaments, vessels, and pictures and carried them to El Paso del Norte.

To what extent the church itself was damaged is not known, but during the attempt to retake the lost province in the following year, one of the soldiers recorded that

> they marched to the pueblo of Santo Domingo where they found things in the same condition as in the others. All the churches had been demolished and burned, and yet in all of them, as had been stated, the Indians' kivas had been built. The apostates had rebuilt the principal stretch of wall (*lienzo*) of Santo Domingo for a fortress and living quarters. The Spanish saw in this pueblo a large number of masks and idolotrous objects.[5]

Perhaps, Kubler queried, the church was rebuilt prior to 1696 and ruined in the incidents of that year; or perhaps the remains of the old structure were extended and refurbished in the construction of 1706.[6] The site of the pueblo was shifted to the current location around 1700. Some time after the arrival of Fray Antonio Zamora in 1740—1754 is a date suggested in one "vague" report—a larger church was constructed at the padre's own expense. "Thus in 1776 Santo Domingo had two churches, side by side facing south, an old one relegated to burials and passage to and from the convento, and a thick-walled newer one, both 'in full view of the Rio de Norte,'" explained John Kessell.[7]

Tamarón visited the mission in 1760 and commented more on the state of the souls than on the condition of the structures. The next reports, these in the usual excruciating detail, were those of Domínguez in 1776. "Father Zamora," he began,

> built it [the church] out of his alms. It is adobe with very thick walls, single-naved, and the outlook and main door are due south. The choir loft is in the usual place and like those of the Rio Arriba missions, and the entrance is an ordinary single leaf door with a key. It is approached by a stairway of small beams between the walls of the two churches mentioned. This begins from the front corners of both and is open toward the cemetery. In the choir there is a good large niche for the musicians, who, at Father Zamora's expense, keep two guitars and three violins there.[8]

There were only rudimentary furnishings for the church. "For further adornment of the good work which I have been describing, Father Zamora had

19–2

19–3

19–4

19–2
SANTO DOMINGO
1880
In this early photograph two churches—
both subsequently destroyed—are visible. Although suffering from erosion,
the bell arch displays an exaggerated
vertical note surpassing that of the old
San Juan church.
[Museum of New Mexico]

19–3
SANTO DOMINGO
1917
Taken away by flood, the new church
has been rebuilt in a safer location and
stands in good condition—neatly
plastered.
[Museum of New Mexico]

19–4
SANTO DOMINGO
circa 1907–1910
The clerestory is oriented toward the
west, receiving the afternoon light.
[Museum of New Mexico]

a small altar screen in perspective painted on the
wall at his own expense. Although it is an ordinary
painting in tempera, it is very pretty and carefully
done. It is in two sections and does not reach the
ceiling."[9] This reredos, which features an image of
the patron Santo Domingo carved in the round,
had been painted by a father named Camargo and
shipped from Mexico.

The plan of the pueblo differed noticeably from
the layout of the other pueblos except, perhaps, for
a weak formal simultaneity to that of Acoma. Instead of the more typical plaza-centered arrangement, Santo Domingo was, and still is, arranged in
roughly parallel linear blocks.

> The pueblo consists of six blocks, or buildings, of
> dwellings. Of these, two stand one after the other
> below the right corner of the new church, and face
> due east overlooking the church and convent to their
> left side on the north and to the south side on their
> right side. The four remaining blocks face due south
> with their backs to the church and convent. They are
> all separate from one another, with a street in the
> form of a cross dividing the four.[10]

There was, however, a plaza in the pueblo: "The
houses have upper and lower stories like those I described at Tesuque, and these are better arranged
than the ones there, with a beautiful plaza overlooked by the last ones mentioned between their
facades and those of the church and convent."[11]

An 1880 plan by Bandelier is reproduced as Figure 51 in Kubler's *The Religious Architecture of New
Mexico* and depicts this arrangement in basically the
same position, although the supposed beauty of the
plaza is difficult to glean from Bandelier's sketch.
The depredations of the Comanche and other
Plains Indians had on rare occasions penetrated as
far as the Rio Grande valley, and so, as at Taos, "the
whole pueblo is surrounded by a rather high adobe
wall with two gates; this is for resistance against the
enemy [Indians], for day by day they show more
daring against the natives of this kingdom."[12] Fray
Juan Agustín de Morfi was warmer in recording the
conditions in 1782: "The church is large and beautiful and attractively decorated and painted. The
house of the priest is roomy and comfortable."[13]

When the American Zebulon Pike was escorted
from Santa Fe to Chihuahua for interrogation, he
had the opportunity to stop at Santo Domingo. He
described his visit in a diary entry dated Friday,
March 5, 1806, and did so in a rather casual tone,
considering the harsh conditions in which he was
traveling: "When we entered it [the church], I was
much astonished to find enclosed in mudbank walls
many rich paintings, and the Saint (Domingo) as

large as life, elegantly ornamented in gold and silver.... We then ascended into the gallery, where the choir are generally placed to procure the charming view frequently mentioned by visitors." [14] An unsigned 1806 inventory stated that the church had "just been repaired, well roofed with boards, the vigas very striking with their corbels and carved decoration." [15]

The church occupied a site nearby the bank of the Rio Grande, that is, northwest of the pueblo. In time the church sat directly on the banks of the river, which continually wore away at the available land. A mission report of 1831 listed floodwaters in 1780, 1823, and 1830 when two unnamed churches were lost. [16] The threat was relatively constant. John Bourke mentioned the heavy rains of the summer in 1881 in several of his journal entries, often adding that repairs to the church were necessary as a result. His sketch of the old Santo Domingo presented the structure much as its successor appears today, except that the gable then sheltered two bells instead of one. [17] In 1881 through 1884 the very existence of the structure and the western part of the pueblo was continually threatened by the river's waters. On each occasion, with levees built to protect the building and a last-minute subsiding of high waters, the church was spared. In 1885 the last grace period expired. *The Santa Fe New Mexican Review* ran a headline in 1885 exclaiming, "The Raging Rio Grande Is About to Take the Church at Santo Domingo." And then it finally happened: on Thursday, June 3, 1886, the river reached the church and began its destructive undermining. First to go was the main new church, then the old one, and finally the convento. Anything that could be removed had been removed, including all mobile ornamentation, paintings, and other furnishings. The earth structure of the buildings succumbed to the turbulent waters and became part of the riverbed or bank or was carried downstream.

Father Noel Dumarest, a young French priest, was assigned the custody of Santo Domingo on January 1, 1895, as part of his ministry at Peña Blanca. Through his prompting a new church was constructed, this time safely *east* of the pueblo on rising ground. It maintained the traditional ground-hugging adobe nave with a twin-towered facade, and although a new structure, it immediately occupied a comfortable position in the community. Given the ravages of Archbishop Lamy's campaigns for putting archdiocese architecture in a more "polite" style, it does indeed seem a wonder that the church was built in the usual manner. "Judging from the improvements upstream at San Juan,"

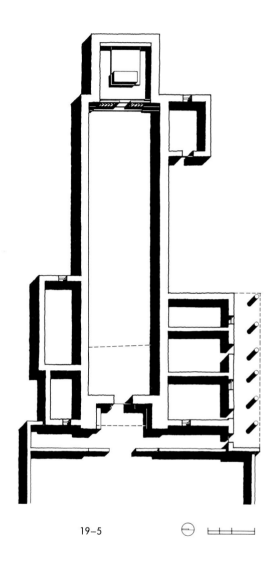

19–5

19–5
SANTO DOMINGO, PLAN
[Sources: National Park Service Remote Sensing; and historical photographs]

John Kessell succinctly put it, "one might have expected the new Santo Domingo church to rise with peaked windows, gabled roof, and slender white steeple."[18] Somehow the building escaped this fate. Perhaps Dumarest was in no bargaining position as to style—he was both too young and too new on the job—or maybe the traditional ways of Santo Domingo pueblo forced continuity rather than innovation.[19]

The church of Santo Domingo is rather small in comparison to, say, San Felipe nearby, but the congregation at the time the building occurred was probably smaller. Domínguez listed the population of the village in 1776 as 136 families with 528 persons,[20] and the population had not drastically changed in the intervening century.

The last church, like its predecessors, is a single-naved structure. The choir loft above the entry to the nave continues a spatial sequence that begins between the towers. Because of the building's orientation to the west, the effect of the functioning clerestory is felt only in the afternoon when the declining sun directs its light on the altar. The windows on the south side of the nave, however, somewhat counteract the effect of the limited clerestory light.

The sanctuary is inset, raised, and articulated, but it is not battered inward as at several other pueblo churches. A lively, three-part altarpiece dominates the front of the church and illustrates the continuing tradition of santos in New Mexico. Free and simple, the colors and painting techniques derive their effect from feeling in gesture rather than sophistication in modeling. The lattice altar rail and several other details, like the frames of the reredos, reflect the Victorian penchant for ornamentation, rather than the simple and direct execution of traditional construction.

On the exterior the principal, western facade is composed of two towers with a balcony between, much in the manner of nearby San Felipe or the rebuilt Cochiti. But unlike the earth tones of most of the church, the western elevation is rendered more emphatic by the use of white and color. Painted decorations exhibiting the same feeling as woven patterns are painted over the white background. The large beams that span the opening (in 1982) are colored in green, white, and red; the geometric designs are intricate and handsome and reinforce the presence of the main doorways. A stepped motif integrates the dado wainscot with the frame around the lower and upper balcony doors. Also on the balcony are the two familiar horses that

Hesse tried in vain to have eradicated with whitewash (see San Felipe).

One enters the church through the enclosed campo santo at the west of the church. Earthen and bare except for a single wooden cross, the enclosed court marks the collective summation of the hundreds of graves on this site or on that land once west of the pueblo reclaimed by the river.

Writing in 1929, Earle Forrest noted that each year at the fiesta on August 4 the church was put in order: "It is cleaned and whitewashed, and two large horses are painted by native artists on the front [of the church]."[21] The annual dance is still held in August, and it has grown into one of the main attractions of the summer season. Several hundred dancers may participate, and a crowd of thousands fills the pueblo. There is a strange mixture of cultural institutions at this time: the Anglo tourist, often in strange garb; the commercial aspects of the fair; the amusement park rides and sno-cones; the presence of the faithful at the church; and, of course, the dancers emerging from the kivas clad in costumes that date back centuries. A curious, sometimes tawdry blend, it directly reflects the juxtaposition, or collision, of the cultures and values from which New Mexico has been fashioned.

SAN FELIPE PUEBLO

SAN FELIPE

1605; 1706 (new site); c. 1801

The earthen architecture of a pueblo looks so resolute and wedded to the site that it is difficult to believe that at some time in the past those buildings might not have been there. The structures read as geometric landforms, while the plaza spaces and alleys recall a slightly more confined and formalized version of the canyons that surround the site. Seen from the elevated bank across the river, San Felipe elicits just this feeling: as if it had always been in just this place, in more or less the same form.

But this is not the case. The pueblo has actually been moved at least twice since the time of the Spanish entrance into the province. In 1540 Coronado passed through this land on his move north and found the pueblo at the foot of Tamita Mesa. Some fifty-one years later Castaño de Sosa stopped at the village and christened it San Felipe, overlying its native Keres name of Katishtya. Apparently there is no translation for the name; Hesse, for one, said he had never been able to discover one.[1]

On Oñate's entry into the territory, the various religious personnel were assigned their posts and duties. Fray Cristóbal de Quiñones was assigned to San Felipe, and it was he who supervised the construction of the pueblo's first church, built in 1605. He died two to four years later and was buried inside the mission.[2]

Benavides described San Felipe only as part of his generalized description of the Keres, saying that it probably contained a joint population of "more than four thousand souls, all baptized" and that it possessed three "very spacious and attractive churches and conventos."[3] Some few decades later San Felipe was specifically credited with "350 souls, a good church and the provision for public worship is very well arranged."[4] Like nearby Santo Domingo, it boasted a choir, an organ, and other musical instruments.

After the Pueblo Revolt and the Spanish retreat to El Paso, the San Felipe church fell victim to the whim and revenge of the natives and the elements. When Vargas reentered the province, he found the pueblo relocated on the top of the adjacent mesa, no doubt for protection against both the predictable return of the Spanish and the other hostile Indian groups. Thereafter, a church was built on this elevated site, a small church of stone measuring twenty by fifty-four feet set in the northeast corner of the plaza. Although down to its foundations, and immediately adjacent to the eroded edge of the mesa, the ruins of the church are still visible in a 1967 aerial photograph.

Either Vargas was successful in goading the inhabitants into coming down from their mesa top to

20-1

20-2

20-1
SAN FELIPE
San Felipe has one of the best-defined
plazas of all the pueblos. The church,
at the lower left, is long and low, its
walled campo santo enclosing a square
courtyard.
[Dick Kent, 1960s]

20-2
SAN FELIPE
The ruins of the early church on the
mesa are still visible in this aerial
photograph.
[Dick Kent, 1960s]

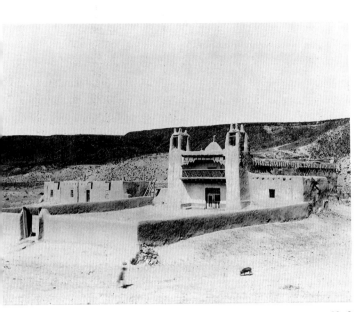

20–3

20–3
SAN FELIPE
1899
A classic example of the two-tower facade type, San Felipe has aged gracefully in this turn-of-the-century view.
[Adam C. Vroman, Museum of New Mexico]

20–4
SAN FELIPE
circa 1935
Exposed to erosion in four sides, the pillars of the towers appear badly worn. Note also the geometric painted ornament around the doors and the carved and overscaled corbels supporting the roof of the balcony.
[T. Harmon Parkhurst, Museum of New Mexico]

20–5
SAN FELIPE
1919
The attenuated length of the nave about which Domínguez commented late in the eighteenth century is apparent when viewed from the flank.
[Museum of New Mexico]

the more manageable lands along the river, or they realized that the probability of attack by other natives had been greatly reduced with the return of the Spanish. In either case there was no longer any need for living in this defensive and inconvenient position distant from water and fields. And so San Felipe pueblo was moved to its present location, somewhat reversing the migration pattern of the Anasazi at Mesa Verde, as they shifted downward from the mesa into the caves.

The pueblo today is formed around a single, highly defined square and slightly concave plaza that orients to the river to the east. Some time shortly after 1700, probably near 1706, a church was built at the new site south of the pueblo, and here it remains.

Fray Juan Álvarez reported in January 1706 that both the pueblo's residential structures and kivas and the new church "are being built, the latter having been moved down from a high mesa."[5] This early structure proved insufficient for the needs of the community, and a larger church was constructed in 1736 through the efforts of Fray Andrés Zeballos. Little attention, however, was paid to the convento in which he lived, adding, in retrospect, greater commitment to his vows of poverty. In 1743 a Franciscan successor, Fray Pedro Montaño, set to remedy the priest's living conditions, which he found deplorable. Montaño prided himself on the results:

> All this [fixing the convento, stables, corrals, all of which were in ruinous condition] I repaired and put in order, raising the walls anew, cleaning out and leveling everything that was uneven and full of sand for the most part, all at a cost of great diligence and care, and labor in order to incline the Indians. I stayed with them in person like a shadow, not even giving them the time to go and eat, so that they might not get away and quit their labor.[6]

Kubler specified that roof repairs directed by Andrés Zeballos were undertaken in 1736 and involved "the use of 84 *canales* or drain spouts, probably signifying a church of some size."[7]

Tamarón passed by in 1760 but offered no description of San Felipe; he seemed intent on getting on to Santo Domingo. Domínguez, however, with his usual thoroughness, left a complete description of the church, convento, and pueblo:

> The church is adobe with thick walls, single-naved, with the outlook and main door to the east. . . . The sanctuary is marked off by four steps made of wrought beams. . . . It is as wide as the nave and as much higher as the clerestory demands. The choir loft is in the usual place and like those of the mis-

20–4

20–5

sions that have them. Its entrance is from the flat roof of the convento. On the right side there are three poor windows with wooden gratings which face south.[8]

There was no covering on the floor: "It was bare earth, its interior dark."[9] There were at the time ninety-five Indian families with 406 persons living in the pueblo.[10]

Shortly after 1801 Fray José Pedro Rubí de Celis assumed the administration of the mission. Writing in 1808, he noted that "the church was rebuilt with its two new towers,"[11] implying that until that time there had been only the planar facade typical of early postrevolt religious building. In 1782 the status of the church was reduced to that of a visita of nearby Santo Domingo. The control of the church was removed from the hands of the Franciscans in 1823 as the missions were secularized by the Mexican government; but on July 9, 1900, the Franciscans returned to the pueblo, serving San Felipe from nearby Peña Blanca.

Father Jerome Hesse left us with a somewhat ironic and amusing incident of life in San Felipe pueblo and the Indian's relation to the church. It tells of Christmas 1912 and poignantly illustrates the amalgam of native and Christian beliefs at this most sacred of holidays. Like the Christmas story of Isleta by Elsie Parsons (see Isleta), the anecdote also illustrates the relationship between architecture and dance, structure and movement, and prayer and belief. Father Jerome wrote, "I entered the church where I found the altar tastefully decorated. Before the altar the Indians had erected a hut of cedar twigs, covered with a roof of straw." (This was similar to structures built outdoors to house a shrine or serve other religious purposes—for example, the structures built each year as part of the dance on August 4 at Santo Domingo pueblo, erected at the head of the principal dance plaza.)

> A dance? in church? before the crib? What a scandal, a desecration, a sacrilege! someone might say. And the benches? Are they removed? Well, there are no benches. . . . The Indians squat on the floor, not even a wood floor, but just Mother Earth. The interior of an Indian church is very bare, at least at San Felipe and Santo Domingo. Four adobe walls, whitewashed within, an adobe roof, generally leaking in places, with an adobe floor: truly not unlike the stable of Bethlehem. A few simple boards nailed together to form an altar, a statue of St. Philip, a few mural paintings to serve as ornaments, and you have a complete Indian church.[12]

If decoration was spare at San Felipe, segments of the church were whitewashed, but whitewashing

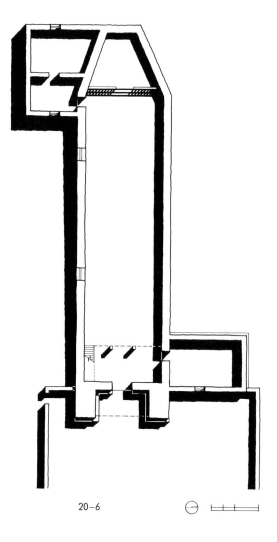

20–6

20–6
SAN FELIPE, PLAN
[Sources: National Park Service Remote Sensing; and historical photos]

was usually restricted to that segment of the principal facade between the towers or to a wainscot on the interior, while the balance of the church remained the color of the earth. A similar practice is still evident at Picuris, where only the facade is painted white, although the balance of the structure is an earthen color. At Laguna the entirety is white, although it was probably not always so. The whiteness makes a lasting impression in the dusty lands of New Mexico as almost every structure, whether made of earth or not, acquires a chromatic layer of dust that joins it to the countryside.

Although the towers were eroding in 1915, Prince was nonetheless impressed by the brilliance of San Felipe and noted its "dazzlingly white appearance"; he also remarked that "it is cared for most faithfully, being whitened every year until it glistens in the bright sunlight."[13] There were other benefits to whitewashing, which Hesse described in a 1920 article. Hesse was troubled by the two horses painted on the upper balcony of the eastern facade, a motif also present at Santo Domingo and occasionally at other churches. "Horses, stationed at the entrance of a church," he reasoned,

> are not very conducive to devotion, so I asked the parishioners to obliterate them through a coat of whitewash. The feast of St. Philip, patron of San Felipe, was near at hand, when, according to "costumbre" (custom) the church is annually whitewashed both inside and outside. The Indians' love for the horse is well known; and "cabellitos" are objects of their superstitious veneration. . . . What happened? The church was simply not whitewashed, for the Indians had no time! Excuses are never wanting to the Indian.[14]

The church of San Felipe is an impressive structure but is more impressive from the flank than from the front. The facades of the Spanish mission churches, other than those of the Salinas district and perhaps Acoma, rarely achieve the scale or proportions necessary for lifting them from their bases. Nor are they integrated into the pueblo in such a way that their increased mass is sufficient to create a striking contrast. In pueblos such as Zia or Laguna, for example, when the pueblo is contemplated as a unit, the church may actually read more strongly from a distance. In these conditions the church, a reflection of native construction method, becomes a part of the architecture of the pueblo, however different the form.

Height was not the means, nor was span the tool to increase the church's volume, and the heights of postrevolt churches rarely exceeded their widths. Length was the sole variable, and with it the church

size, determined by the number of the congregation. San Felipe is nearly one hundred twenty feet long, an exceptional dimension for an architectural method that historically had produced living spaces on the order of twelve to fifteen feet square.

As Kessell noted, there are more vigas in place today than at the time of the Domínguez visit, suggesting that the church was extended during the 1801 remodeling, at which time the twin towers were added to the facade.[15] The marvelous photograph taken in August 1919 from the southwest, where the nave is played against the lower convento to the south, illustrates the feel of the long, literally shiplike nave and the characteristic bump of the tapered apse as it rises to accommodate the transverse clerestory. This photo also shows the seriously eroded towers, particularly the pinnacles of the open belfries, which suffered under rain and wind from all four directions. The church was refurbished after 1920, probably on more than one occasion, as it usually appears in good condition in photos.

The images of the horses that troubled Father Jerome still grace the entry facades, although they were missing from a Parkhurst photograph from the 1930s. By that time the convento had all but melted into the landscape, and a small structure (baptistry/sacristy) appended the nave to the north.

With the importation of commercial paints came a greater palette of colors. Today the facade and its wooden brackets are painted in lively hues: turquoise tipped with red. The horses have returned, and the dado and stepped sky altar motif of the wainscot are worked in yellow. Even from the opposite bank of the Rio Grande, the church creates an unmistakable impact.

ZIA PUEBLO

NUESTRA SEÑORA DE LA ASUNCIÓN

1610–1628?; 1693

The mission church of Nuestra Señora de la Asunción at Zia rests on its mesa like a lion in its lair and looks eastward. Like Laguna, the church's golden white form contrasts markedly with the surrounding earthen colors of the pueblo, and also like Laguna, its visual primacy within the pueblo is assured by position and scale. The Espejo expedition reached Zia and found five towns in Cumanes province. Zia was the principal settlement, "having eight plazas or market places, and houses plastered or painted in many colors."[1] The pueblo occupied a site along the Jemez River and was built on the ruins of an earlier village. The houses, unlike those of most other pueblos, integrated basalt rock with the adobe mud, thereby replacing construction of purely adobe brick. The Indians were cautious and kindly to the strangers, at least initially, and provided them with provisions and even cotton *mantas* (blankets).

Under Oñate's pressure, the pueblo swore allegiance to the Spanish crown and the Catholic church at a meeting held at the Santo Domingo pueblo in July 1598. Fray Alonso de Lugo was placed in charge of Zia in 1598, and the first church followed soon thereafter. The convent was first mentioned in July 1613 and was probably founded by Fray Cristóbal de Quirós in 1610. Although the mission of San José de Giusewa maintained its own resident priest until its demise circa 1630, Santa Ana remained a visita of Zia and had been as early as 1614. Benavides mentioned seven churches in the province; Prince assumed that at least three of them must have been Jemez, Santa Ana, and Zia.[2] Then came the revolt of 1680 and the supposed ruin of the church.

In 1687 Governor Domingo de Cruzate, in an abortive attempt to retake New Mexico, attacked the pueblo in what was to be one of the bloodiest battles between the Spanish and the Indians.[3] Even allowing for inflation of numbers, the Indian losses must have been considerable. Cruzate claimed that about six hundred Indians were killed and that the seventy remaining were sentenced to ten years of slavery, "except for a few old men who were shot in the plaza."[4] It is no surprise that the villagers, recalling the horror of those previous few years, submitted peacefully to Vargas and agreed to rebuild the church. A large cross was erected in the main plaza, the stone base of which remains to this day.

When the mission was first established in 1598, it was dedicated to San Pedro and San Pablo. When the church was refounded in 1692, its attribution was changed to Nuestra Señora de la Asunción. Vargas found the church in the normal postrebel-

21–1

21–2

21–1
ZIA PUEBLO
The church and pueblo from the air.
[Dick Kent, 1960s]

21–2
NUESTRA SEÑORA DE LA ASUNCIÓN
1923
From the north the church—low and
heavy—appears almost as a geological
formation.
[Odd Halseth, Museum of New Mexico]

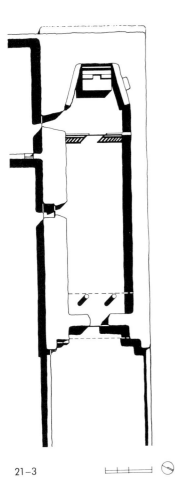

21–3

21–3
NUESTRA SEÑORA DE LA ASUNCIÓN,
PLAN
[Source: Kubler, *The Religious Architecture*]

21–4
NUESTRA SEÑORA DE LA ASUNCIÓN
1923
The unrestored Neo-Gothic altarpiece shines under the roof light.
[Odd Halseth, Museum of New Mexico]

21–5
NUESTRA SEÑORA DE LA ASUNCIÓN
1923
The choir loft (east) end at the time of the 1920s restoration.
[Odd Halseth, Museum of New Mexico]

lion condition: the roof and wooden elements were burned or destroyed, as were portions of the walls. But this symbolic desecration of sacred structures seemed to have satisfied the Indians in almost all instances, and pragmatically inclined, they used the four enclosing walls as corrals or cattle pens.

In the case of the Zia, however, the natives were not occupying the same site at the time of the Reconquest but had shifted some ten miles or so away from the old pueblo. Vargas wrote, "I ordered them to reoccupy their said pueblo, since the walls are strong and in good condition and also the nave and main altar of the church are in good condition, only lacking the wooden parts, which I ordered them to cut at the time of the next moon." Vargas promised them a saw, "so that they would be able to cut the said wood for the church and convent."[5] The church was rebuilt, and in its current form dates from this time to near the end of the seventeenth century.[6] Custos Juan Álvarez noted in 1706 that the church building "is now at a good height,"[7] which suggests that the rebuilding had not proceeded as quickly as Vargas had predicted or that, following the typical cycle, after a few years of neglect the church structure was once again in need of repairs.

John Kessell quoted at length Fray Manuel Bermejo, who, writing in 1750, claimed credit for another major rebuilding effort: "[I worked] personally with the Indians, without the help of said gentlemen [government officials], as I am doing at present on the church that I have begun from the foundation up and on the repair of the convento which was falling in ruins."[8] In all probability this did not extend to the actual reconstruction of the church from the foundations up but constituted only extensive reparation. (If Bermejo was dealing with the adobe erosion known as coving, in which the edge of the structure at the ground was undermined by splashing and undercutting, he would have indeed been working from the ground up.)

In 1760 the weary Bishop Tamarón made no comment on the church, merely saying that Zia "is two long leagues from Santa Ana over dunes and sandy places."[9] The 1750 census showed that there were about five hundred inhabitants in Zia, a considerable decline from its pre-European days of the village with eight plazas. As usual, it was Domínguez who provided the first really detailed description of the church:

> The church is adobe with very thick walls with the door to the east. . . . The sanctuary is marked off by two steps made of wrought beams and from there to the center it measures 6 varas, being as wide as the

nave and as much higher as the clerestory demands. Choir loft like those mentioned before. It has four windows with wooden gratings on the Gospel wall, facing south, and one in the choir. The nave is roofed with forty good corbeled beams, and the clerestory rises along the length of the one facing the sanctuary, whose roof consists of eight beams like the foregoing.[10]

Domínguez credited Fray Francisco Xavier Dávila with the rebuilding of the church. Dávila was in residence at Zia during part of the 1750s and early 1760s and may have been responsible for yet another rebuilding effort.[11]

The convento was meager and basic, as were its furnishings.[12] In 1806 the church and its possessions were inventoried by Fray Mariano José Sánchez Vergara. He specifically noted an altarpiece commissioned in 1798 by Víctor Sandoval and Dona María Manuela and ascribed to the same santero who painted the reredos at Laguna (hence called the Laguna Santero): "This is all that this church possesses, and everything is in need of repair. To do so there are no settlers and funds to tap. Unless some measure is taken for this purpose nothing will improve."[13] Nothing ever improved in the battle against time and the elements, and the particularly annoying problem of the roof parapet meant that the outcome could be a stalemate at best. From the day of its completion, the church began to deteriorate, sometimes at an alarming rate.

Lieutenant Bourke, on the scene in 1881, also included Zia in his rounds. Matter-of-factly he stated, "Front of ruined church of the Virgin. . . . Interior going rapidly to decay. . . . The ceiling is riven pine slabs, and according to Jesus (son of the pueblo governor), is "muy viejo" (very old). The nave measured from the floor of the altar to the main door is 37 paces in length. Earthen ollas [ceramic jugs] are in position as holy water fonts."[14] By this time the church's roof had been lowered and the nave shortened (in comparison to Domínguez's description). The balconied facade might have been the result of rebuilding undertaken at this time.

Bourke was less kindly with his evaluation and verdict: "Interior rapidly going to decay. . . . The wooden figure of the Savior on the Cross must have been intended to convey to the minds of the simple natives the idea that our Lord had been butchered by Apaches. If so, the artist had done his work well."[15] Americans rarely took kindly to Hispanic-Indian imagery, whether to the "barbarity" of the designs at Cochiti that Prince cited or the not-infrequent comments about the "gory dolls" that filled the various altars.

21–4

21–5

Bandelier, in his *Final Report* of 1888, wrote, "The church is large and the outer walls are asserted to be those of the church prior to 1680, the new walls being built inside of them. The appearance justified the presumption of old age. And in his *Journals*, he noted, "The site may be the same but the church is probably a more recent edifice though erected on old foundations."[16] This remains the commonly accepted explanation except that the extent of the prerebellion walling has not been precisely determined. There is a double thickness of wall apparent on the south wall, however. Kessell offered the traditional story that the vigas for the roof had been cut too short.[17] Rather than return to the mountains and recut, rehaul, and reseason the timber, the builders added an additional thickness of wall within the old one, thereby rendering the spans of the vigas sufficiently long.

There was no priest in residence in 1881. From 1890 on Zia was served from Jemez, giving testimony to the fact that the importance and the population of the pueblo had both declined, at least in the eyes of the church.

In the 1890s the church was once again in need of repairs. Photographs taken in the early 1920s, just before restoration, show light coming through the holes in the roof. The Committee for the Preservation and Restoration of New Mexico Mission Churches gave priority to Zia because of its historic importance and its perilous condition. Work began in earnest in 1923 under the direction of Odd S. Halseth of the Museum of New Mexico and artist Jozef G. Bakos, a member of Los Cinco Pintores. Although this sounds curious to us today, artists in and around Taos and Santa Fe were quite interested in (a somewhat romanticized version) of New Mexico's past and were informed as to certain historical aspects of the missions as well. Painters such as Carlos Vierra, who executed a series of paintings of the "restored" missions, became de facto authorities on mission architecture and life, although their knowledge of the churches was limited.

The old roof was removed and three vigas were found to require replacement. Interestingly their ends were creosoted and packed with loose stones to foster the increased passage of air and to facilitate evaporation of excess moisture. A new roof was laid over a two-inch concrete slab, and work was completed in December 1923.[18] During the renovation work a fragment of the Victorian Gothic altar screen was removed, and the old reredoses, attributed to the Laguna Santero, were revealed. "Part of these are primitive French and part Spanish, according to Father Bernard of Jemez."[19] Subsequent investigation by E. Boyd changed the attribution. In the 1930s the old images were "restored," somewhat ineffectually, by Zia artist Andrés Galzán.[20]

Today Zia appears the most solid and substantial of all the missions, its low and long profile and ultra-thick walls the absolute objectification of permanence. The walls are almost six feet thick in places, with corner buttresses adding to their commodity; these walls could support a much larger and higher building. That the ceiling is a mere twenty or so feet high only adds to the impression of density. There is a shallow porch formed by the balcony that extends between the two towers on the eastern facade and the choir loft within. The clerestory still functions, and the original earthen floor remains. East of the church and forming its entrance court is the campo santo. Filled with a single cross and loose earth, it looks as if it has been filled to maintain a level plane. Here the faithful were buried, while persons of higher rank were buried within the nave of the church. Leslie White noted that the density of bodies already interred required disturbance of the old by the new but that this practice did not seem to bother the Indians to any considerable degree.[21] Unlike Isleta, there is no division along a center line continuing from the nave for distinguishing gender.

From a distance Nuestra Señora de la Asunción glows in the sunlight, particularly in the early morning or the late afternoon. The church has been stuccoed with cement plaster with a decidedly golden rust tint to it, making Zia one of the most beautifully colored and textured of those churches that have undergone the questionably beneficial process of hard plastering. Somehow, in spite of the density of its surface, the unavoidable cracks, and the consequent patching, the building radiates confidence and security and promises to occupy its site for another two or three centuries.

21–6

21–7

21–6
NUESTRA SEÑORA DE LA ASUNCIÓN
1899
At the turn of the century, only the
church facade was whitewashed.
[Adam C. Vroman, Museum of New
Mexico]

21–7
NUESTRA SEÑORA DE LA ASUNCIÓN
circa 1917
The figures of the small horses mark the
entrance of the otherwise deteriorating
structure.
[Museum of New Mexico]

JEMEZ SPRINGS

SAN JOSÉ DE GIUSEWA

(c. 1600); 1621–1622; 1625–28;
abandoned c. 1630

The mere bulk of San José de Giusewa set in the hillside, its height, and its commanding proportions evoke the very image of stability, and its presence high on the canyon hillside seems inevitable. Yet missionary efforts on the site lasted hardly two decades, leaving only the piled stonework as a testament to the ambition and hope of its founders.

When an offshoot of the Coronado expedition under the direction of Francisco de Barrio-Nuero ascended the Jemez Mountains in 1541, it came on a community settled in several diverse units. At that time there may have been as many as eleven distinct villages occupying sites along the Jemez River and the canyons to the east roughly centered around what is today called the Jemez Hot Springs. Casteñeda gave the number of pueblos as ten; Espejo, seven; and Oñate, nine.[1] Giusewa means "place of boiling waters" in Towa, a reference to the hot springs found nearby. According to Paul Walter, by 1709 the Jemez Indians had abandoned the Giusewa site and had built their present pueblo further down the canyon.[2] Religious work in the Jemez district was assigned to Fray Alonso de Lugo, who concentrated his efforts in the canyon where the ruins of the church of San José now rest.

Spanish missionary policy required the sedentary residence of the Indians, a policy that in turn demanded the consolidation of scattered villages. In New Mexico this policy was usually unnecessary because the Indians were already resident in sufficiently dense pueblos linked to fields under cultivation. In the Jemez district, however, the missionaries were few (only one in the beginning), and the distances to be traveled between the various pueblos were too great to maintain either rigorous religious or military control. With continued efforts at concentrating settlement, the Spanish were relatively successful in consolidating the indigenous peoples into three pueblos: Astialakwa, Patoqua, and Gyusiwa (Giusewa).[3] Of these, the third was the largest and was thus the center of religious life. Scholes believed that Fray Alonso resided at one of the pueblos, probably Giusewa, and must have erected at least a rudimentary chapel some time around 1600.[4] From 1601 to 1610 the mission probably suffered intermittent abandonment, and Christianization attempts ultimately failed.

Fray Jerónimo de Zárate Salmerón was appointed custos of the New Mexican missions and was assigned to Jemez in 1617, although Scholes dated his arrival no earlier than 1621.[5] Undaunted by the apparent lack of success of his predecessors, Zárate Salmerón claimed that he executed no fewer than 6,566 baptisms in his time there. He no doubt im-

22–1

22–1
SAN JOSÉ DE GIUSEWA
1880
The ruins of the church seen from
across the valley.
[John K. Hillers, Museum of New
Mexico]

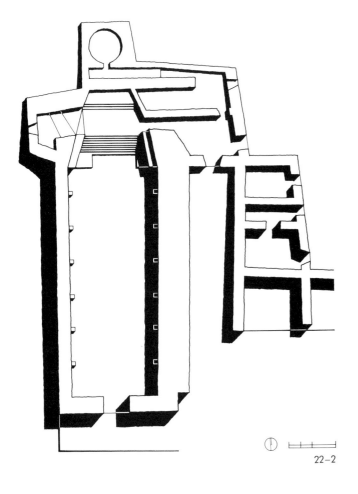

22–2

22–3

proved the condition of the Lugo structure or perhaps began a new church of his own in 1621–1622, with construction completed in 1625–1628.

Zárate Salmerón founded a second congregation called San Diego de la Congregación, another mission, in 1622. One year later the church and its convento were in ruins and the congregation scattered. In spite of his considerable faith, he left the district shortly thereafter because of the unsettled conditions.

The Jemez and the Navajo were traditional enemies, and the presence of the Spanish among the former did little to quell their basic mutual animosity. Fray Martín de Arvide assumed charge of the venture at Jemez in 1628 and reassembled those Indians who had abandoned their reductions. Little is known of his contributions toward mission construction, although Kubler stressed that a church had been built prior to Arvide's arrival.[6] When Benavides visited the area about 1629, he noted that the Jemez people had been "almost depopulated by famine and wars," but he described the church itself (credited to Zárate Salmerón) as sumptuous and beautiful and the convento as interesting.[7] Notwithstanding Benavides's positive and somewhat optimistic description, the institution failed once again and was abandoned sometime shortly after 1630.

There are few references to San José from this period to the 1680 revolt, which has led historians to believe that from 1630 on the newer San Diego became the active congregation and that, as Scholes contended, San José was abandoned sometime between 1632 and 1639. A 1664 copy of a report from 1642 remarked that "the pueblo of Jemez has a splendid church, a good convento, a choir organ, and 1,860 souls under its administration," but this description referred to the new church of San Diego.[8]

The church of San Diego endured. Founded in 1622, it was burned in 1623 and was rebuilt by Martín de Arvide in 1626 or 1628. Fray Juan de Jesús María was fatally shot in the shoulder with an arrow while at the altar and was buried there, but he was later disinterred by Vargas after the Reconquest. "The difficulties with regard to confessions and catechism continue," recorded Tamarón in 1760, but he said nothing of the church itself.[9] Kubler noted a new church built at Jemez in 1856; Bourke recorded "that it had collapsed about ten days ago" in 1881.[10] Presently located in the pueblo of Jemez some few miles downriver, a structure was built in 1919 in a style hardly of the Hispanic tradition.

22–4

22–2
SAN JOSÉ DE GIUSEWA, PLAN
[Source: Kubler, *The Religious Architecture*]

22–3
SAN JOSÉ DE GIUSEWA
The thickened base of the facade strengthens the sense of entry and permanence.
[1981]

22–4
SAN JOSÉ DE GIUSEWA
The floor of the nave was cut into the hillside, with the rubble removed in the process deposited at its lower end.
[1981]

248

22–5

22–6

22–5
SAN JOSÉ DE GIUSEWA
1852
In this mid-nineteenth-century litho-
graph San José is treated romantically,
the ruins and hillsides cut from the same
material.
[From: James Simpson, *Journal*,
Museum of New Mexico]

22–6
SAN JOSÉ DE GIUSEWA
In spite of the cut-and-fill system used
to flatten the slope, the altar (chancel)
end of the church was elevated more
than the usual few steps.
[1981]

The church of San José de Giusewa, even in its fragmented state, provides an excellent picture of the sanctuary at the time of its construction in the early seventeenth century. By New Mexican standards it is an extremely large edifice, measuring some one hundred eleven feet in length and almost thirty-four feet in width. Its somewhat hybrid plan consists of a single nave with a stubby western transept that possibly served as a subsidiary chapel. The canyon is relatively narrow at the church's site (the intersection of a stream and the Jemez River) and provided little available flat land for construction. As a result, part of the nave was dug into the adjacent hillside, while other areas had to be filled. The floor of the church was built in two levels with a space in between filled with ashes and charred wood. This technique was used to absorb any water seeping in through the walls or the floor because excavation into the hillside interrupted the drainage pattern of underground waters moving toward the stream.

The church was built of local sandstone set in an adobe mortar, and its walls were massive: up to six feet thick in places on the west and eight feet on the east. The walls extended five to six feet above the roof level, which suggests that originally a crenellated parapet could have been used for combat from the roof. At the rear of the church an octagonal tower, sometimes interpreted as a chapel, extended about forty-eight feet above the church, with a doorway that gave directly onto the roof. Obviously this church was constructed with an eye as much to the Navajo as to God, continuing a tradition of fortress churches found in Mexico and Old Spain. The roof construction was supported by vigas, and traces have been found of the matting placed above the smaller roof pieces, in turn covered with pine needles and earth to form the final roof surface.

The nave is oriented north-south, directing the principal facade and entry to the south. The hillside is slightly less steep on this side of the canyon, and the exposure to the sun is considerably better, a particularly important feature during the winter months when the surrounding hill cuts off the sunlight early in the day. The presence of the tower and the access to the roof suggest that there was no clerestory, although the evidence is not conclusive. Remaining fragments indicate the presence of a balcony along the front of the church, perhaps also graced by two towers capping the wall, although these were not expressed as buttresses in plan.

The nave is lined with twelve low platforms, twelve by eighteen inches, which are believed to have once served as pedestals for sculpture or light-ing units. The floor is stepped quite drastically in the chancel area, indicating that there have been efforts to minimize excavation. A door in the east connects the nave with the convento. As already noted, flat land on the site was severely limited, and as a result the convento, which included a small chapel, living rooms, kitchen, and sleeping rooms, took a relatively irregular disposition. To the south of the church and forming its forecourt is the burial ground, which once extended almost to the stream.

Although the church was built of stone, its interior was finished with gypsum plaster. Traces of coloring were found during excavation, which indicated that murals had been painted on the base white coat on the interior of the church. These murals were executed al fresco, that is, painted when the plaster was still wet, a technique quite rare in New Mexico. The windows of the church, quite high in the walls, were made of selenite, a micalike rock easily fractured to produce thin translucent panels. A good quantity of fragments of this material was revealed in excavation.

In 1921 two claimants to the property donated the ruins to the School of American Research. In that and the following year a team of archaeologists under the direction of Lansing Bloom excavated the site. From 1935 through 1937 work was continued at Giusewa by the Civilian Conservation Corps. More recent excavation work was performed by the Museum of New Mexico in 1965.

Archaeological investigation of the church has been extensive. Yet only a fraction of the pueblo has been excavated, although it is believed to predate the church by almost three centuries. The site is today owned by the state and administered by the Museum of New Mexico.

ALBUQUERQUE

SAN FELIPE NERI

c. 1706; 1793; 1880s

Albuquerque today displays precious few signs of its original Spanish colonial founding. The city is mostly modern and predominantly postwar modern, as is typical of many Sunbelt cities. Only weak stylistic references or slight vestiges of an adobe tradition or the basically earthen brown color palette of its architecture gives a hint of the villa founded on the banks of the Rio Grande some two and a half centuries ago. Central to that founding was the parish church of San Felipe Neri, although that was not the name of the church when it was first consecrated.

Albuquerque was the third villa to be established in New Mexico, if the first tentative capital of San Gabriel is discounted. Albuquerque's founding directly responded to the domestic needs of the ever-growing number of Spanish settlers trickling into the province after the Reconquest. In the north sixty-six families crowded into the limited confines and agricultural lands in and around Santa Fe, and to meet the problem, Governor Vargas ordered the settlement of "La Villa de Santa Cruz de los Españoles Mejicanos del Rey Nuestro Señor Carlos Segundo" on April 12, 1695. The valley's Indian inhabitants were ordered displaced, and some of the families moved north after the order. (See Santa Cruz.) The founding of the new town helped ease pressure on the capital, yet settlers continued to arrive in the province. Albuquerque, on the other hand, was established to serve settlers already living in the area.

Communication between New Mexico and the mother country was slow, and the authority for gubernatorial appointment rested with the king of Spain on advice from the Council of the Indies. Upon Vargas's death in 1704, as an interim measure the viceroy, duke of Alburquerque, appointed Francisco Cuervo y Valdés as the acting governor. In the principal gesture for which he is remembered, Cuervo y Valdés resettled thirty to thirty-five families on a piece of land along the Rio Grande between Sandia and Isleta pueblos and named it "La Villa Real de San Francisco de Alburquerque"—the last reference was undoubtedly intended to garner some favor from his overlord. The year was 1706. Unfortunately, the acting governor was overstepping the boundaries of his duty in establishing a town since settlements were supposed to be approved by the viceroy and ultimately by the king. Instead of a reward from the viceroy, Cuervo y Valdés received a reprimand. At the same time the patron saint of the nascent villa was changed from San Francisco to San Felipe Neri; the simpler spelling eliminating one *r*—Albuquerque—came with time.

23–1

23–2

23–1
SAN FELIPE NERI
The elaborated tower finials crown the
Neo-Gothicized church.
[1981]

23–2
SAN FELIPE NERI
1881
With its elaborate turrets and white
picket fence, the church appeared quite
Anglo and "proper" in 1881. A look beyond the facade, however, would have
revealed the church's Hispanic origins.
[Ben Wittick, Museum of New Mexico, School of American Research
Collections]

A church was soon constructed, although not on the site where it resides today. The plan of the city was based on the royal ordinances of 1573, which declared that each town should be centered on a plaza mayor, with streets extending from it on the pattern of the gridiron. But New Mexican towns rarely followed the letter of the law. The church itself served a congregation of settlers numbering roughly two hundred thirty-two and included some limited elements of a convento for the priest's use.[1] In his 1760 report on the town, Bishop Tamarón remarked, "This villa is composed of Spanish and Europeanized mixtures. Their parish priest and missionary is a Franciscan friar. . . . There are 270 families and 1,814 persons."[2] There was an adjustment in the number of duties expected of the priest in consideration of the distance between settlements and the difficulties in getting to Santa Fe: "And the title of vicar and ecclesiastical judge of this villa was issued to him [the priest] because of the distance."[3] Tamarón, however, gave no description of the church itself, although he did recount a somewhat amusing incident about the problems caused by the scattering of the ranchos necessary to secure fertile and irrigatable lands:

> Because some of his parishioners are on the other side of the river, this parish priest of Albuquerque, called Fray Manuel Rojo, is obliged to cross it when summoned. This kept him under apprehension, and above all he emphasized to me that when the river froze, it was necessary to cross on the ice. He elaborated this point by saying that when the ice thundered, he thought he was on the way to the bottom, because when one crosses it, it creaks as if it were about to break.[4]

Visiting the *villa real* some sixteen years later, Domínguez provided a complete description of the church structure, noting that it was "adobe with very thick walls, single-naved, with the outlook and main door to the east."[5] The convento faced south. As Bainbridge Bunting pointed out, the present church shares neither this orientation nor these dimensions, indicating that a new church rising on the site in the 1790s modified its orientation.[6]

About the villa of Albuquerque, Domínguez was more positive:

> The villa itself consists of 24 houses near the mission. The rest of what is called Albuquerque extends upstream to the north, and all of it is a settlement of ranches on the meadows of said river for the distance of a league from the church to the last one upstream. Some of their lands are good, some better, some mediocre. They are watered by the said river through very wide, deep irrigation ditches, so much so that there are little beam bridges to cross them. The

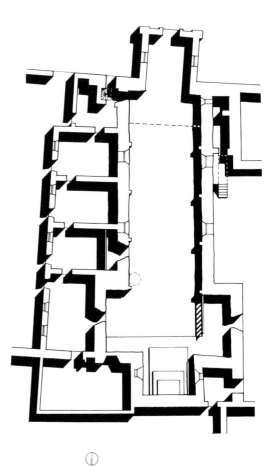

23–3

23–3
SAN FELIPE NERI, PLAN
[Sources: Plan by Arthur H. Lewis, Architects; and measurements by Dorothée Imbert and Marc Treib, 1987]

23–4
SAN FELIPE NERI
1881
The interior of the church before the pressed metal ceiling and arches were added.
[Ben Wittick, Museum of New Mexico, School of American Research Collections]

crops taken from them at harvest time are many,
good and everything sown in them bears fruit.[7]

Its church facade was plain, a two-panel door
"with a good lock" for an entry and two windows
facing south. The clerestory illuminated the nave,
while one window above the entrance lit the choir.[8]
On each side of the nave were two altars, with "poor"
or "badly made" furniture.[9] The condition of the
interior was not good, and Domínguez noted that
all the furnishings were worn. "The floor of this
church is the bare earth," he added, "and its aspect
is gloomy."[10] The square convento fared little better; it was basic and minimal, with "no cloister, but
just a bare patio."[11]

Following the typical New Mexican pattern, the
town dispersed, rather than concentrated, as it developed, and as a result the distance between parishioners increased. The church's substance decayed.
By 1793 a new church or extensive repairs had been
undertaken, mostly with the aid of Indians from
Tome and Valencia. Bunting and Kessell have dated
the present church to this 1793 rebuilding.[12]

For the next century the traditional forms were
retained and maintained in decent repair, although
with the usual lapses of attention. While descriptions are not exact, the church's present-day twin
towers are found in a wood engraving from the
1850s.[13]

Two results of the 1846 American takeover of
New Mexico had a direct impact on the form of San
Felipe Neri. The first was the transference of the
bishopric to Santa Fe, a move that severed ecclesiastical ties with Mexico and created a need for a cathedral worthy of the name. The second was the
arrival of the railroad in the last quarter of the nineteenth century. New Mexico's first bishop, Jean-
Baptiste Lamy, displayed little sympathy for the rudimentary expression of Hispanic churches and the
passion of their art. In place of the traditional adobe
masses came the transplanting of European medieval Gothicism, although its architectural vocabulary was quite varied and indistinct by the time it
reached New Mexico. Gothic touches thus came to
overlay the earthen Hispanic forms in hopes of con-
veying a more polished image and, one assumes,
pride to building and congregation. The railroad,
which provided milled lumber, metal for roofs,
Eastern styles, and stock ornamentation, was the
vehicle by which this architectural refurbishing program was implemented.

Under the direction of Father Joseph P. Mache-
boeuf, who had accompanied Lamy and thereafter
served as parish priest, the look of the church began
to change.[14] In 1868 Italian Jesuits assumed the ad-

23–4

254 ministration of the church and furthered the renovation efforts. A porch was added to the entrance, and the gothicization commenced. An 1881 photograph shows an almost complete transformation. The towers have been stepped, effecting a neat transition from the massive adobe base to the finicky detailing of the two-staged towers. Louvers over the belfry, like those at San Miguel in Santa Fe or the old Isleta church, continue the new architectural program. On the projecting porch there are two small end towers that recall the twin towers of the Santuario of Chimayo and no doubt express the same call to a somewhat lesser degree.

In all, the transformation of the exterior of the church was conclusive. The Gothic version of this adobe mission, with its mouldings, its touches of crenellation, and its pointed, arched, louvered windows, sat comfortably and harmoniously with the picket-fenced plaza it faced, a remade American plaza complete with requisite Victorian bandstand. The Hispanic elements remained, yet each had been overlaid with a hybrid of French, Gothic, and Anglo styles. Ecclesiastical Albuquerque tried passionately to join the United States, architecturally if not temperamentally.

From his journal entry of November 3, 1881, we learn that Bourke was impressed by the remodeling: "The cathedral of Albuquerque is a modern building of good size, double towers in front and of neat and attractive, but not imposing appearance. The interior is kept neat as a pin. It is the only Catholic Church in the Terry [*sic*] provided with pews,— each of these marked plainly with the name of owner or occupier."[15] The same was not the case for the interior of the building, whose traditional aspects belied its origin as a Hispanic New Mexican parish church. The Victorian garb was just that, a reclothing to bring a classic form up to date. Inharmonious in some respects, clumsy in others, the decor lucidly illustrated the state of the territorial architecture idea in the late nineteenth century [Plate 18].

The transverse clerestory was lost with the installation of the metal roof, an addition that canceled the dramatic quality of light on the altar. A wooden floor covered the packed earth that had been the only floor surface for over a century and a half. Perhaps most curious and most ingenious was the manner by which the ceiling disguised the structural vigas and corbels of the eighteenth-century church. In sheathing them with nonstructural, stamped metal ceiling panels, the builders established vague references to both the vault and the then-current construction of the cathedral in Santa Fe, which

23–5

23–6

23–5
SAN FELIPE NERI
The walls have been painted to resemble stone; columns and nonstructural arches overlay the adobe walls.
[New Mexico Tourism and Travel Division, no date]

23–6
SAN FELIPE NERI
Detail of the Victorian pressed metal and painted ornamentation in the sanctuary of the church.
[1986]

provided inspiration for some of the detailing. The arches that sprang from the tops of the pilasters seemed inconsistent, yet harmonious, and the net effect of the package successfully countermanded the usual horizontal progression of the nave. The increased availability of glass from rail shipment permitted larger windows—like those at Ranchos de Taos, for example. If the quality of light was lost by blocking the clerestory, at least the volume of light could be equaled, if not actually surpassed. In commenting on the amount and quality of detailing, Bunting wrote, "The lavish use of sawed boards, and elaborately cut designs for crosses and crockets, finials and tracery show the relish with which the local carpenter availed himself of sharp metal tools and the unlimited supply of finished lumber."[16]

Much of the detailing created its own style and suggested that the builders worked from an interpretation of how "someone had heard things were supposed to be," working perhaps from printed images or verbal descriptions. The plaster walls were painted to look like stone, and the religious icons, as Bunting noted wryly, originated far from the territory: "If the invoice for these statues could be found, it would almost certainly indicate St. Louis as the source of supply, although the ultimate point of origin was undoubtedly some forgotten European plaster works."[17]

The church still retains a choir loft with an intricate railing of milled lumber. A spiral stairway in one of the towers provided access to the choir loft; a more recent stairway was added during the late 1880s–1890s.[18]

San Felipe Neri, like many churches, has had its share of controversy. In the mid-1960s there were plans to expand the church to accommodate a larger congregation and bring its form into accord with the Vatican II decision allowing celebrants more immediate contact and involvement with the mass. These plans, prepared by a Santa Fe architect, would have destroyed not only the feeling of the Victorian version of an adobe but also any feeling of what had been there historically. Restoration, remodeling, and enlargement are all complex processes with no perfect solutions. But in the case of San Felipe Neri, the "real" Victorian forms—which are today being created in an ersatz manner from coast to coast—would have lost out to a characterless 1960s version of Hispanic colonial. If some critics deride the Victorian drapings as dating from an era and a people out of accord with the Hispanic origin of the church's history, what would a future critic think of the complete destruction of both the colonial and the Victorian?

The 1960s remodeling of San Agustín at Isleta—that is, the removal of its turn-of-the-century Gothic appliqué to a restored version of a mission style that never really existed—left San Felipe Neri as the only major New Mexican church illustration of the manifest changes in style that accompanied the American takeover [Plate 19]. Under the gloss of decoration that reveals the church fathers', the parishioners', or the city's aspirations in the late nineteenth century, colonial intention remains discernible, even if the church does not completely reflect eighteenth-century Hispanic building style. The building's mass and cruciform plan; the presence of the choir loft; the positioning, if not the idiom, of the altarpieces; and the twin towers that still bracket the entry all serve as reminders that the foundation of the church and the community is Hispanic. As the proposed remodeling was never executed and close to twenty years have elapsed, perhaps the threat is over; one can only sigh with relief and hope the project will never come to pass.

More recently another problem has arisen. Old Town Albuquerque has become one of those places that seem to have sprouted up like weeds across the United States. Seeking an economic viability for the preservation of historic districts, many of which require extensive maintenance and considerable capital, communities find that the only viable solutions lie in the creation of tourist districts. "Real" functions—necessary services and neighborhood shops—moved out, and their places were filled by tourist-oriented souvenir shops, restaurants, T-shirt stores, and the like. There were also problems with drinking in the vicinity of the church. Church authorities asked the city government on several occasions to restrict the sale of alcoholic beverages within a certain radius of the church's doors. The city did not comply, and in response authorities closed the church at all times other than at mass and devotional services.[19] One can only hope that this problem will be remedied in the not too distant future so that San Felipe Neri, possibly the one authentic element in the quasi-Disneyland atmosphere of Old Town, can be open freely to the public for inspiration, education, and even enjoyment.

ISLETA PUEBLO

SAN AGUSTÍN

1613–1617?; (1690s?); 1923; 1962

Even in subdued light filtered through cloudy skies, the general brilliance is dazzling. As one emerges from the narrow streets of the pueblo, the drastic change in light forces the eyes to close involuntarily for a moment until they can adjust. Across the plaza sits the imposing body of San Agustín, a church that in one form or another has existed on this site for nearly three hundred fifty years. On the hot, glaring days of summer, crossing the plaza is almost an effort. The heat and light make the space seem even larger than it actually is. Finally at the gate of the campo santo the traveler is greeted by a spacious courtyard. The massiveness of the walls becomes more apparent as one enters the church.

Through the doors lies another world: cool even in the hottest weather, dark even in the most intense sunlight. The clerestory casts a splash of light across the crucifix [Plate 16]. The modulation of religious theatrics could hardly be improved, even with the use of greater architectural resources. Perhaps no other church better exemplifies the Franciscan use of two basic New Mexican architectural materials: mud and light.

San Agustín is certainly among the most impressive of the mission churches in New Mexico. It sits on a superscaled plaza and is itself substantial in bulk and dimension; it was built to shelter the entire congregation on feast days and Christmas. In 1915 Isleta was said to be the largest of the Rio Grande pueblos.[1] The southernmost of the Tiwa group, the pueblo originally occupied a small delta or island in the Rio Grande adjacent to its steep banks. Joe Montoya gave the Indian name for the pueblo as Shiahwibak, meaning "knife laid in the ground to play *hwib*," an Indian game.[2] Like Laguna, the Spanish were more content to name the pueblo after its physical setting rather than its Indian name.

Isleta has always been a successful agricultural community situated on fertile and strategically important land. Its lands are distinguished by diversified crops, including fruits such as apricots, pears, and peaches and more common grain stuffs.[3] Its location at the intersection of routes to the north, south, and west was both reinforced and modified with the establishment of the Spanish villa of Albuquerque in 1706, although the pueblo's position on the river as a gateway to the Rio Abajo certainly contributed to its continued economic advances. Even the railroad's arrival was a benefit, albeit a mixed blessing, for nearby the lines divided in two; the first continued east-west, while the second headed south toward El Paso.

Coronado passed through these pueblos in 1540

24–1

24–1
SAN AGUSTÍN
[1986]

and named them the Tiguex group. By 1612 there were twenty Franciscans working as missionaries in the New Mexican province, and one of them, Juan de Salas, was stationed at Isleta. He stayed there almost seventeen years and was responsible for the construction of the first church dedicated to San Antonio de Padua, who had lived as a member of the Franciscan order. By 1629, when Benavides visited the province, a church was standing, probably constructed between 1613 and 1617. Benavides referred to the structure as one of the finest in the province, with a flourishing mission.[4] Roughly two decades later Isleta was documented as having "a very fine church and *convento*. It has very good music and organ."[5] Seven hundred fifty souls were under its administration.

Of course, the Franciscans' Christianization attempts were also beset with certain problems, among them a reluctance on the part of the Indians to detach from the ancient ways. Montoya put it succinctly: "They had become Catholics, paid the taxes and did the work required of them and their reward seemed to be sickness, starvation, exposure to Navajo and Apache attack, and death—not a very good exchange."[6] These, of course, were exactly the problems that plagued all the pueblos in their dealings with Europeans and European culture. While promises of heaven might be ultimately granted, there were certainly no assurances of reward on earth.

The Pueblo Revolt of 1680 also affected Isleta. Governor Otermín, fleeing Santa Fe with about one thousand Spanish refugees, headed south toward Isleta with the intention of meeting up with Lieutenant Governor Alonso García. When the Otermín party arrived, it found the pueblo deserted by its reported two thousand inhabitants. The refugees, now including some Isletans, continued south, eventually overtaking García on August 27 at Alamillo near Socorro. From there the parties continued safely to El Paso del Norte.

A year passed and Otermín set out to retake New Mexico. He managed to regain control of Isleta, although the Indians had first planned to resist but then reconsidered. A segment of his group continued north along the river to Cochiti and Santo Domingo. They returned to Isleta, however, on realizing that they were overextended, with the rear flank unprotected. They also recognized that Isleta itself was vulnerable to the revenge of still-hostile Indians. The party headed south once again to El Paso del Norte, this time accompanied by about one thousand Christian Indians who founded the community of Isleta del Sur, still extant as part of Texas.

24–2

24–2
SAN AGUSTÍN
Aerial view of the pueblo.
[Dick Kent, circa 1957]

24–3
SAN AGUSTÍN
1867
In this early photograph of the church the arched facade of the convento is still visible to the right.
[William Bell, Museum of New Mexico]

How much of the original 1613–1617 church is incorporated into the present structure is open to question, although general opinion holds that the location of the building remains the same. If this is so, there is some justification for claiming that San Agustín is the oldest continuously occupied church in the United States. The body of the structure was repaired in 1706 and again in 1716, although to what degree is speculative. The church was built in the typical single-nave plan of the pueblo churches and originally sported a simple facade with neither towers nor buttresses. In the earliest known photograph of the church, taken in 1867 by Dr. William Bell, the flat facade similar to the old Santa Clara appears. On the corners of the facade are the indications of intended towers, although these features all share the same plane. A single bell sits somewhat uneasily in a single arch at the top of the wall. To the right is a two-story rectory with one of the few known uses of the arch in New Mexican colonial architecture.

The combination of church and convento, even in the earliest reports, impressed visitors. Benavides reported that the church and the convento "were very spacious and attractive."[7] By Tamarón's 1760 visit the patron saint of the church had been changed to San Agustín. There were 107 families, with 304 persons in the village, which was not inundated when the Rio Grande was in flood "because it stands on a little mound. . . . The Isleta church is single naved with an adorned altar."[8] Tamarón seemed pleased with the village, the church, and its management.

Domínguez recorded his mixed reactions during his visitation. He noted the presence of the baptistry to the right of the church and the campo santo fronting it with a surrounding wall, but he ambiguously referred to the interior of the nave as "like that of a rather dark wine cellar."[9] Whether the Franciscan regarded this as a positive or negative quality is not clear. He was less ambiguous about the access to the choir loft, which could be entered only from the exterior of the church through the warrenlike circulation of the convento. "The plan is so intricate that if I describe it I shall only cause confusion. It has upper and lower stories so badly arranged that in proof of the poor arrangement I reveal that the entrance to it all is by a stairway which gives on the corral."[10]

This lack of comprehensive planning and structural integrity suggests that church construction was incremental, with only a general notion of the overall extended form, or that modification proceeded on an ad hoc basis. Even Catholic architec-

24–3

ture reflected Indian construction practice inflected toward Christian purpose. The pueblo walls were rarely aligned directly one above the other, and each floor was regarded as its own integral unit. Through overdesign or oversizing of the beams, not through any consistent support system, structural problems were avoided.

The adobes for the church were prepared on the site, which Montoya credited as the reason for the slight depression in the plaza, a feature shared by the plaza at San Felipe further north.[11] The large vigas were cut in the neighboring Manzano Mountains and were dragged by oxen to the pueblo. San Agustín has a pronounced batter to its walls that at the base measures some ten feet thick. The tapering is beyond the normal deposit of eroded earth at the base of adobe walls and must be considered to have been purposely executed. The four windows are said to be original and appeared in the Domínguez report, although their dimensions have been increased, as can be seen by comparing photographs taken in 1895 and 1981.

The clerestory provides the most important light in the church and grants significance to its interior. The effects of restoration are always problematic, and this has been particularly true at San Agustín. There is no question, however, that the repatriation of the clerestory during restoration reinstated the feeling of the original edifice, even though the increased light entering through the west windows reduced the contrast between the ambient light in the church and the directed light on the sanctuary and altar.

Kubler believed that the transverse clerestory, perhaps the most singular and characteristic feature of New Mexican colonial architecture, was a vestigial remnant or optimistic attempt to recreate the lantern of the baroque prototypes of Spain and the Hispanic New World. This may be the case, but the clerestory nevertheless elucidated the drama of the church and the emotional basis of the religion and played on the fears and feelings of the Indians. Indeed, the conscious manipulation of emotions through architectural design was basic to the missionary effort. The point was to generate wonder. In Mexico this effect derived from scale, ornamentation, and precious materials. None of these properties was available to the New Mexican missionaries. In their place were only mud and light. And yet through the clerestory and other limited means, the presence of God and the definition of the sacred precinct could be manifest. That the church's builders could accomplish this effect through the simplest and most rudimentary of materials is to their lasting credit.

24–4

24–4
SAN AGUSTÍN
1904
By this date, the floor had been covered with boards, a small stove had been added for heat, but—typically—there were no pews.
[Museum of the American Indian, Heye Foundation, Churchill Collection]

24–5
SAN AGUSTÍN
circa 1885
The facade has been restored, and wooden boards protect the tower tops, but the second story of the convento has disappeared.
[Ben Wittick, Museum of New Mexico, School of American Research Collections]

The mud construction of San Agustín, while appearing stable, is actually quite volatile. By the turn of the nineteenth century, with the transference of the New Mexican archdiocese from Durango to Santa Fe and with the importation of French and Anglo styles into the territory, the church registered certain physical changes. By 1881, when Ben Wittick photographed Isleta, the facade had been replastered and its elements reduced to a single entry, a window over the choir loft, and a simple pediment. But two wooden turreted towers were installed on the east and west corners of the principal facade. Their shape then recalled the eastern United States as much as Spanish America; and here was the first instance of a major stylistic change at Isleta. By this time the top story of the convento was so badly deteriorated that it either was pulled down or tumbled of its own accord. The arches, however, remained.

Although originally packed earth, the floor in Whittick's interior photo is covered with sawn boards, another example of American territorial material benefits. Nevertheless, there are no seats or benches, which was the case well into the twentieth century.

Bourke's journal entry of November 2, 1881, complemented the image of the church captured by the photographer:

> People began thronging to Church; not only from the pueblo itself but from the adjacent hamlets. . . . Dozens of kneeling women in their finest raiment [were] in the "campo santo" in front, each with her offerings for the "animas": burning candles, baskets of corn, cakes, fresh bread, "turn-overs," pies, apples, grapes, and slices of watermelons, onions, and canteloupes. The interior of the church was resplendent with the light of candles. Upon the steps of the altar and upon the wooden floor of the nave, there were two or three hundred of these blazing at once which produced an imposing effect.[12]

By the artificial illumination of candles the interior was no less magic.

The church was not without deterioration, however. Perhaps settlement or coving at the bases of the south facade caused structural problems because in a late 1890s photograph by Vroman two thick buttresses are present. Or perhaps these represented the halfway point toward the subsequent remodelings of 1910–1923, certainly the most major in the church's history. The effect of the renovation—conducted by Father Antonine Docher, pastor from 1891 to 1926—was cataclysmic. The church looked strange and uncomfortable, as if wearing foreign and ill-fitting new clothing. Atop the massive adobe

24–5

24–6

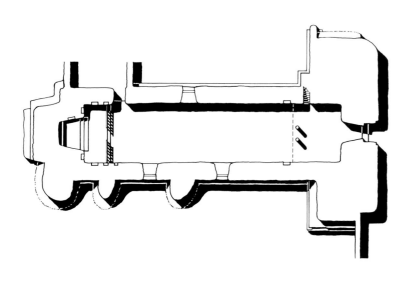

24–7

24–6
SAN AGUSTÍN
1912
By the beginning of the twentieth century, the convento had vanished, and two massive blocks were buttressing the towers.
[Jesse L. Nusbaum, Museum of New Mexico]

24–7
SAN AGUSTÍN, PLAN
[Sources: Kubler, *The Religious Architecture;* and measurements by Dorothée Imbert and Marc Treib, 1987]

24–8
SAN AGUSTÍN
1937
Within twenty years of its cataclysmic renovation, San Agustín began to return to its native soil, the balcony railing being the first of the architectural additions to be lost.
[New Mexico Tourism and Travel Division]

24−8

base were two richly intricate, Neo-Gothic turrets. A tin pitched roof covered the entire church,[13] and a balcony without direct precedent in mission architecture extended along its front. In time even these decorative touches suffered, and by 1931 the porch railing had disappeared, and the ornamentation on the towers had been greatly simplified. In the rear, over the crossing, a curious little brother of the facade towers looked rather out of place and a bit forlorn.

By the 1940s even the porch itself had vanished, which was no great loss functionally as there had been no way to get out to it—except rather precariously over the top of a buttress. The loss of the porch left the church with a rather strange, yet fascinating juxtaposition of architectural styles, a sandwich of historic strata.

The next great rebuilding occurred in 1959 when the church was "restored" to a more cohesive adobe style under the guidance of the controversial priest Frederick A. Stadtmueller and following a design by McHugh and Hooker, Bradley P. Kidder and Associates[14] [Plate 15]. The pitched roof was removed, the clerestory reinstated, and the wooden towers rebuilt with adobe more in keeping with the remainder of the structure. Hard cement plaster was applied to the exterior walls, a mixed blessing that created as many, if not more, problems than it solved. Pews were installed for the first time, the auxiliary convento buildings were renovated, and a general refurbishing was carried on throughout the church itself. If today some of the details seem out of keeping, in particular the harshness of the colors and some of the decorations, one must bear in mind that this church is the home of a living congregation and not a museum.

There was no attempt to "restore" the church in the early sixties, only to remove those elements deemed inharmonious with its adobe construction. Certainly one can be grateful for the removal of the metal roof and the reinstitution of the clerestory, which makes the light quality at Isleta one of the most beautiful and effective of all the mission churches. At the same time, one misses the presence of the discordant wooden elements that were so illustrative of the territorial and early twentieth-century history of San Agustín. In those details, the church was unique. Today only San Felipe Neri in Albuquerque still wears its elaborate Victorian garb, the only major remaining example of this period of mission history.

San Agustín in its three or more centuries of existence has acquired a history and the stripping away of any aspect of history—restoring to a single point in time or to *no* particular point in time, as is the case here—reduces the value of the message. The result is a more consistent piece of adobe architecture, but there is a definite diminution of character. What is lost in the end is a concrete expression of the Victorian period, the architectural expression of a social phenomenon.

Elsie Parsons described a 1925 Christmas service at Isleta. The story is valuable in two respects. First, it illustrates the mixture of Indian ceremony with Catholic ritual and the somewhat indistinct border between the two. And second, it provides one of the relatively few recountings of a church in use.

"The pueblo was illuminated with rows of lanterns on the dwellings augmented by small bonfires on the ground. About ten at night the dancers, arranged by moiety, entered the church in single file. Alternating men and women, they dance-stepped to the altar, then reversed direction toward the choir loft."[15] Since there were few seats and no pews at the time, it was possible to accommodate the dance inside the church itself. The arrangement was, in Parsons' terms, "quadrille-like." The men faced east and women west; then they all shifted so that the men faced south and the women north, but both groups continually maintained their opposing directions. After the dance ended a few people stayed for the mass. About half past ten the following morning the dancers moved from the center of the plaza to the churchyard. Women standing in the churchyard gave gifts to the dancers.

24-10

24-9
SAN AGUSTÍN
Despite the enlarged side windows, present-day San Agustín provides an almost perfect example of clerestory illumination. As the eyes adjust to the darkness, the power of the brilliant sanctuary grows to dominate the interior.
[1986]

24-10
SAN AGUSTÍN
1899
Seen from the apse end, the beauty and fragility of adobe are apparent, especially when the protective coating of mud plaster has been washed away, exposing the individual bricks.
[Adam C. Vroman, Museum of New Mexico]

24-9

THE SALINAS GROUP

ABO

SAN GREGORIO

(1629–1644), abandoned by 1678

New Mexico, the Land of Enchantment, presents several mysteries of settlement that continue unanswered.[1] One of these is the precise reason for the Pueblo settlement of the Salinas plains. The barren land is hardly conducive to burgeoning ranchos and villages, water is relatively scarce, and there is little prominent indigenous vegetation besides the stubby Utah juniper and Rocky Mountain cedar. The reason for Spanish settlement in the valley is more easily answered: the Indians were already living there. Abo, for example, was a thriving community of nearly two thousand inhabitants at the time of the Spanish colonization in 1598. The pueblo managed to extract a satisfactory subsistence from the inhospitable soil and the nuts of the piñon tree, although there was little rainfall or groundwater for irrigation. A small stream south of the pueblo flowed intermittently throughout the year. Joseph Toulouse described the weather, somewhat understatedly, as "sub-humid with a deficiency of moisture all year round."[2] Neither of the mountains nor of a river drainage, "Abo is in the transition zone here identified as Grassland"[3]—a small pad of level ground between the Manzano Mountains to the northwest and the Great Plains to the east.

The native population that settled here at the end of the eleventh century belonged to the Tompiro group, the mountain relatives of the Piro who lived to the south. The pueblo occupied a large parallelogram roughly a thousand feet on its long side and three hundred feet in width and was encircled with a "strong, continuous fortification with only one entrance."[4] The strong wall was a necessity: on the very edge of the pueblo culture, the community was constantly exposed to attack from the marauding Indians of the Plains, one of the factors that led to the eventual destruction and desertion of the villages. The Salinas missions, perched as they were on the delicate edge between existence and dissolution, have been referred to collectively as the "Cities That Died of Fear,"[5] an extreme instance of the problems that beset the Pueblo people as a whole.

Coronado never reached these lands east of the Manzanos; his turning point northward was the Galisteo basin that skirts the Salinas district to the north. Oñate's expedition pivoted at about the same place, and in his stead he sent a small party eastward under the direction of his nephews and lieutenants Juan and Vicente de Zaldívar. They found the pueblo active and thriving, a description difficult to believe in view of subsequent events. When the Spanish colony was established in 1598, the missionaries were assigned custody of the various Indian settlements, and the Salinas missions were

25–1

25–1
SAN GREGORIO
View over the convento ruins toward
the nave. The recesses in the upper part
of the nave walls suggest the stacked
beams they once supported.
[Fred Mang, Jr., National Park Service,
1973]

administered as a single group. Fray Francisco de San Miguel, based at Pecos to the north, assumed jurisdiction over the Salinas efforts but accomplished little: the distances were too great and the available resources too meager. Only in 1626 when Fray Alonso de Benavides acquired charge of the Custody of the Conversion of Saint Paul, which administered evangelical efforts in New Mexico, were the first positive results registered. He was succeeded by Fray Alonso de Peinado, who brought additional priests and supplies in 1609–1610; it was he who established the first permanent mission in the province, at Chilili, around 1614.

Benavides listed Fray Francisco Fonte as "guardián de Abo" until 1635, but it was the arrival of Fray Francisco de Acevedo in 1629, and his subsequent stay at Abo of more than a decade, that marked the first decisive missionary efforts and architectural realization. Fray Francisco "undoubtedly played an important part in the construction of the church whose ruins we see today."[6] He chose Abo as his headquarters based on the substantial size of the community and the available resources. Prior to Spanish contact the Indians lived primarily by subsistence agriculture. The export of piñon nuts, and salt—a commodity precious to the Spanish for mining as well as preserving food—led to a limited economic prosperity for the community, which was able to acquire an organ for the choir loft some years later. After 1630 Las Humanas (Gran Quivira) and Quarai were made visitas of the more prosperous Abo. The church is said to have been named for Åbo, Finland (now Turku), and for its patron, Saint Gregory. This claim is probably fatuous because an Indian village by the name of Abo, on or near the site, existed before the Spanish arrival.[7] The Spanish may, however, have taken a near-phonetic rendition of the Indian term and associated it with the name of one of their known saints.

The construction of the mission complex extended over its entire history of almost half a century. Religious and physical necessity played a significant part in prompting the continuing building program. Recent excavations and study by James E. Ivey, archaeologist and historian with the National Park Service, ascertained that the history of San Gregorio had three major stages. In the first phase, dating roughly from the middle to the end of the 1620s, a convento with a single courtyard was constructed contemporaneously with the first church. This was a simple structure with a single nave terminating in a square apse similar to the church of San Ysidro at Gran Quivira or the earlier form of San Miguel in Santa Fe. Built of stone and set on an

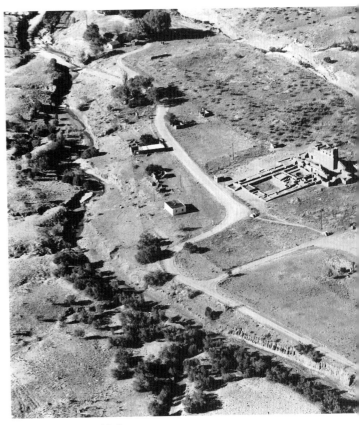

25–2

25–2
SAN GREGORIO
Aerial view of the church and convento ruins.
[Fred Mang, Jr., National Park Service, 1975]

earthen and rubble platform, the church was probably plastered on both the interior and exterior and utilized clerestory lighting. It maintained this form for about twenty years.

Franciscan building programs during the seventeenth century expressed far greater ambitions than those accompanying the Spanish return in the 1690s. The mission churches were intended as structures of magnificence, and until time and resources ran out, building projects almost continually augmented existing structures.

From 1645 to 1649, the second phase, San Gregorio underwent a massive renovation, but it did not follow the somewhat typical pattern of mission development, which began with the rooms of the pueblo, then extended to a small church as a temporary measure, and thereafter culminated in an edifice worthy of the Catholic venture. (The sequence at Gran Quivira illustrates this pattern.) Under the direction of Francisco de Acevedo, the apse end of the old church was demolished to allow for an extension of the nave toward the north. New east and west transepts and an apse in battered form completed the existing structure, which was retained in the renovated church. The convento was also refurbished at this time. The roof was raised, and new walls were thickened to address structural demands placed on them. To strengthen the thinner walls of the first church, buttresses were added.

Although pressures against the Salinas mission group were increasing, in the mid-1650s, the third phase, a reinvigorated effort was mounted to strengthen the religious and economic program. The convento was again rebuilt, and a second courtyard was added primarily for storage and animals; and pens and corrals were constructed to complete the building program. But within ten years the pueblo and the mission would be left untended.

The church building was positioned in the northeast corner of the pueblo on about the only piece of land available for construction. Even in this relatively flat location the land fell in places, and a level floor could be attained only by adding fill to the chapel and convento areas. The mission and its entry faced south, with the sole means of access through the pueblo proper. Here fear joined the Spanish and the Indians in a common bond against Apache raiders.

San Gregorio is a continuous-nave church, although there are two vestigial transepts two-thirds of the way along its length. While not fully developed as transepts, they are a definite inflection to the hall and define the transition to the chancel area

25-3

25-3
SAN GREGORIO
The use of buttresses to stiffen the walls of the nave allowed for a reduction in wall thickness.
[Paul Logsdon, mid-1980s]

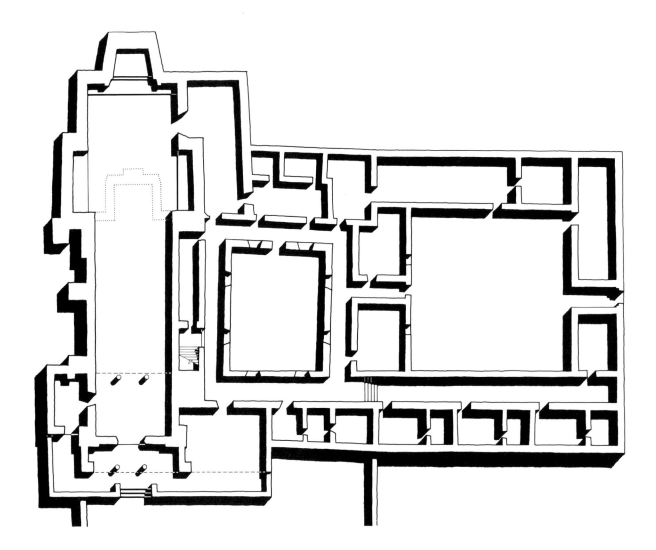

0 4 8 16

25–4
SAN GREGORIO, PLAN WITH
CONVENTO
[Sources: Toulouse, *The Mission of San Gregorio;* and National Park Service measured drawings]

25–5
SAN GREGORIO
The nave and remaining portions of its west wall.
[1986]

25–4

to the north. The nave was built to commodious dimensions, roughly one hundred thirty-two feet in length and in width from about twenty-three feet at the south entrance to almost thirty-two feet at the end of the sanctuary. The nave's walls are almost parallel, which seems to refute Kubler's theory that the nonparallel relation of nave walls in New Mexican churches might have been consistently intended to make the spaces seem longer through optical illusion.[8] Any discernible impact on perception at Abo would work against this intended effect. The church was almost fifty feet in height, and with the exception of today's San Esteban at Acoma, it would have been roughly twice the height of any of the state's existing adobe churches.

On the south a narthex was formed by the extended east and west buttress of the entry facade, and to the right of the main doors a small chapel shared a terrace with the narthex. As a solution to the problem of accommodating the vast population of Abo, the campo santo might have been used in the manner of an atrio, the memory of which was fresh in the minds of the recently transplanted friars. This structure, unlike much of the construction at Abo, was made of adobe, and it is possible that this chapel was used to conduct services during the construction of the church. Until about 1640 an area below the choir loft served as the baptistry, but thereafter a new room was built to the left just inside the entrance. The sacristy, to the right or east, gave onto the sanctuary area, which was raised the typical several steps. Unlike its predecessor, the apse itself was battered inward and turned at a slight angle to the axis of the nave.

San Gregorio was constructed of sandstone, a reflection of earlier Indian building techniques. The area around Abo rests on a geological base of reddish-brown sandstone, a stone already fissured in layers and easily removed without iron technology. In driving to the church today, for example, one can see an eroded bluff cut by the nearby stream that exposes usable building material. Although the walls were to be plastered, the stone that faced the rubble core was selected and positioned to reduce irregularities in the wall surface. The stones, which were rarely larger than one foot square or more than four inches thick, were laid up dry or set in adobe mortar for stabilization. Smaller fragments could be inserted as chinks into the gaps left by stones of irregular profile. As Carleton claimed in 1853, "We saw not a single dressed stone about the ruins."[9] Although stones were not dressed, the smoothest side was usually oriented outward. The construction method was analogous to that used during the

25–5

tenth through thirteenth centuries at the various hamlets in Chaco Canyon.

Although stone is more permanent than adobe, construction time could be considerably longer. In addition to permanence, stone construction required water only for mixing the adobe mortar. Stone also permitted greater wall heights than adobe, which rarely rose above thirty feet. The walls at Abo were remarkably thin—about three to four feet—and were relatively consistent in thickness throughout the church. Buttresses provided additional strength when needed to support the clerestory beams, for example, and a number of engaged external pilasters remain clearly visible on the western side. At the corners, under the bell tower, and in the buttresses an additional mass of five or more feet in thickness stabilized the weight and thrust of the beams. With this system, which drew upon the fortified church of Spain transmitted through Mexico, the celebrants were able to build a structure of considerable dimensions using reasonable quantities of materials.

The ceiling was beamed but did not use round vigas in the more typical manner. Six squared timbers, roughly one foot by one foot in section, were bundled in groups stacked two wide and three deep. Drawing on written sources, Edgar Hewett claimed that "the beams are said to have been the most beautifully carved and most massive in the southwest."[10] On top of the vigas were the smaller savinos, in turn covered by juniper and piñon branches and then thick adobe mud. The mud-plastered roof drained to the west away from the convento. This spanning system, rather than the arches more common in Mexico, reduced the problems of thrust against the side walls and allowed a reduction in mass—hence thinner walls. Had the walls of the nave been splayed, they would also have reinforced the rigidity of the structure, although in comparison to the dead weight of the stone buttresses, this contribution would probably have been negligible. In suggested reconstructions the parapet of the nave walls is usually shown as crenellated, adding to the image of the church as a fortified structure.[11]

The increased height of the transepts, eight feet higher than the nave, allowed for the clerestory's southern orientation, which offered a continuous flow of light throughout the day. The exact height of the roof over the apse is assumed to have been equal to that of the transepts. In the chancel are the remains of three stone altars, all facing north. A choir loft spanned the southern end of the nave. The interior of the church shows remnants of the white gypsum plaster applied to the interior walls.

25–6

25–6
SAN GREGORIO
1938
Excavation and stabilization work in progress.
[Museum of New Mexico]

In some places there are also vestiges of black painted dados, which added to the sense of decoration. Doorways were cut into the walls using wooden lintels rather than arches. The floors were all packed adobe.

East of the church was an extensive convento, one of the largest in New Mexico, organized around two courtyards. Portions of the convento were constructed of adobe, and the floors in many areas were paved with sandstone flags. The "western court is surrounded by corridors into which open living quarters, kitchen storage rooms, and a room set aside for bird pens."[12] In the western courtyard a kiva was built slightly off center, possibly dating from the same time as the church. James Ivey suggested that it had been built with Franciscan approval as a transitional form.[13] It was used as a refuse pit for the convento during later Spanish occupation. The eastern courtyard was used for the friars' livestock, mainly sheep and goats, as well as for storage of goods. The entry doors to the church pivoted on iron pins, which Toulouse claimed to be the only instance of this type found in seventeenth-century New Mexico[14]—although wooden versions of the pivot were in use up to the construction of the Santuario at Chimayo in 1816. Other iron elements, which were necessarily imported from New Spain, were nails, hinges, buttons, and fire tongs, all of which appeared on the list of supposed provisions for the founding of new missions.

The admission of the Spanish into the precincts of the pueblo had the effect of a Trojan horse. Prosperity at first increased through export and trade, but material gain was more than offset by increased attacks by the Plains Indians who fed so viciously on the well-being of the pueblos. Communicable diseases, unknowingly injected into the mainstream through contact with Europeans, also contributed to the downfall of the Tompiro. And then in the late 1660s and 1670s drought and consequent famine attacked the tottering population, whose numbers dwindled quickly. As early as 1671 there were reports of emigration from Abo to the Rio Grande valley near Socorro, and by 1678 the formerly thriving pueblo was vacant and quiet. Only the wind and the Apache visited it. The former, with the infrequent rain, contributed to the erosion of the mission, while the latter probably burned down the church shortly after its abandonment. Excavations of charred timbers bore witness to this supposition.

From about 1800 to 1815 tentative efforts were made to resettle the area around Abo. Houses and utility buildings such as barns, corrals, and pens were constructed for dwelling, ranching, and farming. But these attempts were premature, and heightened Apache raids around 1830 forced the abandonment of the hamlet.

Although known, the Salinas sites were rarely visited thereafter. In December 1853 Major James Carleton, stationed at Albuquerque, took a tour of the Salinas missions and left a detailed description of how they stood at the time. He noted basic dimensions and indicated that there were no finished stones and that the woodwork had been destroyed by fire.[15] Fellow soldier Lieutenant Emory had left a picturesque but somewhat vague record of the ruins in 1848. The site became private property with the American occupation of the territory. Late in the century, with the Plains Indian threat gradually reduced, the land again provided for Hispanic habitation. This time resettlement efforts were successful, and for half a century the Cisneros family held and worked the land around the former mission.

In 1937 the University of New Mexico, already sporting a Spanish Colonial Territorial Revival campus, bought the property and held it jointly with the School of American Research. In 1938 the remainder of the site, on which the apse was located, was donated by Fred Cisneros, and the church buildings became a state monument. From June to December 1938 there were excavations and stabilizations on the site, work that continued through 1939. Late in 1981 the entire property, with Gran Quivira and Quarai, became a joint historical district known as the Salinas National Monument, administered by the National Park Service. In 1988 the name was modified to the Salinas Pueblo Missions National Monument.

QUARAI

NUESTRA SEÑORA DE LA PURÍSIMA CONCEPCIÓN

(1620s?); 1630–1633; deserted by 1677

SECOND CHURCH

1830 (unfinished)

One of the most distinctive characteristics of the earliest New Mexican missions is their seeming disjunction from their sites.[1] At the Salinas missions, such as Gran Quivira and Quarai, for example, huge piles of stone in areas almost devoid of communities appear like the works of some long gone or extraterrestrial peoples or gods. Charles Lummis best captured the scope of the accomplishment in his often-cited quotation about the Salinas missions: "An edifice in ruins, it is true, but so tall, so solemn, so dominant of that strange, lonely landscape, so out of place in that land of adobe box huts, as to be simply overpowering. On the Rhine, it would be superlative, in the wilderness of the Manzano it is a miracle."[2]

Of course, this effect was the builder's intention: a miracle of scale, space, mass, and light meant to impress on the native population the wonders and glory of God. And even in ruins, although now stabilized and partially restored, Quarai resolutely stands its ground against the mountains that form its backdrop.

Coronado did not come this far east before turning his attention northward toward the Great Plains. But during the winter of 1581–1582 an expedition under the leadership of Captain Francisco Sánchez Chamuscado and Fray Agustín Rodríguez reached the five villages forming the Salinas group. These pueblos comprised Tompiro-speaking Tiwa Indians, as did the communities at Abo, Tabira, and Las Humanas. All these tribes were the object of conversion attempts during the early stages of Spanish colonization.

Settlers arrived with Oñate in 1598, at which time the new province was divided into areas of conversion, each assigned to various friars. Their work did not begin immediately, however, and it was not until 1610, when more missionaries arrived in New Mexico, that their efforts commenced in earnest. Governor Oñate had toured the new territory in the late 1590s and had extorted signatures on an "Act of Obedience and Vassalage" at Acolocu pueblo, which is believed to have been situated near Quarai. As part of the Spanish economic and political campaign, the viceroy had declared that the Indians should be gathered into more compact pueblos to facilitate control and conversion and to "promote the welfare of these Indians and facilitate their administration."[3] The Indians would have been only too aware of the latter Spanish motive, and it is doubtful that they would have agreed to the former without coercion. The first conversions and the construction of the earliest church at Quarai are credited to Fray Juan Gutiérrez de la

26–1

26–1
LA PURÍSIMA CONCEPCIÓN
View across the pueblo ruins to the
second church.
[1984]

Chica, who first took up the mission at the Salinas pueblos.[4] The site he chose, or on which he was allowed to build, was a pueblo mound requiring retaining walls and fill to render it suitable for constructing a church.[5]

The best known of the Quarai missionaries is Fray Estevan de Perea, who arrived in New Mexico in 1610. He served two terms as the custodian of the Franciscans and headed the Office of the Holy Inquisition—which applied only to the Spanish—then headquartered at Quarai. The presence of this office in the pueblo led to some degree of turmoil because various conflicts between the civil and the religious authorities over the Indians and other, mostly economic matters were played out here. These problems continued during the residency of Perea's successor, Fray Gerónimo de la Llana, a native of Mexico City who came to Quarai in 1634.

Because the church of Nuestra Señora de la Purísima Concepción dates to the period 1627–1633, it is difficult to determine who was responsible for its construction. The structure was built, however, under Franciscan supervision but almost entirely by Indian labor. It is cruciform in plan, with an altar in each transept. The nave measures a full hundred by twenty-seven feet, making it one of the largest in the state. It originally was forty feet high, nearly twice the height of many of the pueblo churches still extant.[6]

The church is built of a red sandstone similar to that used at Abo. Although the walls were built with minimal amounts of adobe, the mortar contributed little to the stability of the structure, which depended primarily on the dead weight and thickness of the stonework itself. The building units were rather small, commonly one to four inches thick and usually less than one foot square. Given the scale of the unit from which the church was built, the amount of labor required to construct an edifice of this scale must have been staggering.[7]

Like Abo, the nave of the church widens slightly toward the altar, only to converge quite noticeably past the transepts. The ceiling was constructed in the usual manner over vigas taken from the nearby Manzano mountains, although the beam sockets still visible in the walls indicate a clustering of squared vigas rather than the single round ones characteristic of convento and later church construction. The building faces south and slightly west and is believed to have had two towers in its better days. A campo santo extended south from the entrance, and a walled enclosure distinguished this ground from the pueblo to the west.

26–2

26–3

26–2
QUARAI
Aerial view of the church and convento
ruins. The foundation outline of the
1830 church appears on the right.
[Fred Mang, Jr., National Park Service,
1975]

26–3
LA PURÍSIMA CONCEPCIÓN, PLAN
[Source: Wilson, *Quarai State
Monument*]

There was a reasonably large convento at Quarai, the ruins of which abut the east side of the church. The disposition was the familiar square cloister, which included the residence of the friar, storerooms, and offices and which was adjoined by a walled corral for the animals. Much of the pueblo construction aligned with the Franciscan structures, suggesting that they were built or rebuilt after the church.

Inhabitation on the site, ascertained from pottery fragments, dates to 1300, although this earlier occupation had probably ceased by 1350. Perhaps a period of drought forced a temporary abandonment of the pueblo, as occurred in the seventeenth century. Water is found in springs southeast of the church group as well as additional sources about three miles further up the hillside—a remarkably reliable situation for the Salinas area. The pueblo at the time of the Spanish arrival contained about six hundred people, but this number later fell drastically. A description of the building from about 1641 referred to it as a "very good church, organ and choir, very good provision for public worship. 658 souls under its administration."[8] The anomalous presence of an organ demonstrated that although the agricultural yield of the pueblo was limited and meager, the profit derived from trading in textiles, animal products, and salt was considerable.

The pueblo exported salt, piñon nuts, hides, cotton mantas, and livestock.[9] In exchange, the triannual mission supply caravans brought items such as ironwork, chocolate, and "certain things used for the divine cult."[10] Trade with the Plains Indians yielded buffalo meat, hides, and captives in exchange for Pueblo corn and cotton and Spanish horses and iron knives. But peaceful trade with the Plains tribes existed side by side with violent plundering. Indeed, introduction of the Spanish horse led to increased fear in the pueblos of Apache raids. Given this new mobility, the Plains Indians discovered that raiding was more profitable than stock raising and that the risk of retribution was lessened.

By the 1670s a combination of debilitating forces was already wreaking havoc on the Salinas missions. European diseases had continually reduced the population, and when pestilence was not actually present, there was always the fear of its reappearance. Plains Indian attacks were a constant threat. In response to this latter pressure, the Quarai ostensibly attempted a peace treaty with the Apache between 1664 and 1669, but the leaders of the negotiations were found out and hanged. The Apache, no doubt less than pleased by this reversal of events, mounted attacks with renewed vigor. And drought in this last decade reduced the agricultural yield while increasing the pressure of the Plains deprecations; the Apache, too, were hungry. In 1669 Fray Juan Bernal wrote of the Apache forays, the crop failure, and the consequent starvation that prevailed throughout the pueblo. The Spanish requested more arms and troops; some of them were later reduced to eating animal hides merely to subsist. By 1678 all the Salinas missions as well as the pueblos they served had been abandoned. Quarai was most likely deserted by 1677. The Indians probably migrated first to nearby Tajique and then to Isleta, where they had linguistic kin. And then the desert and the elements took their course.

Like Abo, squared beams—here twelve inches deep by ten and a half inches wide—spanned the nave of Quarai about twenty-six feet above the floor.[11] In the transepts and apse the ceiling height was increased by an additional six feet to create the transverse clerestory that illuminated the nave. Facing nearly south, it would have provided almost constant light throughout the day.

The beams supported a field of latillas installed on the diagonal as well as layers of rough fiber matting, earth, and a finished plaster coating sloped to encourage water runoff. In the apse a lower, "false" ceiling thirty feet above the floor created a profile in which the section of the church resembled its plan; in this way the sanctuary was articulated, and its presence as the focus of the church was heightened. Similar to the roof structure, a series of thirty-five-foot-long beams ran continuously through the south wall to form a balcony without and a choir loft within.

The exterior was plastered, concealing the mason's craft and rendering the wall surfaces monolithic. Within the church the walls were covered with white plaster on which decorations "in red, black, gray, yellow, orange and probably blue, white and green" were painted.[12] Although provisions had been made in the masonry structure for the mounting of an altarpiece imported from Mexico, the wall surfaces behind the altar may have been ornamented directly to serve until the time and the means allowed for a more polished work.

Attempts to reinhabit the land around 1800 had been both premature and futile, but by 1815 clusters of houses were beginning to appear around the pueblo of Quarai and what was to become the town of Manzano. By the 1820s sufficient resources and settlers on the Manzano grant were available to establish a congregation, and on August 25, 1829, they petitioned to build their church in Manzano.[13] Within a month, however, the citizens decided that

26—4

LA PURÍSIMA CONCEPCIÓN
The partially restored facade.
[1984]

the new church should be built at Quarai, probably because it had been the religious seat in times past.

Concepción de Quarai was still standing, with portions of its roof and convento nearly intact, well into the nineteenth century. But water damage, rot, and soil that had fallen or blown into the church had rendered the old structure unsafe and unusable. Refurbishing the old structure was not practical, and instead the Spanish settlers began to construct a small church to the southwest. They did not get very far. The instability of the Indian situation in general and an Apache attack in late 1829 or early 1830 instigated a retreat from building efforts at Quarai. The church was left barely protruding out of the ground, with its walls less than two feet in height. On July 6, 1830, the citizens again petitioned the parish priest to move the church to the Plaza de Apodaca at Manzano.

Although still noticeable a half-century later and indicated on Bandelier's sketch map of the site published in 1892, the remnants of the structure had been buried in the intervening century.[14] In 1959 the "lost" church was found by Stanley Stubbs, who mistakenly believed it to be a first church dating from 1615–1620 and similar to San Ysidro at Gran Quivira. A recent study by James E. Ivey provided a logical rationale for the 1829 date based on church patents.

The Apache raid of 1829–1830 also burned the remaining wooden structure of Concepción: openings such as the clerestory and collapsed areas of the roof served as chimneys that intensified and spread the fire. With the covering gone and weakened by the heat of fire, the walls lay prone to attacks by the elements. By the time of the early photographs, the profile of the church had weathered to softened masses, with a deep V cut dividing the towers of the facade.

The site was visited in 1853 by Major James Carleton, who gave the interim report of the church's condition:

> These ruins appear to be similar to Abo, whether as to their state of antiquity, the skill in their construction, their state of preservation or the materials of which they are built. The church at Quarra [sic] is not as long by thirty feet as that at Abo. We found one room here, probably a cloister attached to the church, which was in a good state of preservation [almost two hundred years later]. The beams that supported the roof were square and smooth and supported under each end by shorter pieces of wood, carved into regularly curved lines and scrolls. The earth upon the roof was sustained by small straight poles, well finished and laid in herringbone fashion upon the beams.[15]

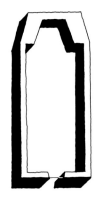

26–5

26–5
QUARAI, THE UNFINISHED 1830
CHURCH, PLAN
[Source: Stubbs, "'New' Old Churches
Found at Quarai"]

26–6
LA PURÍSIMA CONCEPCIÓN
The nave, looking toward the sanctuary.
[1984]

26–7
QUARAI
The church ruins, in 1916, reveal the
extent of subsequent stabilization and
restoration efforts.
[Museum of New Mexico]

The Quarai site was purchased privately in the nineteenth century and was donated to the state of New Mexico in 1913. At that time very limited excavations on the site were undertaken; not until 1934 did a joint team from the University of New Mexico, the Museum of New Mexico, and the Civilian Conservation Corps complete the excavation of the churches. Five years later efforts continued under the auspices of the Works Progress Administration, when archaeological investigations of the pueblos were also carried out. During the course of the 1939–1940 work the walls were stabilized, and new portions, from one to ten feet high in places, were added to them. (The change in the color of the stone makes these newer additions readily identifiable.) The smaller chapel southwest of the main church was discovered in 1959.

Even in ruins, the facade of the church with the remnants of two towers retains a stately presence [Plate 4]. The church was built when religious zeal, resources, and the numbers of the Indian population were all at their zenith. The memories of Mexico, not only of the fortress church but also of the stone and the scale of the naves, were the obvious standard by which the friars reviewed their intentions. When Domínguez visited the province a century later, Mexican churches were still the yardstick he used. The walls at Quarai were uniformly thick, thicker than at Abo, where buttresses were used to lighten construction.[16] Quarai was a "safer" church, more conservative in its building method. Only in the transepts, with the projected clerestory, were the walls thickened to support the increased weight. There remain two clean-cut square openings visible in the ruins, one high on the west wall and the other over the entry lighting the choir loft, the sockets for the beams of which still exist. The interior was flagged with large pieces of sandstone, roughly eighteen to twenty-four inches and as at Abo, the interior was entirely plastered. Just left of the entry is a small projecting structure believed to be the baptistry. The sacristy connects with the eastern transept, which in turn leads to the convento.

Walking through the ruins, one can easily complete the building mentally by supplying the missing roof. But a more difficult task is to imagine the quality of the clerestory light, which would have fallen on the narrow and battered chancel. Given the passage through the walled cemetery, the massive towers, the darkness at the entry, the general feeling of weight and bulk, and the compressive force of the choir loft, that light pouring on the altar must have been convincingly ethereal. As Lummis said, in the Manzano it was a miracle.

26–6

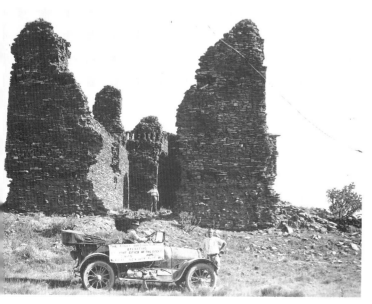

26–7

GRAN QUIVIRA
[LAS HUMANAS PUEBLO]

SAN YSIDRO

1629–1632?

SAN BUENAVENTURA

1659?–1660s

The pueblo of Las Humanas constituted the limit of culture in more than one sense. On the periphery of the Rio Grande pueblos, it was situated on the edge of a vast desert that supported only nomadic raiders. If the sky did not precisely "determine" in these lands, it certainly coerced. Water was measured by its absence, and existence was always marginal. And yet in spite of these severe environmental conditions, a community of several thousand people thrived until the Spanish arrival in New Mexico. This arrival also marked the beginning of a rapidly escalating population decline: about a century later the pueblo would be deserted.

Las Humanas, or Gran Quivira, is one of the three sites that today form the Salinas Pueblo Missions National Monument. Salinas is Spanish for "salt beds", and these were the lands from which the salt so critical for the preservation and flavoring of food and for mining was extracted. From here it was shipped in trade to other parts of the province and to Mexico itself. The land, Lummis related, was not always salty. According to Indian myth, this area was once freshwater lakes, and it abounded with fish, waterfowl, bison, and antelope. But dwelling among the people was one unfaithful wife, "and for her sins the lakes were accursed to be salt forever."[1] Under the unyielding pressure of the heat of the sun, the seas evaporated, leaving the great salt flats east of the mountains.

The remains of Las Humanas pueblo are situated on a gentle rise in the rolling limestone hills that extend eastward from the base of the Chupadera Mesa. The road south from Mountainair continues through this sparsely settled landscape, and the monument is hardly discernible in the surrounding landscape. As one approaches, however, the regularity of San Buenaventura distinguishes it from the adjacent scrub and terrain. It has changed little since Adolph Bandelier wrote about it almost a century ago: "In this arid solitude the massive edifice of the church, with the mounds of the pueblo, look strangely impressive. From the west the church can be seen miles away, a clumsy parallelopiped of gray stone; from the northeast, through vistas of dark cedars and junipers, the ruins shine in pallid light, like some phantom city in the desert."[2]

Based on ceramic evidence, inhabitation on the site began some time between the seventh and eighth centuries, with A.D. 900 the latest probable date.[3] This fortuitous location formed a geographic pivot between the Jornada branch of the Mogollon culture to the south and the Rio Grande Anasazi culture to the west. Interpretation of pottery found during excavations determined that both cultures

27–1

27–1
GRAN QUIVIRA
The ruins of San Buenaventura are to
the right, and San Ysidro is to the left.
[Fred Mang, Jr., National Park Service,
early 1970s]

had a decided effect on the pueblo until the beginning of the fourteenth century, when the culture turned more decidedly toward the Rio Grande. The pueblo's language, like that of nearby Abo, was Tompiro. By the thirteenth century "pueblo groups of 12 or more surface buildings" had been built, with the pit dwellings of earlier eras being retained as the ceremonial kivas.[4] About seven miles west of the pueblo, wells fifteen to twenty-five feet deep provided a more reliable source of water.[5] The current average rainfall is only twelve and a half inches, most of it falling in irregular summer storms and incapable of being retained. But if water is present, the soil can be made to bear.

The group managed to thrive in spite of the severity of geographic and climatic conditions by augmenting agricultural subsistence through chasing deer, quail, bison, and rabbit and growing corn, squash, and beans—none of which required high water consumption.[6] In time geography played a decisive and in this case positive role, positioning Las Humanas as the last commercial outpost between the sedentary pueblo peoples and the nomadic Plains groups. Like Pecos, or to some degree Taos far to the north, Las Humanas became an important trading camp where the Plains Indians exchanged the products of the buffalo for the products of the soil. The pueblo's position, however, ultimately proved to be its downfall as drought and continued demands by nomadic traders for goods brought the pueblo to ruin.

Early Spanish exploration did not reach the Salinas district because the usual route turned north along the Rio Grande nearer present-day Albuquerque. Only with permanent settlement were efforts made to bring the Indians under Spanish hegemony and into the church. In October 1598 Oñate traveled through the country and found three Humano pueblos. In March 1599, Scholes reported, Oñate personally visited the provinces of Abo and Xumanas (the original spelling). Oñate wrote his superiors that he had again visited "the Xumas [*sic*], where within four leagues there are three pueblos, one very large like Cia [Zia] and two smaller ones. [A]nd the two pueblos of the Salinas and the Xumanas all gave obedience to your majesty."[7]

The first friar to begin serious conversion work at the pueblo was Alonso de Benavides. Having preached a sermon in the plaza of the pueblo, he reported, "The Indians are all converted, the majority baptized, and more are being catechized and baptized every day."[8] Benavides explained that there were six churches and conventos operating in the district.

27–2

27–3

Among the pueblos of this nation there is a large one which must have three thousand souls; it is called Xumanas, because this nation often comes there to trade and barter. I came to convert it on the day of San Isidro, archbishop of Seville, in the year 1627, and I dedicated it to this saint on account of the great success that I experienced there on that day. Many were converted, and our Lord delivered me on that day, because these Indians are very cruel. Nevertheless, many leaders were converted, and with their favor, I erected the first cross in this place and we all adored it.[9]

In 1629 Father Francisco de Letrado arrived and is believed to have begun construction on the chapel of San Ysidro, which lies southwest of the main flank of the native structures. Exactly how much he completed during his tenure has not been determined, although Benavides credited him with the building of a church and convento. Archaeological evidence does not seem to bear this out, at least not to the letter, because no remains of a convento have been found in relation to the first chapel. The convento to which Benavides referred was probably a portion of the Indian pueblo that had been modified to provide a residence for the visiting priest, storage areas, and perhaps office space. Letrado left to minister to Zuñi in 1632, and for the next twenty-eight years Las Humanas remained a visita of Abo. The latter was a much larger pueblo—at least in the beginning—and was closer to the Spanish strength and farther from hostile nomad groups. A stream also provided Abo pueblo with an adequate amount of water, in contrast to the marginal and irregular sources of Las Humanas.

Ironically the first and "small" chapel of San Ysidro was among the widest of any New Mexican church, second only to the early construction of San José de Giusewa in the Jemez Mountains. Apparently even the priest supervising the building was not aware of this fact, nor did he possess the necessary knowledge of structure and construction. The span may have exceeded that allowed by the beams and the bearing capacity of the wall supporting them. The chapel, today in ruins, measured 29 feet by 109 feet, a considerable size for a first effort. Located on a falling limestone slope, part of the floor had to be built up and part excavated. Only in the eastern sections was a foundation wall laid, the remainder being built directly on the bedrock of the mesilla. Here, at the entrance (east) end, the walls were three and a half to four feet thick, while the remaining walls were kept between one and a half and two feet thick. (The stone walls at Quarai and Abo, for example, were at least three to four

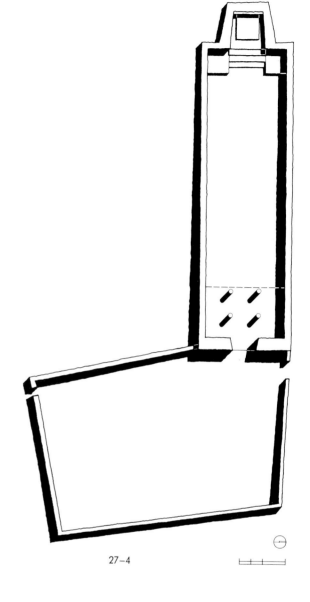

27–4

27–2
GRAN QUIVIRA
View over the pueblo toward the remains of San Buenaventura.
[Fred Mang, Jr., National Park Service, 1973]

27–3
SAN YSIDRO
The first church seen from the exterior of its apse
[1986]

27–4
SAN YSIDRO, PLAN
[Sources: Vivian, *Gran Quivira;* and National Park Service measured drawings, 1986]

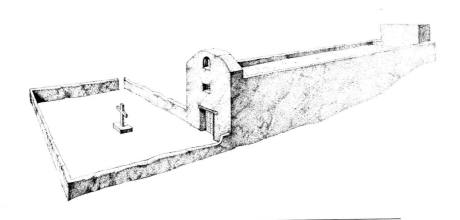

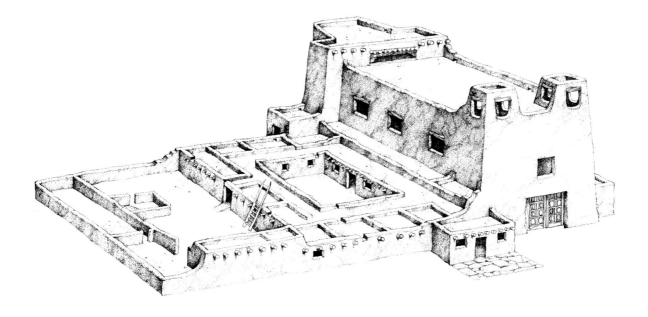

27–5

27–5
GRAN QUIVIRA, HYPOTHETICAL
RESTORATIONS OF SAN YSIDRO (ABOVE)
AND SAN BUENAVENTURA (BELOW)
[Lawrence Ormsby]

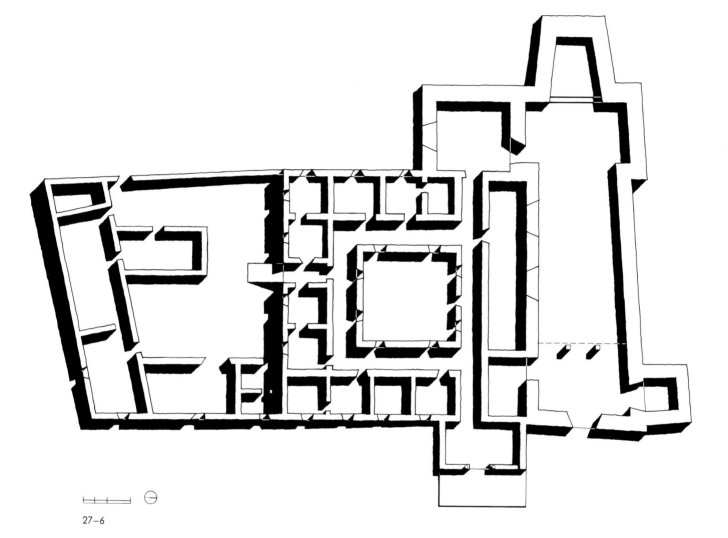

27–6

27–6
SAN BUENAVENTURA AND CONVENTO,
PLAN
[Sources: Vivian, *Gran Quivira;* and
National Park Service measured drawings,
1983]

feet thick and could vary up to a full six feet in places. The system of buttresses at Abo allowed for the relative thinness of the walls.) At San Ysidro the minimal wall thickness courted disaster, and the width of the nave relative to its wall thickness has been offered as evidence that it was Letrado who began construction. If it had been Fray Francisco de Acevedo who supervised construction at Abo, he would have been far more knowledgeable, having had his own church as precedent, and would not have attempted the architectural daring—or ignorance—that transpired at Humanas.

San Ysidro is of the single-nave type without transepts and is oriented on an east-west axis. It was constructed of the local light blue-gray limestone, unworked, but positioned best side out [Plate 5]. The stones were set in a mud mortar, or *caliche*. Along the nave are two rows of what are taken to be foundation stones; Gordon Vivian interpreted these to be the bases of a row of columns that supported the roof beams.[10] Although these posts might have been intended from the start of construction, in effect forming a three-aisle church, they were probably, introduced once the bearing capacity of the walls or the strength of the beams had been tested and found wanting. The pines for the great vigas, which must have been at least thirty-three feet long, could have come only from the Gallinas Mountains at least twenty miles away and were probably positioned on seven-and-a-half-foot centers. On top of these were savinos of the local juniper, used when the span presented no problem. The usual layer of branches topped the construction, carrying the adobe mud for the roof surface. The weight of this building system was considerable and paired with the relative thinness of the walls hastened the collapse of the structure after the pueblo was abandoned in 1670. In the eastern portion of the nave the foundation stones supported columns that carried the choir loft located just inside the entry.

Not much is known about the chapel's fenestration. There were probably one or two high windows in the south wall, a common pattern, but whether there was also a clerestory is impossible to determine because the existing walls are too low for a definitive interpretation. Vivian believed that oiled sheepskin parchment covered the windows because it more easily fit into the window frames than the irregular pieces of selenite of the native tradition.[11] Throughout the centuries tales of buried wealth attached to Gran Quivira (hence its sobriquet), and treasure hunters hastened the natural processes of attrition with their forays and their digging. The floor and altar area of the San Ysidro

27–7

27–7
SAN BUENAVENTURA
The nave of the church, with tapering apse and two shallow transepts
[1984]

chapel were particularly unfortunate victims of such searches.

The altar end of the church still contains the remains of the stone altar and a box believed to have held the vessels of baptism. The font itself was supported on a small stand, the fragments of which lie along the east wall near the choir loft. Remnants of a thin, sandy plaster reveal that the interior of the nave was plastered. Along the base of the wall a wainscot of dull red paint once existed, decorated above a thin black line with designs painted on the white plaster. Similar treatment may be seen today at Acoma and Laguna. Only small fragments of these decorations have been found, however, implying that at least a portion, if not all, of the nave was so decorated.

West of the church's simple planar facade lies the burial ground, which is surrounded by a low stone wall and is focused on a single cross set on a stone base. Like the later San Buenaventura, the stone wall of the church might have been integrated into the circumferential wall of defense around the pueblo.[12]

San Ysidro represents a common second stage in mission development: the extension of development efforts from the existing spaces of the pueblo (first stage) to a small, temporary church for use until a larger structure was warranted. Single-nave buildings of the same type as San Ysidro include one at Tabira (1629), the earliest chapel of San Miguel in Santa Fe, and the "lost" Pecos church from the first two decades of the 1600s.[13] The church of San Buenaventura illustrates the third phase of mission establishments in the New Mexican religious campaigns: substantial edifices meant to endure.

Given the location of Las Humanas in the marginal areas of Pueblo culture, it is difficult to explain why a church this large could have proven insufficient. Rather than increased needs, the deterioration of the existing chapel or the desire for a less marginal position could have instigated the construction of a more ambitious edifice to the west of the old San Ysidro. The population already had seriously declined by the 1660s, perhaps by as much as fifty percent, from the 1627 count of 2,000 people.

During the 1650s the Apache raided the pueblo, destroyed the church, and carried off seventeen women and children as captives.[14] In 1659 Fray Diego de Santander arrived at Las Humanas, found the existing chapel in poor repair—perhaps in ruins—and began construction of the church and convento of San Buenaventura. These structures were still incomplete at the time of his departure

three years later, although he is usually assigned credit for their erection.[15]

Gran Quivira witnessed one of the most exaggerated conflicts between the civil and the religious powers in New Mexico's history. Until Santander began his residency, Las Humanas had been administered from Abo. Nicolás de Aguilar, the *alcalde mayor*, came to the pueblo in the 1660s as a loyal executor of Governor Bernardo López de Mendizábal. Mendizábal had no love for the church, a fact borne out by his continuing program of personal gain at the expense of the religious venture. As Santander was trying to reestablish the position of the church in the pueblo, Mendizábal was waging a campaign against the religious by forbidding the Indians to work on the church's construction. The governor, Charles Hackett noted, "commanded under penalty of death that no Indian work on the structure; but the Indians continued at great risk in the construction of the edifice, for they had no church."[16]

This proscription was fueled by the traditional enmity between the missionaries and the governor's office. Indians working on construction could not be tending flocks, weaving, or growing corn. And if crops and other goods were produced for the religious, the friars were accumulating wealth directly in competition with the governor. The father replied to the governor that a church was needed to bring the word of God to the Indians. Unconvinced about such expenditures of time and resources, the governor replied "that churches with costly ornaments and decoration were not necessary; that a few huts of straw and some cloth ornaments, with spoken masses, were ample."[17] Construction continued, no doubt under the disgusted eye of Aguilar, who kept the governor informed of the pueblo's affairs.

Although the width of San Buenaventura is less than that of its predecessor, almost every other aspect surpassed the earlier structure. The nave is about 27 feet wide, with a length of 109 feet. There are two transepts barely 6 feet in average depth that hardly alter the impression of a single-naved church. The transepts are more symbolic than perceptual, although even these slight extensions allow for use as side altars. Like San Ysidro, the church is aligned on an east-west axis, with entrance again to the east. The original campo santo must have served for burials, as none fronts the second church.[18]

The construction technique remained the same: walls of local limestone laid in mud mortar but this time worked to a wall thickness of five feet or more.

27—8

27—8
SAN BUENAVENTURA
The convento, its first courtyard seen in
the center (walls with window openings)
[1986]

The facade was planar and showed no traces of towers, although the remaining stone walls seen today offer that impression. A central door led directly into the nave through a tapered entrance spanned by a composite wooden lintel. The baptistry lay just to the right of the entry.

Evidence indicates that the building was never finished, although portions of its wooden structure had been installed, including the choir loft at the east end of the nave. This "entablature," as Major Carleton referred to it in 1853, received considerable carving and detail, but the church was never roofed.

Ornamentation, the last stage in the construction of a church, indicates that the edifice was nearly completed, although the corbels and beams were carved prior to installation. Because the span was shorter than San Ysidro's, vigas spared from the Apache desecrations could have been used in roofing the new church. Carleton was clearly impressed by the quality and the amount of carved ornamentation:

> Some of the beams which sustained it [the choir loft], and the remains of the two pillars that stood along under the end of it which was nearest to the altar are still here; the beams in a tolerable good state of preservation—the pillars very much decayed; they are of pine wood, and are very elaborately carved. There is also what perhaps might be termed an entablature supporting each side of the gallery, and deeply embedded in the main wall of the church; this is twenty-four feet long, by, say eighteen inches or two feet in width; it is carved very beautifully indeed, and exhibits not only the greatest skill in the use of various kinds of tools, but exquisite taste on the part of the workmen in the construction of the figures.[19]

The illumination of the church presents other problems of interpretation. Vivian, after Kubler, assumed that there was the typical window illuminating the choir loft from the east as well as one or more windows high on the south side of the nave.[20] The existence of a clerestory cannot be definitely determined by archaeological evidence, although transept-type churches from this time usually possessed a transverse clerestory.

Along with the church, Gran Quivira now boasted a developed support structure. The extensive convento south of the church included a full sacristy with access from the south transept and a complete quadrangle of living and utility spaces. Lying further south was a large corral measuring sixty by fifty-three feet and an adjoining stable area. As the pueblo declined, the mission flocks and herds were moved to Abo, where food and water were more plentiful and the Apache slightly less in evidence.

By the middle of the 1660s conditions had turned even worse. As early as 1663 Alcalde Nicolás de Aguilar had sympathetically reported that "it costs a great deal to get water and it makes a lot of work for the Indians in obtaining it, and the wells are exhausted and there is an insufficient water supply for the people, for their lack of water is so great that they are accustomed to save their urine to water the land and to build walls."[21] The population fell to about one thousand. During the end of the decade no crops were harvested, and starvation became another of the population's miseries: at Las Humanas at least four hundred fifty people died. Those who did not die were seriously weakened and more prone to contract or expire from disease. Fray Juan Bernal, writing in 1669, described the horrible scene of the great number of Indians "lying dead along the roads, in the ravines, and in their huts."[22]

Conditions were no better for the Apache. What had been denied them through trading, they now attempted to extort through attack and theft. But there was little left to steal, except perhaps human life, which could be sold into slavery in exchange for life's necessities. The Apache displayed their rage by destroying the church on September 3, 1670. The situation had become intolerable. In either 1671 or 1672 the pueblo was finally abandoned to the desert, the Apache, and, in time, the Anglos.[23]

The site had sporadic visitors over the centuries. At the time of Major Carleton's visit in 1853, the ruins of the churches were still visible. The pueblo itself had been transformed into a series of earth-covered mounds, only parts of which have yet been excavated. Tales of buried treasure still brought many seekers, and even after the transformation of the site into a national monument in this century, permits were granted for digging. No treasure was ever found.

More scientifically, the School of American Research and the Museum of New Mexico undertook excavations of San Buenaventura commencing in July 1923 under the direction of Edgar L. Hewett. In 1951 National Park Service archaeologist R. Gordon Vivian undertook excavations at Gran Quivira that provided a more complete picture of the chapel of San Ysidro as well as parts of the pueblo proper. Gran Quivira National Monument was established on November 1, 1909; in the fall of 1988 it was incorporated with Abo and Quarai as Salinas Pueblo Missions National Monument.

WEST OF ALBUQUERQUE

LAGUNA PUEBLO

SAN JOSÉ DE LA LAGUNA

c. 1700

As one heads west on Interstate 40, mile after mile of desert and mesa forms slip by almost as a continuous extrusion. Only the rhythm imposed on the topography by the basalt mesas and buttes punctuates the first hundred miles west of Albuquerque. There is a singular exception: Laguna Pueblo. Seen from the road, the pueblo sits squarely on its rise as an island in the land. The stone and adobe buildings are mud plastered to the color of the earth, and homogeneity and harmony pervade the various elements of the village. Atop the stacked dwellings, the visual focus is the bulk and whiteness of the pueblo's church: San José de la Laguna.

The founding of the settlement is not precisely ascertained. Prince and other writers attributed its dating to 1699, but this is only the date of Spanish recognition after the Reconquest. Walter wrote that Laguna was "founded in 1689 by rebel Queres from Santo Domingo, Cochiti, Sia, and evidently Acoma, and may also include some of the Queres which had fled to Hopi Country."[1] Prince asserted that the pueblo's inhabitants were primarily people from Acoma who had entered the area in search of better farming and hunting lands and had eventually founded a permanent settlement augmented by emigrants from Zia and Zuñi.[2] Ellis qualified these interpretations by suggesting that the settlement predated 1698–1699 and that this accepted date was based on the first Spanish identification of July 1699, when Governor Cubero traveled through the district demanding the submission of the native population.[3]

A dam across the San Jose River, which passes at the foot of the rise, formed the lake from which the native name Kawaik derived, translated into Spanish as Laguna. The pueblo was unusual in that farming shared economic importance with sheep raising. According to tradition, the Laguna originated on the other side of the lake, possibly from the Anasazi of the Four Corners region, and settled in their current lands around the beginning of the fifteenth century. Ellis believed that the Spanish initially regarded Laguna as part of Acoma and that this is why we do not have a separate description of the pueblo and its population.[4] By 1706 a small chapel was under construction in Laguna, administered as a visita of Acoma.[5]

Bishop Tamarón visited Laguna on his way from Zia and Jemez to Zuñi and commented at length about the aridity of the land and the difficulty of the journey given that "the sun burned as if it were shooting fire."[6] He was a bit disconcerted about the resident priest's inability to speak and receive confession in the native Keres. Tamarón listed the

28–1

28–1
LAGUNA PUEBLO
The white form of the church crowns
the pueblo hillside.
[1984]

28–2

population at 174 Indian families with 600 persons and 20 families of citizens with 86 persons, which no doubt included the Spanish members of the congregation rather than only those living in the pueblo itself.[7] He also described the mission for the first time: "The church is small, the ornament poor."[8]

Sixteen years later Domínguez found everything "built here . . . made of stone from the hill and mud" and the church "very gloomy."[9] The walls of this simple church were "not very thick," the floor was bare earth, there were only "two poor windows with wooden gratings facing south, and another facing east," and the clerestory illuminated the interior.[10] The convento lay to the south. "Father Claramonte rebuilt all that has been mentioned in the year 1766, for when he came to this mission, he found everything in bad shape, and so he installed many doors and windows."[11] Domínguez showered rare praise on the cloister; "Although walled in, it is light, for when the said father rebuilt it, he arranged a beautiful window on each side."[12] The friar's quarters on the small second story were considered "very pretty," with a view over the cemetery. He also recorded the meager increase in population, now totaling 178 families comprising 699 persons.[13] In the early decades of the nineteenth century reconstruction was instigated under the direction of Fray Mariano Peñón.[14]

De Morfi mentioned nothing of the church structure itself but seemed favorably impressed by the visual aspect of the pueblo, which he saw as "one of the most beautiful which the entire realm has. It is situated on a hill of moulded rock which makes the flooring hard. Its rooms are well arranged and evenly made. The houses are all of stone, all two stories along the upper part, and well constructed. They are very clean and neat within and without, painted and whitened with *enjarre* similar to gypsum."[15] He also devoted about half his entry to the "abundance of snow" in winter, the "little stream fed by a spring" called El Gallo, "pleasing and crystalline water," and the small lake west of the pueblo.[16]

The whiteness of the pueblo and/or its church elicited continual notice from visitors. "Seen from the windows of the cars of the Atlantic and Pacific Rail Road whose track runs within 50 yards of the noble old wreck," wrote Bourke in 1881, "the white-washed walls suggest the idea of a beacon planted in the midst of a restless ocean of strife and angry passion."[17] In a landscape of earthen chroma, white can be as powerful as the sun whose light it reflects.

In descriptions of the social structure of Laguna,

28–3

28–2
SAN JOSÉ
The facade of San José and its campo
santo.
[1986]

28–3
SAN JOSÉ
circa 1917
The whiteness of San José has always
distinguished the church from the ruddy
tones of the pueblo.
[Museum of New Mexico]

writers continually noted the tension caused by
the presence of diverse social elements within the
group. Their origin, for example, derived from the
stock of several pueblo groups. Although the Laguna shared a common language with the Acoma,
there was always some implicit conflict with their
neighbors in the Sky City. In the late nineteenth
century a progressive faction of the pueblo that followed Protestant, rather than Catholic, living patterns caused additional problems. In reaction, a
group of the more conservative elements of the
pueblo emigrated to Isleta pueblo, or nearby Me-
sita, in about 1879. The dissention was also directed
at the church, and there had even been pressure
from the Protestant-linked group to tear the building down. Its preservation is credited to the sacristan Hami:

> His descendants tell of Hami debating the crisis,
> praying, bathing, washing his hair, putting on clean
> clothes, praying again . . . and then going to the di-
> lapidated church which recently had been used as a
> corral for burros. Bracing himself in the doorway, he
> told the Protestant "progressive" crowd which had
> gathered outside that they could pull down the church
> only after they had first killed him, the sacristan. . . .
> Then he set himself to its repair.[18]

The challenge worked and the church remains.

As the century closed Bourke found that the
church, "once the seat of a convent and surrounded
by monastic buildings now in the last stages of ruin,
is itself in fair preservation."[19] The continuing dia-
lectic of decay and repair continued into the twentieth century. During the 1920s Father Fridolin
Schuster of Acoma could "announce joyfully that
the work of placing a roof on the mission church
. . . had been finally completed successfully."[20] As
part of its work recording key structures during the
Depression, the HABS measured and documented
the Laguna church; the remodeling of the convento
followed soon thereafter.

Today, not surprisingly, the pueblo has changed
greatly. Prince listed the population in 1905 as
1,384 and in 1910 as 1,583, indicating that notwithstanding the perils of European contact, the pueblo
has managed not only to hold its own but also to
grow. Prince referred to the pueblo as "the most
prosperous and progressive of Indian communities."
But he qualified his remarks by adding that this
progressive spirit had also fragmented the unity of
the pueblo because "the people who were originally
concentrated in the one town have become scattered in various communities in order to carry on
their farming operations to better advantage. In
consequence of this, the town is almost deserted in

28–4

28–5

28–4
SAN JOSÉ
1885
The second story of the convento (left) still existed in the late nineteenth century.
[F. A. Nims, Museum of New Mexico]

28–5
SAN JOSÉ
1895–1905
By the turn of the twentieth century, the second floor of the convento had almost completely disintegrated, although the church and lower walls appear to have been well maintained.
[Museum of New Mexico]

28–6
SAN JOSÉ, PLAN
[Sources: Kubler, *The Religious Architecture*, based on HABS and field observations by Stephen Glaudemans, Dorothée Imbert, and Marc Treib, 1990]

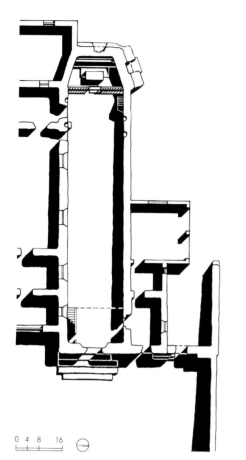

0 4 8 16

28–6

the summer, and even in winter many of the old houses are vacant and going to ruin."[21]

What was already noticeable to Prince in 1915 has continued throughout the twentieth century and has been exacerbated by the federal government's policy of constructing more modern detached housing on the perimeter of the pueblo at the expense of the traditional plaza and core. Seen in Stubbs's aerial photographs of the pueblos published in 1950, the main dance plaza was divided in two sections by a block of houses, which are now gone, leaving the plaza as one space.[22] The church, although dominant in its position and color, sits to the side of the main plaza and with new development is further removed than it had once been.

San José de la Laguna is notable in several ways. On the top of the crest, it serves as a fitting crown to the hill and the land around it. The church was built with a single nave and battered apse. About twenty-three feet wide, the span indicates that the roof vigas came from mountain sources thirty miles distant. Above the vigas and particularly noticeable in the underside of the choir loft are the herringbone latillas beautifully articulated through painting in black, red, and white [Plate 9].

One enters the church through the walled burial ground, passing through a handsome gate topped by a pediment in the form of a stepped sky altar. The yard is bare except for one cross, which commemorates scores of graves left otherwise unmarked. There is only bare earth, terraced to effect a transition between the lower plane of entry and the floor level of the church itself. To the left is the convento structure, still present but reduced from the two-story buildings visible in nineteenth-century photographs. The facade, which recalls the old Santa Clara or Isleta as seen in earliest photographs, is planar, although it is enlivened by a stepped pediment flanked by two small towers at either edge. These recall the twin-towered form to which so many churches once aspired, while they also sensibly compensate for the increased erosion of the corners of the facade by wind and rain.

While the interior is dark, the clerestory having been covered up in subsequent remodelings, the nave is animated by color and ornamentation. The walls are painted with abstract geometric and bird designs in red and black that run along the length of the nave. The floor remains earthen, dry, and cracked and packed through use over centuries; in the sanctuary rugs cover the floor in the traditional manner. In his descriptions Domínguez commented on several occasions that the only real floors in the churches were the rugs or blankets laid down on the

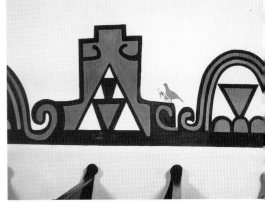

28–8

28–7

28–9

28–7
SAN JOSÉ
The painted ornamentation plays a significant role in completing the church architecture and activating the edge between the wainscot and the upper wall.
[1981]

28–8
SAN JOSÉ
Detail of the animated black and red painted ornament, which mixes abstract, vegetal, and animistic motifs.
[1981]

28–9
SAN JOSÉ
The church interior about 1935.
[T. Harmon Parkhurst, Museum of New Mexico]

altar floor and that these were often the property of the friars, either brought with them or traded or purchased from the Indians.

In addition to the wall paintings, which have the look of recent execution, the church possesses one of the finest altarpieces in New Mexico [Plate 10]. A portrait of Saint Joseph fills the center of the reredos. He is flanked on the right by Saint Barbara, protector against thunder, lightning, and sudden death, and on the left by Saint John Nepocene. Above the altar, projecting at an angle to it, is a panel painted with images from the native religion, that is, the moon, sun, rainbow, and stars. While suggesting native origins, this projection functionally serves to keep dust and dirt from the roof from falling on the altar. The entirety of the piece is so consistently painted and integrated that the seeming discontinuity in iconography is all but completely mitigated. As a whole, the decorations of the church convey the intensity with which the Indians undertook the decoration of the church, although the principal paintings were from the Laguna Santero.[23] In Laguna, perhaps more than in any of the other missions, decoration plays a central role in the feel of the building.

Although Acoma also features some wall paintings, their effect is limited by the immense volume of the nave. At Laguna the decoration is felt more strongly: in the painted wainscot, the reredos that fills and cramps the sanctuary, the blankets or rugs on the floor, the painted latillas, the carved beams of the choir loft, and the elaborate detailing of the corbels. Together, as a suite of decoration, these elements not only unify but also embellish the space and transcend the restricted confines of its physical dimensions and the pervasive darkness.

Prince related the curious story of the enmity caused by a painting of San José said to have been brought to Acoma by its missionary, Fray Ramírez, and given to him by Charles II.[24] The painting was reputed to have supernatural powers, and as a result, or so it was believed, Acoma had grown to prosper. Laguna shared none of Acoma's successes and was troubled by scanty harvests and periodic bouts with sickness and disease. San José was also the patron saint of Acoma—although the church there was dedicated to San Esteban—and Laguna pueblo asked to borrow the painting to effect a reversal in the village's fortunes. Acoma was less than anxious to let the painting go, and only after a season of penance and prayer instigated by the priest did the congregation agree to draw lots to "let God decide." God's decision was to have the painting remain on the mesa. So angered by the decision were

the Laguna parishioners that a group of them broke into the Acoma church and took the painting back to their pueblo. Only with considerable difficulty and with persuasion by Father Mariano de Jesús López was conflict avoided, which finally convinced the Acoma people to be generous with the miraculous image.

Laguna's lot improved, which only added to the faith the Acoma people bestowed on the painting and to their considerable efforts to have it returned. But Laguna adamantly refused. Father Mariano personally talked to the Laguna parishioners at length, imploring them to see reason and acquiesce. But they would not. Finally, Acoma sought legal recourse, and the case reached the Supreme Court of New Mexico as the case of *The Pueblo of Acoma* v. *the Pueblo of Laguna*.

"All we know," Prince wrote, "is that it was hotly contested, and that the lawyers' fees made both pueblos poor." Judge Kirby Benedict decided in favor of Acoma and declared that the painting be returned to its rightful owners. A party from Acoma started out to reclaim the painting; halfway to Laguna, in the canyon that separates the two pueblos, the party found an image of San José "resting against a mesquite tree." Having heard the decision, the story concluded, the saint "was in such a hurry to get back to his home in Acoma that he started out by himself."[25] While the court case is a matter of record, the nature of the incident remains a mystery.

ACOMA PUEBLO

SAN ESTEBAN

c. 1630; 1696–1700; 1924; 1926

West of Albuquerque, past the pueblo of Laguna, and south of Interstate 40 lies Acoma, the Sky City. The approach to Acoma leads through a vast canyon that extends for twenty miles with no apparent exit, its edges severely circumscribed by the steep cliffs and mesas surrounding the valley. There are two principal interruptions to the sweep of the level canyon floor. The first is Enchanted Mesa, a large piece of rock isolated from the surrounding cliffs like a piece of debris left on the beach after a particularly high tide. The second is the mesa on which Acoma pueblo is perched.

The Acoma are said to have first occupied the top of Enchanted Mesa, which is higher still and yet within sight of the mesa top they now inhabit [Plate 1]. One day, legend tells, an enormous storm caused a fissure in the cliff that severed the fragment containing the only access to Enchanted Mesa, a series of foot and hand holes worn in the side of the rock. Up on the butte three old women, either too old or too infirm to work in the fields, were left to finish out their lives. The majority of the people were isolated in the valley below, and they had to seek a new life and a new home in the closest defensive stronghold they could find. And so they began anew on a second piece of rock hardly more, and probably less, hospitable than the first. The settlement of Acoma then parallels and recreates the settlement pattern of Mesa Verde, although here the order of habitation was somewhat reversed. On the summit, some seventy-odd acres, the Acoma Indians built their new pueblo.

It would be difficult, it not impossible, to conjure up a more dramatic, poetic, and less likely place to found a community. Next to nothing of life's necessities, except defense, was found on the cliff top. Water supplies were limited to a cistern pool and incidental accumulations of rainwater. At other times water was brought from the valley floor, carried up the nearly four hundred feet by hand or on the head, in jars from distant springs. There was no agricultural land; in fact, there was almost no soil at all on the mesa. Only sky and protection were abundant.

And yet the setting and those structures that have been constructed and resolutely dwell on this rock strike the basic chords of harmony and inevitability. Lummis was clearly struck by the landscape: "And in its midst lies a shadowy world of crags so unearthly beautiful, so weird, so unique, that it is hard for the onlooker to believe himself in America, or upon this dull planet at all."[1] So steep is the rock surface that it actually overhangs in places. And until well into this century little more than a donkey

29–1

29–1
ACOMA PUEBLO
The Sky City and San Esteban, with the
Enchanted Mesa beyond.
[Dick Kent, 1960s]

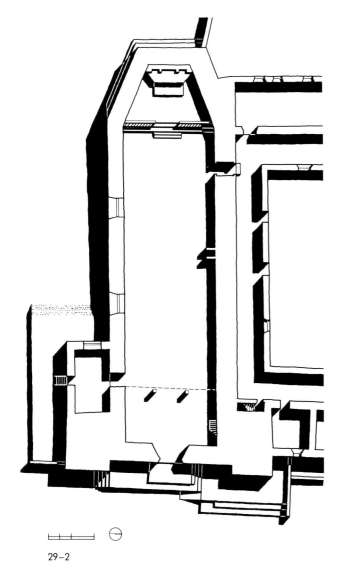

29–2
SAN ESTEBAN, PLAN
[Source: Kubler, *The Religious Architecture*, based on HABS]

29–3
SAN ESTEBAN
The handsome, boatlike shape of the nave seen from the southwest. Without a plaster top coat, the stone and adobe mixture is apparent.
[1981]

path provided access. Before, one climbed a series of handholds with food, building materials, or water. It was not until the 1950s that a road permitting automobile access was cut and then only because a motion picture was being filmed on the site.

Fray Marcos de Niza heard of the pueblo, whose name he learned as Ahuacus, during his travels in 1539. Coronado passed by Acoma. In 1581 Espejo actually visited the pueblo and remained there as a guest for three days.

"The Acomas received the wondrous strangers kindly, taking them for gods,"[2] or so the Spanish chronicles read. In 1598 they became vassals of the Spanish crown after submitting to Oñate's act of obedience and homage. Initially their submission was short-lived. Oñate, experiencing difficulty in his campaigns, dispatched Juan de Zaldívar with some troops to collect supplies at Zuñi. En route they camped below the mesa. "Zaldívar and some of his men," Marc Simmons related,

> were lured to the summit and a horde of painted and befeathered warriors fell upon them. One after another, the sword-swinging Spanish went down, until the few who remained were driven to the edge of the cliff. There was no choice; they jumped. Twenty-year-old Pedro Robledo smashed against the rocky wall, his body tumbling to the base like a broken doll. Three other soldiers landed in sand dunes swept by the winds against the foot of the mesa. They were gathered up, dazed, by the four members of the horse guard who remained below.[3]

Oñate learned of the battle and the death of ten of his men. He dispatched Vicente de Zaldívar from San Gabriel on January 21, 1599, to deal retribution to the Acoma. The battle was bloody, and at its conclusion the Spanish emerged victorious. Hundreds of Acoma were dead. Oñate, intent on establishing a precedent for dealings with Indian uprisings, handed down a series of sentences ranging from mutilation to servitude, even though the pueblo was already decimated. From that time on there was little Acoma reaction against the Spanish.[4]

Acoma was first assigned to Fray Jerónimo de Zárate Salmerón, who kept charge from 1623 to 1626.[5] It is said that Fray Juan Ramírez walked to Acoma from Santa Fe to assume his post as Zárate Salmerón's successor and to live among the Indians for a number of years. To him is usually assigned credit for building the first church. Benavides was clearly astonished by the pueblo, calling it "the most amazing in strength and location that could be found in the whole world. It has to all appearances, more than two thousand houses, in which there

29–3

29–4

29–4
SAN ESTEBAN
The twin towers of the principal facade
seen across the cemetery, with the remnants of the convento to the right.
[1986]

must be more than seven thousand inhabitants."[6] In 1644 the church was described as "the most handsome [in the Custodia?], the paraphernalia of public worship is abundant and unusual; [the church] has a choir and organ; there are 600 souls under its administration."[7] During the Pueblo Revolt the resident friar, Fray Lucas Maldonado, perished while the church was believed to have been destroyed.

Whether the church was demolished completely or damaged at all during the revolt is still a matter of dispute, however. If the church has remained with its original walls on the same site, it has a rightful claim to being the oldest continually used church in New Mexico. Yet there are opinions to the contrary. Walter, for example, said, "Despite tradition, Hodge declares that no trace of it [the original structure] remains today except some carved beams which form part of one of the houses of the old north tier."[8] Today, however, several scholars believe that at least portions of the current structure predate the Reconquest, although a major reconstruction took place between 1696 and 1700. The bell in the northeast tower is inscribed "San Pedro, 1710," but it could have been added at a later date. Fray Juan Álvarez visited Acoma in 1705 and found the inventory scant and a single priest, Fray Antonio Miranda, repairing the church by himself. Domínguez, however, stated that "this church was inaugurated in the year 1725" and tentatively credited Fray Miranda with its construction.[9] The attribution could apply to a substantial renewal of the church, but the exact explanation of how much was rebuilt has remained elusive.

The church of San Esteban of Acoma is an enormous church measuring 150 feet in length and 33 feet in width. It strikes a certain note of irony that this, the largest existing mission structure, serves the most inaccessible congregation. The church is without transepts. At the sanctuary the apse end of the nave angles prominently, extending the sense of its length. The walls are nearly 10 feet thick and built of massive amounts of adobe and stone, approximately twenty thousand tons, according to Riley writing in 1924 at the time of its restoration.[10] A choir loft spans the rear of the nave at the eastern end.

The vigas that support the roof are fourteen inches square and forty feet long. They were reportedly brought to the mesa—but not by horse, ox, or wheel—from the San Mateo Mountains twenty miles distant. The inside height of the nave is almost fifty feet, equaling the loftiness of the Salinas missions, all of which now lie in ruins.

Neither loose rock nor soil was found on the mesa. As a result, it was necessary to import the earth in which to bury the dead. "There are no burials in the church," Domínguez recorded, "because the rock prevents this, and in order to cover it, it was filled with earth to a depth of about half a vara."[11] But loose soil in the campo santo would have been blown away by strong winds, and so a retaining wall of stone brought from the valley was built east of the church (a wall that measures forty-five feet high in places) to form a giant box to contain the good soil for a Christian burial. The ten years' work required to construct the church is impressive, but tradition has it that an additional forty years were spent filling the box. If the pueblo did indeed have 760 Christians in 1705, it should also have had two resident priests. But in 1821 it had none.

On his visitation in 1760 Tamarón was obviously moved by the site and the missionary efforts at Acoma. "It is the most beautiful pueblo of the whole kingdom," he wrote, "with its system of streets and substantial stone houses more than a story high. The priest's house has an upper story and is well arranged."[12] (This convento, arranged in a square and not accessible to the public, still exists.) Atypically, it was sited north of the church—not a good exposure, but where land was available. Tamarón mentioned that Fray Pedro Ignacio Pino had learned enough of the native tongue to listen to confession but required the aid of some seven interpreters to give penance in return. The bishop remarked calmly that the friar "has had to whip them, and he keeps them in order, although he is not up to date with regard to confession."[13] Second only to the discussion of language was Tamarón's expressed amazement at the agility and ability of the women to carry water to the mesa's crest.

Sixteen years later Domínguez expressed unusual respect for the congregation: "There is not even a brook, earth to make adobes, or a good cart road. Therefore, it is necessary to prevent any preconception in order to achieve even a confused notion of this place. This makes what the Indians have built here of adobes with perfection, strength, and grandeur, at the expense of their own backs, worthy of admiration." He noted the entrance to the baptistry (no longer extant) under the choir to the left and the paintings and ornamentation of colored earth that embellished the interior. In total effect, "the interior is pleasant, although bare."[14] The barrenness of the mesa top impressed Domínguez, and he devoted several comments to the provision of water. In the convento, for example, "some little peach trees . . . are watered by hand."[15] The service to the mission friar consisted mostly of water bearing.

29–5

29–5
SAN ESTEBAN
1897
The church, convento, and the retaining wall of the cemetery seen from across the mesa top.
[Museum of the American Indian, Heye Foundation]

29–6

29–6
SAN ESTEBAN
1902
Erosion by wind and rain had taken
their toll on the body of the church
early in the twentieth century. Although
the base—more easily within human reach
—had been maintained, the upper portions of the walls, especially the towers,
were deeply rutted.
[Museum of New Mexico]

29–7
SAN ESTEBAN
circa 1915
The great box containing soil for the
Christian burial reads clearly in the left
portion of the photo.
[Museum of New Mexico]

29–8
SAN ESTEBAN
The convento and San Esteban seen
from the north.
[1981]

29–7

29–8

"Twelve Indian women . . . bring twelve small jars **311** of water to be used daily. . . . The reason for such a large number of water carriers is that the water . . . is very far away, and to avoid frequent trips a good deal is brought at one time.[16] On the summit water assumed the status of currency.

Shortly after Domínguez's visit Acoma became a visita of Laguna due to the ravages of smallpox in the Acoma community. Also, Acoma was isolated and difficult to reach, whereas Laguna stood on the main route between the Rio Grande pueblos such as Isleta and Sandia and the western missions at Zuñi.

"The approach is one of the most romantic imaginable, and brings to the mind of the climber all that he has ever heard or read of ascent in the Andes," Bourke wrote, stopping at Acoma while heading east.[17] "There is an old church of massive proportions but without symmetry or beauty in which Catholic priests still held Divine Service once a month."[18] Since Bourke's watercolor sketch depicted the symmetrical structure much as we see it today, he must have used the word symmetry in its classical associations with proportion. He also referred to a "ruined church of San José de Acoma: 80′ broad, 55′ high, towers 70′ × 13′ broad," a curious note.[19]

By the turn of the twentieth century the condition of the church had reached a critical level. Contemporary photos show that the erosion of the towers and the spalling of the mud plaster from the south wall had caused considerable deterioration. The tower bases were severely eroded by water and wind. With funds from the Committee for the Reconstruction and Preservation of New Mexico Mission Churches, restoration work commenced under the supervision of Lewis Riley and Sam Huddleston acting in conjunction with architect John Gaw Meem in Santa Fe.[20] At that late date the nearest railroad stop was still fifteen miles away at Acomita, which meant that the final part of the journey—and the lifting of building materials to the top of the peñol—had to be accomplished by human and animal strength. First priority was given to the roof, which leaked seriously and threatened the destruction of the nave.

Even in 1924, Riley reported, the younger men of the village lived, not in the Sky City, but in the surrounding settlements at Acomita and McCarty's. The rebuilding was undertaken cooperatively, with a "community effort which could hardly be duplicated among our own people."[21] The water was transported in five-gallon casks and steel barrels and was hauled on donkeys the two miles from the nearest spring. (Acoma still does not have a regular

29–9

29–10

29–9
SAN ESTEBAN
1940
Free of pews and still with earthen floor,
the interior appears monumental.
[Wilder, Taylor Museum, Colorado
Springs Fine Arts Center]

29–10
SAN ESTEBAN
Detail of the upper portion ceiling of
the altarpiece.
[Museum of New Mexico]

source of water.) The women augmented these efforts in the traditional way by bearing water to the precipice in buckets and ollas. The roof work was completed in six weeks using lumber from Arizona and roofing materials from Denver, both brought via rail. "The convento is rapidly falling into ruins, but it preserves as yet most of its former beauty and could be restored with comparatively little expense," Riley wrote.[22] He had also hoped to repair the towers and the exterior plastering, but these had to wait until the works of 1926–1927.

The 1926 restoration was a community effort with cooperative decisions determining the allocation of human resources. On September 12, 1926, it was decided that all members of the pueblo would assemble and for three days pack and carry dirt up to the church site. From September 15 onward there would be a crew of fifteen men, to be rotated each week, who would work on the repairs until the winter weather intervened. On September 9 a large herd of burros was discovered by B. A. Reuter, who had succeeded Lewis Riley as superintendent, and these were commandeered to haul earth. Thus, drawing on the ageless tradition of human and animal labor, the church reconstruction began.

The south wall was given the first attention; the church roof shed its water toward the south, and both this splashing and the water driven back onto the wall surface by the prevailing winds had gouged out a good portion of the structure. This destructive force was exacerbated, of course, by the force of the storms themselves. After repair the canales were extended by five feet to alleviate the problem. The upper part of the wall had receded almost thirty inches between the base and the top, and "it is quite clear that the principal part of this batter is the effect of erosion."[23] The south wall had eroded an average of ten to eighteen inches to a height of about eight feet, seriously undercutting the base of the structure. The west wall of the south tower, taking the brunt of the wind and rain forces, was also seriously undermined.

The church was built primarily of adobe but incorporated some pieces of local rock. It was virtually impossible to get any new rock from the mesa because all the best material had been previously used in house construction. Photographs taken near the end of the restoration or shortly thereafter reveal a very finished and polished version of the Acoma church, looking almost as if the final polishing were a bit too perfect to be comfortable.

Today San Esteban is in a good state of repair following further preservation efforts in 1975 and roof repairs in 1981.[24] The south facade, which is normally out of bounds to visitors, often lacks some of its plaster, as it seems to be an almost impossible task to maintain this skin intact. Morning is the best time to view the church, when the facade catches the sunlight and reflects it back across the campo santo. The interior of the nave is whitewashed and sports a pink wainscot with painted decorations that recall the motifs used on the exquisite pottery for which Acoma is noted. The absence of pews is still noticeable, and the altarpiece provides the single focus to the nave. Above the altarpiece are paintings of the sun and moon, native motifs mixed into the religious framework of Catholic iconography. Acoma remains a world apart.

ZUÑI PUEBLO

NUESTRA SEÑORA DE GUADALUPE

1629–1632; 1692; 1706+; 1968

With Spanish hegemony centered on the upper Rio Grande, the western villages of the Zuñi and the Hopi remained peripheral to the missionary enterprise. The Zuñi village of Hawikuh had been the first to confront the Fray Marcos de Niza party in the mid-1500s. That confrontation resulted in the death of the "scout" Esteban and the ambiguous substantiation of the existence of the Seven Cities of Cíbola. What the friar took for gold may have been only mud and stone seen in the setting sun, but his subsequent report played a pivotal role in the move to colonize what is now New Mexico.

Traces of occupation in the Cíbola cultural area date as far back as the ninth century B.C. and are believed to be signs of a hunting culture; by the beginning of the Christian era it had been superseded by an agrarian-based society.[1] The development of a sedentary agricultural group occasioned a more substantial architecture and led to a conglomerate dwelling with storage spaces that was oriented along a northeast-southwest axis. Although the archaeological evidence does not present an absolutely conclusive picture, the Cíbola villages were probably part of the extensive system of "outlyers" that centered on the Anasazi settlements of Chaco Canyon. Characteristics of the parent culture—at times multistoried, aboveground dwellings and the ceremonial kiva—marked Cíbolan construction well into the thirteenth century.

After this time a shift in site patterns occurred, with the villages transferred to higher elevations, perhaps to capture increased rainfall during an extended period of drought. Paralleling the transference of dwellings from mesa top to cave at Mesa Verde, the Cíbolan pueblo of the late thirteenth century displayed a pronounced defensive form. Against whom is not known. And like the structures of Chaco Canyon and Mesa Verde, the Cíbolan buildings were deserted early in the fourteenth century. As Steven Le Blanc noted, many gaps remain to be breached, and many questions are still to be answered. Over time attrition in population concentrated the people in fewer villages so that by the time of the Spanish entrance in 1540, there were only "six or seven pueblos along the Zuñi River."[2]

The chronicle of Spanish contact with the Zuñi pueblos, while a few years longer than that of other pueblos, is typical. Coronado used the pueblos as his point of departure; he was lured eastward away from the villages by the promise of more immediate reward. Antonio de Espejo crossed Zuñi lands in 1583, followed by Juan de Oñate in 1598. At this time, Oñate obtained the customary "Act of Obedient Vassalage" promising respect for the king and

30–1

30–1
NUESTRA SEÑORA DE GUADALUPE
Seen from the rear, the mass of the
church reveals its plan: a single nave
without transepts.
[1984]

the church.[3] Some thirty years later the first mission was founded. The considerable expedition that reached Zuñi in June 1629 included the provincial governor, Manuel de Silva Nieto, and Custodian Estevan de Perea. The Spanish made a good show of it: "And to give that people to understand the veneration due to the Priests, all the times that they arrived where these were, the Governor and the soldiers kissed their feet, falling upon their knees, cautioning the Indians that they should do the same. As they did; for as much as this example of the superiors can do."[4]

As a setting for the mass and a residence for the religious, "a house was bought. . . . And hoisting the triumphal standard of the Cross, possession was taken. . . . To the first fruits of which there succeeded, on the part of the soldiers, a clamorous rejoicing, with a salvo of arquebusses; and in the afternoon, skirmishings and caracolings of the horses. . . . There were knowing people of good discourse; beginning at once to serve the Religious by bringing him water, wood, and what was necessary."[5] Perea probably confused fear and discretion here with compulsion and acceptance.

The church, however, required a more elaborate expression. "And in order to make this art spectacular, he ordered a high platform to be built in the plaza, where he said mass with all solemnity, and baptized them . . . singing the *Te Deum Laudamos*, etc; and through having so good a voice, the Father Fray Roque—accompanied by the chant—caused devotion in all."[6] Fray Francisco de Letrado succeeded Fray Roque de Figueredo in 1630 or 1631 with three missions under construction in the Zuñi area.[7] Two principal missions were founded at Hawikuh, one dedicated to La Purísima Concepción and the other to Nuestra Señora de la Candelaria at Halona. The third church at Kechipauan never reached completion.[8] Benavides described the churches as "adorned and tidy" and credited the successful work to the devotion of the religious and the financial support of the crown.[9] These successes were short-lived. On February 22, 1632, as Fray Francisco de Letrado attempted to gather the flock into his church, a volley of arrows felled him. A second priest shared his fate five days later. In what was to be their typical response, the Zuñi fled to the protection of the nearby mesa, "Thunder Mountain (called *Dowa-Yallone* by the Zuñis) and fearing retaliation, remained there for three years."[10]

In 1643 the two missions were reestablished, with the priest assigned to Halona. At the very edge of the empire, this assignment was miserable at best. One Fray José succinctly remarked, "If it had been

30—2

30—2
NUESTRA SEÑORA DE GUADALUPE
1880s
Late in the nineteenth century erosion had removed the protective outer layer of plaster, with severe deterioration from the towers and bell arch downward.
[Museum of New Mexico]

30—3
NUESTRA SEÑORA DE GUADALUPE
At the nineteenth century's end Nuestra Señora was quickly falling into ruin, its sagging balcony propped by a single post.
[Hyde Expedition; Negative 4630, courtesy of the American Museum of Natural History, Department of Library Services]

30–3

chosen for a prison for those guilty of the gravest crimes there would have not been a more severe decision."[11]

In the decades just after midcentury the weakening of Spanish power and its distance from the Zuñi nation, compounded by the famine brought on by drought, led to more numerous and violent raids by the Apache. A report ascribed to 1644 implied that the church had been destroyed and the mission abandoned. "The province of Zuñi [was] severely punished for having destroyed churches and *conventos* and for having killed one of the ministers who served in the work of conversion. . . . In this province there are 1,200 Indians who have asked for ministers once again."[12] In 1672 an Apache attack on the village left the missionaries dead and the church again destroyed. The Zuñi joined the rebellion of 1680, during which the resident priest was killed—although certain tales have him abandoning the cloth and joining the tribe.[13]

The church itself was ruined. Again the natives fled to the defensive security of the mesa top and were living there when Vargas coaxed them to return to their fields and restore the church. At the turn of the eighteenth century a detachment of eleven soldiers was dispatched to Zuñi from Santa Fe to maintain order in the village and to ensure the restoration of Nuestra Señora de Guadalupe, which by 1699 had badly deteriorated.[14]

The assignment at Zuñi was never an easy one, and the years of relative calm were also years of dire frustration. By midcentury, two priests served at Halona (a quota that was rarely filled). One incident in 1763 led to three Spanish dead and the traditional Indian departure for the higher elevations. Within two years the priest returned and convinced the Zuñi to again tend their crops. Tamarón was unable to reach Zuñi on his visitation of 1760, thwarted by intense heat and its effect on the pack animals. He was informed, however, that it was the largest pueblo in the province, with 182 families and 664 persons. The patron saint of the mission was Our Lady of Guadalupe, and the "church was good."[15]

Domínguez included Nuestra Señora de Guadalupe on his inspection tour, noting that the walls of the church were "nearly a vara thick." At this time the population was given as 1,617 persons in 396 families,[16] a drastic contrast to Benavides's figure of 10,000 souls living in ten or eleven pueblos a century and a half earlier,[17] although this was probably an inflated figure. The church, as Domínguez described it, was quite typical: built of adobe with a single nave, several steps up to the sanctuary, a choir loft "in the usual place," two windows on the

30–4

30–4
NUESTRA SEÑORA DE GUADALUPE
1890s?
Interior of nave in ruined state. The walls have deposited material into the nave, and portions of the roof have collapsed.
[I. W. Tauber, Museum of New Mexico]

30–5
NUESTRA SEÑORA DE GUADALUPE
Nuestra Señora seen over the cemetery wall.
[1984]

30–6
NUESTRA SEÑORA DE GUADALUPE, PLAN
[Sources: Caywood, *The Restored Mission*, and Smith, "Seventeenth-Century Spanish Missions"]

30—5

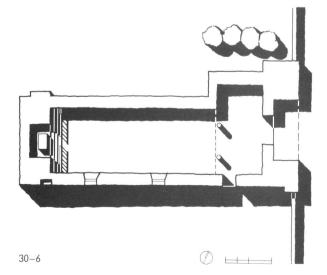

30—6

right side, and a transverse clerestory. The front doors, however, were simpler in construction than the inset entrance beneath the balcony visible in photos from the late nineteenth century. "The door is squared, with a wooden frame instead of masonry, with two paneled leaves, no lock except the cross bar."[18] The convento, configured as a square, abutted the church to the south and was fronted by the portico of a porter's lodge that might have doubled as an open-air chapel.

In the early nineteenth century the Navajo and Apache terror increased, and by 1821 the residence of priests at Zuñi was sporadic. In the past the church had had a considerable impact on the living pattern of the villages, but by midcentury that presence was negligible. The new bishop, Jean-Baptiste Lamy, visited the village in 1863, and priests continued to hold mass only on an irregular basis thereafter. By 1881 the merciless elements had already taken their toll. Bourke sketched the "ruined church."

> The windows never had been provided with panes and were nothing but large apertures barred with wood. The carvings about the altar had at one time included at least half a dozen angels as caryatids, of which two still remained in position. The interior is in a ruined state, great masses of earth have fallen from the north wall; the choir is shaky and the fresco has long since dropped in great patches upon the floor. The presence of five or six different coats of this shows that the edifice must have been in use for a number of years.[19]

A Wittick photograph of 1890 shows the tired form of the old church, its adobe towers withered, its sagging balcony propped by a single post. Some time early in the twentieth century the north wall was rebuilt south of its original location, and new timbers and roofing were installed.[20]

Isleta's Father Docher, writing in 1913, was skeptical of Zuñi piety. "The Zuñis are more numerous," he declared. "But they are half still barbarians."[21] Around 1905 parts of the roof had been rebuilt, and the width of the nave had been reduced by ten feet and its length by twenty—but who accomplished the work is not known.[22] During the 1920s the village was split on whether to reinstate a Catholic mission or a Protestant church; the pro-Catholic force eventually succeeded.

The church standing today, excavated and last restored in the late 1960s by the National Park Service under the direction of Louis R. Caywood, is only a part of the original complex. Once flanked by the structures of the pueblo—then a multistoried configuration recalling the form of today's Taos pueblo—it now stands tall among the houses of the village. The church is basically a single-nave plan without transepts. The campo santo still fronts the church, divided in burial practice with women to the north and men to the south.[23] Replastered in hard stucco, the church shares the color of the surrounding dwellings. Today, it lacks the original sacristy, baptistry, and convento.

Decoration seems to have played an important part in the church's interior. Matilda Coxe Stevenson, the wife of an army officer at nearby Fort Wingate with an interest in ethnography, reported in 1879 that the nave was decorated with Zuñi religious images, the pieces of which Bourke recorded only two years later.[24] Today the church at Zuñi is considerably reduced from its more expansive structure of two centuries ago, its walls displaying a hardness uncharacteristic of the more malleable mud plaster. Inside painted images by Alex Seowtewa enliven the nave. Outside the flowers of the small burial ground provide intense spots of color that relieve the almost monochrome siena of the church, pueblo, and earth itself.

30–7

30–7
NUESTRA SEÑORA DE GUADALUPE
The sculptured forms of the ovens provide a foil for the prismatic mass of the
church.
[1984]

NOTES

PART I

AN ARCHITECTURAL FOOTPRINT ON THE NORTHERN FRONTIER

---

1. Lummis, *The Land of Poco Tiempo*, p. 3.

2. The phrase is from Walter, "The Cities That Died of Fear."

3. These conglomerate structures grew incrementally without any overall plan. Their sense of unity was thus the product of common building materials as well as the result of adding, fitting, and adjusting the part to the whole, rather than subdividing a larger entity into discrete units. This process is characteristic of multiunit folk building throughout the world, where the structure directly reflects the process and to some degree the temporal staging by which it was realized. It becomes even more evident in multistory building construction and is characteristic of the dwellings of the Pueblo culture. See Pike, *Anasazi*; and Nordenskiöld, *The Cliff Dwellers of the Mesa Verde*. For a concise account, see Breternitz and Smith, "Mesa Verde."

4. The expulsion of the Moriscos in 1609–1614 reduced revenues, and the effects of a series of economic depressions from 1623 to 1650 followed by a period of severe inflation from 1664 to 1680 were compounded by a tax system that served only to increase the need for more revenue. Moreover, Spain's standing armies required maintenance, and wars had to be funded. Bottineau, *Iberian-American Baroque*, p. 5.

5. Ibid., p. 6.

6. The necessity for Christianization efforts in Mexico was realized within a few years after the Conquest. In a letter to Charles V dated October 15, 1524, Cortés restated the need for "some religious of good life and example; but, up to the present, only a few have come, or none, so to speak, and, since their coming would be of very great usefulness, I beg Your Majesty to send them with as little delay as possible" (p. 20). Missionaries would be best; the expense of supporting bishops and regular clergy would be excessive. The mission of the "Twelve Apostles," members of the Friars Minor of the Observance, arrived in Mexico City on 17 or 18 June 1524, but more missionaries were needed (p. 21). The conditions in Mexico in the early sixteenth century were not unlike those in New Mexico decades later. "In 1561, the second bishop of New Galacia, Fray Pedro de Ayala, begged Philip II to send him some Franciscans for his poor diocese, because the religious at his disposal were aged and worn out, and the new ones preferred to remain in easier and more agreeable dioceses, such as Mexico and Michoacán" (p. 81). Richard's general description of the Mexican religious enterprise also could serve as a characterization of the evangelical project further north, particularly the patience and flexibility necessary to sustain the spirit in trying circumstances: "one sees the character of moderation and common sense, that defiance of systematic and absolute theology, that eclecticism, which seem to be the dominant traits of the Mexican mission" (p. 95). Ricard, *The Spiritual Conquest of Mexico*.

7. See Kubler, "Two Modes of Franciscan Architecture," pp. 39–48. "When Quiroga became Auditor of New Spain in 1530, his first concern was to realize in America the Utopian speculations of his English contemporary, in two urban creations, one near Mexico City, and the other on the shores of Lake Patzcuaro in Michoacan. Quiroga expressly stated in later life that he had modelled these communities, designated as 'Hospitals,' upon the *Utopia*. They were dedicated to the attainment of Christian perfection, and served to propagate the faith among unsettled groups of new converts. Property was held communally; the Indians were relieved from personal service and tribute; subsistence was provided from agriculture and the exercise of the crafts. . . . The Mendicants adopted its form in their urban foundations

324 throughout western Mexico, and as late as the eighteenth century, the landholding system, the community meetings, and other arrangements were maintained intact in many areas" (p. 45).

8. Mundigo and Crouch, "The City Planning Ordinances," p. 260.

9. Simmons, *New Mexico*, p. 11.

10. The myth of the Seven Cities extended back centuries and was rooted in the Muslim occupation of Spain. In *Universalior Cogniti Orbis Tabula* (1508), Jan Ruysch, a German geographer, told of seven bishops who during the eighth century had fled westward by ship reaching "the island of Antilia (a name echoed today in the Antilles Islands), where each built an opulent city brimming with treasure." Ibid., p. 13. See also Bandelier, *The Discovery of New Mexico*, p. 65.

11. Esteban had been a member of the ill-fated Pánfilo de Narváez expedition to Florida in 1528. Shipwrecked on the west coast of the peninsula, he, Alvar Núñez Cabeza de Vaca, and a few other survivors spent eight years making their way back to Mexico on foot and heard tales of the Seven Cities as they traveled.

12. Bolton, *Coronado, Knight of Pueblo and Plains*, pp. 35–36; cited in Simmons, *New Mexico*, p. 18.

13. This discussion of the Laws of the Indies is adapted from Mundigo and Crouch, "The Laws of the Indies Revisited." A book by the same authors and Garr restated essentially the same material: Crouch, Garr, and Mundigo, *Spanish City Planning*.

14. Prince, *Spanish Mission Churches of New Mexico*, pp. 38–39.

15. Bolton, "The Mission as a Frontier Institution," p. 60.

16. A mission system was established in the late seventeenth century in Pimería Alta, which extended from what is Sonora, Mexico, to Arizona. The system is almost synonymous with the name of the Jesuit Fray Eusebio Kino (1645–1711), who arrived in New Spain in 1687 and is credited with founding more than a dozen churches, including the celebrated San Xavier del Bac in 1700. The expulsion of the Jesuits in 1767 left the missions under Franciscan jurisdiction. Because of distance and hostile conditions, there was virtually no contact between these missions and those along the Río Grande. See Polzer, *Kino Guide II*. For a geographical discussion of the land and its settlement, see Meinig, *Southwest*.

17. Simmons, *New Mexico*, p. 41. As is subsequently noted, Oñate later stood trial for the brutality used in bringing Acoma under control.

18. To effectively administer and control disparate towns in Mexico, the Spanish devised a policy of *reducciones* that condensed the scattered villages into larger units under direct Spanish supervision. According to the Laws of the Indies, "The Spaniards, to whom Indians are entrusted (*encomendados*) should seek with great care that these Indians be settled into towns, and that, within these, churches be built so that the Indians can be instructed into Christian doctrine and live in good order." At first the Indians resisted relocation into nontraditional village clusters but through coercion, threat, and, one assumes, some demonstration of material gain, the reducción became a rather successful institution—at least when viewed from the Spanish side.

19. Bolton, "The Mission as a Frontier Institution," p. 52. For a more extensive study of work policy, see Barber, "Indian Labor in the Spanish Colonies."

20. Simmons, *New Mexico*, p. 55.

21. Kubler, *Mexican Architecture*, p. 136.

22. Prince, *Spanish Mission Churches*, p. 44. The letter describing the situation was written by Fray Escalona to the superior of the Franciscan order in Mexico.

23. "Ultimately, New Mexico's conqueror was to be tried and convicted along with many of his leading officers for a wide variety of crimes. But the most important crime Oñate had committed in the eyes of Spain's rulers was one he was never tried for: that of failing to duplicate the feats of Cortés and Pizzaro in finding Indians of sufficient wealth to swell the bottomless coffers at Madrid." Beck, *New Mexico*, p. 60.

24. Hewett and Fisher, *Mission Monuments*, p. 81.

25. Scholes discussed the origins of the position of *custos* and ascertained when the title was first used. He concluded that although there had been other Franciscans who had earlier headed the missionary program in New Mexico, it was Fray Estevan de Perea who actually served as the first custodian. Scholes, "Problems in the Early Ecclesiastical History," pp. 32–75.

The custody was established in part as a response to the Oñate crisis and to the problems involved with canceling colonization in New Mexico and the concomitant abandonment of those Indians already converted—said to number more than 2,000. "Hence, it was finally decided to turn the colony over to the crown as a mission station with control in the hands of the clergy, the entire area being converted in a *custodia*, with the military there only to protect the missionaries." Beck, *New Mexico*, p. 59.

26. Prince, *Spanish Mission Churches*, pp. 45–49.

27. Spicer, *Cycles of Conquest*, p. 167; cited in Dozier, *The Pueblo Indians*, pp. 48–49.

28. Hewett and Fisher, *Mission Monuments*, p. 102.

29. Walter, "Mission Churches," p. 116.

30. "Against smallpox, measles, whooping cough, and cholera, they had no natural resistance, and they died in droves. . . . Other epidemics in the 1660s further thinned their ranks." Simmons, *New Mexico*, p. 65.

31. Hackett and Shelby, *The Pueblo Revolt;* cited in Dozier, *The Pueblo Indians,* p. 59.

32. "In spite of Popé's commands, many villagers retained their animals, continued to use their carts, refused to pull up their orchards, and some kept little forges in operation to work the scraps of iron and steel that were spoils of the revolt. A few who had been touched deeply by the friars squirreled away religious articles, salvaged from the churches, against the day when the Christians might return." Simmons, *New Mexico,* p. 72.

33. Hackett, *Historical Documents,* vol. 3, p. 132.

34. "Fortified village" is probably too strong a rendering of the term *plaza* in English because it suggests an impregnable outpost built to withstand a major battle or interminable siege. The Spanish word *plaza* in English, which is more commonly associated with an urban space, suggests a town plan that is more social than defensive. This was not the case. See Bunting, *Early Architecture,* p. 63; and Bunting, *Of Earth and Timbers Made,* pp. 6, 17.

35. The site of San Gabriel is marked today only by limited archaeological evidence. For the findings of a 1984 conference at San Juan Pueblo, see *When Cultures Meet,* especially pp. 10–38 and illustrations pp. 45–55.

36. Mundigo and Crouch, "The City Planning Ordinances," p. 248. To situate a forum at the intersection of the two main avenues of the Roman town was not common planning practice, although towns following this model did exist. The parallels with the towns prescribed by the Laws of the Indies are thus limited because the plaza was always intended to create the center of the Hispanic town; from it streets extended. Although in spite of the seeming specificity of their language, the ordinances were ultimately ambiguous and open to both interpretation and adjustment to site conditions. In theory streets led

from the midpoints of the plaza as well as from its corners, but in actual practice street planning varied considerably.

37. "In 1584, finally, among a shipment of forty cases of books . . . four folio copies of a quarto edition of the 'Arquitectura de Vitruvio' arrived, as well as four copies of a quarto edition of the 'Arquitectura de Alberto [sc. Leon Battista Alberti]' and two copies of a folio edition of the 'Arquitectura de Serlio.'" Kubler, *Mexican Architecture,* p. 104.

38. See Kubler, "Open-Grid Town Plans."

39. Article 34. These and all subsequent ordinances are translated in Mundigo and Crouch, "The City Planning Ordinances."

40. Article 35, Laws of the Indies.

41. Article 112, Laws of the Indies.

42. Article 113, Laws of the Indies.

43. Now used as a part of the Museum of New Mexico, the palace no longer represents its former architectural self, having been stripped of its original character and length by time and a restoration early in this century. See Shishkin, *The Palace of the Governors.*

44. Article 124, Laws of the Indies.

45. Article 119, Laws of the Indies.

46. For an extensive discussion of the development of the plaza at Santa Fe, see Wilson, "The Santa Fe, New Mexico, Plaza." Although ostensibly about the style of Santa Fe, Johnson, "The Santa Fe of the Future," included plans of the plaza "as it is today" and "as it should be" (which is, it will be seen, how it once was).

47. Article 122, Laws of the Indies.

48. Article 129, Laws of the Indies; Article 127, Laws of the Indies; and Article 126, Laws of the Indies.

49. Article 133, Laws of the Indies.

50. Domínguez, *The Missions,* pp. 39–40. In his condemnation of the capital, Domínguez expressed views on the character of cities that underlay the Laws of the Indies, that is, a nearly direct correlation

between the political and social entity and urban form. "Surely when one hears or reads 'Villa of Santa Fe,' along with the particulars that it is the capital of the kingdom, the seat of political and military government with a royal presidio, and other details that have come before one's eyes in the perusal of the foregoing, such a vivid and forceful notion or idea must be suggested to the imagination that the reason will seize upon it to form judgments and opinions that it just at least be fairly presentable, if not very good." The actuality of Santa Fe did not bear out this preconception, despite the exceptional setting. Domínguez termed the town "a rough stone set in fine metal." To provide a more suitable example, the friar cited the pueblo of Tlatelolco, a suburb of Mexico City. "Although a pueblo (a less pretentious title than villa) [it] has the very greatest advantages over this villa [Santa Fe]; not superficially, as one might suppose, but indeed in its actual appearance, design, arrangement, and plan, for in it there are streets, well-planned houses, shops, fountains; in a word, it has something to lift the spirit by appealing to the senses." At this point he rendered his verdict on Santa Fe: "This villa is the exact opposite, for in the final analysis it lacks everything" (p. 39).

51. See Bunting, *Early Architecture;* Bunting, *Of Earth and Timbers Made;* Jackson, "New Mexico Houses," pp. 2–5; and Wilson, "When the Room Is the Hall," pp. 17–23.

52. Notwithstanding its height, Pueblo architecture was essentially single-story construction stacked in floors. Walls may or may not have continued through more than one floor, but each roof became a potential building surface for the story above it, allowing for an agglomeration of units that to some degree were structurally independent. Each unit could appear, expand, decay, or even disappear with a minimum of influence on its neighbors. The need for coordinating communal

building efforts was also reduced. Bunting showed how oblique windows at Zuñi overcame some of the difficult conditions created by this piecemeal construction pattern. See Bunting, *Early Architecture*, pp. 32–51, especially Figure 25; and for a description of Pecos, see Kessell, *Kiva, Cross, and Crown*, pp. 8–12.

53. Knowles argued that Anasazi and Pueblo Indian architecture represented building in complete accord with solar and thermal principles. Although the residential blocks on the Acoma mesa follow rules of orientation quite closely, this is the exception rather than the rule. Similarly, Cliff Palace at Mesa Verde also faces south and is thus shaded by the cavern ceiling during the hot summer months. But other clusters such as Spruce Tree House face in many different directions, suggesting that a cave with sufficient building surface was more important than its orientation. See Knowles, *Sun Rhythm Form*.

54. "In warm weather the zaguan was often a family work area, and piles of drying corn, wheat, chile, melons, onions, and tobacco were strewn in it for cleaning or tying in strings; farm tools and drying hides hung from the vigas." Boyd, *Popular Arts*, p. 27.

55. Ibid., p. 23. "Well-to-do Spanish families built *torreones* (towers) next to or near their houses for defensive purposes. Composed of adobe, ledgestone or lava rocks according to their locations, these towers were frontier extensions of medieval European fortified castles, at least in the minds of their owners. They had blank walls with crenellated adobe parapets above the upper room and a few peepholes in the upper walls to shoot through at hostile raiders. Either round or square in shape, the lower room was used to shelter livestock when an alarm of approaching Indians was given. Women, children, and neighbors who had time to reach the tower stayed in the upper room along with the food and water that had been collected for the besieged. Fighting men crouched be-

hind the parapets and endeavored to shoot the enemy with their often inadequate firearms. Nomadic Indians soon learned to hold the Spanish prisoners by staying out of gun range while others of their party drove off whatever human captives and livestock they could find in the neighborhood, seizing corn and other loot and making their escape. At best a torreon might save the lives of its occupants, but more often this method of defense turned out to be the funeral pyre of those who had taken refuge in it." Boyd, *Popular Arts*, p. 23.

56. Although no real tradition of meditative or ornamental gardens developed in the harsh conditions of New Mexico, vegetable gardens and orchards could serve ornamental purposes, particularly when fruit trees came into bloom. At Acoma water was brought to the mesa with great effort to irrigate small peach trees, which no doubt addressed both functional and decorative needs. Domínguez, *The Missions*, p. 192.

57. As a result of the expulsion of the Jesuits in 1767, the mission program in California late in the eighteenth century was placed under Franciscan jurisdiction—but by this time the Franciscans' doctrine had undergone fundamental change. "With this earlier [utopian] urban ideal of the Franciscans for the converted Indian settlements, the later practice of the Order in California has very little in common. Whereas in New Spain and in New Mexico, supervision had served only to regulate an established Indian culture, and to protect the Indians against European exploitation, the Franciscans in California produced a mission discipline fundamentally military in character. Imposed upon primitives, it implied a permanent state of tutelage and a mechanization of society at the expense of inner development. On the other hand, it was a most successful solution to the basic colonial problem —the education of primitives to systematic habits of work." Kubler, "Two Modes of Franciscan Architecture," p. 46.

58. Kubler and Soria, *Art and Architecture*, p. 71.

59. Toussaint, *Colonial Art*, pp. 275–277.

60. The full story of Hispanic-American architecture lies beyond the scope of this book; what concerns us, however, are those church structures built specifically for other remote native populations in the Americas that provide parallels with the churches built later in New Mexico.

61. Wethey, *Colonial Architecture*, p. 18. The churches that were supposedly built on the model of the Gesú in Rome actually displayed a greater affinity for Gothic and Renaissance prototypes. "The truth is that the Jesuit order never officially adopted a specific type of floorplan in Peru or anywhere else" (p. 18).

62. Kubler, *Mexican Architecture*, pp. 105–106. Kubler confirmed that "the vast official documentation for the colony contains almost no reference to drawings prepared in Spain for American use" (p. 105).

63. For the definitive presentation and analysis of the *atrio* and the development of related Mexican religious architecture, see McAndrew, *The Open-Air Churches*; and Toussaint, *Colonial Art*, pp. 25–31, 57.

64. This term *architectural competence* is borrowed from Glassie: "The learning designer develops a set of pure and simple geometric ideas. As thinker, as perceiving, conceptualizing human being, he shatters and rebuilds reality by dint of an inward capacity for sundering and ordering. Without limiting his thoughts in terms of future need, he constructs ideas that are inherently useless but of enormous potential owing to their very simplicity. He relates these essential ideas into a geometric repertoire much the same way the learning speaker develops a set of phonemes or the learning musician develops a scale of notes. The designer's geometric repertoire is not composed of models of the sights of the phenomenal world. It is not a set of abstracted trees or faces, but a set of

simple shapes abstracted beyond any connection with trees and faces. It is an unreflectively held repertoire of geometric entities, elegant summaries of features of shape, such as line or angle or curve." Glassie, *Folk Housing*, pp. 19, 19–40.

65. See Stubbs, Ellis, and Dittert, "'Lost' Pecos Church."

66. Kubler, *The Religious Architecture*, p. 19.

67. While visiting Picuris in 1776, Domínguez recorded the uncertainty of existence on the frontier. The new church would be built, he assured the reader, but its site was to be adjusted to take defense into account. The Comanche raids "are so daring that this father I have mentioned [Don Pedro Fermin de Mendinueta] assures me that he escaped by a miracle in the year '69, for they sacked the convent and destroyed his meager supplies; yet he considered them well spent in exchange for his life and freedom from captivity. . . . Orders were issued for the erection of a new building [church] in a safe place. This is near one block of, but outside, one plaza of the pueblo, with the intention that the convent should be in that block. But according to the plan, all is to be defensible as a unit, for the present space between the church and the block where the convent is to be built will be a cloister." Domínguez, *The Missions*, p. 92.

68. Schuetz, *Architectural Practice*, p. 43.

69. The supplies for each friar establishing a mission included "one ream of paper." Scholes, "The Supply Service," p. 100.

70. "After outlining the foundation with powdered lime, the trench is opened, leveled, and straightened with a mason's square and lines." Schuetz, *Architectural Practice*, p. 21.

71. Kubler cited the surveying practice of "setting cords for a new town," illustrated in *Pintura del Gobernador*, circa 1566. Kubler, *Mexican Architecture*, p. 159.

72. Scholes, "The Supply Service," pp. 103–104.

73. Boyd, *Popular Arts*, p. 48.

74. Ibid., p. 446.

75. Cited in Walter, "Mission Churches," p. 116.

76. The Casa Grande was built by the Hohokam people between A.D. 1300 and 1400. Hand-formed lumps of soil (called "turtle backs" because of their rounded forms) patted into place are believed to be the principal elements of construction. See Wilcox and Shenk, *The Architecture of the Casa Grande*.

77. Lumpkins, "A Distinguished Architect," p. 3.

78. Nelson, *Preservation of Historic Adobe Buildings*. The process of burnishing, more effective when the device is slightly wet, is actually a process of sealing and polishing by gradually redistributing surface particles through continued rubbing. This technique is used to great aesthetic effect in the making of unglazed ceramics as the burnished areas—whether reduced or oxidized—acquire a brilliant shine without glazes.

79. Dickey, *New Mexico Village Arts*, p. 51.

80. Note the resemblance between this technique and the function of foundation stones. Halseth, "Report of Repairs," pp. 10–12.

81. "There is no heading for the nave of this church, because its adornment is so soulless that I consider it unnecessary to describe anything so dead. Nevertheless, although its chief resemblance is to a culverin because of its length and narrowness, it also resembles a wine cellar, and it contains two poor benches provided by Father Fray Sebastian Fernandez." Domínguez, *The Missions*, p. 115.

82. Kubler, *The Religious Architecture*, p. 34. Ivey, however, stressed the importance of block and tackle in church construction: "It is frequently forgotten that such equipment was known to virtually every Spaniard in the New World, since all had arrived there on board ships

with innumerable pulleys, winches, and other lifting devices in constant use." He dismissed Kubler's interpretation that one nave wall's greater thickness was due to its use as a lifting surface: "Shear legs or some similar system of lifting had to have been used in the construction of the Salinas missions, contrary to the statements of George Kubler." Most of the beams had intricate carvings and were finished before they were installed. "If finished beams had been rolled to a wall top and then dragged into position, as depicted by Kubler, they would have been extensively damaged on the finished surfaces and edges. Instead they had to be lifted clear of the walls and lowered into position." Ivey, *In the Midst of Loneliness*.

83. Bunting and Conron, "The Architecture of Northern New Mexico," p. 27.

84. Hesse, "The Missions of Cochití and Santo Domingo, N.M.," p. 27.

85. See Toulouse, *The Mission of San Gregorio*. It was more common for doors to be mounted on wooden pivots than on metal hinges. "A pintle hinge would be fashioned from a stile extended beyond the top and bottom rails of the door, and allowed to rotate in a socket carved from the door frame. Such a pintle pivot door is known in New Mexico as a *zambullo*." Holmes, "Architectural Woodwork," p. 18.

86. Domínguez, *The Missions*, pp. 198–199.

87. Lummis, *The Land of Poco Tiempo*, p. 6.

88. "Like the alabaster window panes of Ravenna's Byzantine churches, selenite is not transparent but is translucent, giving a subdued bath of light to the interior. Electric bulbs dangling from a cord, fluorescent tubes and plastic shades that have been installed in several chapels to replace obstructed clerestory windows give, in comparison, sorry lighting." Boyd, *Popular Arts*, p. 48.

328

89. Inventory of goods from Glascow and Brother, St. Louis, which consisted mostly of clothing and food stuffs: "3 half boxes window glass 8 × 10. 3 half boxes window glass 10 × 12." Ibid., p. 325.

90. Kubler, *The Religious Architecture*, p. 67.

91. Ibid., pp. 69–70.

92. Domínguez, *The Missions*, p. 205.

93. For additional information on wooden chests, see Boyd, *Popular Arts*, pp. 246–265; Taylor and Bokides, *Carpinteros and Cabinetmakers*; and Dickey, *New Mexico Village Arts*, pp. 50–82.

94. Adams and Chavez (Domínguez's translators and editors) defined the term *first fruits* as follows: "*Primicias*. A voluntary Annual offering from the harvests and herds, seldom requested from the poor and never from the Indians" (p. 355). Yet Domínguez's entry on "How He [the Franciscan] Acquires Necessities" for Picuris stated, "Although it comes out the same everywhere according to the usual method and by exchange, this father says that here, in order not to deprive himself of the little grain he acquires by harvests and first fruits and perhaps an obvention or two, most of it comes from the royal alms in chocolate, linen, or winding sheets." Domínguez, *The Missions*, p. 96.

95. Domínguez, *The Missions*, pp. 192, 193.

96. "The Cubero document does not say whether the convent was actually south of the church or viceversa; because the south would be the better protected side, we can suppose almost with certainty that the Fathers used the higher church structure as a wind and weather break on the north. Invariably they chose the sheltered side for their convents in all the missions. Chavez, "Santa Fe Church and Convent Sites," p. 93. Acoma is another very apparent example of the pattern Chavez described.

97. Domínguez, *The Missions*, p. 27.

98. Ibid., p. 48.

99. Ibid., p. 93.

100. Lange, *Cochiti*, pp. 419–420. "The new burial ground was opened about the turn of the century. This occurred after a severe epidemic of 'Los Frios,' mountain fever, and another of malaria had plagued Cochití in the 1890s and the early 1900s. At that time, numerous deaths in the village, sometimes five or six a day, filled the *campo santo* immediately in front of the church, and the new burial ground west of the pueblo was consecrated. Like the Indians, the Spanish families at Cochití have used both *campo santos*" (p. 419).

101. Kubler, *The Religious Architecture*, p. 75.

102. McAndrew, *The Open-Air Churches*, p. 349.

103. Toulouse, *The Mission of San Gregorio*, p. 61, n. 7.

104. Dickey, *New Mexico Village Arts*, p. 59.

105. Bolton, "The Mission as a Frontier Institution," p. 64. As late as 1853 "the New Mexico woman's preference for sitting on the floor, even if she had 'American' furniture," made an impression on foreign eyes. W. W. H. Davis, *El Gringo, or New Mexico and Her People*; cited in Boyd, *Popular Arts*, p. 43.

106. Domínguez, *The Missions*, p. 65.

107. This development is traced in Mather, *Baroque to Folk*.

108. "The Laguna santero, working just at the end of the 18th century, was a true folk artist in his use of tempera pigments and abandonment of perspective and realism for two-dimensional treatment of his subjects." Boyd, *Popular Arts*, p. 162. See also Wroth, *Christian Images*, pp. 69–92.

109. Boyd, *Popular Arts*, p. 275.

110. Ibid., p. 118; and Wroth, *Christian Images*, pp. 47–50.

111. Boyd, *Popular Arts*, p. 118.

112. Domínguez, *The Missions*, p. 66.

113. Cited in Boyd, *Popular Arts*, p. 125.

114. Ibid., p. 275. Among the metal goods at Abiquiu Domínguez found "a saw. A lever. Two crowbars, so worn out that they are no longer useful. A plane. All came from the King, and the said inventory so records them. Still another crowbar. Adze. Chisel, but Father Fernandez did not find this, for they say it is lost, and so there is nothing but what has been listed before." Domínguez, *The Missions*, p. 123.

115. Simmons and Turley, *Southwestern Colonial Ironwork*, pp. 22–32.

116. Scholes, "The Supply Service," pp. 100–109.

117. Boyd, *Popular Arts*, p. 64.

118. "Epistle side, *lado de la epistola*. The right side of the altar as one faces it, where the Epistle of the Mass is sung or recited; hence, the entire right side of the church." Domínguez, *The Missions*, p. 355. Thus, the gospel side is to the left.

119. Domínguez, *The Missions*, pp. 308–310.

120. Cited in Bolton, "The Mission as a Frontier Institution," p. 63. "[He] was able to report fourteen monasteries, serving fifty-odd pueblos, each with its school, where the Indians were taught not only to sing, play musical instruments, read, and write, but, as Benavides puts it, 'all the trades and polite deportment,' all imparted by 'the great industry of the Religious who converted them'" (p. 63).

121. Domínguez, *The Missions*, p. 67.

122. Bloom, "Bourke on the Southwest X," p. 251.

123. Ibid., p. 197.

124. "Among the Mendicant builders, the incidence of formal architectural education, low everywhere in Europe at the period, remained very rare in Mexico. . . . Architectural education, then, among the Mendicants, remained highly informal, guided by no theory other than that which could be assimi-

lated from reading and from experienced men in civilization and monastic life. The new quantum that must not be overlooked, however, is the presence in Mexico after 1550 of men bearing an academic, book-formed standard of classicizing taste in architecture." Kubler, *Mexican Architecture*, p. 128.

125. Ibid., p. 104.

126. Schuetz, *Architectural Practice.*

127. Ibid., pp. 50–51.

128. Ibid., p. 21, n. 9.

129. Manucy, *The Houses of St. Augustine*, p. 27.

130. Kessell, *The Missions of New Mexico*, p. 156.

131. Wroth, *The Chapel of Our Lady of Talpa*, p. 43, n. 15.

132. "Except for two known cases, New Mexico had no native vocations from 1600 to 1800. The reason is obvious. As a mere military outpost, the Spanish population never got educational help or facilities from the Crown; moreover, the number of people and their economy were kept down at a miserable low level by the poverty of the land and the continuous Indian invasions." Archdiocese of Santa Fe, *Lamy Memorial*, p. 23.

133. Ellis, *Bishop Lamy's Santa Fe Cathedral*, p. 65.

134. Cited in Boyd, *Popular Arts*, p. 163.

135. Weigle, *The Penitentes*, pp. 8–13.

136. Wroth, *The Chapel of Our Lady of Talpa*, p. 44, n. 17.

137. See Bunting, Lyons, and Lyons, "Penitente Brotherhood Moradas." "Penitente observances usually require not only a *morada*, or meetinghouse, but also a separate chapel which serves as the place of communal observances involving not only Brothers but also members of the families and guests. The *morada* itself is more exclusive and usually more isolated. It is the center for the Brothers and their private penitential practices (necessarily private since the strictures of Bishop Zubiria in 1833). During

Holy Week both structures, the chapel and the *morada*, are utilized, the chapel is the *deposito* (depository) for the Virgin Mary and the dwelling for the women and children, while the men are in retreat for the week (or longer) in the *morada*." Wroth, *The Chapel of Our Lady of Talpa*, p. 44, n. 17.

138. Although much of the current sculpture is sold to collectors as sculpture, rather than as devotional images, the Cordova woodcarving tradition continues, producing some of the finest works sold each year at the Spanish market in Santa Fe. The buyer sees there familiar names—Ortiz, López, Córdova—suggesting that ideas and craft are still transmitted through family lines. See Briggs, *The Wood Carvers.*

139. Dickey, *New Mexico Village Arts*, p. 183.

140. Simmons, *New Mexico*, p. 120.

141. The shift in the siting of the church from the periphery to the center of the plaza accompanied the deterioration of the architecturally defined plaza, and with it, a further weakening of the influence of the distant Laws of the Indies. Like the stylistic modifications upon the church fabric encouraged by physical isolation, climate, and later the change in government, the town pattern as a whole was evolving. See Jackson, *Landscape Autoguide*, p. 19.

142. Kubler, *The Religious Architecture*, p. 105.

143. Ibid., pp. 22–23. A flat earthen roof fit between parapets can be a truly satisfactory solution only in a climate without rain. Because the parapet is exposed to the elements on three surfaces, because water collects on the roof surface and infiltrates the joint between roof and parapet, the connection will always remain problematic and will require constant vigilance. Any sloping roof that extends over the walls will function more competently than a flat earthen roof—hence the widespread popularity of the pitched roof once metal sheeting became available.

144. Johnson Nestor Mortier & Rodríguez, Architects, Santa Fe, surveyed Catholic churches built before 1940 during 1984–1988. A second phase of the study is in progress.

145. The construction and conversion of Old or New Santa Fe style buildings reached epidemic proportions during the 1930s. John Gaw Meem was the most prominent among the architects working in the "historical" idiom, his work including stylistic renovations as well as new construction. The architectural gloss he applied to the Presbyterian Church in Santa Fe in 1939 was so extreme that even a regular churchgoer might have mistaken what had been a Neo-Gothic building for a colonial Catholic church. See Bunting, *John Gaw Meem.* For Cristo Rey, see Krahe, *Cristo Rey.*

146. For the story of artists in New Mexico during the 1920s and 1930s, see Robertson and Nestor, *Artists of the Canyons and Caminos;* and Eldredge, Schimmel, and Truettner, *Art in New Mexico.*

147. Carlos Vierra's paintings of the missions appear in Walters, "Mission Churches"; and in Hewett, *Mission Monuments.* In "New Mexico Architecture," Vierra argued for a regional architecture and condemned the Anglo remodeling of Cochiti as "benevolent vandalism." "Exterior arches have no place in this architecture—peak roofs are no part of it, and steeples—impossible. Peak roofs, steeples, the Roman arch of the Spanish colonial, and the Moorish arch were ruled out through the limitations of adobe as material in which these forms could not endure" (p. 46).

148. Because of the nature of adobe, there have been significant changes to the churches recorded by the HABS during the nearly half-century that has elapsed since the work was undertaken. A comparison of the plan of Isleta in this book and the HABS drawing (a plan based on it is published in Kubler, *The Religious Architecture*) will show that one of the major but-

330 tresses has been removed. Many other changes in the structures are less drastic; but the buildings continue to evolve. Drawings of Acoma Pueblo—but, unfortunately, not of San Esteban—have been published in Nabokov, *Architecture of Acoma Pueblo.*

149. The Santa Fe Planning Department's *Design and Preservation in Santa Fe* tried to remedy some of the flaws in the Historical Style Ordinance, principally to develop guidelines for a coherent townscape rather than for aesthetically correct (if artificial) individual buildings.

150. Ruskin chided the reader (and the scraper): "Do not let us deceive ourselves in this important matter; it is *impossible*, as impossible as to raise the dead, to restore anything that has ever been great or beautiful in architecture that which I have above insisted upon as the life of the whole, that spirit which is given only by the hand and the eye of the workman, never can be recalled. Another spirit may be given by another time, and it is then a new building; but the spirit of the dead workman can not be summoned up, and commanded to direct other hands, and other thoughts." Ruskin, *The Seven Lamps of Architecture,* p. 184.

151. Owings, "Las Trampas," pp. 30–35.

152. Bunting, "San Agustín de la Isleta," pp. 14–16.

153. Kessell, *The Missions of New Mexico,* pp. 219–220.

154. One should not be too optimistic, however, as buildings of mud exist in a state of constant crisis. Picuris collapsed in the late 1980s; and several smaller churches have been allowed to deteriorate or have been bulldozed when there was no other alternative. Given the problems of continual care that adobe structures require, the existence of the smaller structures will always be tenuous.

155. Hesse, "The Missions of Cochití and Santo Domingo, N.M.," p. 30.

156. Bloom, "Bourke on the Southwest X," pp. 262, 279.

157. Dozier, *The Pueblo Indians,* p. 50.

158. Lummis, *The Land of Poco Tiempo,* p. 3.

159. Bandelier, *The Delightmakers* (a thinly veiled anthropology).

160. Meinig, *Southwest,* p. 74.

PART II: **THE CHURCHES**

SANTA FE: **SAN MIGUEL**

1. "Almost every town in Spain has its ermitas, small chapel-like buildings or shrines, often on hilltops or in other out-of-the-way places, not unlike the late nineteenth century Penitente moradas of New Mexico. In the case of San Miguel, 'outlying chapel' seems a better rendering than 'hermitage.' After its rebuilding in 1710, San Miguel was no longer called an ermita." Kessell, *The Missions of New Mexico,* p. 57, n. 29, n. 30. Johnson-Nestor, *San Miguel Chapel,* p. 3.

2. See Stubbs and Ellis, *Archeological Investigations.*

3. Simmons, "Tlascalans," p. 102.

4. Ibid., p. 108.

5. Cited in Prince, *Spanish Mission Churches,* p. 72.

6. Scholes, "Church and State," pp. 297–342.

7. Kubler, *The Rebuilding of San Miguel,* p. 9.

8. Ibid., p. 21.

9. A document listing the payment to workers was discussed in ibid., p. 6.

10. Ibid., p. 5.

11. Adams, *Bishop Tamarón's Visitation,* pp. 46–47.

12. Domínguez, *The Missions,* p. 38.

13. De Morfi, "Geographical Description," pp. 91–92.

14. Kessell, *The Missions of New Mexico,* pp. 50–51. Boyd stated that Don Antonio José Ortiz, who funded repairs to the Parroquia and the construction of the Rosario chapel,

also contributed to repairs at San Miguel undertaken in 1798. Boyd, *Popular Arts,* p. 33.

15. Bloom, "Bourke on the Southwest VII," p. 303.

16. See Johnson-Nestor, *San Miguel Chapel.*

17. The dating of the "oldest house" is also questionable. As the principal body of San Miguel dates from the 1710 rebuilding, both Acoma and at least parts of Isleta and other churches are actually older and could claim the title. St. Augustine, Florida, also claims to possess the "oldest house."

SANTA FE: **LA PARROQUIA; THE CATHEDRAL OF SAINT FRANCIS**

1. Crouch, Garr, and Mundigo, *Spanish City Planning,* pp. 14–15. Ordinance 126 stated, "In the plaza, no lots shall be assigned to private individuals; instead they shall be used for the buildings of the church and royal houses and for city use" (pp. 14–15). In later years at least two chapels were built on the plaza: Nuestra Señora de la Luz (La Castrense) on the south side and the Chapel of the Vigiles (Holy Trinity) on the west. Prince, *Spanish Mission Churches,* p. 68.

2. See also Wilson, *The Santa Fe, New Mexico, Plaza.*

3. Kubler, *The Religious Architecture,* p. 100.

4. Chavez, *The Santa Fe Cathedral,* unpaged.

5. Hodge, Hammond, and Rey, *Fray Alonso de Benavides,* p. 68.

6. Ibid.

7. Kubler, *The Religious Architecture,* p. 100.

8. Scholes, "Documents for the History of the New Mexican Missions," pp. 46–47.

9. Chavez, "Santa Fe Church and Convent Sites," p. 91.

10. Boyd, *Popular Arts,* pp. 36–37. The structure was razed in 1714 to give the plaza a more proper figure. By this time, however, the entire palace was in such an extremely

poor condition that demolition and rebuilding were contemplated. Shiskin, *The Palace of the Governors*, pp. 17–18.

11. Prince, *Spanish Mission Churches*, p. 73.

12. Adams, *Bishop Tamarón's Visitation*, p. 46.

13. Domínguez, *The Missions*, p. 39.

14. Ibid., p. 39.

15. Ibid., pp. 13–14.

16. Ibid., p. 13.

17. Sena, "The Chapel of Don Antonio José Ortiz," pp. 355–356.

18. Ibid., p. 356; Chavez, *The Santa Fe Cathedral*, unpaged.

19. Ellis, *Bishop Lamy's Santa Fe Cathedral*, pp. 66–69, 77. Ellis offers a detailed investigation not only of the cathedral but also of all the structures that preceded it.

20. Abert, *Report . . . 1846–47*, pp. 454–455; cited in Kessell, *The Missions of New Mexico*, pp. 38–39.

21. Calvin, *Lieutenant Emory Reports*, p. 59.

22. Ellis, *Bishop Lamy's Santa Fe Cathedral*, p. xii.

23. Ibid., p. 11.

24. *Daily New Mexican*, January 3, 1873; cited in Ellis, *Bishop Lamy's Santa Fe Cathedral*, p. 2.

25. Ellis, *Bishop Lamy's Santa Fe Cathedral*, p. 20.

26. Both characterizations were cited in ibid., p. 16.

27. Ibid.

28. Ibid., p. 32: "The original Mouly plan had called for stone towers 100 feet high, without spires."

29. Ibid., p. 28.

30. Ibid., p. 35.

31. Defouri, *Historical Sketch of the Catholic Church in New Mexico*, pp. 143–146; cited in Kessell, *The Missions of New Mexico*, p. 42.

32. Bloom, "Bourke on the Southwest VII," pp. 303, 307.

33. Kessell, *The Missions of New Mexico*, p. 43; Bunting, *John Gaw Meem*, p. 117.

34. Chavez assigned credit for the design to Urban C. Weidner, Jr. Chavez, *The Santa Fe Cathedral*, unpaged.

SANTA FE: **EL ROSARIO**

1. The statue was kept in the small chapel in the Palace of the Governors until the reconstruction of the Parroquia in 1714. Boyd, *Popular Arts*, p. 331.

2. Ibid., p. 332.

3. The annual procession is held the second Sunday after Trinity or the Sunday after Corpus Christi and carries the Conquistadora from the cathedral to the Rosario.

SANTA FE: **NUESTRA SEÑORA DE GUADALUPE**

1. Archives of the Archdiocese of Santa Fe.

2. Twitchell, *Leading Facts of New Mexico History;* cited in Prince, *Spanish Mission Churches*, p. 188. Defouri, *Historical Sketches of the Catholic Church in New Mexico;* cited in Prince, *Spanish Mission Churches*, p. 117.

3. Kubler, *The Religious Architecture*, p. 101.

4. Abert, *Report of the Secretary of War, communicating . . . a report and map . . . of New Mexico*, pp. 39–40; cited in Kubler, *The Religious Architecture*, p. 102.

5. Bloom, "Bourke on the Southwest VII," p. 321.

6. Prince, *Spanish Mission Churches*, p. 119.

7. Ibid., p. 121.

SANTA FE: **NUESTRA SEÑORA DE LA LUZ [LA CASTRENSE]; CRISTO REY** 331

1. Domínguez, *The Missions*, p. 40.

2. Hodge, Hammond, and Rey, *Fray Alonso de Benavides*, p. 68.

3. Adams, *Bishop Tamarón's Visitation*, p. 46.

4. Ibid., p. 47.

5. Von Wuthenau, "The Spanish Military Chapels," p. 187.

6. Adams, *Bishop Tamarón's Visitation*, p. 47.

7. Domínguez, *The Missions*, p. 40.

8. Ibid., p. 34.

9. Ibid.

10. Ibid.

11. "Although the stone altar screen at La Castrense unquestionably was the model for later wooden examples in New Mexico, the designers of these did not attempt to reproduce the flat pilasters decorated all over with carving. Instead they made full rounded, salomonic pillars of an earlier period." Boyd, *Popular Arts*, p. 60.

12. Ibid., p. 34.

13. De Morfi, "Geographical Description," p. 91.

14. Kessell, *The Missions of New Mexico*, p. 45.

15. Guevara, Santa Fe, March 2–April 8, 1818, Archives of the Archdiocese of Santa Fe; cited in ibid., p. 45.

16. Krahe, *Cristo Rey*, p. 26.

17. Adams cited the memoirs of Colonel Perea, "who visited Santa Fe as a boy in the winter of 1837–38: Opposite the Palace stood the military church, called La Castrense, then the handsomest building of its kind in the capitol city. This house of worship was most gorgeously adorned within with pictures of saints and other portraits, some of which were said to be very valuable. The altar in every appointment was very tastefully adorned, and was a thing of dazzling beauty." Allison, "Santa Fe as it appeared during the winter in the years 1837 and 1838," p. 177; cited in Adams, "The Chapel," pp. 338–39.

18. Bieber, "The Papers of James J. Webb, Santa Fe Merchant, 1844–1861," p. 276; cited in ibid., p. 339.

19. Abert, *Western America*, p. 41; cited in Kessell, *The Missions of New Mexico*, pp. 45–46.

20. Ibid., p. 47.

21. Ibid., p. 48.

22. From Krahe, *Cristo Rey*, p. 24; cited in Chauvenet, *John Gaw Meem*, p. 83.

23. Bunting, *John Gaw Meem*, p. 125.

TESUQUE PUEBLO: **SAN DIEGO**

1. For a discussion of architectural planning in relation to the surrounding landscape, see McCaffrey and Needham-McCaffrey, "Old as the Hills."

2. See Knowles, *Sun Rhythm Form*.

3. Dutton, *Let's Explore Indian Villages*, p. 25.

4. Hodge, *Handbook of American Indians*, p. 735.

5. Walter, "Mission Churches," pp. 119–120.

6. Kessell, *The Missions of New Mexico*, pp. 61–62.

7. De Morfi, "Geographical Description."

8. Adams, *Bishop Tamarón's Visitation*, p. 54.

9. Ibid.

10. Domínguez, *The Missions*, p. 51.

11. Ibid., p. 48.

12. Ibid., p. 49.

13. Ibid., p. 50.

14. Ibid., p. 47.

15. Ibid.

16. Hewett and Fisher, *Mission Monuments*, p. 119, Walter, "Mission Churches," p. 119.

17. Prince, *Spanish Mission Churches*, p. 280.

18. Conversation with author, July 1981.

19. Kessell, *The Missions of New Mexico*, p. 62.

SAN ILDEFONSO PUEBLO: **SAN ILDEFONSO**

1. Stubbs, *Bird's-Eye View*, pp. 47–48.

2. Hewett and Fisher, *Mission Monuments*, p. 69; Walter, "Mission Churches," p. 119.

3. Kubler, *The Religious Architecture*, p. 122.

4. Hodge, Hammond, and Rey, *Fray Alonso de Benavides*, p. 68.

5. Kubler, *The Religious Architecture*, p. 122.

6. Adams, *Bishop Tamarón's Visitation*, p. 65.

7. Domínguez, *The Missions*, p. 64.

8. Ibid., p. 65.

9. Ibid., p. 68.

10. Kessell, *The Missions of New Mexico*, p. 78.

11. Bloom, "Bourke on the Southwest XI," p. 66.

12. Prince, *Spanish Mission Churches*, p. 277.

13. Walter, "Mission Churches," p. 119.

14. Kessell, *The Missions of New Mexico*, p. 81, n. 4.

SANTA CLARA PUEBLO: **SANTA CLARA**

1. According to Prince, *Spanish Mission Churches*, the Indian name for the village is Kah-po, translated as either "enclosed water," "wild rose," or "eyeball" (p. 292).

2. Scholes, "Documents for the History of the New Mexican Missions," p. 47.

3. Adams, *Bishop Tamarón's Visitation*, p. 64.

4. Domínguez, *The Missions*, p. 114.

5. Ibid.

6. Ibid., p. 116.

7. Ibid., p. 119.

8. Kessell, *The Missions of New Mexico*, p. 116.

9. Bloom, "Bourke on the Southwest X," p. 256.

---

10. Forrest, *Missions and Pueblos*, p. 72.

11. Prince, *Spanish Mission Churches*, p. 295.

12. Walter, "Mission Churches," p. 116.

13. Photo by Edward Ruda taken September 1962, facing p. 294 in Prince, *Spanish Mission Churches*.

14. Stubbs, *Bird's-Eye View*, p. 43.

15. Compare color photo by Robert B. McCoy (c. September 1976) facing p. 173 in Prince, *Spanish Mission Churches*, with photo by the author taken July 1981.

SAN JUAN PUEBLO: **SAN JUAN BAUTISTA; OUR LADY OF LOURDES**

1. Prince, *Spanish Mission Churches*, p. 290.

2. Ortiz, *Handbook of North American Indians*, vol. 9, pp. 278–281, 292.

3. Ibid., p. 280.

4. Kessell, *The Missions of New Mexico*, p. 90.

5. Domínguez, *The Missions*, p. 89, n. 6—Villagra was quoted as having said, "In memory of those noble sons who first raised in these barbarous regions the bloody Tree upon which Christ perished for the redemption of mankind."

6. Hodge, Hammond, and Rey, *Fray Alonso de Benavides*, pp. 68–69.

7. Prince, *Spanish Mission Churches*, p. 41.

8. Hewett and Fisher, *Mission Monuments*, p. 69.

9. Prince, *Spanish Mission Churches*, p. 284.

10. "I made this copy of the original which is in the archive of the Secretariat of the Indies, and it agrees with the original. Madrid, May 24, 1664. (signed) Fray Bartolomé Márquez (rubric), Secretary-General of the Indies." Document in the Archivo General de las Indias, *legajo* 60-3-6, *Mexico. Ecclesiastical, 1664*; cited in Scholes, "Documents for the History of the New Mexican Missions," pp. 46–51.

11. "The second document, which is a report to the officials of the Hacienda in Mexico City, describes the status of the missions during the years 1663–66 and contains a statement of the needs for the future." Ibid., pp. 51–58.

12. Ortiz, *Handbook of North American Indians*, vol. 9, pp. 278–281. Domínguez, *The Missions*, p. 85.

13. Domínguez, *The Missions*, p. 86.

14. Adams, *Bishop Tamarón's Visitation*, p. 63.

15. Hewett and Fisher, *Mission Monuments*, p. 109.

16. Domínguez, *The Missions*, p. 86. Kessell gave the dimensions as 22 by 110 feet. Kessell, *The Missions of New Mexico*, p. 10.

17. Domínguez, *The Missions*, p. 87.

18. Ibid., p. 84.

19. Ibid., p. 86.

20. Ibid., p. 88.

21. Ibid., p. 90.

22. Kessell, *The Missions of New Mexico*, p. 94.

23. Ibid.

24. Bloom, "Bourke on the Southwest X," pp. 269, 260.

25. Kessell, *The Missions of New Mexico*, p. 94.

26. Prince, *Spanish Mission Churches*, p. 289.

27. Forrest, *Missions and Pueblos*, p. 82.

SANTA CRUZ: **SANTA CRUZ**

1. Prince, *Spanish Mission Churches*, p. 305.

2. Forrest, *Missions and Pueblos*, p. 73.

3. Prince, *Spanish Mission Churches*, p. 307.

4. Domínguez, *The Missions*, p. 248.

5. Kessell, *The Missions of New Mexico*, p. 82.

6. Santa Cruz Parish, *La Iglesia de Santa Cruz*, p. 13.

7. Prince, *Spanish Mission Churches*, p. 307.

8. Adams, *Bishop Tamarón's Visitation*, p. 63.

9. Ibid.

10. Kessell, *The Missions of New Mexico*, p. 82.

11. Kubler, *The Religious Architecture*, p. 103.

12. Domínguez, *The Missions*, pp. 72–73.

13. Ibid., p. 73.

14. Ibid., p. 74.

15. Ibid., p. 82.

16. Ibid., p. 84.

17. Kessell, *The Missions of New Mexico*, p. 82; Kubler, *Religious Architecture*, p. 103.

18. "Visitation of Fray José Mariano Rosete, 1796," #1360; cited in Santa Cruz Parish, *La Iglesia de Santa Cruz*, p. 15.

19. "Report of Fray Josef Benito Pereyro, 1808," #1191; cited in ibid., p. 16.

20. Kessell, *The Missions of New Mexico*, p. 83.

21. Ibid.

22. "Inventory of Father Juan de Jesús Trujillo, 1867," Reel #57, Frames #450–456; cited in Santa Cruz Parish, *La Iglesia de Santa Cruz*, p. 19.

23. Kessell, *The Missions of New Mexico*, p. 84.

24. Bloom, "Bourke on the Southwest X," p. 250.

25. Ibid., pp. 250–251.

26. King, "Santa Cruz Church," pp. 49, 74.

27. Ibid., p. 49.

28. Bloom, "Bourke on the Southwest X," p. 252.

1. Prince, *Spanish Mission Churches*, p. 316.

2. De Borhegyi, "The Miraculous Shrines," pp. 9–11. I have relied heavily on this study in my discussion of the Santuario.

3. Prince, *Spanish Mission Churches*, p. 317.

4. De Borhegyi, "The Miraculous Shrines," p. 11.

5. Ibid., p. 6.

6. Prince, *Spanish Mission Churches*, p. 317.

7. De Borhegyi, "The Miraculous Shrines," p. 13. El Potrero was actually held as common pasturage for the settlers.

8. Boyd, *Popular Arts*, pp. 69–70.

9. Ibid., p. 15.

10. De Borhegyi, "The Miraculous Shrines"; Briggs, *The Wood Carvers*.

11. De Borhegyi, "The Miraculous Shrines," pp. 21–22.

12. Read presented a telling of the story that was more kindly to the Church and that explained Prince's vehement presentation as an expression of benign ignorance. "It is true that Father Francolón (parish priest at Santa Cruz) acting under instructions of his superior Archbishop Lamy, called on Doña Carmen and asked for a conveyance of the Santuario chapel to the Catholic church, explaining to her that he had been directed by his superior to request from her the conveyance; that if this was not done no further religious services were to be held in the chapel, neither would it be recognized as a church unless it was placed under the control of the ecclesiastical authorities. To Father Francolón's proposition the señora refused to accede. Then it was that Archbishop Lamy ordered Catholic religious services in the Santuario discontinued, and the matter ended then and there. It is not true that an excommunication, total or partial, followed." Read, "El Santuario de Chimayó," p. 84.

13. Chauvenet, *John Gaw Meem*, p. 68.

334

14. De Borhegyi, "The Miraculous Shrines," pp. 18–20.

15. Parsons, *Isleta*, pp. 415–416.

16. Boyd, "Señor Santiago de Chimayó," p. 29.

17. Simmons, *New Mexico*, p. 79.

LAS TRAMPAS: **SAN JOSÉ DE GRACIA DE LAS TRAMPAS**

1. Harris, "The Preservation of Art," Appendix.

2. Cited in ibid., p. 6.

3. Ibid., Appendix.

4. Domínguez, *The Missions*, pp. 99–100.

5. Ibid.

6. Harris clarified this point by noting that José González, "a displaced native of Sonora," repainted these works of an earlier date. Harris, "The Preservation of Art." Also see Kessell, *The Missions of New Mexico*, p. 102.

7. Bloom, "Bourke on the Southwest X," pp. 274–275.

8. Owings, "Las Trampas," p. 32.

9. Kessell, *The Missions of New Mexico*, p. 105.

PICURIS PUEBLO: **SAN LORENZO**

1. Forrest, *Missions and Pueblos*, pp. 83–84.

2. Hodge, Hammond, and Rey, *Fray Alonso de Benavides*, p. 70.

3. Kubler, *Religious Architecture*, pp. 108–109.

4. Scholes, "Documents for the History of the New Mexican Missions," p. 50.

5. Kubler, *Religious Architecture*, pp. 108–109.

6. Forrest, *Missions and Pueblos*, p. 83.

7. Kessell, *The Missions of New Mexico*, p. 97.

8. Ibid.

9. Picuris, Fragments of Inventory Book, 1743–67; cited in ibid., p. 99.

10. Ibid., p. 98.

11. Ibid.

12. Ibid.

13. Domínguez, *The Missions*, p. 92.

14. Ibid.

15. Ibid., p. 95.

16. Zubiría, Santa Clara, July 18, 1883; cited in Kessell, *The Missions of New Mexico*, p. 99.

17. Bloom, "Bourke on the Southwest X," p. 275.

18. "Recently it was torn down nearly to ground level and rebuilt by the pueblo over a two year period." Boyd, *Popular Arts*, p. 64.

19. Victor Johnson, architect, conversation with author, June 24, 1986.

RANCHOS DE TAOS: **SAN FRANCISCO DE ASÍS**

1. A recent book—D'Emilio, Campbell, and Kessell, *Spirit and Vision*—documented the history of the church and its attraction as a subject of paintings, graphics, and photographs. See also Robertson and Nestor, *Artists of the Canyons and Caminos*, 1976.

2. See O'Keeffe, *Georgia O'Keeffe*, unpaginated.

3. Kubler, *The Religious Architecture*, p. 103.

4. Domínguez, *The Missions*, pp. 112–113.

5. Ibid., p. 113.

6. De Morfi, "Geographical Description," p. 97.

7. Boyd gave the date as 1815. Boyd, *Popular Arts*, p. 352.

8. Kessell, *The Missions of New Mexico*, p. 109. In a more recent publication Kessell assigned an autumn 1815 date for the consecration. Kessell, "Born Old," p. 119.

9. Boyd, *Popular Arts*, p. 352.

10. Field, *Matt Field on the Santa Fe Trail*, p. 42.

11. Kubler believed that window size may have increased two to three times. Kubler, *The Religious Architecture*, pp. 47–48.

12. Hooker, "To Hard Plaster or Not?" pp. 11–16.

13. Johnson-Nestor, *A Report on the Exterior Plaster*.

14. Robert Nestor, architect, conversation with author, August 1981.

15. Pogzeba, *Ranchos de Taos*, p. ix.

TAOS PUEBLO: **SAN JERÓNIMO**

1. Walter, "Mission Churches," p. 122.

2. Hodge, Hammond, and Rey, *Fray Alonso de Benavides*, p. 71.

3. Wroth, *The Chapel of Our Lady of Talpa*, p. 15.

4. Adams, *Bishop Tamarón's Visitation*, p. 56. The 1750 census listed 146 households with 456 persons, including some Apache.

5. Ibid., p. 57.

6. Kubler, *Religious Architecture*, p. 113.

7. Bishop Lamy reliably affirmed as much, on the evidence of the records he consulted in Santa Fe. Ibid., p. 114.

8. Domínguez, *The Missions*, p. 110.

9. Ibid., p. 103.

10. Ibid., p. 108.

11. Adams, *Bishop Tamarón's Visitation*, pp. 57–58.

12. Ibid., p. 58.

13. Cited in Boyd, *Popular Arts*, pp. 356–359.

14. Chavez, *Archives of the Archdiocese of Santa Fe, 1678–1900*, p. 157; cited in Wroth, *The Chapel of Our Lady of Talpa*, p. 22.

15. Prince, *Spanish Mission Churches*, p. 253.

PECOS PUEBLO: **NUESTRA SEÑORA DE LOS ANGELES DE PORCIÚNCULA**

1. Nordby, "The Prehistory," p. 7.

2. Ibid., pp. 10–11.

3. Kessell, *Kiva, Cross, and Crown*, pp. 54–55.

4. Winship, *Annual Report of the Bureau of Ethnology*, p. 523; cited in ibid., p. 136.

5. Bezy, "The Geology of Pecos," p. 25. Domínguez also commented on the Pecos water sources: "Along the small plain between the sierra and the pueblo a very good river of good water and many delicious trout runs from north to south, but the water is not taken for use in the pueblo because it is about half a league away and there is very great danger from the Comanches. Therefore they have opened some wells of reasonably good water below the rock, and that is used for drinking and other purposes." Domínguez, *The Missions*, p. 213.

6. Hewett and Fisher, *Mission Monuments*, p. 141.

7. The untangling of the succession of church building at Pecos is relatively recent and credited to National Park Service archaeologist Jean Pinckley, who died in 1969. Her findings have been reported by Hayes, *The Four Churches*. Kessell, *Kiva, Cross, and Crown*, provided an exhaustive chronicle of the pueblo's history.

8. Kessell, *Kiva, Cross, and Crown*, p. 84; Kessell, *The Missions of New Mexico*, p. 230, n. 2.

9. Kessell, *Kiva, Cross, and Crown*, p. 104.

10. Ibid., p. 122.

11. Ibid., p. 123.

12. Hayes, *The Four Churches*, p. 3. Benavides wrote, "Another four leagues in the same northerly direction one finds the pueblo of Peccos [*sic*], which has more than two thousand Indians, well built houses three and four stories high, and some even more. . . . It is mountainous country, containing fine timber for construction, hence

these Indians apply themselves to the trade of carpentry and they are good craftsmen, since the minister brought them masters of this craft to teach them." Hodge, Hammond, and Rey, *Fray Alonso de Benavides*, p. 67.

13. Ibid., p. 67.

14. Hayes, *The Four Churches*, p. 4.

15. Cited in ibid., p. 4.

16. Cited in ibid., p. 6.

17. Simmons, *New Mexico*, p. 63.

18. Scholes, "Documents for the History of the New Mexican Missions," pp. 47–48.

19. Kessell, *Kiva, Cross, and Crown*, p. 272.

20. Ibid., pp. 254–255.

21. Hayes, *The Four Churches*, p. 9.

22. Kessell, *Kiva, Cross, and Crown*, p. 272.

23. Audiencia de Guadalajara legajo 141; cited in Hayes, *The Four Churches*, p. 11.

24. Ibid., p. 13.

25. Kessell, *The Missions of New Mexico*, p. 224.

26. Kessell, *Kiva, Cross, and Crown*, p. 272.

27. Adams, *Bishop Tamarón's Visitation*, pp. 48–49.

28. Domínguez, *The Missions*, p. 210.

29. Ibid., pp. 209, 212.

30. De Morfi, "Geographical Description," p. 93.

31. Kessell, *Kiva, Cross, and Crown*, p. 349.

32. Ibid., p. 458.

33. Prince, *Spanish Mission Churches*, p. 47.

34. Calvin, *Lieutenant Emory Reports*, pp. 53–54.

35. Hewett and Fisher, *Mission Monuments*, p. 141.

36. Cited in Kessell, *Kiva, Cross, and Crown*, p. 476.

37. Ibid., p. 481.

COCHITI PUEBLO: **SAN BUENAVENTURA**

The pueblo of Cochiti does not permit photography.

1. Forrest, *Missions and Pueblos*, p. 111.

2. Lange, *Cochití*, p. 9.

3. Ibid.

4. Forrest, *Missions and Pueblos*, p. 112.

5. Hodge, Hammond, and Rey, *Fray Alonso de Benavides*, p. 65.

6. Scholes and Bloom, "Friar Personnel and Mission Chronology," pp. 335, 66.

7. Scholes, "Documents for the History of the New Mexican Missions," p. 47.

8. Prince, *Spanish Mission Churches*, p. 145.

9. Ibid., p. 146, gave the date as April 21.

10. Hackett, *Historical Documents*, vol. 3, p. 375.

11. Adams, *Bishop Tamarón's Visitation*, p. 65. The 1750 census listed only 371 people.

12. Domínguez, *The Missions*, p. 155.

13. Ibid., pp. 155–156.

14. Ibid., p. 156.

15. Ibid.

16. Kessell, *The Missions of New Mexico*, p. 156.

17. Ibid.

18. Ibid.

19. Bloom, "Bourke on the Southwest XIII," p. 235.

20. Prince, *Spanish Mission Churches*, p. 138.

21. Hesse, "The Missions of Cochití and Santo Domingo, N.M." p. 27.

22. Walter, "Mission Churches," pp. 122–123.

23. Forrest, *Missions and Pueblos*, p. 119.

24. Kessell, *The Missions of New Mexico*, p. 158.

25. Forrest, *Missions and Pueblos*, pp. 119–120.

336 SANTO DOMINGO PUEBLO:
SANTO DOMINGO

The pueblo of Santo Domingo does not permit photography.

1. Forrest, *Missions and Pueblos*, p. 120. Prince, *Spanish Mission Churches*, p. 155, gave the spelling as Guypuy.

2. Kubler, *The Religious Architecture*, p. 108.

3. Hodge, Hammond, and Rey, *Fray Alonso de Benavides*, p. 65.

4. Scholes, "Documents for the History of the New Mexican Missions," p. 47. The copy was dated 1664, although Scholes believed it to be an addition from 1642.

5. De Herrera, Camp on the Río del Norte, December 21, 1681; cited in Kessell, *The Missions of New Mexico*, pp. 128–129.

6. Kubler, *The Religious Architecture*, p. 108.

7. Kessell, *The Missions of New Mexico*, pp. 129, 134, n. 4.

8. Domínguez, *The Missions*, p. 131.

9. Ibid., p. 132.

10. Ibid., p. 137.

11. Ibid.

12. Ibid.

13. De Morfi, "Geographical Description," p. 98.

14. Prince, *Spanish Mission Churches*, p. 159.

15. Inventory, Santo Domingo, July 28, 1806; cited in Kessell, *The Missions of New Mexico*, p. 134, n. 5.

16. Ibid., p. 132.

17. Bourke's sketches are reproduced in Kessell, *The Missions of New Mexico*. See Plate XII for his drawing of Santo Domingo in 1881.

18. Kessell, *The Missions of New Mexico*, p. 133.

19. Ibid.

20. Domínguez, *The Missions*, p. 138.

21. Forrest, *Missions and Pueblos*, p. 123.

SAN FELIPE PUEBLO: **SAN FELIPE**

The pueblo of San Felipe does not permit photography.

1. Forrest, *Missions and Pueblos*, p. 124; and Hesse, "San Felipe and Its Inhabitants," p. 35. Hesse gave the native name as Katestya.

2. Forrest, *Missions and Pueblos*, p. 124.

3. Hodge, Hammond, and Rey, *Fray Alonso de Benavides*, p. 65.

4. Scholes, "Documents for the History of the New Mexican Missions," p. 47.

5. Hackett, *Historical Documents*, vol. 3, p. 375; cited in Kessell, *The Missions of New Mexico*, p. 161.

6. Montaño, November 26, 1743; cited in ibid., p. 161.

7. Kubler, *The Religious Architecture*, p. 108.

8. Domínguez, *The Missions*, pp. 160–161.

9. Ibid., p. 161.

10. Ibid., p. 165.

11. Kessell, *The Missions of New Mexico*, p. 162.

12. Hesse, "Christmas 1912 with the Indians of San Felipe and Santo Domingo, N.M." p. 30.

13. Prince, *Spanish Mission Churches*, p. 163.

14. Hesse, "San Felipe and Its Inhabitants," p. 35.

15. Kessell, *The Missions of New Mexico*, p. 165, n. 4.

ZIA PUEBLO: **NUESTRA SEÑORA DE LA ASUNCIÓN**

The pueblo of Zia does not permit photography.

1. Prince, *Spanish Mission Churches*, p. 171.

2. Ibid., p. 172.

3. Given by Prince as 1687; by White as 1688.

4. White, *The Pueblo of Sia*, p. 172.

5. Espinosa, *First Expedition of Vargas*, p. 177.

6. Kessell, *The Missions of New Mexico*, p. 174.

7. Ibid.

8. Ibid., p. 175.

9. Adams, *Bishop Tamarón's Visitation*, p. 66.

10. Domínguez, *The Missions*, pp. 171–172.

11. Ibid., p. 172.

12. The population of 416 persons indicates that there had been a reduction of almost 25 percent during the previous twenty-five years.

13. Vergara, Zia, July 21, 1806; cited in Kessell, *The Missions of New Mexico*, p. 180, n. 5.

14. Bloom, "Bourke on the Southwest XIII," pp. 222–223.

15. Ibid., p. 222.

16. Bandelier, *Final Report*, p. 196, and Bandelier, *Journals*, 1885–88, p. 276; both cited in Kessell, *The Missions of New Mexico*, p. 174.

17. Ibid.

18. Halseth, "Report of Repairs," pp. 10–12.

19. Ibid., pp. 11–12.

20. Kessell, *The Missions of New Mexico*, p. 176.

21. White, *The Pueblo of Sia*, p. 215.

JEMEZ SPRINGS:
SAN JOSÉ DE GIUSEWA

1. Scholes, "Notes on the Jemez Missions," p. 61.

2. Walter, "Mission Churches," p. 121.

3. Forrest, *Missions and Pueblos*, p. 134.

4. Scholes, "Notes on the Jemez Missions," 1939, p. 62.

5. Ibid., p. 64.

6. Kubler, *The Religious Architecture*, p. 82.

7. Hodge, Hammond, and Rey, *Fray Alonso de Benavides*, p. 69.

8. Scholes, "Documents for the History of the New Mexican Missions," p. 48.

9. Adams, *Bishop Tamarón's Visitation*, p. 66.

10. Kubler, *The Religious Architecture*, p. 89; Bloom, "Bourke on the Southwest XIII," p. 227. The heavy summer rains of 1881 had taken their toll on a number of the churches.

ALBUQUERQUE: **SAN FELIPE NERI**

1. Bunting and McHugh, "The San Felipe Neri Affair," p. 9.

2. Adams, *Bishop Tamarón's Visitation*, p. 43. Adams provided the 1750 census figures as 191 families comprising 1,312 people.

3. Ibid., p. 44.

4. Ibid.

5. Domínguez, *The Missions*, p. 145.

6. Bunting and McHugh, "The San Felipe Neri Affair," p. 9.

7. Domínguez, *The Missions*, p. 151.

8. Ibid., p. 145.

9. Ibid., p. 147.

10. Ibid., p. 149.

11. Ibid., p. 151.

12. Bunting and McHugh, "The San Felipe Neri Affair," p. 9; Kessell, *The Missions of New Mexico*, p. 142.

13. Kessell, *The Missions of New Mexico*, p. 143.

14. Prince, *Spanish Mission Churches*, p. 242.

15. Bloom, "Bourke on the Southwest," p. 199.

16. Bunting and McHugh, "The San Felipe Neri Affair," p. 11.

17. Ibid., p. 12.

18. Ibid.

19. In 1987 the church was open daily from 1 to 3 in the afternoon and was monitored by volunteers.

ISLETA PUEBLO: **SAN AGUSTÍN**

1. Prince, *Spanish Mission Churches*, p. 190.

2. Montoya, *Isleta*, p. 8.

3. Prince, *Spanish Mission Churches*, p. 190.

4. Hodge, Hammond, and Rey, *Fray Alonso de Benavides*, p. 64.

5. Scholes, "Documents for the History of the New Mexican Missions," p. 49.

6. Montoya, *Isleta*, p. 9.

7. Hodge, Hammond, and Rey, *Fray Alonso de Benavides*, p. 64.

8. Adams, *Bishop Tamarón's Visitation*, pp. 70–71.

9. Domínguez, *The Missions*, p. 203.

10. Ibid., p. 205.

11. Montoya, *Isleta*, p. 9.

12. Bloom, "Bourke on the Southwest XIII," pp. 196–197.

13. Two skylights in the metal roof permitted light to filter through the clerestory. Kessell, *The Missions of New Mexico*, p. 233, n. 6.

14. The enmity between the pueblo and Stadtmueller culminated in his removal, *in handcuffs*, by the pueblo administration in 1965. "Nine years later, in 1974, Archbishop Robert F. Sanchez reelevated Isleta to parish status, and a resident priest, the first since Stadtmueller, moved back into the rectory." Ibid., p. 221.

15. Parsons, *Isleta*, p. 303.

1. For this section I have relied heavily on the work of Toulouse, *The Mission of San Gregorio de Abó;* and on Ivey, *In the Midst of Loneliness.* This detailed text offers an extremely thorough discussion of the history of the pueblos and missions and the results of on-site excavation, and it includes some radical interpretations that question long-held opinions. Mr. Ivey provided me with an advance draft of the book, drawings from which the plans were prepared, and several hours discussing his findings. I am most grateful to him for all his help.

2. Toulouse, *The Mission of San Gregorio*, p. 5.

3. Ibid.

4. Forrest, *Missions and Pueblos*, p. 147.

5. Walter, "Mission Churches," p. 117.

6. Toulouse, *The Mission of San Gregorio*, p. 4.

7. Whiffin, "The Manzano Missions," p. 219. In addition, the name for the Finnish city is actually Åbo, pronounced "Oh-bo."

8. Kubler, *The Religious Architecture*, pp. 37, 69–70. "

9. Carleton, "Diary of an Excursion," p. 301.

10. Hewett and Fisher, *Mission Monuments*, p. 160.

11. Ibid., p. 164. The painting—and illustrations from this period, which should always be taken with some caution—was executed by Regina Tatum Cooke with the WPA Museum Extension Project. For increased verity, see Ivey, *In the Midst of Loneliness.*

12. Ivey, *In the Midst of Loneliness*, p. 219. Ivey suggested that some construction taken for bird pens was actually a privy.

13. Ivey, *In the Midst of Loneliness*, pp. 415–421.

14. Toulouse, *The Mission of San Gregorio*, p. 9.

15. Carleton, "Diary of an Excursion," pp. 300–301.

338 QUARAI: **NUESTRA SEÑORA DE LA PURÍSIMA CONCEPCIÓN; SECOND CHURCH**

1. For this section I have depended primarily on two publications by Wilson: *Quarai State Monument* and "Quarai." Ivey, *In the Midst of Loneliness*, was also a rich source of detailed information.

2. Lummis, *The Land of Poco Tiempo*, p. 225.

3. Wilson, *Quarai State Monument*, unpaginated.

4. Alternate spellings include Quarra, Cuara, and Querac.

5. Ivey, *In the Midst of Loneliness*, p. 111. Ivey credited the design and construction to Gutiérrez de la Chica.

6. Senter, "The Work on the Old Quarai Mission," stated that the walls "originally stood as high as sixty feet" (p. 170).

7. Ibid. "Only the twenty workmen laboring on the church this summer can adequately appreciate the effort involved in the building of this imposing edifice."

8. No date or source given. Wilson, *Quarai State Monument*, unpaginated.

9. Ibid.

10. Ibid.

11. Ivey, *In the Midst of Loneliness*, p. 129.

12. Ibid., p. 144.

13. Ibid., pp. 243–247.

14. Ibid., p. 329.

15. Carleton, "Diary of an Excursion," p. 302.

16. Senter, "The Work on the Old Quarai Mission": "The sturdy walls averaging four and a half feet thick are as much as ten feet in width at the base" (p. 170).

GRAN QUIVIRA: **SAN YSIDRO; SAN BUENAVENTURA**

1. Lummis, *The Land of Poco Tiempo*, p. 222.

2. Cited in Hewett and Fisher, *Mission Monuments*, p. 172.

3. Vivian, *Gran Quivira*, pp. 142–143, is a comprehensive report and interpretation of the pueblo and its churches. See also Hayes, "The Missing Convento of San Isidro," pp. 35–40; and Ivey, *In the Midst of Loneliness*.

4. Vivian, *Gran Quivira*, p. 145.

5. Carroll, Fulfer, and Schofield, "Gran Quivira."

6. Ibid.

7. Scholes and Mera, "Some Aspects of the Jumano Problem," pp. 276–277; cited in Vivian, *Gran Quivira*, p. 14.

8. Hodge, Hammond, and Rey, *Fray Alonso de Benavides*, p. 66.

9. Ibid.

10. Vivian, *Gran Quivira*, p. 71.

11. Ibid., p. 73.

12. Toulouse, *The Mission of San Gregorio*, p. 65, n. 7.

13. Vivian, *Gran Quivira*, pp. 63–68.

14. Wilson, *Quarai State Monument*, unpaginated.

15. National Park Service, "Gran Quivira," brochure, no date.

16. Hackett, *Historical Documents*, volume 3, p. 161.

17. Ibid., pp. 188–189.

18. In an October 24, 1986, letter National Park Service historian James Ivey informed me that all three Salinas missions "have a plaza on the opposite side of the church from the convento, with main wall locations and alignments echoing the general size of the convento complex."

19. Carleton, "Diary of an Excursion," p. 307.

20. Vivian, *Gran Quivira*, p. 73.

21. Cited in ibid., p. 1.

22. Ibid., p. 29.

23. Álvarez wrote in 1705 about the 1670s and the finish of the settlements: "They burned the church, profaned the holy vessels, and mocked the images, and the same happened in the pueblo of Humanas. The six pueblos of the Salinas were abandoned." #110; cited in Wilson, *Quarai State Monument*, unpaginated.

LAGUNA PUEBLO: **SAN JOSÉ DE LA LAGUNA**

1. Walter, "Mission Churches," p. 119.

2. Prince, *Spanish Mission Churches*, p. 203.

3. Ellis, "An Outline," pp. 325–328.

4. Ibid., p. 327.

5. Domínguez, *The Missions*, p. 183, n. 2.

6. Adams, *Bishop Tamarón's Visitation*, p. 67.

7. Ibid. The 1750 census recorded 65 Indian households with 520 persons.

8. Ibid.

9. Domínguez, *The Missions*, p. 183.

10. Ibid.

11. Ibid., p. 185.

12. Ibid.

13. Ibid., p. 187.

14. Kessell, *The Missions of New Mexico*, p. 193, n. 3.

15. De Morfi, "Geographical Description." p. 102.

16. Ibid., pp. 102–103.

17. Bloom, "Bourke on the Southwest XII," p. 372.

18. Ellis, "An Outline," p. 343.

19. Bloom, "Bourke on the Southwest XII," p. 373.

20. "Acoma and Laguna," p. 60.

21. Prince, *Spanish Mission Churches*, p. 202. Several separate villages had been long-standing: Paquate, founded in 1767, and Encinal, founded by 1831, for example.

22. See Stubbs, *Bird's-Eye View*.

23. Boyd, *Popular Arts*, pp. 155–169.

24. Prince, *Spanish Mission Churches*, pp. 209–213; also "Pueblo of Laguna," pp. 34–36. "Some years ago Father Juillard wanted to have the painting restored by an artist, but the Indians would not have their treasured picture depart a second time from the Pueblo, and there it hangs, a tattered mass, dimmed and well nigh unrecognizable" (p. 35).

25. Prince, *Spanish Mission Churches*, pp. 212–213.

ACOMA PUEBLO: SAN ESTEBAN

1. Lummis, *The Land of Poco Tiempo*, p. 42. Lummis was convinced that the Acoma myths were accurate, although a complete vindication of his assertions came only after an 1897 expedition to the top of Enchanted Mesa found evidence of early inhabitation. See Houlihan and Houlihan, *Lummis in the Pueblos*, pp. 62–64, for a more complete telling of the incidents.

2. Hewett and Fisher, *Mission Monuments*, p. 187.

3. Simmons, *New Mexico*, p. 39.

4. Given that the pueblo regained its strength in several years, some scholars believe that the reports of Benavides, the battle, and the retributions have been exaggerated.

5. Hewett and Fisher, *Mission Monuments*, p. 84.

6. Hodge, Hammond, and Rey, *Fray Alonso de Benavides*, p. 48.

7. Scholes, "Documents for the History of the New Mexican Missions," p. 47.

8. Walter, "Mission Churches," p. 123.

9. Domínguez, *The Missions*, p. 189. Adams's and Chavez's note 1 on that page outlines the building chronology.

10. Riley, "Repairs to the Old Mission," p. 8.

11. Domínguez, *The Missions*, p. 190.

12. Adams, *Bishop Tamarón's Visitation*, p. 69.

13. Ibid., pp. 69–70.

14. Domínguez, *The Missions*, p. 189.

15. Ibid., p. 190.

16. Ibid., p. 192.

17. Bloom, "Bourke on the Southwest XII," p. 361.

18. Ibid.

19. Ibid., p. 364.

20. See Chauvenet, *John Gaw Meem*, pp. 27–42.

21. Riley, "Repairs to the Old Mission," p. 6.

22. Ibid., p. 9.

23. Reuter, "Restoration of Acoma Mission," p. 83.

24. Kessell, *The Missions of New Mexico*, p. 201.

ZUÑI PUEBLO: NUESTRA SEÑORA DE GUADALUPE

1. For this and subsequent information I have relied on LeBlanc, "The Cultural History of Cibola." pp. 2–8.

2. Ibid., p. 8.

3. Hart, "A Brief History," pp. 20–30.

4. Bloom, "Fray Estevan de Perea's *Relación*," p. 228.

5. Ibid., pp. 223–229.

6. Ibid., p. 234.

7. Smith, "Seventeenth-Century Spanish Missions," p. 6.

8. Ibid.

9. Hodge, Hammond, and Rey, *Fray Alonso de Benavides*, p. 74.

10. Crampton, *The Zunis of Cibola*, p. 33.

11. Hart, "A Brief History," p. 23.

12. Scholes, "Documents for the History of the New Mexican Missions," p. 50.

13. Crampton, *The Zunis of Cibola*, p. 40. The myth tells that on his reconquest expedition, Vargas found a room with two candles burning—the work of the priest who had chosen to live with the Zuñi at the time of the Pueblo Revolt.

14. Ibid., p. 45. Other sources dated the return from the mesa to as late as 1699.

339

15. Adams, *Bishop Tamarón's Visitation*, p. 60.

16. Domínguez, *The Missions*, p. 202.

17. Hodge, Hammond, and Rey, *Fray Alonso de Benavides*, p. 74.

18. Domínguez, *The Missions*, p. 197. Caywood, *The Restored Mission*, p. 10, supported Cushing's claim (1881) that the church was built between 1775 and 1780.

19. Bloom, "Bourke on the Southwest VIII," pp. 114–115.

20. Caywood, *The Restored Mission*, p. 14.

21. Docher, "The Quaint Indian Pueblo," p. 29.

22. Kessell, *The Missions of New Mexico*, p. 212.

23. Burials placed the heads toward the east. Leighton and Adair, *People of the Middle Place*, p. 79.

24. Stevenson, "The Zuñi Indians"; cited in Crampton, *The Zunis of Cibola*, p. 57.

340

BIBLIOGRAPHY

"Abo Mission Repair Begun." *El Palacio* 44 (1938): 167.

"Acoma and Laguna." *El Palacio* 15 (1923): 60.

Adams, Eleanor B. "The Chapel and Confradia of Our Lady of Light in Santa Fe." *New Mexico Historical Review* 22 (1947): 327–41.

Adams, Eleanor B., ed. *Bishop Tamarón's Visitation of New Mexico, 1760.* Albuquerque: Historical Society of New Mexico Publications in History, 1954.

———. Fray Silvestre Velez de Escalante. "Letter to the Missionaries of New Mexico." *New Mexico Historical Review* 40 (1965): 319–32.

Ahlborn, Richard Eighme. *The Penitente Moradas of Abiquiú.* Washington, D.C.: Smithsonian Institution Press, 1986.

Allison, W. H. H. "Santa Fe As It Appeared During the Winter of the Years 1837 and 1838." *Old Santa Fe 2* (1914–1915): 170–83.

"Another Play by Mrs. Bloom." *El Palacio* 14 (1923): 170–71.

Archdiocese of Santa Fe. *Lamy Memorial: Centenary of the Archdiocese of Santa Fe.* Santa Fe, N.M.: Archdiocese of Santa Fe, 1950.

Ayres, Atlee B. "The Earliest Mission Buildings of San Antonio, Texas." *American Architect* 124 (1924): 170–78.

Baird, Joseph Armstrong, Jr. *The Churches of Mexico, 1530–1810.* Berkeley and Los Angeles: University of California Press, 1962.

Bandelier, Adolph F. *The Delightmakers.* New York: Dodd, Mead, and Company, 1890.

———. *The Discovery of New Mexico by the Franciscan Monk Friar Marcos de Niza in 1539.* Translated and edited by Madeleine Turrell Rodack. Tucson: University of Arizona Press, 1981. First published in *Revue d'Ethnographie* (1886).

———. "Quivera," parts 1 and 2. *Nation* 49 (1889): 348–49, 365–66.

Bannon, John Francis, ed. *Bolton and the Spanish Borderlands.* Norman: University of Oklahoma Press, 1974.

Barber, Ruth Kerns. "Indian Labor in the Spanish Colonies." *New Mexico Historical Review* 7 (1932): 105–43, 233–72, 311–47.

Beck, Warren A. *New Mexico: A History of Four Centuries.* Norman: University of Oklahoma Press, 1963.

Beck, Warren A., and Ynez D. Haase. *Historical Atlas of New Mexico.* Norman: University of Oklahoma Press, 1979.

Bezy, John V. "The Geology of Pecos." *Exploration* (1981): 23–25.

Bloom, Lansing B. "Bourke on the Southwest." *New Mexico Historical Review*, Part I, 8 (1933): 1–30; Part II, 9 (1934): 33–77; Part III, 159–83; Part IV, 273–89; Part V, 375–435; Part VI, 10 (1935): 1–35;

Part VII, 271–322; Part XIII, 11 (1936): 77–122; Part IX, 188–207; Part X, 217–82; Part XI, 12 (1937): 41–77; Part XII, 337–79; Part XIII, 13 (1938): 192–238.

———. "Fray Estevan de Perea's *Relación.*" *New Mexico Historical Review* 8 (1933): 211–35.

———. "New Mexico Under Mexican Administration, 1821–1846." *Old Santa Fe* 1 (1913–1914): 3–49, 131–75, 235–87, 347–68; 2 (1914–1915): 4–56, 119–69, 223–77, 351–80.

Bolton, Herbert Eugene. "The Mission as a Frontier Institution in the Spanish American Colonies" (1917). In *New Spain's Far Northern Frontier: Essays on Spain in the American West, 1540–1821*, edited by David J. Weber, 49–66. Albuquerque: University of New Mexico Press, 1979.

Bottineau, Yves. *Iberian-American Baroque.* Translated by Kenneth Martin Leake. New York: Grosset and Dunlap, 1970.

Boyd, E. *The New Mexico Santero.* Santa Fe: Museum of New Mexico Press, 1969.

———. "The Plaza of San Miguel del Vado." *El Palacio* 77 (1972): 17–26.

———. *Popular Arts of Spanish New Mexico.* Santa Fe: Museum of New Mexico Press, 1974.

———. "Señor Santiago de Chimayó." *El Palacio* 63, (1956).

Boyle, Bernard Michael, ed. *Materials in the Architecture of Arizona, 1870–1920.* Tempe: College of Architecture, Arizona State University, 1976.

Breternitz, David A., and Jack E. Smith. "Mesa Verde: 'The Green Table.'" In *Rocky Mountain and Mesa Verde National Parks.* National Parkways series, vols. 3 and 4. Casper, Wyo.: World-wide Research and Publishing, 1975.

Briggs, Charles L. *The Wood Carvers of Córdova, New Mexico: Social Dimensions of an Artistic "Revival."* Knoxville: University of Tennessee Press, 1980.

Brody, J. J. *The Chaco Phenomenon.* Albuquerque, N.M.: Maxwell Museum of Anthropology, 1983.

Bullock, Alice. *Mountain Villages.* Santa Fe, N.M.: Sunstone Press, 1981.

Bunting, Bainbridge. *Early Architecture in New Mexico.* Albuquerque: University of New Mexico Press, 1976.

———. *John Gaw Meem: Southwestern Architect.* Albuquerque: University of New Mexico Press, 1983.

———. *Of Earth and Timbers Made: New Mexico Architecture.* Albuquerque: University of New Mexico Press, 1974.

———. "San Agustín de la Isleta." *New Mexico Architect* 2 (1960): 14–16.

———. *Taos Adobes.* Santa Fe: Museum of New Mexico Press, 1975.

Bunting, Bainbridge, and John P. Conron. "The Architecture of Northern New Mexico." *New Mexico Architect* 8, nos. 9–10 (1966).

Bunting, Bainbridge, Thomas R. Lyons, and Margil Lyons. "Penitente Brotherhood Moradas and Their Architecture." In *Hispanic Arts and Ethnohistory in the Southwest*, edited by Marta Weigle, 31–79. Santa Fe, N.M.: Ancient City Press, 1983.

Bunting, Bainbridge and John W. McHugh. "The San Felipe Neri Affair." *New Mexico Architect* 8 (1966): 8–17.

Burke, James Wakefield. *A Forgotten Glory: The Missions of Old Texas.* Waco, Tex.: Texian Press, 1979.

Cairns, Trevor. *Europe Finds the World.* Cambridge: Cambridge University Press, 1973.

Calvin, Ross. *Sky Determines.* 1948. Reprint. Albuquerque: University of New Mexico Press, 1965.

Calvin, Ross, ed. *Lieutenant Emory Reports.* 1951. Reprint. Albuquerque: University of New Mexico Press, 1968.

Caperton, Thomas J., and LoRheda Fry. "Links to the Past: New Mexico's State Monuments." *El Palacio* 83 (1977): 9–13.

Carleton, Major James Henry. "Diary of an Excursion to the Ruins of Abó, Quarra, and Gran Quivira, in New Mexico." In *Ninth Annual Report.* Washington, D.C.: Smithsonian Institution, 1855.

Carroll, Tom, Glenn Fulfer, and Sue Schofield. "Gran Quivira, Salinas National Monument." Southwest Parks and Monuments Association with the National Park Service, brochure. No date.

Castano de Sosa, Gaspar. "Pecos Pueblo: December 31, 1590." *Exploration* (1981): 26–27.

Caywood, Louis R. *The Restored Mission of Nuestra Senora de Guadalupe de Zuni.* National Park Service (no place of publication), 1972.

Cervin, Olaf Z. "The Spanish Mexican Missions of the United States." *Architectural Record* 14 (1903): 181–204.

Chapman, Richard C., and Jan V. Biella. "Four Thousand Years on the Southern Pajarito." *Exploration* (1980): 6–11.

Chauvenet, Beatrice. *John Gaw Meem: Pioneer in Historic Preservation.* Santa Fe: Museum of New Mexico Press, 1985.

Chavez, Fray Angelico. "The Conquistadora Is a Paisana." *El Palacio* 57 (1950): 299–307.

———. *La Conquistadora: The Autobiography of an Ancient Statue.* Paterson, N.J.: St. Anthony Guild Press, 1954.

———. "New Mexico Place-Names from Spanish Proper Names." *El Palacio* 56 (1949): 367–82.

———. "Saint's Names in New Mexico Geography." *El Palacio* 56 (1949): 323–38.

342 ———. *The Santa Fe Cathedral.* Rev. ed., Santa Fe, N.M., 1978.

———. "Santa Fe Church and Convent Sites in the Seventeenth and Eighteenth Centuries." *New Mexico Historical Review* 24 (1949): 85–93.

Clark, David L. *Spatial Archaeology.* London: Academic Press, 1977.

Crampton, C. Gregory. *The Zunis of Cibola.* Salt Lake City: University of Utah Press, 1977.

Crouch, Dora P., Daniel J. Garr, and Axel I. Mundigo. *Spanish City Planning in North America.* Cambridge, Mass.: MIT Press, 1982.

Crouch, Dora P., and Axel I. Mundigo. "The City Planning Ordinances of the Laws of the Indies Revisited. Part 2: Three American Cities." *Town Planning Review* 48, no. 4 (1977).

Cushing, Frank H. *My Adventures in Zuñi.* 1882. Reprint. Palmer Lake, Colo.: Filter Press, 1967.

De Borhegyi, Stephen F. "The Miraculous Shrines of Our Lord of Esquípulas in Guatemala and Chimayó, New Mexico." *El Palacio* 60 (1953).

DeBuys, William. *Enchantment and Exploitation: The Life and Times of a New Mexico Mountain Range.* Albuquerque: University of New Mexico Press, 1982.

D'Emilio, Sandra, and Suzan Campbell. "Mission of Beauty: The Art of Ranchos de Taos Church." In *Spirit and Vision: Images of Ranchos de Taos Church,* by Sandra D'Emilio, Suzan Campbell, and John L. Kessell, 1–30. Santa Fe: Museum of New Mexico Press, 1987.

D'Emilio, Sandra, Suzan Campbell, and John L. Kessell. *Spirit and Vision: Images of Ranchos de Taos Church.* Santa Fe: Museum of New Mexico Press, 1987.

De Morfi, Juan Agustín. "Geographical Description of New Mexico, 1782." In *Forgotten Frontiers: A Study in the Spanish Indian Policy of Don Juan Bautista de Anza, Governor of New Mexico, 1777–1787,* edited by Alfred Barnaby Thomas, 87–115. Norman: University of Oklahoma Press, 1932.

Denver Art Museum. *Santos of the Southwest.* Denver, Colo.: Denver Art Museum, 1970.

Dickey, Roland F. *New Mexico Village Arts.* 1949. Reprint. Albuquerque: University of New Mexico Press, 1970.

Docher, The Reverend A. "The Quaint Indian Pueblo of Isleta." *Santa Fe Magazine* 7, no. 7 (1913): 29–32.

Domínguez, Fray Francisco Atanasio. *The Missions of New Mexico, 1776.* Translated and edited by Eleanor B. Adams and Fray Angelico Chavez. Albuquerque: University of New Mexico Press, 1956.

Dozier, Edward P. *The Pueblo Indians of North America.* New York: Holt, Rinehart and Winston, 1970.

Duell, Prentice. "The Arizona-Sonora Chain of Missions." *Architect and Engineer* 66 (1921): 1, 65–81; 2, 67–77; 3, 62–72.

Dutton, Bertha P. *Let's Explore Indian Villages: Past and Present.* 1962. Reprint. Santa Fe: Museum of New Mexico Press, 1970.

Eldredge, Charles C., Julie Schimmel, and William H. Truettner. *Art in New Mexico, 1900–1945: Paths to Taos and Santa Fe.* Washington, D.C.: National Museum of American Art, Smithsonian Institution, 1986.

Ellis, Bruce. *Bishop Lamy's Santa Fe Cathedral.* Albuquerque: University of New Mexico Press, 1985.

———. "The 'Lost' Chapel of the Third Order of St. Francis in Santa Fe." *New Mexico Historical Review* 53 (1978): 59–74.

Ellis, Florence Hawley. "An Outline of Laguna Pueblo History and Social Organization." *Southwestern Journal of Anthropology* 15 (1959): 325–47.

Ellis, Richard N. *New Mexico, Past and Present.* Albuquerque: University of New Mexico Press, 1979.

Ely, Albert Grim. "The Excavation and Repair of the Quarai Mission." *El Palacio* 39 (1935): 133–44.

Espinosa, J. Manuel. *First Expedition of Vargas into New Mexico, 1692.* Albuquerque: University of New Mexico Press, 1940.

Field, Matthew C. *Matt Field on the Santa Fe Trail.* Edited by John Sunder. Norman: University of Oklahoma Press, 1960.

Forrest, Earle R. *Missions and Pueblos of the Old Southwest.* 1929. Reprint. Glorieta, N.M.: Rio Grande Press, 1979.

Gebhard, David. "Architecture and the Fred Harvey Houses." *New Mexico Architect* 6 (1964): 18–25.

———. "R. M. Schindler in New Mexico—1915." *New Mexico Architect* 7 (1965): 15–21.

Gerald, Rex E. *Spanish Presidios of the Late Eighteenth Century in Northern New Spain.* Santa Fe: Museum of New Mexico Press, 1968.

Gibson, Charles, ed. *The Spanish Tradition in America.* New York: Harper and Row, 1968.

Glassie, Henry. *Folk Housing in Middle Virginia.* Knoxville: University of Tennessee Press, 1975.

Goss, Robert C. "The Churches of San Xavier, Arizona, and Caborca, Sonora: A Comparative Analysis." *Kiva* 40 (1975): 165–79.

———. "The Problem of Erecting the Main Dome and Roof Vaults of San Xavier del Bac." *Kiva* 37 (1972): 117–27.

H., Fray H. "Glimpses into the History of the Catholic Church in New Mexico." *The Franciscan Missions of the Southwest* (1918): 24–31.

Hackett, C. W., ed. *Historical Documents Relating to New Mexico.* 3 vols. Washington, D.C.: Carnegie Institution, 1923–1937.

Hallenbeck, Cleve. *Spanish Missions of the Old Southwest.* Garden City, N.Y.: Doubleday, Page and Company, 1926.

Halseth, Odd S. "Report of Repairs on Zia Mission: October 29 to December 8, 1923." *El Palacio* 16 (1924): 10–12.

Harris, Louise A. "The Preservation of Art, Architecture, and Artifacts of Las Trampas, New Mexico." Master's thesis, University of New Mexico, 1967.

Hart, E. Richard. "A Brief History of the Zuni Nation." *Exploration* (1983): 19–25.

Hayes, Alden C. *The Four Churches of Pecos.* Albuquerque: University of New Mexico Press, 1974.

———. "The Jumanos Pueblos." *Exploration* (1982): 11–15.

———. "The Missing Convento of San Isidro." *El Palacio* 75 (1968): 35–40.

Henderson, Rose. "A Primitive Basis for Modern Architecture." *Architectural Record* 54 (1923): 188–96.

Hesse, Fray Jerome. "Christmas 1912 with the Indians of San Felipe and Santo Domingo, N.M." *Franciscan Missions of the Southwest* (1913): 28–33.

———. "The Missions of Cochití and Santo Domingo, N.M." *Franciscan Missions of the Southwest* (1916): 27–30.

———. "San Felipe and Its Inhabitants." *Franciscan Missions of the Southwest* (1920): 35–39.

Hewett, Edgar L. "Hispanic Monuments." *El Palacio* 45 (1938): 53–67.

Hewett, Edgar L., and Reginald G. Fisher. *Mission Monuments of New Mexico.* Albuquerque: University of New Mexico Press, 1943.

Historic Santa Fe Foundation. *Old Santa Fe Today.* 1972. Reprint. Albuquerque: University of New Mexico Press, 1978.

Hodge, Frederick Webb. *Handbook of American Indians North of Mexico.* Bulletin 30, vol. 2. Washington, D.C.: Bureau of American Ethnology, 1910.

Hodge, Frederick Webb, George P. Hammond, and Agapito Rey, eds. *Fray Alonso de Benavides' Revised Memorial of 1634.* Albuquerque: University of New Mexico Press, 1945.

Holmes, Viviana Nigro. "Architectural Woodwork of Spanish Colonial New Mexico." *New Mexico Studies in the Fine Arts* 10 (1985): 17–22.

Hooker, Van Dorn. "To Hard Plaster or Not?" *New Mexico Architect* 19 (1977): 11–16.

Horgan, Paul. *The Centuries of Santa Fe.* Santa Fe, N.M.: William Gannon, 1976.

Houlihan, Patrick T., and Betsy E. Houlihan. *Lummis in the Pueblos.* Flagstaff, Ariz.: Northland Press, 1986.

Ivey, James E. *"In the Midst of Loneliness": The Architectural History of the Salinas Missions.* Santa Fe, N.M.: Southwest Cultural Resources Center Professional Papers, no. 15. In press.

———. "We've Got It, Tom: The Search for the First Church at Abó, Salinas Pueblo Missions National Monument, New Mexico." Unpublished ms.

Jackson, John Brinckerhoff. *Landscape Autoguide: Tours 1, 2, and 3.* 1962. Reprint. Santa Fe, N.M.: *Landscape,* 1963.

———. "New Mexico Houses." *Mass* 2 (1984): 2–5.

James, George Wharton. "The Franciscan Mission Buildings of California." *Craftsman* 5 (1904): 321–35.

———. "Old Missions of New Mexico and Arizona." *Franciscan Missions of the Southwest* (1913): 5–16.

Jenkins, Myra Ellen. "The Pueblo of Nambe and Its Lands." In *The Changing Ways of Southwestern Indians: A Historic Perspective,* edited by Albert H. Schroeder. Glorieta, N.M.: Rio Grande Press, 1973.

Jenkins, Myra Ellen, and Albert H. Schroeder. *A Brief History of New Mexico.* Albuquerque: University of New Mexico Press, 1974.

Johnson, Ross B. *Pecos National Monument, New Mexico: Its Geologic Setting.* Washington, D.C.: U.S. Government Printing Office, 1969.

Johnson, William Templeton. "The Archaic Architecture of New Mexico." *Journal of the American Institute of Architects* 7 (1919): 65–70.

———. "The Santa Fe of the Future." *El Palacio* 7 (1916): 33–41.

Johnson-Nestor, Architects. *Holy Cross Church Renovation Master Plan Report.* Santa Fe, N.M., 1974.

———. *San Miguel Chapel: Historic Structure Report and Master Plan.* Santa Fe, N.M., 1978.

———. *A Report on the Exterior Plaster: St. Francis of Assisi Church, Ranchos de Taos, N.M.* Santa Fe, N.M., March 17, 1979.

Jordan, Louann, and St. George Cooke. *El Rancho de las Golondrinas: Spanish Colonial Life in New Mexico.* Santa Fe, N.M.: Colonial New Mexico Historical Foundation, 1977.

Kelly, Henry W. "Franciscan Missions of New Mexico, 1740–1760." *New Mexico Historical Review* 15 (1940): 345–68; 16 (1941): 41–69, 148–83.

Kessell, John L. "Born Old: The Church of San Francisco at Ranchos de Taos." In *Spirit and Vision: Images of Ranchos de Taos,* by Sandra D'Emilio, Suzan Campbell, and John L. Kessell, 115–24. Santa Fe: Museum of New Mexico Press, 1987.

———. *Kiva, Cross, and Crown: The Pecos Indians and New Mexico, 1540–1840.* Washington, D.C.: Department of the Interior, National Park Service, 1979.

———. *The Missions of New Mexico Since 1776.* Albuquerque: University of New Mexico Press, 1980.

344 ———. "The Presence of the Past: Pecos Pueblo." *Exploration* (1981): 12–14.

Kidder, Alfred Vincent. *An Introduction to the Study of Southwestern Archeology.* New Haven, Conn.: Yale University Press, 1924.

King, Scottie. "Santa Cruz Church: A Vigorous Renewal." *New Mexico Magazine* (November 1980): 46–49.

"Kivas Found in Quarai Monastery." *El Palacio* 40 (1936): 122.

Knowles, Ralph. *Sun Rhythm Form.* Cambridge, Mass.: MIT Press, 1981.

Krahe, The Reverend Daniel W. *Cristo Rey: A Symphony in Mud.* Albuquerque, N.M.: Lourdes School Press, 1940.

Kubler, George. "Gran Quivira-Humanas." *New Mexico Historical Review* 14 (1939): 418–21.

———. Introduction to *Santos: An Exhibition of the Religious Folk Art of New Mexico.* Fort Worth, Tex.: Amon Carter Museum of Western Art, 1964.

———. *Mexican Architecture of the Sixteenth Century.* New Haven, Conn.: Yale University Press, 1948.

———. "Open-Grid Town Plans in Europe and America." In *Urbanization in the Americas, From Its Beginnings to the Present,* edited by Richard P. Schaedel, Jorge E. Harday, and Nora Scott Kinzer. The Hague: Mouton, 1978.

———. *The Rebuilding of San Miguel at Santa Fe in 1710.* Colorado Springs, Colo.: Taylor Museum, 1939.

———. *The Religious Architecture of New Mexico in the Colonial Period and Since the American Occupation.* 1940. Reprint. Albuquerque: University of New Mexico Press, 1972.

———. "Two Modes of Franciscan Architecture: New Mexico and California." *Gazette des Beaux Arts* 23 (1943): 39–48.

Kubler, George, and Martin Soria. *Art and Architecture in Spain and Portugal and Their American Dominions, 1500–1800.* Baltimore, Md.: Penguin Books, 1959.

Lange, Charles H. *Cochiti: A New Mexico Pueblo, Past and Present.* 1959. Reprint. Carbondale: Southern Illinois University Press, 1968.

Larcombe, Samuel. "Plaza del Cerro, Chimayó, New Mexico: An Old Place Not Quite on the Highway." In *Hispanic Arts and Ethnohistory in the Southwest,* edited by Marta Weigle, 171–80. Santa Fe, N.M.: Ancient City Press, 1983.

Lawrence, F. S. "The Old Spanish Missions in and About San Antonio." *American Architect* 124 (1923): 444–50.

Lazell, Carleen. "Early Spanish-Pueblo Revival Architecture at the University of New Mexico, Albuquerque." *New Mexico Studies in the Fine Arts* 10 (1985): 23–29.

LeBlanc, Steven. "The Cultural History of Cibola." *Exploration* (1983): 2–7.

Leighton, Dorothea C., and John Adair. *People of the Middle Place: A Study of the Zuni People.* New Haven, Conn.: Human Relations Area Files, 1966.

Lewis, Brother B. *Oldest Church in the U.S.: The San Miguel Chapel.* 1957. Reprint. Santa Fe, N.M.: San Miguel Chapel, 1968.

Lister, Robert, and Florence Lister. *Chaco Canyon.* Albuquerque: University of New Mexico Press, 1981.

Lummis, Charles F. *The Land of Poco Tiempo.* 1893. Reprint. Albuquerque: University of New Mexico Press, 1952.

Lumpkins, William. "A Distinguished Architect Writes on Adobe." *El Palacio* 77 (1972): 3–10.

McAndrew, John. *The Open-Air Churches of Sixteenth-Century Mexico.* Cambridge, Mass.: Harvard University Press, 1969.

McCaffrey, Robin H., and Janet Needham-McCaffrey. "Old as the Hills." Master's thesis, Massachusetts Institute of Technology, 1978.

Manucy, Albert. *The Houses of St. Augustine, 1565–1821.* Saint Augustine, Fla.: Saint Augustine Historical Society, 1962.

Mather, Christine. *Baroque to Folk.* Santa Fe: Museum of International Folk Art, 1980, exhibition catalog.

Mays, Buddy. *Indian Villages of the Southwest.* San Francisco, Calif.: Chronicle Books, 1985.

Meinig, D. W. *Southwest: Three Peoples in Geographical Change, 1600–1970.* New York: Oxford University Press, 1980.

Meyet, Fray Theodosius. "The Cathedral of St. Francis, Santa Fe, New Mexico." *Franciscan Missions of the Southwest* (1921): 14–22.

Miller, Nory. "Back to Basics: San Francisco de Asís, Ranchos de Taos, N.M." *Progressive Architecture* (November 1981): 83–85.

Mills, George. *The People of the Saints.* Colorado Springs, Colo.: Taylor Museum, no date.

Minge, Ward Alan. *Acoma: Pueblo in the Sky.* Albuquerque: University of New Mexico Press, 1976.

Montoya, Joe L. *Isleta Pueblo and the Church of St. Augustine.* Isleta, N.M.: Saint Augustine Parish, 1978.

Morand, Sheila. *Santa Fe Then and Now.* Santa Fe, N.M.: Sunstone Press, 1984.

Morley, Sylvanus Griswold. "Santa Fe Architecture." *Old Santa Fe* 2 (1914–1915): 273–301.

Morrow, Irving F. "The Mission of San Luis Obispo." *Architect and Engineer* 62 (1920): 73–79.

———. "San Juan Bautista." *Architect and Engineer* 59 (1919): 42–75.

Mundigo, Axel I., and Dora P. Crouch. "The City Planning Ordinances of the Laws of the Indies Revisited. Part I: Their Philosophy and Implications." *Town Planning Review* 48, no. 3 (1977).

———. "The Laws of the Indies Revisited." *Town Planning Review* 48, no. 4 (1977).

Murphy, Dan. "Salinas: A View Through Time." *Exploration* (1982): 6–10.

Nabokov, Peter. *Architecture of Acoma Pueblo: The Historic American Building Survey Project.* Santa Fe, N.M.: Ancient City Press, 1986.

Nelson, Lee H., ed. *Preservation of Historic Adobe Buildings.* Preservation Briefs 5. Washington, D.C.: Technical Preservation Services Division, Department of the Interior, 1978.

Noble, David Grant. *Ancient Ruins of the Southwest: An Archeological Guide.* Flagstaff, Ariz.: Northland Press, 1981.

———. *New Light on Chaco Canyon. Exploration* (1986).

Nordby, Larry. "The Prehistory of the Pecos Indians." *Exploration* (1981): 5–11.

Nordenskiöld, Gustaf. *The Cliff Dwellers of the Mesa Verde.* 1893. Reprint. Translated by D. Lloyd Morgan. Glorieta, N.M.: Rio Grande Press, 1979.

Nuttall, Zelia. "Royal Ordinances Concerning the Laying Out of New Towns." *Hispanic American Historical Review* 4 (1921): 743–53.

O'Keeffe, Georgia. *Georgia O'Keeffe.* New York: Viking Press, 1978.

"The Old Missions of New Mexico." *Architectural Review* 6.

Oppelt, Norman T. *Guide to Prehistoric Ruins of the Southwest.* Boulder, Colo.: Pruett Publishing Company, 1981.

Ortiz, Alfonso. *The Tewa World: Space, Time, Being, and Becoming in a Pueblo Society.* Chicago: University of Chicago Press, 1974.

Ortiz, Alfonso, ed. *Handbook of North American Indians: Southwest.* Washington, D.C.: Smithsonian Institution, 1979.

Owings, Nathanial Alexander. "Las Trampas: A Past Remembered." *New Mexico* (July–August 1970): 30–35.

Parsons, Elsie Clews. *Isleta, New Mexico (the Pueblo of Isleta).* c. 1926. Reprint. Albuquerque: University of New Mexico Press, Calvin Horn Publishers, 1974.

Parsons, Francis B. *Early Seventeenth-Century Missions of the Southwest.* Tucson, Ariz.: Dale Stuart King, 1975.

Pearce, T. M. *New Mexico Place Names: A Geographical Dictionary.* Albuquerque: University of New Mexico Press, 1965.

Pearl, George Clayton. "Tradition and the Individual Talent: The Architecture of John Gaw Meem." *El Palacio* 82 (1976): 23–34.

"Pecos Repairs Begun." *El Palacio* 45 (1938): 82–83.

Pike, Donald. *Anasazi: The Ancient People of the Rock.* New York: Crown Publishers, 1974.

Pogzeba, Wolfgang. *Ranchos de Taos: San Francisco de Asis Church.* Kansas City, Mo.: Lowell Press, 1981.

Polzer, Charles W., S. J. *Kino Guide II: His Missions, His Monuments.* Tucson, Ariz.: Southwest Mission Research Center, 1982.

Prince, L. Bradford. *Spanish Mission Churches of New Mexico.* 1915. Reprint. Glorieta, N.M.: Rio Grande Press, 1977.

"Pueblo of Laguna." *Franciscan Missions of the Southwest* (1916): 31–37.

Read, Benjamin M. "El Santuario de Chimayo." *El Palacio* 3 (1916): 81–84.

Reuter, B. A. "Restoration of Acoma Mission." *El Palacio* 22 (1927): 79–87.

Ricard, Robert. *The Spiritual Conquest of Mexico: An Essay on the Apostolate and the Evangelizing Methods of the Mendicant Orders in New Spain.* Translated by Leslie B. Simpson. Berkeley and Los Angeles: University of California Press, 1966.

Riley, L. A., II. "Repairs to the Old Mission at Acoma." *El Palacio* 18 (1925): 2–9.

Robertson, Edna, and Sarah Nestor. *Artists of the Canyons and Caminos: Santa Fe, The Early Years.* Lawton, Utah: Peregrine Smith, 1976.

Ruskin, John. *The Seven Lamps of Architecture.* 1848. Reprint. New York: Farrar, Straus and Giroux, 1979.

Saile, David G. "Making a House: Building Rituals and Spatial Concepts in the Pueblo Indian World." *Architecture Association Quarterly* 9 (1977): 72–81.

Sanford, Trent Elwood. *The Architecture of the Southwest: Indian, Spanish, American.* New York: Norton, 1950.

Santa Cruz Parish. *La Iglesia de Santa Cruz de la Canada, 1733–1983.* Santa Cruz, N.M.: Santa Cruz Parish, 1983.

Santa Fe, Planning Department. *Design and Preservation in Santa Fe: A Pluralistic Approach.* Santa Fe, N.M.: Santa Fe Planning Department, 1977.

Scholes, France V. "Church and State in New Mexico, 1610–1650." *New Mexico Historical Review* 11 (1936): 9–76, 145–78, 283–94, 297–349; 12 (1937): 78–106.

———. "Documents for the History of the New Mexican Missions in the Seventeenth Century." *New Mexico Historical Review* 4 (1929): 45–58, 195–201.

———. "Notes on the Jemez Missions in the Seventeenth Century." *El Palacio* 44 (1938): 61–102.

———. "Problems in the Early Ecclesiastical History of New Mexico." *New Mexico Historical Review* 7 (1952): 32–75.

345

346 ———. "The Supply Service of the New Mexico Missions in the Seventeenth Century." *New Mexico Historical Review* 5 (1930): 93–115, 185–210, 386–404.

Scholes, France V., and Lansing B. Bloom. "Friar Personnel and Mission Chronology, 1598–1629." *New Mexico Historical Review* 19 (1944): 319–36; 20 (1945): 58–82.

Schuetz, Mardith. "Proportional Systems and Ancient Geometry." *Southwest Mission Research Center Newsletter* 14 (1980): 2–7.

Schuetz, Mardith K., trans. *Architectural Practice in Mexico City: A Manual for Journeyman Architects of the Eighteenth Century.* Tucson: University of Arizona Press, 1987.

S[chuster], Fray F[ridolin]. "The Acoma Indians." *Franciscan Missions of the Southwest* (1918): 42–45.

———. "El Dia de los Muertos (All Souls Day) at the Indian Pueblo of Sia." *Franciscan Missions of the Southwest* (1914): 43–47.

———. "The Pueblo of Acoma." *Franciscan Missions of the Southwest* (1918): 42–45.

Scott, Hunter D. "Pueblo-Mission Architecture." *Masterkey* 2 (1928): 15–24.

Scully, Vincent. *Pueblo: Mountain, Village, Dance.* New York: Viking Press, 1975.

Sena, Jose. "The Chapel of Don Antonio José Ortiz." *New Mexico Historical Review* 13 (1938): 347–59.

Senter, Donovan. "The Work on the Old Quarai Mission." *El Palacio* 37 (1934): 169–74.

Shalkop, Robert L. *The Folk Art of a New Mexican Village.* Colorado Springs, Colo.: Taylor Museum, 1976.

Sherman, John. *Santa Fe: A Pictorial History.* Norfolk, Va.: Donning Company/Publishers, 1983.

Shiskin, J. K. *The Palace of the Governors.* Santa Fe: Museum of New Mexico, 1972.

Simmons, Marc. "History of Pueblo-Spanish Relations to 1821." In *Handbook of North American Indians: Southwest,* edited by Alfonso Ortiz, 178–93. Washington, D.C.: Smithsonian Institution, 1979.

———. *New Mexico: A Bicentennial History.* New York: Norton, 1977.

———. "Pecos Pueblo on the Santa Fe Trail." *Exploration* (1981): 2–4.

———. "Settlement Patterns and Village Plans in Colonial New Mexico." In *New Spain's Far Northern Frontier: Essays on Spain in the American West, 1540–1821,* edited by David J. Weber, 97–116. Albuquerque: University of New Mexico Press, 1979.

———. "Tlascalans in the Spanish Borderlands." *New Mexico Historical Review* 39 (1964): 101–10.

Simmons, Marc, and Frank Turley. *Southwestern Colonial Ironwork: The Spanish Blacksmithing Tradition from Texas to California.* Santa Fe: Museum of New Mexico Press, 1980.

Smith, Edward W. *Adobe Bricks in New Mexico.* Socorro: New Mexico Bureau of Mines and Mineral Resources, 1982.

Smith, Miguel C. Leatham. "The Santuario de Guadalupe in Santa Fe and the Observations of Fr. Esteban Anticoli, S. J." *New Mexico Studies in the Fine Arts* 10 (1985): 12–16.

Smith, Watson. "Seventeenth-Century Spanish Missions of the Western Pueblo Area." *Smoke Signal,* no. 21 (Spring 1970).

Society for Restoration and Preservation of the New Mexican Missions. "Imperilled Monuments of Early American History." Brochure.

Spears, Beverly. *American Adobes: Rural Houses of Northern New Mexico.* Albuquerque: University of New Mexico Press, 1986.

Steen, Charlie. "An Archeologist's Summary of Adobe." *El Palacio* 77 (1974): 29–38.

———. "Prehistory of the Northern Plateau." *Exploration* (1980): 17–19.

Stineman, Norman M. "Spanish Mission Architecture in Railway Passenger Stations." *The Architect and Engineer* 62 (1920): 75–79.

Stroessner, Robert. *Santos of the Southwest.* Denver, Colo.: Denver Art Museum, 1970.

Stubbs, Stanley A. *Bird's-Eye View of the Pueblos.* Norman: University of Oklahoma Press, 1950.

———. "'New' Old Churches Found at Quarai and Tabira (Pueblo Blanco)." *El Palacio* 66 (1959): 162–69.

Stubbs, Stanley A., and Bruce T. Ellis. *Archeological Investigations at the Chapel of San Miguel and the Site of la Castrense, Santa Fe, New Mexico.* Monographs of the School of American Research. Santa Fe: Museum of New Mexico, Laboratory of Anthropology, 1955.

Stubbs, Stanley A., Bruce T. Ellis, and Alfred E. Dittert, Jr. "'Lost' Pecos Church." *El Palacio* 64 (1957): 67–92.

Sunset Books Editorial Staff. *The California Missions: A Pictorial History.* Menlo Park, Calif.: Lane Book Company, 1964.

Taylor, Lonn, and Dessa Bokides. *Carpinteros and Cabinetmakers: Furniture Making in New Mexico, 1600–1900.* Santa Fe: Museum of International Folk Art, Museum of New Mexico, 1983.

Toulouse, Joseph H., Jr. *The Mission of San Gregorio de Abó: A Report on the Excavation and Repair of a Seventeenth-Century New Mexico Mission.* Santa Fe, N.M.: School of American Research, 1949.

Toulouse, Joseph H., III. "The Mission of San Gregorio de Abó." *El Palacio* 45 (1938): 103–7.

Toussaint, Manuel. *Colonial Art in Mexico.* Translated and edited by Elizabeth Wilder Weismann. Austin: University of Texas Press, 1967.

Townson, Duncan. *Muslim Spain.* Cambridge: Cambridge University Press, 1973.

Twitchell, Ralph E., ed. *Colonel Juan Bautista de Anza: Diary of His Expedition to the Moquis in 1780.* Historical Society of New Mexico Publication no. 21. Santa Fe, N.M., 1918.

———. *Historical Sketch of Governor William Carr Lane, Together with Diary of His Journey, 1852.* Historical Society of New Mexico Publication no. 20. Santa Fe, N.M., 1917.

———. *Old Santa Fe: The Story of New Mexico's Ancient Capital.* Chicago: Rio Grande Press, 1925.

Vierra, Carlos. "New Mexico Architecture." *Art and Archaeology* 7 (1918): 37–49.

———. "Our Native Architecture in Its Relation to Santa Fe." *El Palacio* 4 (1917): 7–11.

Vivian, Gordon. *Gran Quivira: Excavations in a 17th-Century Jumano Pueblo.* Washington, D.C.: Department of the Interior, National Park Service, 1979.

Von Wuthenau, A. "The Spanish Military Chapels in Santa Fe and the Reredos of Our Lady of Light." *New Mexico Historical Review* 10 (1935): 175–94.

W., Fray A. "The Zuni Indians." *Franciscan Missions of the Southwest* (1916): 11–21.

Walter, Paul A. F. "The Cities That Died of Fear." Paper 35. Santa Fe, N.M.: School of American Research, 1946.

———. "Mission Churches in New Mexico." *El Palacio* 5 (1918): 114–23.

Warren, Nancy. *New Mexico Style: A Source Book of Traditional Architectural Details.* Albuquerque: University of New Mexico Press, 1986.

Weber, David J., ed. *New Spain's Far Northern Frontier: Essays on Spain in the American West, 1540–1821.* Albuquerque: University of New Mexico Press, 1979.

Weigle, Marta. *The Penitentes of the Southwest.* Santa Fe, N.M.: Ancient City Press, 1970.

Weigle, Marta, ed. *Hispanic Arts and Ethnohistory in the Southwest.* Santa Fe, N.M.: Ancient City Press, 1983.

Weigle, Marta, and Peter White, eds. *The Lore of New Mexico.* Albuquerque: University of New Mexico Press, 1988.

Wethey, Harold E. *Colonial Architecture and Sculpture in Peru.* Cambridge, Mass.: Harvard University Press, 1949.

When Cultures Meet: Remembering San Gabriel del Yunge Oweenge. Santa Fe, N.M.: Sunstone Press, 1987.

Whiffin, Marcus. "The Manzano Missions." *Architectural Review* 133 (1963): 219–21.

White, Leslie A. *The Pueblo of Sia, New Mexico.* Smithsonian Institution, Bureau of American Ethnology Bulletin no. 184. Washington, D.C.: U.S. Government Printing Office, 1962. Reprint. Albuquerque, N.M.: Calvin Horn Publisher, 1974.

Wilcox, David R., and Lynette O. Shenk. *The Architecture of the Casa Grande and Its Interpretation.* Arizona State Museum Archaeological Series no. 115. Tucson, Ariz., 1977.

Wilkinson, Catherine. "Planning a Style for the Escorial: An Architectural Treatise for Philip of Spain." *Journal of the Society of Architectural Historians* 44 (1985): 37–47.

Wilson, Christopher Montgomery. "The Santa Fe, New Mexico, Plaza: An Architectural and Cultural History." Master's thesis, University of New Mexico, 1981.

———. "When the Room Is the Hall." *Mass* 2 (1984): 17–23.

Wilson, John P. "Quarai: A Turbulent History." *Exploration* (1982): 20–25.

———. *Quarai State Monument.* Santa Fe: Museum of New Mexico Press, 1977.

Wilson, Skip. *New Mexico One Hundred Years Ago.* Albuquerque, N.M.: Sun Publishing Company, 1980.

Woodbury, Richard B. "From Chaos to Order: A. V. Kidder at Pecos." *Exploration* (1981): 15–22.

Wroth, William. *The Chapel of Our Lady of Talpa.* Colorado Springs, Colo.: Taylor Museum, 1979.

———. *Christian Images in Hispanic New Mexico.* Colorado Springs, Colo.: Taylor Museum, 1982.

Wyllys, Rufus Kay, ed. "Padre Luís Velarde's *Relación* of Pimería Alta, 1716." *New Mexico Historical Review* 6 (1931): 111–57.

Yates, Steven A., ed. *The Essential Landscape: The New Mexico Photographic Survey.* Essays by John Brinckerhoff Jackson. Albuquerque: University of New Mexico Press, 1985.

Designer: Marc Treib
Compositor: G&S Typesetters, Inc.
Text: 10/12 Janson
Display: Futura
Printer: Sandler/Becker, Inc.
Binder: Sandler/Becker, Inc.